Artificial Intelligence with Statistical Pattern Recognition

Edward A. Patrick, M.D., Ph.D.
James M. Fattu, M.D., Ph.D.

Prentice-Hall, Inc.
Business and Professional Division

Englewood Cliffs
New Jersey

Prentice-Hall International, Inc., *London*
Prentice-Hall of Australia Pty. Ltd., *Sydney*
Prentice-Hall Canada Inc., *Toronto*
Prentice-Hall of India Private Ltd., *New Delhi*
Prentice-Hall of Japan, Inc., *Tokyo*
Prentice-Hall of Southeast Asia Pte. Ltd., *Singapore*
Whitehall Books, Ltd., *Wellington, New Zealand*
Editora Prentice-Hall do Brasil, Ltda., *Rio de Janeiro*
Prentice-Hall Hispanoamericana, S.A., *Mexico*

First printing... 1986

Editor: George E. Parker

Library of Congress Cataloging-in-Publication Data

Patrick, Edward A.
Artificial intelligence with statistical pattern recognition.

Bibliography
Includes index.
1. Artificial intelligence. 2. Pattern perception—Statistical methods. I. Fattu, James M. II. Title.
Q335.P36 1986 006.3 85-12319

ISBN 0-13-049131-4

Printed in the United States of America

Dedication

To the children —
May they use intelligence wisely.

Preface

Chapter 1 introduces the book and discusses selected aspects of the knowledge base structure. Included as part of the knowledge base structure are primitives, features, feature value, complex features, categories, concept formation, subsystems, and a total system. Highlighted are **CONSULT-I®** (Patrick, 1979; Patrick *and others* 1979 a & b; Patrick and Fattu, 1985), **CONSULT LEARNING SYSTEM®**, and **The OUTCOME ADVISOR®** (Patrick, 1975, Patrick and Fattu, 1985). **CONSULT-I®** is a unique expert system implementing artificial intelligence **(AI)** with statistical pattern recognition **(SPR). CONSULT LEARNING SYSTEM®** and **The OUTCOME ADVISOR®** process hard data to learn (create knowledge) by example and by Concept Formation. This knowledge can then be incorporated into **CONSULT-I®**. Integration of **SPR** and **AI** began as early as 1965 (Patrick, Patrick *and others*, 1970).

CONSULT-I® is used throughout this book as a reference for comparing classification systems.

Definitions used to integrate **AI** with **SPR** are introduced in Chapter 2. These include: intelligence, scientific method, statistics, patterns, knowledge, hierarchy, inference, learning, discovery, causality, concepts, focus, primitives, features (findings, attributes), classes, categories, complex classes, only classes, actions, states, category conditional probability density functions, reasoning, deduction, induction, heuristics, meta-knowledge, consciousness, and types of learning.

Various types of learning are presented in Chapter 2, along with an introduction to a theorem on a posteriori probability by Patrick (1983). It is a new form of structuring learning without a teacher; it handles multiple classes active at the same time, using Deduction. It also applies to the Concept Formation of patterns of a Category never previously seen.

Chapter 3 provides definitions and methods used to study **SPR,** while Chapter 4 does the same for **AI** as applied to classification systems. For **SPR,** the reader is introduced to feature space, class space, the derivation of Bayes theorem, the difference between statistically independent events, linear independence, and a spanning set. A category space is defined with constructs of only classes and complex classes for the new theorem. Studies from **AI** include propositional calculus, predicate calculus, first order logic, axiomatic formulation, semantic networks, causal networks, control strategy, search procedures, blind search, breadth-first search, depth-first search, heuristic state-space search, production systems, and reasoning. *Heuristics or rules from* **AI** *are incorporated in constructing the category conditional probability density function of* **SPR.** Discussions include frames and inductive inference.

Chapter 5 presents derivation of the theorem on a posteriori probability presented by Patrick in 1983. The theorem provides for concept formation through statistical dependence among categories. Several propositions are presented concerning this statistical dependence. Formation of complex classes as concepts is extensively discussed.

In the theorem by Patrick, features need not be statistically dependent. Furthermore, this theorem on a posteriori probability provides that categories are mutually exclusive but statistically dependent through their features during concept formation. Underlying classes need not be mutually exclusive. This is a significant departure from Bayes theorem where classes must be mutually exclusive, and there is no distinction between classes and categories.

Chapters 6, 7, and 8 set the stage for engineering the category conditional probability density function (c.c.p.d.f.) in Chapter 9. Chapter 6 provides a historical perspective for engineering hierarchical knowledge structures for classification systems. Chapter 7 provides new results for knowledge base structures. Included in the discussion are events, classes, categories, complex classes, the event conditional probability density function, and the mixture probability density. Models are presented for complex classes including fuzzy set approximations and optimum calculation of complex class a posteriori probability.

Chapter 8 deals with fundamental properties of features (findings, attributes) which draw on **SPR.** Features are discussed as Type Ø features, Type 1 features, higher-order complex features that may involve solutions of simultaneous physical equations, insignificant features, missing features, dependence among features, Rule-in features and Can't features.

The category conditional probability density function (c.c.p.d.f.) in Chapter 9 is the *inference function in* **CONSULT-I®** which measures the closeness of a pattern (called the recognition sample) to categories in the knowledge base. In **CONSULT-I®** knowledge in the c.c.p.d.f. is stored by probabilistic inference rules or constellations called columns with minicolumn modifications. While probabilistic, columns can be viewed as inductive conjunctions of production rules guided in their construction by the field of knowledge about the category. Statistical dependence among features for a category exists within the column and additional local dependence is imposed by minicolumns (packets of knowledge). *A minicolumn may correspond to simultaneous physical equations.*

Categories (in particular complex classes) not previously seen during training are generated by deduction if required. This engineered c.c.p.d.f. is an integration of **SPR** and **AI.**

The process of selecting the next feature automatically (feature selection) is introduced in Chapter 10. The viewpoint is that automatic feature selection should change the system's behavior but cannot enhance classification performance. Ultimate system performance is determined by engineering the c.c.p.d.f. Feature selection in Chapter 10 begins with optimal approaches from SPR followed by suboptimal approaches. The latter can include goal directed feature selection such as implemented by production rules. A practical application of feature selection as discussed is selecting the next test based on a column or minicolumn of a category so as to increase expected performance at least possible cost.

Chapter 11 deals with the integration of **CONSULT-I®** subsystems into a *TOTAL SYSTEM*. Discussion begins with defining the parameters of a total classification system. These parameters include subsystems, categories, classes, features, columns, and primitives. Methods include (activation) rules for activating subsystems or category modules which are compatible with either a subsystem or the total system. These category modules can be integrated to form the total system likelihood functions. The steps in developing a total system are then discussed.

Chapter 12 considers inference functions as *closeness* measures and the comparison of classification systems. The first closeness measure discussed is that of **CONSULT-I®** under development for over a decade (Patrick, 1972; Patrick, Shen, and Stelmack, 1974; Patrick and Shen, 1975; Patrick, 1983; Fattu and Patrick, 1983; Patrick and Fattu, 1984; Fattu *and others*, 1985; Patrick *and others, 1985*). Using the

CONSULT-I® closeness measure, various systems are compared including the measure of belief used in **MYCIN** (Shortliffe, 1976; Cerutti and Timó Pieri, 1981); the **PROMISE** closeness measure (Gini and Gini, 1980); the closeness measure of **CASNET/EXPERT** (Kulikowski and Weiss, 1982; Weiss *and others,* 1978); the closeness measure of **INTERNIST** (Miller *and others,* 1982; Myers *and others,* 1982; Pople, 1982).

In Chapter 13 **CONSULT-I®** is visualized in part by using three-dimensional constructions. Chapter 14 discusses considerations when training expert systems using the **CONSULT-I®** model. Considerations include the effect of observation error on the c.c.p.d.f., differences between probability of true observed false and false observed true, examples of training probabilities with unequal observation error, the effect on probability where a feature is observed false given other features are observed true. Other considerations are a priori category probabilities, number of training samples for each feature of a category, and correction constants.

Chapter 15 deals with discovering knowledge using **The OUTCOME ADVISOR®** and **CONSULT LEARNING SYSTEM®.** These systems provide for off line or on line learning of knowledge "by example" utilizing hard data (records) or can be used as true classification systems utilizing hard data. *Using a new definition of correlation to define a new closeness measure, records or examples not part of the initial data base are generated by Deduction that looks like the Findings.* This allows classification of Findings never previously seen and is an important bridge between Artificial Intelligence and Statistical Pattern Recognition.

Chapter 16 discusses **The OUTCOME ADVISOR®, CONSULT LEARNING SYSTEM®** and **CONSULT-I®** from a viewpoint of evolving intelligence.

Basic to Hyperspace are Features (dimensions) with Feature values. One Feature can be used to index Categories for a Classification system. Inference of Outcomes from a Condition is a basic operation in the Hyperspace. Repetition is essential for certain Inferences where a Closeness measure must be learned. This shows the limitation of conventional Artificial Intelligence without Statistical Pattern Recognition. A Closeness measure itself is an inference which must be learned. The Closeness measure used in **The OUTCOME ADVISOR®** and **CONSULT LEARNING SYSTEM®** does not require that Feature values be ordered.

Acknowledgments

Many individuals have influenced this work. It is impossible to express gratitude to all of them. A few of these people are:

The graduate students: Paula Detterman, R. Uthurusamy, Leon Shen, George Carayannopoulos, Frank Stelmack, F. P. Fischer, Lou Liporace, Friend Bechtel, Pete Costello, Bob Agnew, C. R. Steinem, Edward Patrick, Jr.

Nicholas A. Fattu, Sr. for editing and constructive criticism, Nicholas Fattu, Jr. for assistance with literature review, and David Blomberg.

Subsystem developers: Chuck Emmerman, John G. Patrick, Peter Franklin, Clair Wood, Neil Angerman, William R. Patrick, Allen Stein, Anabel Newman, Sharon Andrews, Jo Guth, Michael Dowling, William Sutton. Leo Leverage of the American Medical Association for joint effort in interfacing a video disk system to **CONSULT.**

Editing by Suzanne Fattu, the foresight of Picker International through Michael Hinds and Joe Williams, invaluable help from Andy Green, A. V. Lakshiminarayanan and Raymond E. Gangarosa, and Alfred Roy Fitz.

Inspiration and support from Henry J. Heimlich and Neil A. Armstrong, and Stephen D. Dragin and George E. Parker of Prentice-Hall. And finally, software development, etc. by Edward A. Patrick, Jr. and John G. Patrick.

Theorems

1-1 Bayes Theorem

Comments

$$p(B|A) = \frac{p(A|B)p(B)}{p(A)}$$

(Bayes, 1763)
Basic formula

$$p(\gamma_i^*|\mathbf{x}) = \frac{p(\mathbf{x}|\gamma_i^*)p(\gamma_i^*)}{\sum_{j=1}^{M} p(\mathbf{x}|\gamma_j^*)p(\gamma_j^*)}$$

$\gamma_1^*, \ldots, \gamma_M^*$ mutually exclusive.
Problem: nothing is said about engineering $p(\mathbf{x}|\gamma_j^*)$
No provision to learn about a category from other categories.

$$p(\mathbf{x}|\gamma_i^*) = \int p(\mathbf{x}|\mathbf{b}_i,\gamma_i^*)\, p(\mathbf{b}|\mathbf{x}_1, \ldots, \mathbf{x}_n)d\mathbf{b}$$

(Yakowitz and Spragins; 1966 to 1969 and others) Learning by example: $\mathbf{x}_1, \mathbf{x}_2, \ldots, \mathbf{x}_n$

$$p(\mathbf{b}|\mathbf{x}_1,\mathbf{x}_2, \ldots,\mathbf{x}_n) = \frac{\left[\sum_{i=1}^{M} p(\mathbf{x}|\mathbf{b}_i,\gamma_i^*)P_i\right] p(\mathbf{b}|\mathbf{x}_1, \ldots, \mathbf{x}_{n-1})}{\sum_{i=1}^{M} p(\mathbf{x}|\gamma_i^*)P_i}$$

Learning without a teacher (Type 1). M & P_i's can be unknown as can $\mathbf{b}_1,\mathbf{b}_2, \ldots,\mathbf{b}_M$.

(Patrick 1965, 1968)

$$\mathbf{b} = [\mathbf{b}_1, \mathbf{b}_2, \ldots,\mathbf{b}_M, P_1, \ldots,P_M]$$

1-2 Patrick's Theorem

(Patrick, 1983)

$$p(\omega_i|\mathbf{x}) = \frac{p(\mathbf{x}|\omega_i^*)P(\omega_i^*) + \sum_{\omega_i \,\varepsilon\, \Omega_\xi^*} p(\mathbf{x}|\Omega_\xi^*)\, P(\Omega_\xi^*)}{p(\mathbf{x})}$$

See Section 5-3

- $\omega_1,\omega_2, \ldots,\omega_M$ *not* mutually exclusive

- Multiple classes at same time†
- Features statistically dependent
- Inference function engineered
- Categories statistically dependent during learning

but

$$p(\mathbf{b}|\mathbf{x}_1, \ldots, \mathbf{x}_n) = \frac{\left[\sum_{i=1}^{M_1} p(\mathbf{x}|\omega_i^*, \mathbf{b}_i)P_i + \sum_{\xi=1}^{M_2} p(\mathbf{x}|\Omega_\xi^*, \mathbf{b}_\xi)P_\xi\right]}{p(\mathbf{x}_n|\mathbf{x}_1, \ldots, \mathbf{x}_{n-1})} p(\mathbf{b}|\mathbf{x}_1, \ldots, \mathbf{x}_{n-1})$$

(Patrick, 1983; Patrick and Fattu, 1984)

See Section 5-18-2

- A new form of learning without a teacher (Type 2).
- Concept formation deduction)

For use in the above iterative equation,

$$p(\mathbf{x}_n, \Omega_\xi^*|\mathbf{b}_\xi, \mathbf{x}_1, \ldots, \mathbf{x}_{n-1}) = g_\xi\left(\{p(\mathbf{x}, \omega_i|\mathbf{x}_1, \ldots, \mathbf{x}_{n-2}, \mathbf{b})\}_{i=1}^{M_1}\right)$$

expresses statistical dependence between stage $(n-2)$ and stage $(n-1)$.

In **CONSULT-I**® the c.c.p.d.f. is engineered as

$$p(\mathbf{x}|\gamma_i^*) = \sum_{k=1}^{K} \prod_{\xi=1}^{L_{I(k)}} p(x_\xi|\gamma_{i_k}^*) \left[\prod_{u=1}^{U(k)} \prod_{s=1}^{S_k(u)} p_{i_{k_s}}^u\right] p(\gamma_{i_k}^*|\gamma_i^*)$$

for each category γ_i^*, including only classes and complex classes. $\gamma_{i_k}^*$ is the subcategory of category γ_i^*. Proper engineering provides it with the following properties as discussed throughout the book.

†$\omega_i \varepsilon \Omega_\xi^*$ means the ξth unique combination of classes where one of the classes is ω_i. Ω_ξ^* is called complex class, ω_i^* is called an Only class.

- statistically dependent and independent features
- Missing features
- Insignificant features
- Typical and atypical presentation (emphasizes dependent features)
- A priori category probability
- A priori subcategory probability or fuzzy set rules
- Expert knowledge
- Hard data knowledge
- Feature values need not be ordered
- Type Ø and Type 1 features
- Common sense constraints
- Can generate pattern representation for a category never previously seen
- Performs induction
- Performs deduction

Symbol	*Interpretation*
$\mathbf{x} = [x_1, x_2, \ldots, x_L]$	Feature vector
$\dot{\mathbf{x}}_{n_\xi}$	Sequence of n_ξ vector samples (records) from category γ_ξ^*
p	Probability density or "probability of"
$\exists$	There exists
ε, $\in$	Is in
$\notin$	Is not in
$\forall$	For all
δ_{ij}	Delta function, $\delta_{ij} = 1, i = j$, $\delta_{ij} = Ø, i \neq j$
$A\|B$	Event A conditioned on event B
a/b	Scalar a divided by scalar b

Symbol	*Interpretation*
$\binom{a}{b}$	$\frac{a!}{b!\,(a-b)!}$, binomial coefficients
M_1	Number of *only classes* ω_i^* in category space
M_2	Number of *complex classes* Ω_i^* in category space
$M = M_1 + M_2$	Number of categories in the category space limited to *only classes* and *complex classes*
$\cup$	Union, Or
$\cap$	Intersection, And
$\sum_{j=1}^{L}$	Sum of terms indexed by $j = 1, \ldots, L$
$\{\ \}$	Collection of, set of
$A + B \quad A \cup B$	Sum or union of two sets A, B
$A - B$	Difference of two sets A, B
$\mathrm{B} \in \mathrm{A}$	B is a subset of A
$AB \quad A \cap B$	Product or intersection of two sets, A and B
S	Certain set
$\bar{A} = S - A$	$\bar{A}$ is complement of A
$AB = \emptyset$	Mutually exclusive sets
$\lVert\mathbf{x}\rVert$	Norm of vector $\mathbf{x}$
$(\mathbf{x}, \mathbf{y})$	Inner product of vector $\mathbf{x}$ and $\mathbf{y}$
$\lVert\mathbf{x}\rVert \triangleq \left[\sum_{i=1}^{L} x_i^2\right]^{1/2}$	Euclidean norm (for L-tuple $\mathbf{x}$)
$d^2(\mathbf{x}, \mathbf{y})$ $\lVert\mathbf{x} - \mathbf{y}\rVert^2 = \lVert\mathbf{x}^2\rVert + \lVert\mathbf{y}^2\rVert - 2\,\mathrm{Re}(\mathbf{x}, \mathbf{y})$	Normed vector space distance for inner product vector space

Symbol	*Interpretation*
$A, B, C, D \ldots$	Sets (sometimes used as scalars or constants)
$A^c, \bar{A}$	Complementary set to set A
$\triangleq$	Means "is equal to by definition"
iff	If and only if (sufficient and necessary)
$\Rightarrow$	Implies
$(\emptyset, 1)$	Part of real line, $\emptyset < x < 1$
$E_Y[y]$	Expectation of a random variable Y having values y
$\mathcal{Y}$	Category space
$\mathcal{V}$	L-dimensional vector space
$\mathcal{C}$	Class space
$\mathfrak{X}$	Feature space
$\mathcal{F}$	Category feature relationship space
$\mathcal{S}$	Total system
$\mathcal{S}_s$	Subsystem s within the total system
$\mathfrak{X}_s$	Feature space for subsystem $\mathcal{S}_s$
M_s	Number of categories in subsystem s of total system
M_{c_s}	Number of classes in subsystem s of total system
L_s	Number of features in subsystem s of total system
K_s	Number of columns for each category in subsystem s of total system
C	Constant accounting for insignificant feature of a c.c.p.d.f. module

Symbol	*Interpretation*
$\mathcal{L}_i$	Likelihood function for *i*th category
S	Number of subsystems in the total system
$\mathbf{x}_s = \{x_{s_j}\}$	$x_{s_j} = 1$ if *j*th primitive is included in subsystem *s*, Ø otherwise
$\boldsymbol{\gamma}_s^* = \{\gamma_{s_i}^*\}$	$\gamma_{s_i}^* = 1$ if *i*th category γ_i^* is included, Ø otherwise
$\boldsymbol{c}_s = \{c_{s_i}\}$	$c_{s_i} = 1$ if ith class included, Ø otherwise
$\boldsymbol{s}_s = \{s_e\}$	$s_e = 1$ if subsystem *e* is associated with reference subsystem $\boldsymbol{s}$
$\mathbf{d}_{s_i}^* = \{\gamma_{s_{i_{e_\xi}}}^*\}$	$\gamma_{s_{i_{e_\xi}}}^* = 1$ *if category* $\boldsymbol{\gamma}_{s_i}^*$ in subsystem *s* depends on category $\gamma_{e_\xi}^*$ in subsystem *e*. $\boldsymbol{d}_s^* \triangleq \{\boldsymbol{d}_{s_i}\}$
$\gamma^*(s)$	Set of intermediate categories for subsystem *s*
$\boldsymbol{\gamma}_i^* \ \varepsilon \ \boldsymbol{\gamma}$	*i*th category in category space
$\omega_i \ \varepsilon \ \mathcal{C}$	*i*th class in class space
$\boldsymbol{\omega}_\xi^*$	Only class ω_ξ, a special category in the category space where ω_ξ is a class in the class space
(ω_i, ω_j)	Class ω_i AND Class ωj, which is the complex class Ω_{ij}^*
$(\omega_i, \bar{\omega}_j)$	Class ω_i BUT NOT Class ω_j, which is ω_i^*, an only class
Ω_{ij}^*	Complex class incorporating classes ω_i and ω_j
*	Superscript * denotes a category as opposed to a class
$\boldsymbol{\gamma} = \{\gamma_i^*\}_{i=1}^M$	Category γ_i^* in the category space can be an only class or a complex class

Symbol	*Interpretation*
$\mathcal{C} = \{\omega_i\}_{i=1}^{M_1}$	Class space; ω_i is a class in the class space
$\mathcal{F} = \{p(\mathbf{x}\vert\gamma_i^*)\}_{i=1}^{M}$	Category–feature relationship space (a cross-product space, $\mathfrak{X}\gamma$); $p(x\vert\gamma_i^*)$ is a c.c.p.d.f. in the category–feature relationship space, $\mathcal{F}$
$\mathcal{A}$	Primitive space
$\gamma_{i_k}^*$	kth subcategory of γ_i^*
$P(\gamma_i^*)$	A priori probability of category γ_i^*
$P(\gamma_{i_k}^*)$	A priori probability of subcategory $\gamma_{i_k}^*$ of category γ_i^*
$\mathbf{x} = [\mathbf{x}_D, \mathbf{x}_I]$	For *training* vector
$\mathbf{x}_D$	Subset of statistically dependent features in training vector
$\mathbf{x}_I$	Subset of statistically independent features in training vector
$\mathbf{x} = [\mathbf{x}_p, \mathbf{x}_M]$:	For *recognition* vector (pattern to be recognized or classified)† The Findings.
$\mathbf{x}_p$	Present features in recognition vector
$\mathbf{x}_M$	Missing features in recognition vector
Type Ø feature x_1	Values $x_{11}, x_{12}, \ldots, x_{1V}$ mutually exclusive but not necessarily ordered
Type 1 measurement x_1 (for convenience referred to as a Type 1 feature; also a complex feature because it is a function of features)	Values $\mathrm{x}_{11}, \mathrm{x}_{12}, \ldots, \mathrm{x}_1\mathrm{V}$ (embedded features) themselves are binary features each having a value either T(true) or F(false); probability of true is between Ø and 1; probability of false is between Ø and 1

†There are features with values present ($\mathbf{x}_p$) and features with values missing ($\mathbf{x}_M$).

Symbol	*Interpretation*
Insignificant Type Ø feature for a category	No value of the feature present in a recognition vector can convey information about the category
Insignificant Type 1 feature for a category	An embedded feature with binary values T(true), F(false), where F is probable with probability approaching one

Additional Notation for Inference Functions and Estimation

Symbol	*Interpretation*
$p(\mathbf{x})$	Probability density function (p.d.f.) for random vector $\mathbf{x}$; a total probability density; a mixture density.
$p(\mathbf{x}\|\gamma_\xi^*)$	Probability density function given category γ_ξ^*; also called ξth category conditional probability density function which is characterized by the vector set of parameters, $\mathbf{b}_\xi$; that is, given $\mathbf{b}_\xi$, this probability density function is completely known.
$p(\mathbf{x}\|\gamma_\xi^*, \mathbf{b}_\xi)$	ξth category conditional probability density function which is characterized by the vector set of parameters $\mathbf{b}_\xi$; that is, given $\mathbf{b}_\xi$, this probability density function is completely known
$\mathbf{m}_\xi^* \triangleq$	$E[\mathbf{x}\|\gamma_\xi^*]$; sometimes one of the parameters in $\mathbf{b}_\xi$ (a mean vector)
$\mathbf{\Sigma}_\xi^* \triangleq$	$E[(\mathbf{x} - \mathbf{m}_\xi)(\mathbf{x} - \mathbf{m}_\xi)^t\|\gamma_\xi^*]$, Conventional definition of correlation
$N(\mathbf{x}\|\mathbf{m}_\xi, \Sigma_\xi^*)$	Multidimensional Gaussian probability density function
n_ξ	Number of training samples from category γ_ξ^*

Symbol	*Interpretation*
$d(\mathbf{x})$	A decision rule assigning $\mathbf{x}$ to category $d(\mathbf{x})$; an inference function
$L(j, i)$ or L_{ji}	Loss incurred when the decision rule $d(\mathbf{x}) = \gamma_j^*$ but $\mathbf{x}$ is from category γ_i^*
α^ξ	$\alpha^1, \alpha^2, \ldots, \alpha^n$ are the parameters characterizing $f_1(\mathbf{x}), f_2(\mathbf{x}), \ldots, f_n(\mathbf{x})$, respectively
$p(AB) = p(A)p(B)$	Required for sets A, B to be statistically independent
$p(B\|A) = p(B)$	If A, B are statistically independent
$h(\mathbf{x})$	$\sum_{\xi=1}^{M} f(\mathbf{x}\|\alpha^\xi)P(\gamma_\xi^*)$ is a mixture of M functions in the family $\mathcal{F}$ of functions

Additional Notation on Measurements

Observation Space or Measurement Space:	Space for a finite number of measurements $w_1, w_2, \ldots, w_L$, where a measurement can be a set of feature values
Feature Space:	Space with points $\mathbf{x} = [x_1, x_2, \ldots, x_L]$, where x_j is the jth feature which may be in a set for a measurement
Feature Value:	x_{j_v} is the vth value of featue x_j
Type Ø Feature:	The feature values x_{j_v}, $v = 1,2, \ldots, V$ are mutually exclusive and exhaustive; a Type Ø feature is a measurement; the feature values may or may not be ordered on the real line
Type 1 Feature:	The feature values are $x_{j_v} = T$ (True) $x_{j_v} = F$ (False); this is a binary feature

Symbol	*Interpretation*
Type 1 Measurement:	Consists of "embedded" Type 1 features
Complex Feature:	A function of respective feature's *values*
	Examples of complex features:
$r = x_{1_v} \| x_{10_v}$	• Ratio of the values of two Type Ø features (example is for feature 1 and feature 10) when both features have ordered values
# of trues in $\mathbf{x}_{10}$	• Number of (embedded) Type 1 features having True values in a Type 1 measurement
# of trues with probability > threshold in $\mathbf{x}_{10}$	• The number of (embedded) Type 1 features having true values with probability exceeding a threshold, True: 1; False: 2
$\mathbf{Ax} = \mathbf{d}$	Simultaneous solution of linear equations provides a complex feature reflecting a priori problem knowledge. For L dimension with rank of A — L, dependent variables are the output
r = # of feature with maximum probability	

Additional Notation on Hypercubes (or Constellations) for Category

Column:	A set of functionals (which can be probability density functions) specialized to a category's presentation; $\gamma^*_{\xi_k}$ is the kth column of category ξ; it may be called a subcategory; it is statistical or fuzzy
Minicolumn:	Set of one-dimensional functions (which can be probability density

Symbol	*Interpretation*
	functions) corresponding to any subset of features; $\gamma^*_{\xi_{k_u}}$ denotes the uth minicolumn of the *k*th column of category $\gamma^*_{\xi_{k_u}}$; it may be called a subsubcategory; it is called fuzzy. Also, a minicolumn can be a surface generated by nonlinear equations.

Additional Notation Used in Artificial Intelligence
Propositional Calculus or Artificial Intelligence Operations

$\wedge$, &	And, conjunction
$\vee$	Or, disjunction
$\neg$, ~	Not, negation
$\rightarrow$, $\Rightarrow$	Implies
$\equiv$, $\Leftrightarrow$	Equivalent (Logical Equivalence)
$\forall$	For all
$\exists$	There exist
/|\	Or node in an and/or graph
A	And node in an and/or graph
IF (Condition) then (Action)	Production rule
Context data structure	Includes condition part of production rule of a production system
Interpreter	Program in a production system that decides which production rule to process next
Predicate	That which is confirmed or denied; the (condition) in a production rule
$\leftrightarrow$	Term rewriting
$\searrow$	Exception (symmetric difference)
F	A set of facts

Symbol	*Interpretation*
H	Hypothesis (an inductive assertion)
$\|>$	Specialization (Deduction)
$\|<$	Generalization (Induction)
$\|=$	Reformulation
D_i	Concept description
K_i	A predicate asserting the name of a concept (a class)
$\overset{\cdots}{\cdots}\!>$	The implication linking a concept description with a concept name
e_i	Description of an object
E_i	Predicate that is true only training E_i of K_i

A.I. Predicates Constructed from A. I. Operations

$\neg\neg A{:}A$	$A\&A{:}\ A$
$A\&B{:}A$	$A\&B{:}\ B$
$A\vee B{:}A$	A and $B{:}A\&B$
$A\&{:}B\&$	$A\vee B{:}B\vee A$
$A\vee B{:}\ \neg(\neg A\&\ \neg B)$	$A\rightarrow B{:}\ \neg A\vee B$
$A\rightarrow B{:}\ \neg B\rightarrow\neg A$	$A\rightarrow B$ and $A{:}B$
$A\vee(B\vee C){:}\ (A\vee B)\vee C$	$A\&(B\&C){:}\ (A\&B)\&C$
$A\vee(B\&C){:}\ (A\vee B)\&(A\vee C)$	$A\&(B\vee C){:}\ (A\&B)\vee(A\&C)$
$A\rightarrow B$ and $B\rightarrow C{:}\ A\rightarrow C$	$A{:}A\vee X$ (X any expression)

Contents

1

Total System, Subsystems, Categories, Complex Features, Features, Primitives, and Other Aspects of Knowledge Base Structure

1-1 INTRODUCTION

1-1-1 About the Book

Artificial Intelligence with Statistical Pattern Recognition discusses classification systems with considerable detail on methodology, theory, and practical implementation. An objective is to integrate methods of knowledge representation and rules of inference from Artificial Intelligence (**AI**) with the mathematical or probabilistic methods from Statistical Pattern Recognition (**SPR**), including formal decision theory. A second objective is to describe two types of operational systems resulting from research and development. At one end of the classification system spectrum are learning systems. Examples are **The OUTCOME ADVISOR®** and **CONSULT LEARNING SYSTEM®**, consisting of the programs and hard data knowledge. These are designed to make complex inferences or multiple classifications, given a particular logical event defined in terms of findings. From the **AI** standpoint **The OUTCOME ADVISOR®** or **CONSULT LEARNING SYSTEM®** are learning systems which learn by example and concept formation; also, they are inference systems. From the SPR standpoint **The OUTCOME ADVISOR®** and **CONSULT LEARNING SYSTEM®** are systems in which the user interactively sets in motion a process that generates distribution free models for a posteriori probabilities of outcomes, and the a posteriori probabilities are estimated from the data in the knowledge base. Alternatively, estimates of likelihoods of categories can be computed. Appropriate a priori probabilities also are provided from the hard data. Both **The OUTCOME ADVISOR®** and **CONSULT LEARNING SYSTEM®** are expert systems if trained with expert samples rather than hard data. The **CONSULT LEARNING SYSTEM®** is more advanced than **The OUTCOME ADVISOR®** in that (1) the **CONSULT LEARNING SYSTEM®** utilizes complex features and (2) multiple classes can be active at the same time. It also can deal with special features, called *Index features,* which have large numbers of values.

At the other end of the decision-making spectrum is the expert system. An example is **CONSULT-I®** (Patrick, 1983; Fattu and Patrick, 1983a; Patrick, 1979; Fattu *and others,* 1982; Franklin and Angerman, 1983; Emerman and Patrick, 1983; Fattu and Patrick, 1983b; Patrick *and others,* 1979a,b; Fattu *and others,* 1983, 1985) (Patrick and Fattu, 1984), (Blomberg *and others,* 1984), which is an expert system capable of computing true a posteriori probabilities of categories. The **CONSULT-I®** system integrates methods of **AI** and **SPR**. The underlying procedure for the integration is the category conditional probability density function (c.c.p.d.f.) from **SPR**. Logical rules for induction, deduction, and hierarchical knowledge representation from AI are integrated with methods from SPR for marginal probability density projection, iterative inference, a priori probabilities, and concept formation. This integration allows engineering a category conditional probability density function which is not a conventional mathematical functional (Patrick, 1972). The functional is an inference function that can be trained with uncertain typical and atypical representations of a category and can, through deduction or induction, generate representations of the category never previously seen by **CONSULT-I®**. This latter ability to form knowledge not previously in the knowledge base is recognized in AI as intelligence.

The uncertain typical and atypical representations for a category can be supplied to **CONSULT-I®** as expert knowledge obtained from individual experts, textbooks, research papers, or by organized knowledge collection projects.

Because knowledge from experts is uncertain, the system named **CONSULT LEARNING SYSTEM®** was devised to have a compatible knowledge base structure with that of **CONSULT-I®**. The **CONSULT LEARNING SYSTEM®** accepts hard data and converts it to the form of knowledge representation required by **CONSULT-I®**, i.e., sets of probability estimates. Like **The OUTCOME ADVISOR®**, the **CONSULT LEARNING SYSTEM®** is a system which learns by example, but is capable of learning the hierarchical form of knowledge required by **CONSULT-I®**. It also can "generate" records never previously seen by concept formation.

The **CONSULT LEARNING SYSTEM®** has been applied to multidimensional sensitivity and specificity analysis of thyroid disorders (Blomberg *and others,* 1984, 1985), and Nuclear Magnetic Resonance (NMR) imaging in a multicenter program (Stein *and others,* 1984).

The OUTCOME ADVISOR®, **CONSULT LEARNING SYSTEM®** and **CONSULT-I®** can be developed and used as independent classification systems and expert systems. **CONSULT-I®**, however, is designed to be a relatively very fast decision-making system to be used on line whereas **CONSULT LEARNING SYSTEM®** is designed to process data off line for delivery to the **CONSULT-I®** knowledge base. **The OUTCOME ADVISOR®** is designed to operate on line or off line, making inference or calculating conditional probabilities of events.

1-1-2 Applications

The methods and theory for classification systems apply to many problem areas. Considerable emphasis has been given to (1) medical decision making, referred to in **AI** as AIM (Artificial Intelligence in Medicine) and in **SPR** (Statistical Pattern Recognition) as MPR (Medical Pattern Recognition). More recently, **CONSULT-I®** and its companions have been used in education for (2) diagnosis of learning disorders (Fattu *and others,* 1983). Other applications include (3) diagnosis of equipment failure (equipment failure and repair), (4) signal recognition in communications, (5) agriculture pattern recognition, (6) recognition of images such as biological cells, (7) recognition of military patterns, (8) process control, (9) geology, (10) business such as Credit and Bad Debt, (11) recreation, such as fishing, (12) military target recognition, (13) marketing, and many others. Other expert systems include **PROSPECTOR** for geology (Duda *and others,* 1979), **DENDRAL** for mass spectroscopy (Buchanan and Feigenbaum, 1978), **MACSYMA** for symbolic integration (Mathlab Group, 1977), **DART** for Computer Fault Diagnosis (Bennett and Hollander, 1981), **R1** (McDermott, 1982) and **R1**-Soar (Rosenbloom *and others,* 1985) for configuration of computer systems and **BATTLE** for the military (Slagle *and others,* 1984, 1985).

Some other medical and nonmedical expert systems are described in Feigenbaum and McCorduck (1983), Hayes-Roth *and others* (1983), Barr and Feigenbaum (1981, 1982), and Winston and Prendergas (1984).

AIM (or **MPR**) is a very fruitful application for **CONSULT-I®** and its companions. Medicine is emphasized in this book with respect to examples, applications, and comparison of systems. References to scientific research may not include all relevant works from the decision-making literature, for which we apologize. Reviews of historical interest in medical decision analysis are in Patrick (1979), Patrick *and others* (1974), Wardle and Wardle (1978), Wagner *and others* (1978), Krischer (1979).

A classification system is a basic component in such applications as computer vision (or image processing) for biological cell processing (Prewitt, 1976; Li and Fu, 1980; Patrick *and others,* 1972a) and so on. This book is applicable to these areas.

1-1-3 The Goal of Operational Systems

The theory and methodology in the book have been used in the research and development of **The OUTCOME ADVISOR®**, **CONSULT LEARNING SYSTEM®**, **CONSULT-I®**, and **CONSULT TOTAL SYSTEM™**. A considerable amount of the theory has resulted from research aspects of the projects and has not been previously published. Objectives have been designing operational systems. At times the reader may visualize material as complicated mathematics or symbols in certain sections; nevertheless, this mathematics represents complex but practical inference implementations. An alternative would be to describe, using words or phrases, the rules or procedures implemented in a computer. This does not promote scientific comparison of systems.

1-1-4 Diagnostic Performances versus Behavior

Diagnostic performance is a measure of the accuracy with which categories are recognized, given their features (attributes, findings, or pattern properties). Formal decision making provides the guidance for ultimate decision making. The ultimate constructed inference function or rule placing a set of feature values in a category needs to be identified for the system. Explanations which hide the structure of the decision-making functions are not acceptable.

In AIM there has been some interest in designing decision-making systems which have humanlike behavior (Barr and Feigenbaum, 1981; Barr and Feigenbaum, 1982; Simon, 1977). Humanlike behavior should not be confused with diagnostic performance. A system may be judged to have considerable humanlike behavior but relatively poor diagnostic performance and even be relatively slow. Most SPR decision-making systems have not been designed to have humanlike behavior but rather have been designed to optimize diagnostic performance.

Alternatively they may complement human behavior or interact with such behavior.

In AIM, a system's humanlike behavior usually results from a suboptimum procedure of automatic *feature selection* which can involve a focus on a subset of categories. Because of automatic feature selection, the system can ask for a next feature value based on those already supplied. Methods for (optimum) automatic feature selection have been extensively studied in **SPR** (Lasker, 1970; Cobelli and Salvan, 1975; Knill-Jones *and others,* 1973; Taylor, 1970; Gorry and Barnett, 1968; Gorry *and others,* 1973; Patrick, 1979; Warner *and others,* 1972; Belforte *and others,* 1980; Morgan *and others,* 1980; Fu, 1968). Ben-Bassat and Teeni (1985) evaluated models for feature selection incorporating heuristic rules. Studies have shown that optimum automatic feature selection can be very slow when on line and can introduce uncertainties which lead to decreased diagnostic performance. Alternatively, rigorously tested rules for feature selection can be used on line.

Feature extraction is the process of obtaining the feature values for a pattern to be classified. For example, in medical diagnosis feature extraction occurs during the physical examination and includes obtaining characteristics of heart sounds, lung sounds, a breast lump, abdominal tenderness, and so on. The expert physician performs feature selection, feature extraction, and diagnostic decision making followed by feature selection with feature extraction and so on (Wallstein, 1981; Christensen-Szalanski and Bushyhead, 1981; Balla, 1982; Balla *and others,* 1983; Bjerregaard *and others,* 1983; Gomez *and others,* 1981; DeDombal *and others,* 1974b; DeDombal *and others,* 1972; Kassirer and Gorry, 1978; Gorry, 1976; American Board of Internal Medicine, 1979). During this process the physician may have a focus consisting of a set of categories which guides the feature selection and extraction. The feature extraction aspect of this process is crucial to human behavior. Feature extraction by clinicians varies (DeDombal, 1976) and can influence the performance of a system (Bjerregaard *and others,* 1983; Lindberg, 1981).

Automatic feature selection in the absence of automatic feature extraction can be of superficial value for diagnostic decision making. *A system can be designed with highest diagnostic performance without the need for feature selection.*

1-1-5 Total System versus Subsystem

An application area may consist of a *total system* whose knowledge base includes all categories and features for the application area. A *subsystem* has a knowledge base consisting of a subset of these categories and features. Examples of subsystems of interest in medical diagnosis include thyroid (Fattu *and others,* 1982; Fattu and Patrick, 1983; Alperovitch and Fragu, 1977; Kulikowski and Ostroff, 1980; Coomans *and others,* 1983), breast diseases (Franklin and Angerman, 1983), drug poisons (Emmerman and Patrick, 1983), drug interactions (Roach *and others,* 1985), electrolyte disorders (Patil *and others,* 1981, 1982; Bleich, 1972), abdominal pain (DeDombal *and others,* 1974; Boom *and others,* 1983; Fieschi *and others,* 1982; Robinson *and others,* 1983; DeDombal *and others,* 1972), neurology (Salamon *and others,* 1976; Reggia *and others,* 1980), EEG (Jagannathan *and others,* 1982), jaundice (Knill-Jones, 1975), ventilator management (Fagan *and others,* 1979), pulmonary function test interpretation (Aikins *and others,* 1983), infectious diseases (Shortliffe, 1976; Evans *and others*, 1985), digitalis therapy (Gorry *and others,* 1978; Swartout, 1983), rheumatology (Kingsland *and others,* 1983; Adlassnig *and others*, 1985), hematology (Engle *and others,* 1976; Fattu and others, 1985; (Lindberg *and others,* 1981), chest pain (Patrick *and others,* 1977; Goldman and Weinberg, 1982; Ludwig and Heilbronn, 1983; Diamond and Forrester, 1979), ophthalmology (Weiss *and others,* 1977; Kastner and Weiss, 1981), protein electrophoresis (Weiss *and others,* 1981; Weiss *and others,* 1983), oncology (Shortliffe *and others,* 1981; Barnett *and others,* 1981; Wirtschafter and Carpenter, 1979), Liver (Lesmo, 1983), Interpretive Laboratory Reporting (Smith *and others*, 1984). Medical logic sectors (**HELP** system) have been implemented using Bayesian statistics in a large data base management system (Pryor *and others,* 1983) to name but a few.

It is desirable to be able to integrate two or more subsystems such as abdominal pain and pelvic mass obtaining combined subsystems containing a category or feature which otherwise would not be available in the diagnostic system. There are numerous applications in medical diagnosis for which a single subsystem (AI or SPR) is useful; there are other applications for which combining two or more subsystems is useful. Combined subsystems including a total system can be designed using the procedures presented in this book as is done in the **CONSULT TOTAL SYSTEM®**. For example, an Abdominal Pain System is being designed by Patrick, Fattu, Detterman and Blomberg which has feedback from CONSULT Subsystems including Anemia, Electrolytes, Acid Base, Liver, Renal, and Cardio-Pulmonary. Another example is an Electroytes system which has feedback from a CONSULT ACID BASE Subsystem (Patrick *and others*, 1985).

1-1-6 Completeness and Repetition

Completeness is obtained when the knowledge base of a subsystem or combined (networked) subsystems contains the categories and features required for the problem definition, and diagnostic performance is acceptable. Completeness can be more important than humanlike behavior.

Completeness may require concept formation of categories not previously in the knowlege base. As an example, complex classes are like and/or unlike categories already in the knowledge base. Although categories are required to be mutually exclusive they can be statistically dependent during concept formation. Learning new categories by concept formation requires knowledge of significant and insignificant features of previously inferred categories. This requires repetition, an area studied in SPR.

1-1-7 A Theorem on A Posteriori Probability (Patrick)

New results presented in this book include aspects of a theorem on a posteriori probability by Patrick (Patrick, 1983). Previously, attention was restricted to the well-known Bayes theorem, which is a simplistic but powerful inference function derived from axiomatic probability theory. Patrick (1972) noted that a whole framework is required for computing a posteriori probability. An important aspect of this framework is the category conditional probability density function, the construction of which involves knowledge base structure. Patrick, Shen, and Stelmack noted in 1974 that the concept of a complex class describes multiple diseases active at the same time. They also noted that statistical independence of features should not in general be assumed in applying Bayes theorem. This has also been noted by others, including Winkler (1982).

Bayes theorem has frequently been criticized (Feinstein, 1977; Shortliffe, 1983; Szolovitz *and others,* 1978; Pople, 1982; Shortliffe *and others,* 1979) with the assertion that it requires classes to be mutually exclusive; and therefore, if a class is a disease, multiple diseases cannot be active at the same time for application of Bayes theorem to medical diagnosis. Patrick has long pointed out (1972) that Bayes theorem has limited application in classification systems. Rather, he suggested that attention should be given to a Bayes framework (1972), which is a major departure from Bayes including the c.c.p.d.f. for statistically dependent features. Recognition of the limitation of Bayes led to the development, over a period of 20 years, of the new theorem on a posteriori probability by Patrick (Patrick, 1983; Patrick and Fattu, 1984).

Another aspect of a posteriori probability inference is the formation (or learning) of previously unknown categories. The distinction between a class and category will be made shortly. In **AI** this currently is called concept formation or learning by discovery but was extensively studied as unsupervised learning (or learning without a teacher) by Patrick in 1965. Many different types of learning without a teacher were described by Patrick in 1972. Types of learning in view of the new theorem are discussed by Patrick and Fattu (1984).

The theorem on a posteriori probability by Patrick (1983) distinguishes between classes and categories. Categories are mutually exclusive but classes may not be. A category is a combination of classes. A basic category is called an *only class,* an event consisting of one class without any other classes. A *complex class* involves two or more classes active at the same time; i.e., a complex class is a category corresponding to the event that certain classes occur with other classes.

A diagnostic decision-making problem formulation begins with the creation of classes in the knowledge base. Features with feature values are described for these classes. The decision space may initially (a priori) consist of the categories called only classes and may not contain complex classes. The new theorem on a posteriori probability describes the formation of new categories, which are complex classes, during inference or a posteriori probability iteration. This formation of new categories is concept formation and is a new form of learning without a teacher.

Just as in Bayes theorem, the theorem on a posteriori probability by Patrick (1983) requires that categories be mutually exclusive. Using the notation of the theorem by Patrick, in Bayes theorem the categories *are* the classes. In the theorem by Patrick, the underlying classes are related only to the categories. Although the categories are mutually exclusive, the underlying classes need not be mutually exclusive. The theorem by Patrick (1983) has the added component of concept formation, which is achieved because *categories can be statistically dependent.* This results because there are sequences of training sessions in which classes or categories already described in the knowledge base are active (supervised learning or learning with a teacher). This results in statistical inference about the feature space about *new* category concepts (Patrick and Fattu, 1984).

The supervised training periods would be called inductive learning in **AI.** But the concept formation of new categories requires SPR ideas of statistical dependence or correlation. Starting with existing classes and categories, concepts are formed of what new categories can "look like" in terms of feature values. The statistical repetition in one training session compared with that of another results in a description of areas of insignificance and significance in the feature space for a category concept. *Then, when that previously unseen category occurs, it can be recognized through deductive inference.*

For example, suppose there are two classes ω_1 and ω_2, and the two only classes denoted ω_1^* and ω_2^* are described by examples. What is known about the concept of a complex class Ω_{12}^*? It is assumed that an example of Ω_{12}^* has never been seen. The concept of Ω_{12}^* is that it is different, with respect to some features, from either ω_1^* or ω_2^* but also like ω_1^* and ω_2^* with respect to some features. During inductive learning of ω_1^* and ω_2^*, statistical knowledge is obtained about respective regions of insignificance and/or significance for ω_1^* and ω_2^* in the feature space. These regions of insignificance are where Ω_{12}^* does not look like ω_1^* and does not look like ω_2^*. Thus any prospective sample from Ω_{12}^* is statistically dependent on those from ω_1^* and ω_2^*.

In summary, *the theorem on a posteriori probability by Patrick* (1983) *provides that categories are mutually exclusive but statistically dependent during concept formation. Underlying classes may not, through their features, be mutually exclusive.* The underlying classes lead to the formation of a complex class (concept) which is statistically dependent on the previous knowledge of the classes in the form of only class knowledge.

1-1-8 Implementation

Inductive learning with a teacher is time consuming and left to the **CONSULT LEARNING SYSTEM®** or **The OUTCOME ADVISOR®**. It is here that basic knowledge of only classes and some complex classes is obtained. Fast inference or decision making then can be done in **CONSULT-I®** using this knowledge.

Concept formation for generation of previously unseen complex classes is the most time-consuming procedure of all. Performing it on line using hard data may be time consuming. There are, however, certain basic procedures of concept formation discussed in this book that can be used to recognize complex classes by deduction on line (Chapter 7).

1-1-9 Philosophy of AI and SPR

Consider that AI is a collection of methods for describing knowledge base structure collection and logical rules for induction and deduction, while SPR is a collection of methods for a posteriori inference, concept formation by learning without a teacher, and statistical methods. Integration of these two collections, AI and SPR, facilitates concept formation or learning by discovery. An objective of this book is to discover how to integrate **AI** and **SPR**.

1-2 PREVIEW OF KNOWLEDGE BASE STRUCTURE

Useful reviews of knowledge base structure are in Patrick (1972, 1979) and Brodie *and others* (1984).

1-2-1 Primitives, Features, and Complex Features (Concepts)

A *primitive* denoted y_ξ is a basic characteristic (level 1) of a category. A *feature value* denoted x_{j_v} (level 2) is the next higher level characteristic in the hierarchy. A *feature* x_j "owns" a set of feature values, one of which is true for a given pattern from a category. There are different kinds of features. A *Type Ø feature* is defined to have values which are mutually exclusive (not necessarily orderable). A *Type 1 feature* is defined as a set of binary features where a binary feature is either True or False. The value of a Type 1 feature is one of the possible combinations of True or False values for all the features in the set (a probability function of these values). These features in the set also are referred to as *embedded features* of a Type 1 feature. All values of a Type 1 feature may not be allowed and/or determined by other feature values using *frames.* Frames can be connected by tree structure or network structure. Other types of features including complex features are defined and developed in Chapter 8.

The above definitions are from **SPR** (except a frame is from **AI**). In the hierarchy there is a *complex feature value* (level 3) defined in **SPR** studies by Patrick, Shen, and Stelmack (1974). A complex feature value is a function of feature values. The complex feature is at the initial level in the hierarchy where *concept formation* can take place. A *complex feature* can be a ratio, sum, maximum, minimum, dependent output of a set of simultaneous linear or nonlinear equations, or a complex mathematical equation. Concept formation is a phrase from **AI** (Michalski and Stepp, 1983; Barr and Feigenbaum, 1982) and its counterpart in **SPR** is learning without a teacher, although in this book we allow for concept formation with a teacher.

Primitives and features are the basic characteristics of a category and are supplied a priori (**SPR**), i.e. by being told (**AI**). They can be added to or modified by a teacher. As a concept, the complex feature value can be formed with or without a teacher. At the initial level in the hierarchy, learning is possible without a teacher.

A complex feature value can be a category; but more generally it is a concept in the hierarchical description of a category. It is convenient at times to have named a Type 1 feature, with its embedded Type 1 features, as a *measurement* because it embodies a number of properties of a pattern. Thus we can, in general, use the name measurement to refer to a Type Ø measurement or a Type 1 measurement. Then a Type Ø measurement is a feature and a Type 1 measurement has embedded binary features. To be precise, this definition of measurement versus features should be used, but it is difficult to escape the convenience of referring to both Type Ø and Type 1 measurements as features. Type Ø, Type 1, and certain "intelligent" complex features are the features given most attention in this book. A special Type Ø feature called an *Index feature* is defined as one that can have a very large number of values. Such a feature usually does not provide a finding for a pattern in a category. Rather, an Index feature has values used to index the categories or all subcategories of the categories. For example, in **CONSULT LEARNING SYSTEM®** we may wish to make an inference given a category or subcategory. In this case an Index feature value simply indexes the given category or subcategory.

Consider this: In **CONSULT-I®**, categories are defined a priori and inferences (decisions) are made about the categories given findings. On the other hand, in **CONSULT LEARNING SYSTEM®** or **The OUTCOME ADVISOR®**, categories usually are not defined a priori, but they *could be* using the values of a category feature. The values of the category feature then can index various subsets of records in the data base of the **CONSULT LEARNING SYSTEM®**; each subset is for a different category. This has application in using **CONSULT LEARNING SYSTEM®** to learn probabilities in the category conditional probability density function of **CONSULT-I®**. The categories in **CONSULT-I®** correspond to the values of a category feature or Index feature in **CONSULT LEARNING SYSTEM®**. Another application of an Index feature is to use its values to describe Diagnosis Related Groups (DRGs) (Yale, 1981; New Jersey State Department of Health, 1980; Title Six, Social Security Act Amendment, 1983) or Major Diagnosis Categories (MDCs) for medical reimbursement. For this example, given a DRG or MDC, inferences can be made about cost, length of stay, quality of nursing, etc., as suggested by Detterman (1984). Other examples of applications using a category feature include: indexing a large number of actions (such as treatments), indexing the names of doctors for DRGs, and names of individuals being evaluated.

An interesting question is, Why can't all features used in **CONSULT LEARNING SYSTEM®** be Index or category features? The reason they usually cannot is explained as follows: To learn an inference by example or discovery we need training—repetition. This repetition increases confidence. If all features in **CONSULT LEARNING SYSTEM®** are category features, then where is the training? We are trying to learn about events, in this case categories and dependencies of other events on these categories. Thus, for a category there must be examples, and these examples are described by features which are not category features. Usually, the number of values of a feature, which is not an Index feature, is much less than that for a category feature. Again, this is done in order to be able to collect enough data to achieve a certain confidence.

In conclusion, Index features are useful to index sets of data where the number of sets can be relatively large. Also, the values of a category feature are a focus for inference, such as categories to be decided or categories to be conditioned on. Dependencies among features which are not category features are learned for the category conditioned on. Given the category, inferences are made about other noncategory feature values.

Another kind of feature is called an *Ownership feature*. An ownership feature can be viewed as "crossing" subsystems in **CONSULT LEARNING SYSTEM®** or **OUTCOME ADVISOR®**. For example, in medicine, endocrine subsystems could correspond to thyroid, adrenal, and pituitary. Records may be collected in each of these subsystems for each patient. Then, the record in respective subsystems is said to be *owned* by the patient. As another example, MDCs could be considered as subsystems, with the set of DRGs for each MDC representing the values of a category feature for the subsystem. A particular patient could have multiple MDCs describing an illness, each with a DRG. The patient's record thus is characterized by an ownership property which crosses the subsystem. That is, the patient owns certain MDCs with DRGs and then any other feature values in the respective subsystems. If a patient has multiple records, then that patient owns each record which in turn owns their projections in the respective subsystems.

Another example of an ownership feature is certification in residency programs. Suppose it is desirable to keep track of the experiences of a resident in each specialty area (subsystem) such as obstetrics, surgery, emergency medicine, internal medicine, and cardiac intensive care. A record owned by a resident for an experience may consist of an experience in emergency medicine and cardiac intensive care. One can ask for the experience of a resident for any event in any subsystem. We stress that the inference being done in this example is minimal; it is nothing more than data storage and retrieval. Most data base management systems operate at this level. Both **CONSULT LEARNING SYSTEM®** and **The OUTCOME ADVISOR®** can operate at this level but it utilizes only a minimal amount of their capability. Their real power is the ability to infer about an event(s) given another event (set of findings) while Learning by Example or Discovery.

We now return to the theory and development of the more sophisticated classification systems.

1-2-2 Examples of Primitives, Features, and Complex Features

In medical classification, an example of a primitive is diastolic blood pressure between 86 to 90. A Type Ø feature for diastolic blood pressure is the *set of ranges,* 81 to 85, 86 to 90, 91 to 95, 96 to 100, and so on. A Type Ø feature also could be called a *fuzzy set.* For a discussion of fuzzy sets, see Zadah, 1982, Zadah, 1979; Adlassnig, 1980; Cerutti and Timó Pieri, 1981; Wechsler, 1976; Smets *and others,* 1977; Fattu and Patrick, 1983; Patrick, 1979; Esogbue, 1983; Clive *and others,* 1983; Negoita, 1985.

A simple example of a complex feature value is diastolic hypertension, defined, for example, as any value range *above* 95. This is achieved by the logical OR (disjunction) operation of feature values.

Define another Type Ø feature as age and define a complex feature value as diastolic blood pressure above 90 for one age range, above 95 for another age range, and so on. This is now a more complicated concept for diastolic hypertension.

The complex feature value diastolic hypertension at the level in the hierarchy can be a category or only a concept in the formation of a category. For example, the category renal hypertension is at a higher level (say, level 4) in the hierarchy but includes the concept of diastolic hypertension, a concept at level 3.

Possible formed categories in the development of the example would not include renal hypertension from level 4 and diastolic hypertension from level 3. This has been accomplished with a teacher, but not much more has been accomplished than naming nodes in a hierarchical network for knowledge representation. The construction relating nodes in the network is the category conditional probability density function (c.c.p.d.f.) denoted $p(\mathbf{x}|\gamma_i^*)$, where γ_i^* denotes the *i*th category and $\mathbf{x}$ is a vector or set of feature values for a pattern of the category (SPR). In AI an analogous construct is called a STAR (Michalski, 1983) but it does not allow for a probabilistic description of pattern occurrences.

The c.c.p.d.f. is an inference from feature values (primitives) to a category. When categories occur during concept formation, they can interact. This interaction is described by classes which have a proper place in the hierarchy horizontal with categories. There are class conditional probability density functions for inference of classes. Also, there is contructed a relationship between a particular category called a complex class and certain classes. Another construction is that of a particular relationship between a particular category called an only class and a class.

1-2-3 Categories and Actions

Categories denoted γ_i^* are in the *decision space* (or classification space). As in the previous example, they can be inferred from multiple levels in the knowledge base hierarchy. Often, *all* possible categories are defined a priori by a teacher. They can be added to later by a teacher. For example, suppose we want to form a new category which is a combination of two existing categories. This problem is surrounded by a lot of confusion in medical classification. In particular, Bayes theorem (**SPR**) requires that categories be mutually exclusive (cannot occur together). If categories are diseases, then the next conclusion is that Bayes theorem does not apply when two diseases are active at the same time. *Bayes theorem does allow for learning without a teacher* (Patrick, 1979; Patrick, 1972), *which is concept formation of new categories, but not from existing categories or concepts.* This describes the problem. A proposed solution is a new theorem on a posteriori probability (Patrick, 1983) with inference of categories where a new category can be formed from previous concepts. These previous concepts are not directly categories but are something else we call classes.

Actions can have one-to-one relationships with the categories, subcategories, or subsubcategories or sets of them. In medical diagnosis an action can be a treatment or a next test. An action can be viewed as a form of feature selection where the feature selection is "hard wired" to a category (subcategory, subsubcategory). This is a simple form of feature selection which is fast and which is useful in many applications.

A more complicated action is one which depends on multiple categories. For example, the action could depend on the highest ranking (in terms of a posteriori probability) categories. There are many possibilities. For example, perform the action indicated by the highest-ranking category and, depending on the response, perform the action indicated by the next-ranking category, and so on. If known, perform the action indicated for the two (or more) top-ranking categories. Methods useful here include production rules, trees, and networks.

As suggested above, feature selection is an action designed to obtain the next feature value minimizing probability of error or risk (i.e., leading to classification). For this type of action (feature selection) we have a criterion with which to select the action. An action should be governed by a criterion, such as to minimize error, obtain the best image, or to implement previously discovered actions.

In conclusion, a useful method to determine an action is a *causality relationship* between a category (categories) and the action. Causality is discussed further in Section 2-1 of Chapter 2. More complicated methods include the optimum feature selection method.

1-2-4 Theorem on A Posteriori Probability (Patrick)

The basic concept in the theorem on a posteriori probability by Patrick (1983) is the class. One kind of category is a class by itself called an *only class* denoted ω_i^*; another kind of category is a combination of classes called a complex class and denoted Ω^*_ξ. Categories are mutually exclusive as in Bayes theorem but there is an additional proposition in the theorem by Patrick: *Categories are statistically dependent during concept formation.* This *statistical dependence* is a new aspect of SPR and does not exist in **AI.** Thus concept formation without a teacher requires SPR where statistical dependence is used to determine regions of significance and insignificance in the feature space.

Concept formation using the theorem on a posteriori probability by Patrick can take place at any level in the hierarchy where concept formation is possible. Again, we point out that the theorem can be implemented at multiple levels.

1-3 THE CLASSIFICATION PROBLEM

The basic classification problem is to calculate the probability with which a set of feature values (findings) belongs to a particular pattern of category γ^*_i. Closeness is measured by a closeness measure, but not an ordinary Euclidean type of distance measure. The closeness measure involves concepts, logical rules, concept formation, induction, deduction, and statistics. Nevertheless, it is a closeness measure. It will be interesting to describe the **CONSULT-I®** closeness measure and use it to describe closeness measures used by **INTERNIST** (Miller *and others,* 1982; Myers *and others,* 1982; Pople, 1982), **MYCIN** (Shortliffe, 1976), **EXPERT (CASNET)** (Kulikowski and Weiss, 1982; Weiss *and others,* 1978), Weiss and Kulikowski, 1984, and **PROMISE** (Gini and Gini, 1980).

1-4 THE KNOWLEDGE BASE STRUCTURE

The knowledge base structure proceeds from primitives to feature values to complex feature values; this marks the first level of concept formation as categories. At each ascending level, concepts can be defined and formed; and categories can be assigned, as desired, to concepts.

Each concept has a concept–feature relationship, a viewpoint from **SPR.** In this book we integrate the proposition of a concept-conditional probability density function from **SPR** with the rules and heuristics of **AI** to form an integrated concept–feature relationship.

This concept–feature relationship involves subconcepts, miniconcepts collectively described as *hypercubes* of knowledge. The

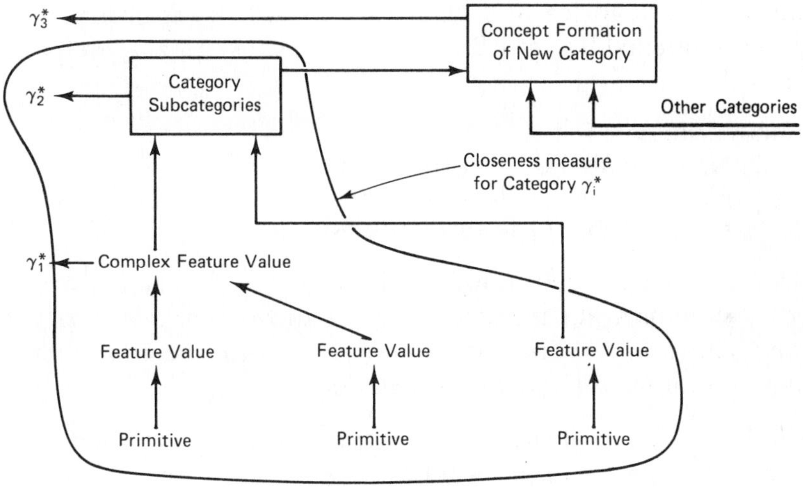

FIGURE 1.1. Diagram of Knowledge representation from primitive to category, with possible intermediate concept formation of a Complex Feature value as a Category.

hypercubes of knowledge for concepts are both trained and potential. The trained aspects reflect both typical and atypical presentations obtained through induction. The potential aspects are those presentations generated by deduction.

To capture all this in a diagram is difficult. But, consider the hierarchy in Figure 1.1. The closeness measure relating a category γ_i^* to feature values is illustrated. The construction of this closeness measure begins with the *weighted conjunctions of disjunctions of weights for respective features*. Features may be eliminated from the conjunction and replaced by a complex feature value or other concepts.

All features, complex features, and concepts are included in the conjunction unless they are *insignificant*.

1-5 TOTAL SYSTEM MODEL

1-5-1 Definitions

The classification problem varies with the applications; but in general, notation is needed for a model ranging from where the total system is a single subsystem, consists of two or three subsystems, or consists of many subsystems. A total classification system (Chapter 11) consists of

L features, M categories, and M_c classes. Knowledge is grouped into S subsystems indexed by $s = 1,2, \ldots ,S$, where subsystem $\mathcal{S}_s$ is characterized as follows:

Subsystem $\mathcal{S}_s$

M_s: Number of categories in subsystem $\mathcal{S}_s$

M_{c_s}: Number of classes in subsystem $\mathcal{S}_s$

L_s: Number of features in subsystem $\mathcal{S}_s$.

A method is needed to index all categories, classes, features, and other subsystems and categories of other subsystems *associated with or affecting subsystem* $\mathcal{S}_s$. This is accomplished with vectors, where the terms in { } indicate those items included:

$\mathbf{x}_s = \{x_{s_j}\}, x_{s_j} = 1$ if jth feature (primitive) is included in { }, insignificant otherwise

$\boldsymbol{\gamma}_s^* = \{\gamma_{s_i}^*\}, \gamma_{s_i}^* = 1$ If ith category γ_i^* is included in { }, insignificant otherwise

$\mathscr{C}_s = \{\mathscr{C}_{s_i}\}, \mathscr{C}_{s_i} = 1$ if ith class is included in { }, insignificant otherwise

$\mathbf{s}_s = \{s_{s_e}\}, s_{s_e} = 1$ if subsystem $\mathcal{S}_e$ is associated with reference subsystem $\mathcal{S}_s$, insignificant otherwise

A category $\gamma_{s_i}^*$ in reference subsystem $\mathcal{S}_s$ can depend on categories in other subsystems. This dependence is indicated by

$\mathbf{d}_{s_e}^* = \{\gamma_{s_{i_{e_\xi}}}^*\}, \gamma_{s_{i_{e_\xi}}}^* = 1$ if category $\boldsymbol{\gamma}_{s_i}^*$ in subsystem $\mathcal{S}_s$ depends on category $\boldsymbol{\gamma}_{e_\xi}^*$ in subsystem $\mathcal{S}_e$.

Then $\mathbf{d}_s \triangleq \{\mathbf{d}_{s_i}\}$ is called a set of intermediate categories for subsystem $\mathcal{S}_s$. It is part of the knowledge base structure of the total **CONSULT-I®** system.

1-5-2 Insignificant Features

The number of features for a total medical classification system can be quite large,† perhaps 20,000 (Gordon, 1970). The number of primitives used in an Internal Medicine system contains over 4000 binary features, **Caduceus** (Miller *and others,* 1982; Miller, 1984). Yet a category such as appendicitis is described by a relatively few number of

†This estimate is much too high, including incidental and redundant features not very sensitive or specific for the diseases.

Subsystem	1	2	S
	$\{\gamma^*_{1_i}\}$	....	....
	$\mathbf{x}_1$	....	....
	....	$\{\gamma^*_{2_i}\}$	....
	....	$\mathbf{x}_2$	....
	....	....	$\{\gamma^*_{s_i}\}$
	....	....	$\mathbf{x}_s$

FIGURE 1.2. Illustration of significant features and categories of subsystems. The dotted lines indicate features or categories not significant for a subsystem.

features, perhaps 10 to 15 or even fewer. A *significant feature* for category γ_i^* is defined as one for which a value of the feature can affect the a posteriori category probability relative to that for other categories.

Illustrated in Figure 1.2 are the categories and features of S subsystems in a total system. The features $\mathbf{x}_s$ are significant for subsystem $\mathcal{S}_s$, but all other features in the total system are insignificant for that subsystem.

The *proposition of an insignificant feature* will be defined and described from the SPR viewpoint in Chapters 8 and 9. This proposition is important for establishing the viewpoint that features $\mathbf{x}_s$ are in subsystem $\mathcal{S}_s$ *and* the total system (Chapter 11).

The proposition of an insignificant feature requires learning. You can be told which features are significant for a category. On the other hand, "learning by example" to determine which features are insignificant for a category can be accomplished using **The OUTCOME ADVISOR®** or **CONSULT LEARNING SYSTEM®**.

The proposition of insignificance is applied when constructing and computing the closeness measure (inference function) for category $\gamma^*_{s_i}$. The construction must be such that only significant features affect $\gamma^*_{s_i}$.

Example:
Suppose the category $\gamma^*_{s_i}$ is appendicitis in an abdominal pain subsystem $\mathcal{S}_s$. Features significant for appendicitis are: location of abdominal pain, time course of abdominal pain, location of abdominal tenderness, white blood cell count, decreased appetite, evidence of peritoneal irritation and a negative history of appendectomy. Insignificant features can be concepts of other diseases such as a bloody nose, a finger amputation,

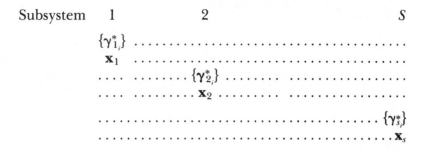

fractured rib, arthritis, and so on. These other features are significant for categories in other subsystems but not for appendicitis. Clearly, a pattern of appendicitis is described by a few significant features. An appendicitis model can be constructed for placement in a subsystem or total system. This is called a *category module* (see Section 11-10-3).

1-6 TOTAL SYSTEM PROCESSING

1-6-1 Introduction

There is a distinction to be made between system performance and system behavior. In this section we preview different combinations of performance and behavior for a classification system.

1-6-2 Optimum Performance, Interactive Behavior with Preformed Concepts

Let all concepts (complex features and categories) be formed so that the closeness measure for each category γ_ξ^* in terms of the feature vector $\mathbf{x}$ can be computed. A recognition vector $\mathbf{x}$ (Findings) containing feature values for patterns from an unknown category is processed. Most feature values for the pattern to be recognized are *missing*. For each category γ_ξ^*, the a posteriori probability is computed as $p(\gamma_\xi^*|\mathbf{x})$. This system, properly constructed, will have optimum performance. Its behavior is not rigid because the user can input any subset of nonmissing features to the system.

Although it may not be obvious, the system is intelligent because in computing $p(\gamma_\xi^*|\mathbf{x})$ it has to perform different kinds of *deductive inferences* because usually it has not seen $\mathbf{x}$ before. At the same time it performs inductive inference by computing conjunctions of feature values or concepts; furthermore it does this with some certainty because previous typical and atypical presentations are stored as *statistical hypercubes*.†

A second processing can be accomplished with one or more previously missing features next utilized as input.

Processing time can be relatively fast. Parallel processing always can be traded or added to decrease processing time.

---

†A hypercube is another name for a cluster of patterns for a category. The cluster of patterns is a subcategory of the category. The engineering of this hypercube is referred to as a column because it is a column of Fuzzy Sets of numbers.

Extensive studies in SPR suggest that *no system can have better diagnostic performance than the above, it can only have different behavior.* This presumes the utilization of all available knowledge in order to achieve convergence in the absence of an unlimited number of training samples.

1-6-3 Optimum Performance, Feature Selection with Preformed Concepts

A feature selection system (see Chapter 10) differs in behavior from the previous system (preformed concepts). The user supplies a feature value and after that the system requests or suggests additional feature values. The next feature selected (whether Type Ø or Type 1) is always the one expected to give best classification performance. The behavior is more humanlike than in the previous system (Section 1-6-2), and even though optimum diagnostic performance is possible, there are problems. The first problem is processing time, which can be *very* long. Another problem is that the human user, while *perhaps* liking the system's humanlike behavior, may have reasons for inputting different features from those requested by the system. A user override method could be used, making the system interactive; but a lot of processing time has been wasted. There are applications where sequential feature selection clearly is undesirable, including applications where a fixed number of feature values will be supplied and answers must always be supplied for completeness.

The feature selection process can be modified suboptimal so as to decrease processing time, but the quality of feature selection can decrease to a level of being useless. If no regard is given to classification performance, the system may appear very humanlike.

1-6-4 Concept Formation

1-6-4-1 On Line versus Off Line

Off-line concept formation utilizes a set of training samples to learn a new concept at one level or concepts at multiple levels. This can be learning by example (learning with a teacher) or learning by discovery (learning without a teacher). This is **SPR** and is explained by the new theorem on a posteriori probability (Patrick).

At the first category level of concept formation the new concept will be a complex class. Once formed, this concept (which is a feature) becomes a "feature value" for categories at the next highest level (if there is one). This is where learning without a teacher becomes difficult. With a teacher, the categories affected at higher levels in the hierarchy are known so that proper updates of category feature relationships are achieved. Going beyond a single level of concept formation during one training session is a "big bite."

On-line Concept Formation using a simple recognition sample requires that at the first category level of concept formation a concept is generated by deduction. This deduction uses rules established a priori. It is not possible to proceed to a next higher level in the hierarchy with this single observation.

It is reasonable to do concept formation off line; and this is the way human researchers usually do it. As mentioned, concept formation on line at a single category level can be practical. This can be used to "generate complex classes," for example, to see if two diseases active is more likely than one disease active. This will be accomplished using a priori rules for concept formation by deduction. These rules are developed in Chapters 5, 6, and 9.

1-6-4-2 Repetition for Concept Formation

Concept formation requires repetitive training sessions. This is an aspect of **SPR.** It is especially true in classification problems where there are uncertainties. But studies show that proper integration of uncertainties from multiple features leads to decreased category uncertainty (Patrick, 1972). Again, these are **SPR** aspects.

In human learning one may get a "glimpse" of a new concept from a single example; but to develop certainty in the concept requires repetition (which is **SPR**). This especially is true because correlations among features are unknown and must be learned by repetition.

1-6-5 Focus for a Differential Diagnosis

There are various ways to obtain a focus for differential diagnosis.

1-6-5-1 Activation Rules

Activation rules (Patrick, 1979; Patrick *and others,* 1974) are devised to activate one or more subsystems based on the findings. Categories from these subsystems are then processed using propositions for interacting among the subsystems. There are many practical examples where activation of a single subsystem solves the problem.

Classification performance is optimal while behavior is interactive in selecting the subsystem. In medicine Activation of such subsystems as Chest Pain, Abdominal Pain, Anemia, Bleeding, or Diarrhea are very practical examples. A **Total System** is not required and would be inefficient. However, a subsystem such as Abdominal Pain does benefit from networking outputs from other subsystems such as Anemia, Liver Function Disorders, Electrolytes, and Acid Base. Networking provides a practical means of building a **TOTAL System** with subsystems.

1-6-5-2 Focus of Small Size

A focus of small size, say four to six categories, can be used. The a posteriori probabilities of all categories in the focus are computed. **AI** rules exist for eliminating categories from the focus, selecting the next feature and then the next category to add to the focus, and an eventual stopping rule (threshold).

The behavior here is humanlike but processing time can be very, very slow, with 1986 computers. Proof as to when a solution to the search is obtained is not available.

If the feature-selection operation is eliminated, the system can reduce to that of Section 1-6-2. Eliminating the human behavior leads to optimum performance. Concept formation on line using a single recognition sample can be included.

A focus also can be used to select two of the classes for which to investigate the a posteriori probability of a complex class of these classes. With M_1 classes there are

$$\binom{M_1}{2} = M_1!/2!(M_1-2)!$$

complex classes to investigate. Processing time can be relatively high. An alternative is user interaction where a specific complex class (two classes) is selected for investigation. For a problem with, say, 5 classes there may be ten complex classes to investigate, which is reasonable. A three-class problem of chest pain (MI, Coronary Insufficiency, Chest Pain Noncardiac Cause) has three complex classes of two classes. Thus, there are three only classes, three complex classes, for a total of six categories in this example. A complex class of three classes can also exist but the user may not wish to address this complexity.

2

Definitions and Historical Review

2-1 DEFINITIONS USED IN INTEGRATING ARTIFICIAL INTELLIGENCE WITH STATISTICAL PATTERN RECOGNITION

The reader is reminded that this book deals with classification (diagnostic) systems. Within the context of this book the following definitions are useful at the outset:

Intelligence. Intelligence is defined as a capacity for *reasoning,* understanding, knowledge of an event or circumstance, gathering or distribution of information. Reasoning is defined as the process of forming conclusions, judgments, or inference from facts or premises.

Artificial. Artificial is defined as produced by man; made in imitation or as a substitution. Thus, the term Artificial Intelligence (**AI**) is defined.

Scientific Method. The scientific method is defined as a method of research in which a problem is identified, a hypothesis is formulated, relevant data is gathered, and the hypothesis is *empirically* tested. **The OUTCOME ADVISOR®** and **CONSULT LEARNING SYSTEM®** described later in this book are modern systems for helping with the scientific method. Today people have access to enormous and varied information and have the ability to pose problem models. The scientific method provides that learning or estimation takes place *against a model.* The model is judged on its empirical performance. For example, the model may be used to process samples to learn a knowledge base to be used in an expert learning system as in the **CONSULT LEARNING SYSTEM®**. Then the system is tested with new, previously unseen, samples to obtain experimental probabilities of error.

Learning by examples about insignificance and significance of events has its roots in statistical pattern recognition (**SPR**). The regions of significance are in the feature space, and are related to propositions essential for concept formation, a topic discussed later in Section 2-3.

Statistics. Statistics is a science that deals with the collection, classification, analysis, and interpretation of numerical facts or data, and by using mathematical theories of probability, identifies order and regularity among aggregates of more or less disparate elements.

Pattern. A pattern is composed of a number of elements or objects arranged in some format. In this book a pattern is said to be composed of a set of feature values, sometimes referred to as attributes or findings. A Pattern is the same as a Record or vector sample.

Statistical Pattern Recognition. Statistical Pattern Recognition (**SPR**) deals with descriptions of patterns such as diseases. Patterns are grouped by category, and variability within a category is described mathematically. Uncertain knowledge about patterns in a category is accounted for by an inference function called the category conditional probability density function (c.c.p.d.f.). Procedures for Learning are studied in **SPR**.

Knowledge. Knowledge is defined as whatever can be ascribed to an agent (Minsky, 1963; Tsotsos, 1982; Newell, 1982) and includes what it is and how it can be used. For example, in computer vision studies it is primarily spatial (between, above, to the left of) or shape (curvature, shape type, e.g., conelike). It can be temporal (involving time), it can involve motion, or be a procedure ("how to"). For systems described as consultation systems, classification systems, decision-making systems, expert systems, inference systems, diagnostic systems, hypothesis generating systems, important knowledge includes the features and feature values used to describe categories. Other important knowledge includes typical and atypical presentations describing the categories and rules for deduction and induction to form previously unseen presentations of categories and new categories.

Hierarchy. A hierarchy is a system of things ranked one above the other. In **CONSULT-I®** a knowledge hierarchy includes in ascending order: feature values, complex feature values, subclasses, classes, categories (only classes, complex classes), subcategories, subsystems, and a total system. A hierarchy is a concept which itself consists of concepts; for example, *categories are concepts.* A category may or may not be present a priori in the hierarchy, but it can be generated through learning, sometimes learning without a teacher (a method of learning to be discussed). For example, complex classes and only classes are concepts which may be generated in the knowledge base rather than inserted a priori.

Inference. Inference is the process of deriving from an assumed premise either the strict logical conclusion or one that is to some degree probable. Inference is a basic proposition for AI or SPR classification systems. Elementary examples of inference include the production rule and decision tree. More complex examples include a column in **CONSULT-I®**. If the premise is a set of feature vectors $\mathbf{x}_1$, $\mathbf{x}_2, \ldots, \mathbf{x}_n$ and the logical conclusion is a category γ_i^*, a well-studied method of inference from statistical pattern recognition is expressed by

$$p(\gamma_i^*|\mathbf{x}_1,\mathbf{x}_2,\ldots,\mathbf{x}_n) = \frac{p(\mathbf{x}_n|\gamma_i^*, \mathbf{x}_1,\ldots,\mathbf{x}_{n-1})\, p(\gamma_i^*|\mathbf{x}_1, \mathbf{x}_2,\ldots,\mathbf{x}_{n-1})}{p(\mathbf{x}_n)}$$

more conveniently written

$$p(\gamma_i^*|\dot{\mathbf{x}}_n) = \frac{p(\mathbf{x}_n|\gamma_i^*, \dot{\mathbf{x}}_{n-1})\, p(\gamma_i^*\, \mathbf{x}_{n-1})}{p(\mathbf{x}_n)}$$

where

$$\dot{\mathbf{x}}_n = (\mathbf{x}_1,\mathbf{x}_2,\ldots,\mathbf{x}_n)$$

which means that the probability of category γ_i^* given n samples can be expressed as an update of that probability which existed given $n - 1$ samples. This shows how inference can be updated but provides no details about knowledge representation. The above is an extremely important and powerful method of inference following from Bayes theorem, but as pointed out by Patrick in 1972, the most extensive engineering requires representing $p(\mathbf{x}_n|\gamma_i^*,\mathbf{x}_1,\ldots, \mathbf{x}_{n-1})$. This book deals with such knowledge engineering.

Learning. A dictionary definition of learning is *the process of acquiring knowledge or skills* whereas in psychology it is *the modification of behavior through training*. Different kinds of learning are discussed in Section 2-2. In this book, learning means to acquire knowledge for classification systems with the objective of optimal classification accuracy.

Discovery. Discovery is the process of acquiring knowledge of something previously unknown. Discovery is a time-consuming process for humans, including converting the discovered knowledge to a form useful for other humans or a computer. Most knowledge known to us was discovered by others. A computer can be helpful in discovery, especially with human interaction. It is not surprising that learning by discovery is a most difficult task for computers.

Learning by discovery can be considered a more difficult form of learning. For instance, learning using supervised examples with a previously constructed model is not as difficult as when the samples are unsupervised for the same model. More difficult yet is learning involving concept formation of new categories as described by the theorem on a posteriori probability (Patrick, 1983; Patrick and Fattu, 1984). These three kinds of learning are illustrated in Figure 2.1. Both of the two highest levels of learning in Figure 2.1 involve learning without a teacher and can be considered learning by discovery.

The lowest level learning in Figure 2.1 uses the model that there are M categories $\omega_1^* = \omega_1, \omega_2^* = \omega_2, \ldots, \omega_M^* = \omega_M$, and samples are available from each (supervised) of them to learn their respective c.c.p.d.f.s. The second level of learning presumes that some or all of the categories do not have training samples precisely identified as being from those categories (Pearson, 1902; Robbins, 1948; Teicher, 1960; Patrick, 1965, 1968, 1972; Fralick, 1967; Spragins, 1966; Yakowitz, 1969; Patrick and Costello, 1970; Cooper and Cooper 1964; Patrick and Carayanopoulos, 1970; Patrick and Shen, 1975; Patrick *and others,* 1975).

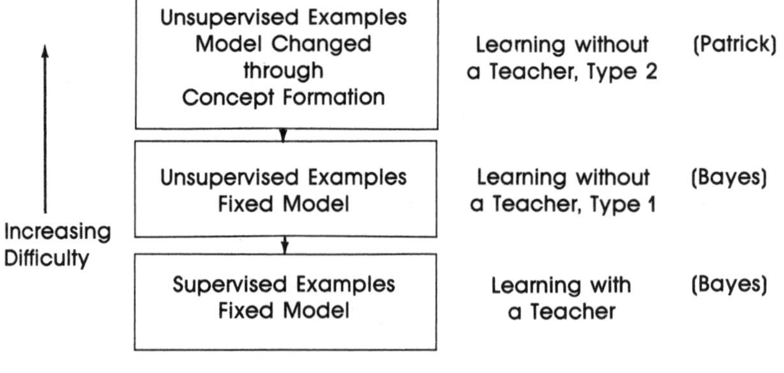

FIGURE 2.1. Three kinds of learning from examples.

The highest level of learning in Figure 2.1 is a departure from Bayes and requires the theorem on a posteriori probability by Patrick. At this level of learning the model can change because new categories can be formed by concept formation. Learning the correlation among features of patterns for a category can lead to learning by discovery, in this case the discovery of patterns never previously seen.

Causality. Causality implies that some outcome (future) must be present given a condition (current). A causality relationship is knowledge. Causality is vital to everyday life in that we can expect an action to have a certain or at most somewhat uncertain effect. We expect a particular response from the action of treating a disease. Another example of causality is the category–feature relationship in the form of a category conditional probability density function.

Concept and Concept Organization. A concept is described as "all that is characteristically associated with or suggested by a term." A concept can be represented by a tree, graph, network, or combinations of these. A concept involves knowledge and causality. A concept can involve a hierarchy or inference. A causality relationship itself is knowledge.

Attention or Focus. Attention or focus implies withdrawal from some things in order to deal effectively with others. For example, a feature or complex feature can be a focus. A subset of categories can be a focus. A subset of actions can be a focus.

Feature. A feature is an attribute such as color, size, age, shape, lab test, intensity, energy, power, and so on. It is a basic property of a pattern.

Class. A class is a number of objects or patterns regarded as forming a group by reason of common attributes (features, findings). A class of objects may include two different kinds of categories as described below.

Category. In philosophy, a category is defined as a classification that is basic and not susceptible to further analysis. Accordingly, we permit a class to consist of categories. Causality knowledge about the relationships of a pattern's attributes for a category is the only way that pattern categories can be distinguished. To be strictly consistent, we should let the basic classifications be a subcategory or subsubcategory.

Complex Class. We define a complex class as a category consisting of patterns where each pattern has attributes common to two or more classes. Initially Patrick *and others* defined a complex class to represent multiple diseases "active at the same time" (1972, 1975, 1979).

Only Class. An only class consists of objects or patterns where each pattern has attributes common to only one class. The term *only class* is not entirely adequate because it sounds peculiar; it does, however, describe the category and the concept.

State. State is defined as a condition with respect to structure. As used here it has nothing directly to do with patterns. It can be used to describe how far along the system is in decision making or how many features have been processed.

Optimum. Optimum means the best or the most favorable degree, condition, or amount. In **SPR,** minimizing probability of error or risk often are used as optimum criteria. Other criteria are minimizing cost, minimizing length of stay, maximizing priority, and so on. In *Decision Analysis in Medicine,* Patrick (1979) defines multidimensional criteria involving both cost and risk. Putting a man on the moon was successful but many optimum criteria were not satisfied. So success may not necessarily require certain optimum criteria.

Category Conditional Probability Density Function. In addition to causality knowledge about the relationships of a pattern's features (attributes), we are interested in the relative frequency with which a particular pattern or *subset of patterns* occurs. This relative frequency or probability also is knowledge. This statistical knowledge may be essential in ultimately rank-ordering category likelihoods. Human intelligence handles statistical knowledge poorly. Therefore, artificial intelligence with statistical pattern recognition can be expected to make decisions better in this regard than humans. In fact, whenever decisions are made with uncertainty they usually involve statistical pattern recognition.

Reasoning. A system is said to reason if it can do something it has not been explicitly told how to do. In artificial intelligence, reasoning often involves the generation of a focus of classes on which to concentrate, the next feature for which to obtain a value, or what a new record of a new category could look like. This, of course, involves conclusions or inference.

Deduction. Deduction is the process of going from the general to the specific. In the case of categories of patterns, it is the process of generating previously unseen patterns from typical and atypical representations. An important deduction operation is the process of generating a new pattern differing from a previously seen pattern only in that certain features are missing. This operation is not as simple as it might seem when the relative frequency of patterns is to be preserved. An important Deduction is generating the probability that a category could produce a pattern never previously seen.

Induction. Induction is the process of going from the specific to the general. In **CONSULT-I®**, outputting from one subsystem to another subsystem is an example of inductive inference. At a lower level in the knowledge hierarchy, a column with or without minicolumn modifications is an example of inductive inference. Later, when we discuss different forms of learning, other aspects of induction will be considered. At times there is a "thin line" between induction and deduction and at times they are "worlds apart."

Heuristic. A heuristic is a rule for generating new knowledge or new representations of knowledge. The new knowledge itself can be a heuristic. Both a domain of operation and a control structure are implied. A heuristic is a model. In mathematics and statistical pattern recognition, models are precisely described whereas in artificial intelligence they often are loosely described mathematically but implemented in a computer, the latter avoiding precise definition.

An example of using heuristics is that of constructing a model using rules for a category conditional probability density function $p(\mathbf{x}|\gamma_i^*)$. In pure statistical pattern recognition the conditional probability density function is estimated using a parametric or nonparametric model and training samples. This conditional probability density function then is used to "generate" previously unseen samples.

Heuristics are models implying learning already has taken place. They can be used to provide relationships for constructing a conditional probability density function which will, by deduction, generate patterns given only typical and atypical representatives of the category. Since the category is known, this is learning with a teacher. On the other hand, learning without a teacher (discovering new categories) also can use heuristics (models) to generate, by deduction, new categories. This appears to be going from the general to the specific (deduction) but in the sense that new categories are being generated it appears like induction.

Meta-Knowledge. Meta-knowledge is self-knowledge, as for example what rule(s) to try given a problem state. A method of learning can involve knowledge that a new pattern "is not like" patterns in any existing category. A system's meta-knowledge is its knowledge about its own knowledge. As another example, the system can know it does not utilize a particular feature or feature value. Meta-knowledge might be in the form of thresholds, distance measures, or alternative models to use for complex features or category conditional probability density functions. Meta-knowledge can consist of a closeness measure and threshold to infer that a previously unseen pattern of a category must be a new subcategory (column, cluster). Meta-knowledge is the ability to generate the probability that a category could produce a particular pattern.

Consciousness. Consciousness is awareness of activity including existence, thoughts, and surroundings. Meta-knowledge would seem to be a component of consciousness. What happens when a machine has increasing capability for concept organization and formation, knowledge representation, focusing, decision making, and interacting among subsystems? The answer would not seem to be consciousness no matter how much meta-knowledge the machine has. On the other hand, anthropologist Pierre de Chardin wrote in the *Phenomenon of Man* (1965) that consciousness may be a physical concept, like the boiling point of water, which exists when a critical level of complexity is reached.

Correlation. Correlation is conventionally defined in probability theory, statistics, and **SPR.** We allow a new definition of correlation as the Correlation level of a pattern with Findings. This Correlation level reflects how much a pattern looks like Findings even if there is not a complete match.

2-2 TYPES OF LEARNING

2-2-1 Introduction

To reiterate, a dictionary definition of learning is *the process of acquiring knowledge or skill,* whereas in psychology it is *the modification of behavior through training.* Various types of learning have been studied and will be described here, following an outline similar to that provided by Michalski, Carbonell, and Mitchell in *Machine Learning: An Artificial In-*

telligence Approach (1983). The types of learning overlap, and this will be indicated where appropriate. Our theme is directed toward the classification problem and the marriage of artificial intelligence with statistical pattern recognition.

2-2-2 Rote Learning

Rote learning does not involve inference. It is the storing of knowledge such as features, feature values, and category feature relationships. Retrieval of this knowledge is possible. For example, such retrieval in **CONSULT-I®** also is called **BASIC CONSULTING** and consists of presenting the feature values of a particular category presentation. Rote learning is basic to both **AI** and **SPR**.

2-2-3 Learning by Instruction

Learning by instruction consists of the storing of rules for induction and deduction and the ability to apply these rules to generate new patterns. The implication is that the rule was learned "off line" by induction. Then "on line" deductive learning provides inference or decisions. Learning by Instruction is limited to acquiring or storing the rules.

2-2-4 Learning by Analogy

This is acquiring new knowledge to represent a pattern in a way successfully used in the past. An example is a method for generating a new subcategory of a category to characterize new patterns, analogous to past generations. The method might consist of a closeness measure or likelihood to indicate that the new patterns more likely belong to a new subcategory. The methods or rules for learning by analogy were learned "off line" by induction. Learning by analogy may be a special case of learning by instruction. The methods of learning by analogy may be likened to rules used in learning by discovery. This method of learning is found both in **AI** and **SPR**.

2-2-5 Learning from Examples (*Learning with a Teacher*)

Learning with a Teacher or supervised learning is based on knowing the class or category of patterns. These patterns, known to be of that class or category, then can be used to learn about the class or category. A model of the class or category is required. Examples of two products under development since 1978 which learn from examples are **The OUTCOME ADVISOR®** and **CONSULT LEARNING SYSTEM®** described in this book. Learning from example is inductive learning, proceeding from pattern examples or cases to a trained system which then can make deductive decisions or inferences. This form of learning has been extensively studied in SPR and to a lesser extent in AI.

2-2-6 Learning from Discovery (*Learning without a Teacher*)

This can be the most difficult form of learning. It is learning new subcategories of categories or new categories. It has been shown that a certain amount of a priori knowledge is required for this type of learning. This a priori knowledge may be rules of deduction from learning by analogy. It was shown in 1966 to 1969 by Spragins (1966) and Yakowitz (1969) that a necessary and sufficient condition to learn without a teacher is that the categories be *linearly independent.* Thus, rules used to learn by discovery must impose such a priori knowledge on the problem. This form of learning was initially studied in statistical pattern recognition (Patrick, 1965; Fralick, 1967; Spragins, 1966; Yakowitz, 1969; Patrick, 1968; Patrick and Costello, 1970; Cooper and Cooper, 1964; Patrick and Carayanopoulos, 1970; Patrick *and others* 1967), but knowledge of the problem dates back to 1902 (Pearson), 1948 (Robbins), and 1960 (Teicher).

In this book a new aspect of learning without a teacher is presented as the theorem on a posteriori probabilities by Patrick. Here, concept formation of new categories takes place. As in Bayes theorem, which applies to classical learning without a teacher, categories are mutually exclusive; but in the theorem by Patrick, they also are statistically dependent during concept formation. This allows for complex classes (such as multiple diseases active at the same time) to be generated by concept formation. Products which learn by discovery are the **CONSULT COMPLEX CLASS GENERATOR™** and the **CONSULT SUBCATEGORY GENERATOR™**.

2-2-7 Learning Insignificance from Relative Frequency

This is a form of learning that, to our knowledge, previously has not been directly discussed in artificial intelligence literature. It is important in both learning from examples and learning by discovery.

Basic artificial intelligence does not account for relative frequency of patterns. Is relative frequency of patterns knowledge? The answer is yes—more important knowledge than it may at first appear. Relative frequency of different subsets of patterns (categories, subcategories) takes time to acquire. This knowledge is discovered in the feature space, not the category space or class space. Discovery of what part of the feature space is insignificant for a category is, we believe, one of the most important concepts for intelligence and reasoning. *When, for example, the insignificant part of the feature space for a category such as an only class is known, the way is open for learning another category (complex class) involving the same class.* Holes are created in the feature space, for the category, corresponding to regions of insignificance.

As another example, knowledge that certain features are insignificant for a category is central to eliminating much of the universe of attributes or features which could characterize patterns in that category.

If the feature space of previously learned categories and that of potential categories is known to be nonoverlapping for respective categories, then repetition more than once to learn new categories by concept formation is unnecessary. This presumes that categories of patterns are completely nonoverlapping in the feature space. That is, *classification is presumed deterministic.* In medical disease classification this generally is not the case, especially early in the diagnostic process.

Learning correlation from relative frequency is a new important upshot of the integration of **SPR** with **AI.** We do not mean correlation in the standard statistical sense. Rather it is the probability that a category could produce a pattern like specified findings. This requires determining the Correlation level of known patterns from the category with the Findings.

2-2-8 The Knowledge in a Category Conditional Probability Density Function (c.c.p.d.f.)

The knowledge in a category conditional p.d.f. includes the feature values significant for that category and the feature values insignificant for the category. Also, weights corresponding to feature values are appended. Very important but elusive is that all this is learned, to some level of significance. *Knowledge about insignificant feature values includes a measure of the degree to which the feature values are known to be insignificant.*

As an extreme illustration of learning by example, suppose that each training pattern is declared a category. This is very uninteresting learning since each case of a category is exactly alike (one concept category). No knowledge of relative frequency of patterns is possible. This may be described as equivalent to the values of a category feature (see Section 1-2-1 of Chapter 1).

It takes time and training examples to declare that a region of feature space is insignificant for a category. But once acquired, *this knowledge for one category can be used to learn about another category involving the same class.*

As part of the new theorem on a posteriori probability, we consider learning classes with a teacher (from examples). This includes learning the insignificant regions in the feature space for the classes. Once this is accomplished the stage is set to use a model to generate a description of a new category which is a complex class involving both classes. Also, models are used to generate the corresponding only classes (categories).

Learning insignificance from relative frequency takes time and cases because there must be an acceptable level of confidence that the region in the feature space indeed is insignificant. This level, incidentally, is itself knowledge.

2-3 EXAMPLE OF CONCEPT FORMATION IN THE THEOREM ON A POSTERIORI PROBABILITY (PATRICK)

2-3-1 Introduction

The theorem on a posteriori probability (Patrick, 1983) is developed extensively in this book. The theorem is derived after introducing in Chapter 3 definitions, axioms, and results from probability theory. In the current section an example is presented to illustrate what is meant by concept formation. The example is for instance where patterns are described by only three features x_1, x_2, x_3, denoted collectively by the feature vector $\mathbf{x}$.

In the examples there are two classes denoted ω_1 and ω_2. But these classes are "intermediate concepts," not themselves in the decision space. What *is* in the decision space are three catgories defined:

$\omega_1^* = (\omega_1,\bar{\omega}_2)$: means class ω_1 but not class ω_2

$\omega_2^* = (\omega_2,\bar{\omega}_1)$: means class ω_2 but not class ω_1

$\Omega_{12}^* = (\omega_1,\omega_2)$: means class ω_1 and class ω_2.

The *concepts* ω_1^* and ω_2^* are called *only* classes, while the concept Ω_{12}^* is called a *complex* class. The superscript * denotes a category.

In this example there are training samples from respective training sessions. For the first training session samples or patterns or examples are available from category ω_1^*. During a second training session samples are available from category ω_2^*.

Now, categories ω_1^*, ω_2^*, and Ω_{12}^* are mutually exclusive as in Bayes theorem. We will show how to learn the concept Ω_{12}^* by discovery without a teacher. *During the learning process there are statistical dependencies among the categories, a property not present in Bayes theorem.*

If, for example, ω_1^* is a single disease and ω_2^* another single disease, Ω_{12}^* is a complex disease involving the two basic disease processes. There is a statistical dependence in the feature space among Ω_{12}^* and ω_1^* and ω_2^*. *This statistical dependence is essential for concept formation and requires SPR.*

2-3-2 Examples of Application of the Theorem on A Posteriori Probability (Patrick, 1983)

Example with Two Classes

Consider that there are three features x_1, x_2, x_3, two classes ω_1, ω_2, and that the first two training sessions provide samples for ω_1^* and ω_2^* as outlined previously.

During the first training session supervised samples from only class ω_1^* generate ω_1^* as points along with x_1 axis shown in Figure 2.2a.

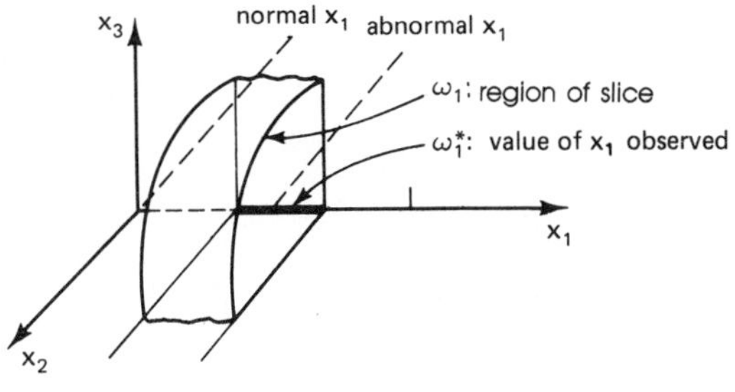

(a)

FIGURE 2.2a. First Training Session generates ω_1^* with feature x_1 significant. Class ω_1 looks like category ω_1^*. Features x_2 and x_3 are insignificant for ω_1^*.

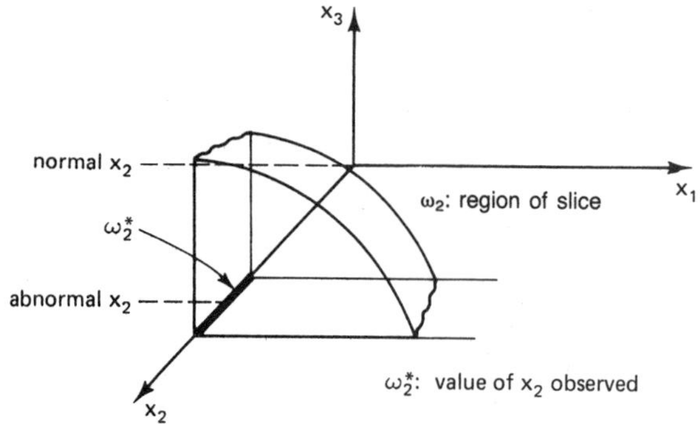

(b)

FIGURE 2.2b. Second Training Session generates ω_2^* with feature $\mathbf{x}_2$ significant. Class ω_2 looks like category ω_2^*. Features $\mathbf{x}_1$ and $\mathbf{x}_3$ are insignificant for ω_2^*.

Class ω_1 is the intermediate concept of all samples which could look like those in ω_1^*. That is, the samples must have values of x_1 as shown but features x_2 and x_3 have uniformly random values for the examples. Important knowledge would be that values of x_2 and x_3 are insignificant for ω_1^* in that they are uniformly distributed.

During the second training session supervised samples from only class ω_2^* generates ω_2^* as points along the x_2 axis shown in Figure 2.2b. The concept of class ω_2 is illustrated using the same reasoning as for the first training session. Features x_1 and x_3 are insignificant for ω_2^*.

Without further training, there exists the concept that $\Omega_{12}^* = (\omega_1,\omega_2)$ *lies in the shaded area of Figure 2.2c.* It is possible but unlikely that Ω_{12}^* lies in the entire vertical column since neither ω_1^* nor ω_2^* were observed to

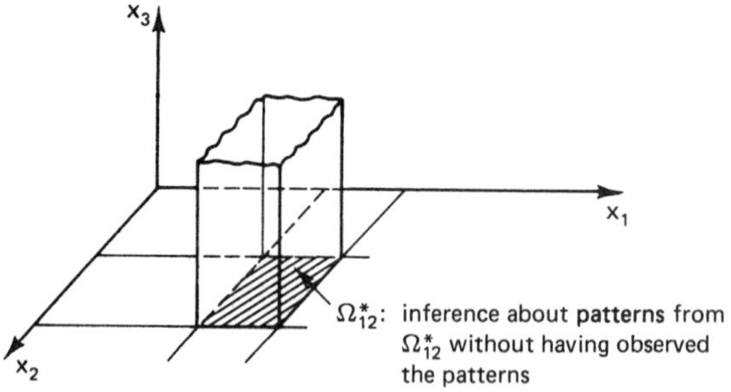

(c)

FIGURE 2.2c. At the end of the second training session there exists the concept of Ω_{12}^*, a complex class.

have values of x_3 other than zero. This suggests the crosshatched area in the x_1, x_2 plane of Figure 2.2c as the concept Ω_{12}^*. The actual probability density illustrations would require a fourth axis in Figures 2.2a and 2.2b and is not shown. For Figure 2.2a, probability density is limited to the region shown along the x_1 axis and need not be uniform, but is uniform along the x_2 axis and x_3 axis. An analogous situation exists for Figure 2.2b.

The first two training sessions are inductive learning sessions. If a future recognition sample were to fall in the shaded area of Figure 2.2c one can deduce that it is from the complex category Ω_{12}^* rather than only classes ω_1^* or ω_2^* even though an example from Ω_{12}^* has never been observed. *Categories ω_1^*, ω_2^*, and Ω_{12}^* are mutually exclusive in that any future recognition sample can be from only one of these categories.*

These conclusions presume that the model applies. The model presumes that there are regions of significance and insignificance in the feature spaces of the two only categories. It further presumes that a potential category Ω_{12}^* looks like both ω_1^* and ω_2^* in that a pattern from Ω_{12}^* would have feature values of x_1 like ω_1^* and feature values x_2 like ω_2^*; at the same time ω_1^* and ω_2^* are different because x_2 is insignificant for ω_1^* while x_1 is insignificant for ω_2^*.

Now we will illustrate the statistical dependence referred to previously. Suppose that the set of two training sessions for ω_1^* and ω_2^* includes a following third session where samples are observed from Ω_{12}^* and that the model is correct in that the samples from Ω_{12}^* indeed fall in the shaded area of Figure 2.2c. Going further, repeat over and over these three sessions. We observe a statistical dependence in that as samples from ω_1^* and ω_2^* occur as described, the following sample from Ω_{12}^* always falls in the shaded area of Figure 2.2c.

If during learning, $\mathbf{x}_1$ is from ω_1^*, and $\mathbf{x}_2$ from ω_2^*, then x_3 from Ω_{12}^* has conditional probabilities

$$p((\mathbf{x}_3,\Omega_{12}^*)|(\mathbf{x}_1,\omega_1^*), (\mathbf{x}_2,\omega_2^*)) = p(\mathbf{x}_3,\Omega_{12}^*) \qquad \text{Bayes}$$
$$p((\mathbf{x}_3,\Omega_{12}^*)|(\mathbf{x}_1,\omega_1^*), (\mathbf{x}_2,\omega_2^*)) \neq p(\mathbf{x}_3,\Omega_{12}^*) \qquad \text{Patrick}$$

illustrating the statistical dependence among categories in Patrick which is not present in Bayes.

The dependence is statistical because we have verified only to some confidence that Ω_{12}^* *look like* ω_1^* and ω_2^* as illustrated. Further, to some level of confidence, we have verified how Ω_{12}^* *does not look like* ω_1^* *or* ω_2^*. The following example further illustrates the statistical dependence.

2-3-3 Example: Only Classes (Categories) with Subcategories

For this example suppose that each only class has two subcategories as illustrated in Figure 2.3a. The four shaded areas in Figure 2.3a are a concept of the likely domain of Ω^*_{12} in the feature space.

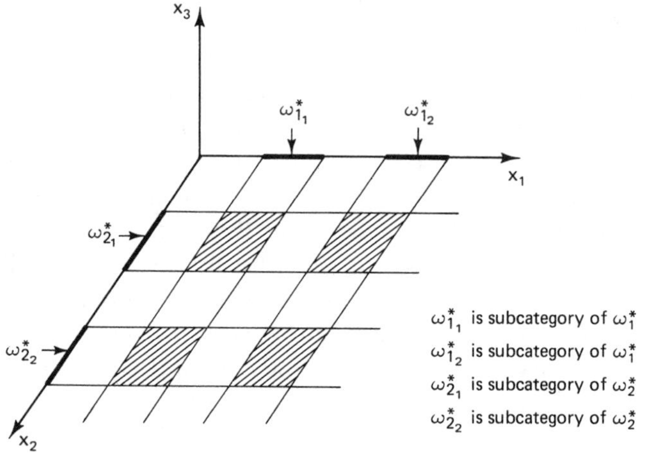

(a)

FIGURE 2.3a. Each Only Class has two subcategories. Inference about Ω^*_{12} is represented by the two-dimensional shaded areas.

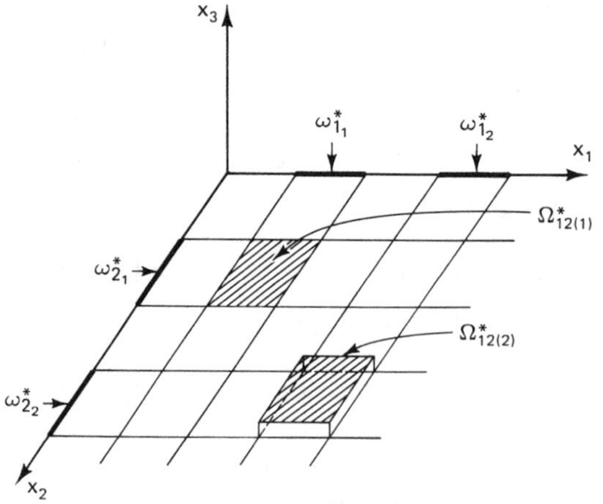

(b)

FIGURE 2.3b. After examples of Ω^*_{12} are observed, inference of Ω^*_{12} is more precise about the subcategories than in Figure 2.3a.

When the experiment of observing multiple sets of three training sessions is performed, suppose that only two shaded areas for the domain of Ω^*_{12} occur as illustrated in Figure 2.3b. Those two shaded areas illustrate concepts of subcategories of Ω^*_{12} denoted respectively $\Omega^*_{12(1)}$ and $\Omega^*_{12(2)}$. These two subcategories of Ω^*_{12} have different values for feature x_3. Clearly, patterns in Ω^*_{12} depend upon properties of ω^*_1 and ω^*_2. This dependence involves subcategories of ω^*_1 and ω^*_2. This type of statistical dependence could be learned by **CONSULT LEARNING SYSTEM®**. In fact, inference about Ω^*_{12} may be incomplete without it. This is a statistical dependence.

Thus, *during concept formation there can be statistical dependence among categories. This is a distinction between the theorem on a posteriori probability by Patrick and that by Bayes* (Bayes theorem).

2-3-4 Historical Perspective of the Theorems on A Posteriori Probability by Bayes and Patrick

Bayes' mathematical work was done in 1763. Robbins in 1948 first studied mixtures which are the framework for statistical learning without a teacher. Then Teicher in 1960 to 1963, Patrick in 1965, Fralick in 1967, Yakowitz and Spragins in 1966 to 1969 studied the problem. Thus, the mathematics and statistics of learning without a teacher was not studied until 185 years after Bayes' work. The previous studies of a posteriori probability computation without a teacher (Patrick, 1965, 1968; Fralick, 1967; Patrick and Costello, 1970; Patrick and Shen, 1975; Patrick and Liporace, 1970; Yakowitz, 1969) did not provide for concept formation through defining classes in addition to the categories (which are mutually exclusive). Patrick and Carayannopoulos came closest to this type of concept formation in a paper in 1970.

The previous studies showed that to learn without a teacher something should be known a priori that makes the possible concepts different. We see from the new theorem by Patrick that a new concept can appear because of a new dimension (feature) or some degree of certainty that there is something different in this concept's feature space from previously discovered concepts.

Returning to the example illustrated in Figures 2.2a,b,c, note that it first was necessary to form the intermediate concepts of ω_1 and ω_2 before forming the concept of Ω^*_{12}. *The intermediate concepts of* ω_1 and ω_2 (theorem by Patrick) *expanded the dimensionality and provided for searching for evidence to discover* Ω^*_{12}.

Another viewpoint for the example illustrated in Figures 2.2a,b,c, is that at the end of the two training sessions there exist two simultaneous expressions for Ω_{12}^*:

$$\Omega_{12}^* = \omega_1 - \omega_1^*$$

$$\Omega_{12}^* = \omega_2 - \omega_2^*$$

The solution Ω_{12}^* to these two simultaneous expressions are points in the column shown in Figure 2.2c.

The intermediate concepts ω_1 and ω_2 are in the class space fundamental to the theorem by Patrick but not present in Bayes. The classes in Ω_{12}^* are the "glue" which relates the categories in the category space, whether these categories be only classes or complex classes. That "glue" reflects our understanding how concepts can look alike and not alike either in terms of feature values (findings) or relative frequency of feature values. The "glue" may be that for a new concept two features x_1 and x_2 should have values varying in a predictable way such as the ratios or products suggested by Patrick (1972, 1979). To learn by discovery that x_1 and x_2 do indeed obey such a relationship requires samples—repetition.

3

Mathematics and Probability Theory for Statistical Pattern Recognition

3-1 INTRODUCTION

In this chapter, definitions and methods used in the study of statistical pattern recognition are presented; and then in Chapter 4 the same is done for studies in artificial intelligence. Considerable overlap in problems being studied is another justification for integrating statistical pattern recognition with artificial intelligence. Basic to **SPR** and knowledge base structure for classification problems are features, complex features, categories, and classes. To study them properly requires sets, set operations, mutually exclusive sets, and so on. To be precise, it is important to understand the feature space, category space, class space, and the cross product of category space with feature space. Eventually a classification system's diagnostic performance must be improved and to accomplish this requires understanding of decision-making theory, not just use of formulas, models, or algorithms which classify findings.

For example, Bayes theorem is a complete classification algorithm just as is a heuristic or blind use of production rules. The reader is presented with the basics and derivation of Bayes theorem for inference. It is important to understand the derivation of Bayes theorem and not just its "blind use" as a formula. Relative frequency is discussed because it is a basic method of learning or obtaining knowledge, called learning by example in **AI.**

We discuss the difference between statistically independent events, linear independence, and a basis or spanning set. These are important considerations when studying features in a knowledge base structure.

Patrick *and others* (1970) reported on constructing features for use in an automatic detection and classification system involving Artificial Intelligence and estimation. Category classification performance depends on separating category representations as far apart as possible in feature space. Thus, Kanal (1974) also stressed that studies of features and their values from **SPR** need to be incorporated with **AI** to obtain best results.

New constructs called only classes and complex classes (which are "coupled" with features) are derived for use in the theorem on a posteriori probability by Patrick.

3-2 SETS, SET OPERATIONS, MUTUALLY EXCLUSIVE SETS, EXHAUSTIVE SETS, EVENTS

An understanding of set operations is important for many aspects of **AI** with **SPR.** For example, derivation of Bayes theorem or the theorem by Patrick utilizes set theory. Construction of rules for complex class formation can use set theory. Set theory is a symbolic method for describing "things" related to "other things" and appeals to common sense. We all use sets whether or not we admit it or understand them. Sets are useful for communicating models to others.

3-2-1 Sets

A set is a collection of objects denoted $\xi_1, \xi_2, \ldots, \xi_n$, and the set is denoted

$$A = \{\xi_1, \xi_2, \ldots, \xi_n\}, \tag{1}$$

where { } means "collection of" or "set of." It is convenient to use an index $i = 1, 2, \ldots, n$ to account for the objects in a set:

$$A = \{\xi_i\}_{i=1}^{n}. \tag{2}$$

An *element* ξ_i in the set is denoted

$$\xi_i \in A: \quad \xi_i \text{ is an element of } A. \tag{3}$$

An element ξ_i *not in* the set A is denoted

$$\xi_i \notin A: \quad \xi_i \text{ is not an element of } A. \tag{4}$$

Sets will be used to describe collections of features, collections of categories, collections of classes, events which are logical combinations of feature values, and so on.

3-2-2 Set Operations

A set A equals a set B if and only if (iff) each element of A is an element of B and each element of B is an element of A. This *Equality* operation is denoted:

$$B = A: \quad \text{Equality of Two Sets.} \tag{5}$$

The *Sum* or *Union* of two sets is a set whose elements are the elements of A and the elements of B, but elements in both set A and set B are not included twice in the sum (Union). This operation is denoted

$$A + B: \quad \text{Sum}$$

or

$$A \cup B: \quad \text{Union.} \tag{6}$$

The *difference* of two sets,

$$A - B: \quad \text{Difference.} \tag{7}$$

is the set of elements in A less those elements in B which also are in A.

A *subset* B of A, denoted

$$B \ \varepsilon \ A: \quad \text{B is a subset of } A, \tag{8}$$

is the set where every element of B also is an element of A. The Product or Intersection of two sets A and B, denoted

$$AB: \quad \text{Product of } A \text{ and } B \text{ (intersection, AND)}$$

or

$$A \cap B: \quad \text{Intersection of } A \text{ and } B, \tag{9}$$

is a set consisting of all elements in *both* set A and set B.

The set of *all possible elements* or the *certain event*, denoted

$$S: \quad \text{Set of All Possible Elements,} \tag{10}$$

is the collection of all elements in any and all sets.

The *complement* of a set A is the set $\bar{A}$ containing all elements of S which are not in A:

$$\bar{A} = S - A: \quad \text{Complement of } A. \tag{11}$$

The complement of a set is important in concept formation where regions of insignificance are learned.

3-2-3 Mutually Exclusive Sets

Two sets A and B are *mutually exclusive* (m.e.) or disjoint if they have no common elements:

$$A\ B = \emptyset: \quad \text{Sets } A \text{ and } B \text{ Mutually Exclusive}$$

or

$$A \cap B = \emptyset \tag{12}$$

For example, categories are sets of patterns for which the patterns in a set are mutually exclusive. A pattern is an element of the set of presentations of a category (or class).

3-2-4 Laws for Set Operations

The Laws for set operations are as follows:

$(A + B) + C = A + (B + C)$:		Associative Law.	(13)
$A + B$	$= B + A$:	Commutative Law of Addition.	(14)
$A\ (B + C)$	$= (AB) + (AC)$:	Associative Law of Product.	(15)
$(AB)\ C$	$= A\ (BC) = ABC$:	Commutative Law of Product.	(16)

3-2-5 Extensions to Multiple Sets

Let

$$A_1, A_2, \ldots\ldots, A_M = \{A_j\}_{j=1}^{M} \tag{17}$$

be M sets such that

$$A_j \ \varepsilon\ S \ \forall\ j \tag{18}$$

where

$$\forall: \quad \text{For all.} \tag{19}$$

The sets in (17) are *exhaustive* if

$$\bigcup_{j=1}^{M} A_j = S, \text{ the whole space.} \tag{20}$$

The sets in (17) are mutually exclusive if

$$A_j \cap A_k = \emptyset \qquad \forall \text{ pairs } j,\ k. \tag{21}$$

Sets satisfying (20) and (21) are said to be *mutually exclusive and exhaustive*. For example, the set of all categories in the decision space are mutually exclusive.

The intersection of M sets is denoted

$$\bigcap_{j=1}^{M} A_j \tag{22}$$

and is the set of elements common to each set.

The laws of set operation apply to multiple sets. Examples of other set relationships devised from the basic set operations include

$$\begin{aligned} A - B &= A\,B \\ A \cap \bar{A} &= \emptyset \\ A + \bar{A} &= S \\ S \cap A &= A \\ \emptyset &= \text{null set without any element.} \end{aligned} \tag{23}$$

Define

$$\text{num}(A) = \text{Number of objects in } A. \tag{24}$$

Then other set operations include

$$\begin{aligned} \text{num}(A + B) &\leq \text{num}(A) + \text{num}(B) \\ \text{num}(AB) &\leq \text{num}(A) + \text{num}(B). \end{aligned} \tag{25}$$

3-2-6 Event: A Special Set Operation

An Event is:

any object ξ_i in S
any set A_j ε S
any subset of a set A_j
any set defined by combinations of set operations on objects ξ_i. (26)

Examples

Examples of events are categories, classes, subcategories, focus of categories for a differential diagnosis, and so on. The values of a feature or complex feature are events. Values of a Type Ø feature (see Chapter 8, Section 8-7) are events which are mutually exclusive and exhaustive. An event can be the logical AND of certain features with the logical OR among values of the features, a procedure used in **The OUTCOME ADVISOR®**, **CONSULT LEARNING SYSTEM®**, and **CONSULT-I®**. An event can be either the Condition or the Outcome of Inference. An example of a simple event is the single value of a Category feature which is a Category.

3-3 MULTIPLE SPACES (CATEGORY SPACE, FEATURE SPACE, DECISION SPACE, CLASS SPACE)

A set of elements

$$S_e \tag{27}$$

is said to characterize the eth space where $e = 1,2, \ldots$. Of particular interest are two spaces called, respectively, the category space and the feature space. Set operations and laws apply to respective spaces individually.

The idea of labeling spaces helps us to account for different kinds of things. For example, in general, categories are different from features and classes and require special rules.

3-3-1 Category Space

The category space is

$$\boldsymbol{\gamma} = \{\gamma_i^*\}_{i=1}^{M}, \quad \text{a set of mutually exclusive elements.} \tag{28}$$

A category γ_i^* can be
an *only class* (to be defined)
a *complex class* (to be defined). (29)

The set of *only classes* and set of *complex classes* are each a subset of the category space. The superscript * indicates category and distinguishes a category from a class.

3-3-2 Class Space

The class space consists of a set of classes

$$\{\omega_i\}_{i=1}^{M_1}: \quad \text{Class space.} \tag{30}$$

For $M_1 = 2$,
an *only class* is a single element of Ω, denoted

$$\omega_i^* = (\omega_i, \bar{\omega}_j): \quad \textit{Only class } \omega_i. \tag{31}$$

which means class ω_i but not class ω_j.

The complex class space consists of a set of all possible combinations of classes (the example below is for $M_1 = 2$):

$$\Omega_{ij}^* = \{\omega_i, \omega_j\} \ \forall \ i, j\text{: Complex class space.} \tag{32}$$

The set

$$\Omega_{ij}^*\text{: } \textit{Complex class} \tag{33}$$

is appropriately defined.

Medical Example

Consider that an individual has hearing loss in the left ear. Is this a class or a category? The answer is that it is a class consisting of two categories. Let

$$\omega_i\text{: Hearing loss left ear}$$
$$\omega_j\text{: Hearing loss right ear.}$$

Then

$$\omega_i^* = (\omega_i, \bar{\omega}_j)\text{: Hearing loss only left ear}$$

is the *only class* hearing loss in the left ear but no hearing loss in the right ear. Likewise

$$\omega_j^* = (\omega_j, \bar{\omega}_i)\text{: Hearing loss only right ear}$$

and

$$\Omega_{ij}^* = (\omega_i, \omega_j)\text{: Hearing loss left ear and hearing loss right ear.}$$

The categories ω_i^*, ω_j^*, and Ω_{ij}^*, are mutually exclusive and cannot occur together yet the two classes ω_i and ω_j can occur together as Ω_{ij}^*. It follows that

$$\omega_i = \omega_i^* + \Omega_{ij}^*$$

is the union of two events and thus it is hearing loss left ear which can occur two ways.

Little has been presented or discussed so far in this chapter to show how to *infer* Ω_{ij}^* *from* ω_i^* *and* ω_j^*. The reader may wish to think about how that could be done. At this point we have noted that classes can occur together but that categories cannot; but no inference facility has been devised other than the previous equation which relates elements of sets; but it does not show us how to "generate" a complex class from only classes.

These constructions are axiomatic. At some point we have to describe how knowledge of events is learned, i.e., how we arrive at Ω_{ij}^* in terms of ω_i and ω_j and how ω_i and ω_j are learned from ω_i^* and ω_j^*. *This learning involves another dimension,* time, or relative frequency. This dimension is appended as probability (starting in Section 3-5), and examples were presented in Chapter 2.

When the category space is exhausted by *only classes* and *complex classes,* it follows that (for general M_1) γ consists of

$$\begin{aligned} &\omega_i^*, \quad i = 1, 2, \ldots, M_1 \\ &\Omega_\xi^*, \quad \xi = 1, 2, \ldots, M_2 = (M - M_1). \end{aligned} \tag{34}$$

The sets

$\{\omega_i^*\}$ are mutually exclusive among themselves and mutually exclusive of

$\{\Omega_\xi^*\}$ which are mutually exclusive, and all sets taken together are exhaustive.

It follows that

$$\omega_i^* = (\omega_i, \neg\omega_j, \neg\omega_k, \ldots .) \tag{35}$$

where $\neg\omega_j$ is the same as $\bar{\omega}_j$, and the *null category* is

$$(\neg\omega_i, \neg\omega_j, \ldots). \tag{36}$$

Description of Figure 3.1 (Only Class in Category Space ($M_1 = 2$))

The classes

$$\{\omega_\xi\}_{\xi=1}^{M_1}$$

are elementary events. Consider again an example where $M_1 = 2$. The points in the category space are mutually exclusive and exhaustive. A three-dimensional (three features) illustration is shown in Figure 3.1. In this example the classes are taken as binary feature values; i.e., along one axis the values are ω_i and $\neg\omega_i$, along another axis ω_j and $|\omega_j$. The event ω_i as the union of ω_i^* and Ω_{ij}^* is illustrated.

Note that the classes are not mutually exclusive (can occur together) while only classes ω_i^* and ω_j^* are mutually exclusive.

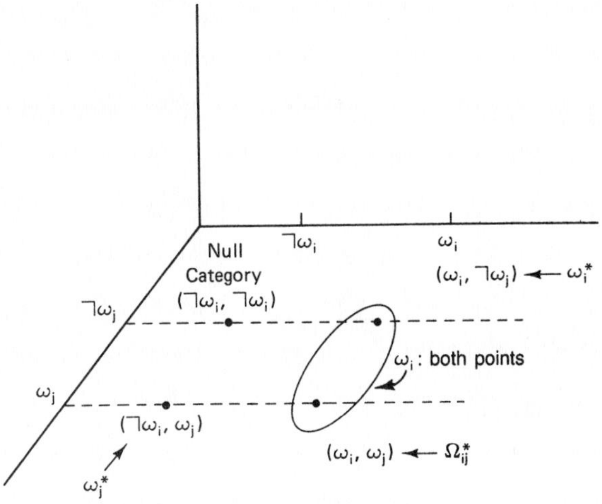

FIGURE 3.1. Only Class ω_i^* in the Category Space ($M_1 = 2$) Classes and a complex class are illustrated.

Suppose we "know" ω_i^* and ω_j^*, meaning that we know the patterns for these Only Classes shown in Figure 3.1. How do we create the concept of a Complex Class? The first model that comes to mind is that the complex class should be both like and dislike each only class.

Finally,

$$\omega_i = (\omega_i, \omega_j) \cup (\omega_i, \neg\omega_j) \qquad (37a)$$
$$\omega_i^* \triangleq (\omega_i, \neg\omega_j) \qquad (37b)$$
$$\omega_j^* \triangleq (\omega_j, \neg\omega_i)$$

and

$$(\omega_i, \omega_j) \text{ is the event class } \omega_i \text{ and class } \omega_j$$
$$(\omega_i, \omega_j) \triangleq \Omega_{ij}^*. \qquad (38)$$

Description of Figure 3.2 ($M_1 = 3$)

In this example there are three classes and the third class is taken as a binary feature with values along the vertical axis. The only classes ω_i^*, ω_j^*, and ω_k^* are illustrated as is

$$\Omega_{ijk}^* = (\omega_i, \omega_j, \omega_k),$$

a complex class.

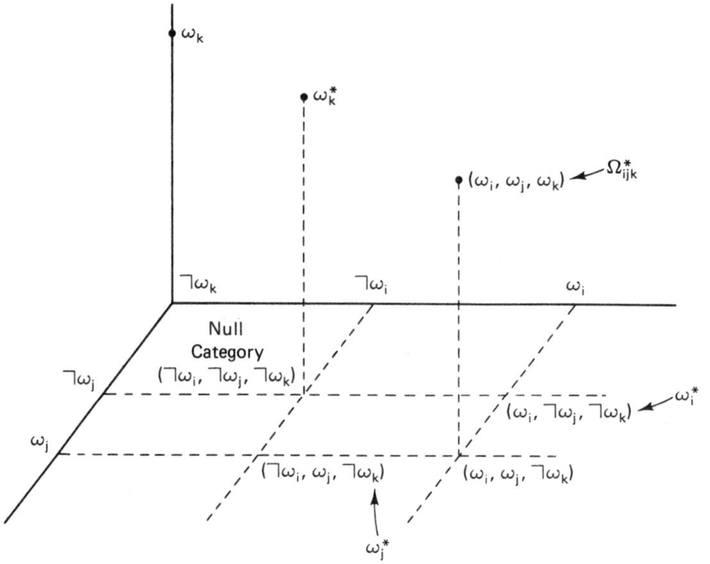

FIGURE 3.2. Complex class and only classes in the Category Space ($M_1 = 3$).

3-3-3 Subcategories

A *subcategory* of a category γ_i^* is denoted

$$\gamma_{i_k}^*, \quad k = 1, 2, \ldots, K. \tag{39}$$

If the category γ_i^* is an *only class* ω_i^* then the subcategory can be denoted

$$\omega_{i_k}^*. \tag{40}$$

If the category is a *complex class* Ω_ξ^*, then the subcategory can be denoted

$$\Omega_{\xi_k}^*. \tag{41}$$

Subcategories are a subset of patterns for the category. In **CONSULT-I®** an inference function relates a pattern's properties to a category in terms of subsets of inferences for a subcategory. *A category is said to occur if any of its subcategories occurs.* Subcategories are important for accurate classifications since action can be dependent on the particular subcategory.

3-4 FEATURE SPACE

3-4-1 Illustration of the Feature Space

The categories just discussed are in the category space. A space is a mathematical convenience where symbols can be used to describe definitions, constructions, and so on. Categories are concepts that somehow must be described. The basic descriptors of a category are through its attributes or feature values.

The feature space as discussed here is essential for the integration of **SPR** and **AI.** The feature space consists of points that are current or potential patterns. A particular set of points is a category or a class. The reader familiar with vector theory can visualize a pattern as a particular vector **x**, as illustrated in Figure 3.3. In general a category of patterns cannot be illustrated with this simplicity, especially as the number of features becomes large. Usually it is not practical to store all possible patterns of a category, but there are exceptions. Fortunately, it is unnecessary to store all possible patterns as long as there is facility for processing stored patterns to deduce the probability of previously unseen (not stored) patterns. This need arises, for example, when a set of findings are to be classified but there are categories without patterns corresponding to the findings.

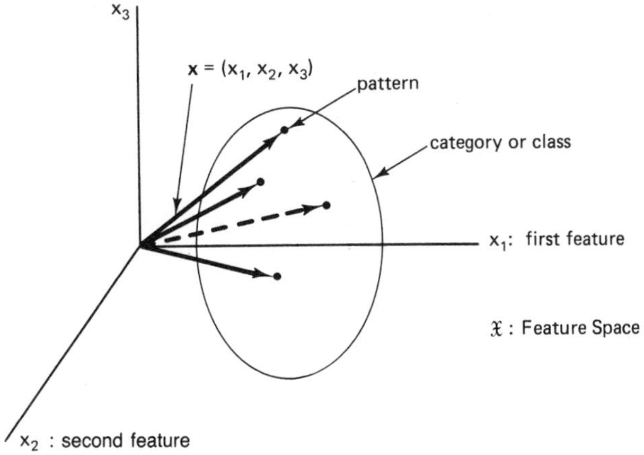

FIGURE 3.3. Illustration of patterns as feature vectors in the feature space.

Formally denote the feature space by a symbol $\mathcal{X}$ and a pattern or vector in this space by $\mathbf{x}$, a standard notaion for a vector. The feature space actually is a set of points and thus a feature vector $\mathbf{x}$

$$\mathbf{x} \in \mathcal{X},$$

is an element of a set $\mathcal{X}$. The feature space $\mathcal{X}$ will be discussed further as an L-dimensional *vector space,* i.e.,

$$\mathbf{x} \in \mathcal{V}_L.$$

A vector space has been extensively studied (Patrick, 1972) in terms of how to make projections and combinations, how to measure closeness between patterns, and so on.

3-4-2 Category–Feature Relationships

For each category $\gamma_i^* \varepsilon \boldsymbol{\gamma}$, there is a set of points in the feature space $\mathcal{X}$ for which a functional is defined:

$$p(\mathbf{x} \mid \gamma_i^*), \qquad \mathbf{x} \ \varepsilon \ \mathcal{X}, \gamma_i^* \ \varepsilon \ \boldsymbol{\gamma}. \tag{43}$$

This defines the *category–feature relationship.* The ellipse in Figure 3.3 encloses patterns for categories γ_i^*, and there are rules to relate each pattern to its feature values. There exists a family $\mathcal{F}$ of $p(\mathbf{x} \mid \gamma_i^*)$, and $\mathcal{F}$ is the *category–feature relationship space.* That is, $\mathcal{F}_i$: $p(\mathbf{x} \mid \gamma_i^*) \ \varepsilon \ \mathcal{F}$. It is not accidental that we have chosen p for the functional because it is to denote the probability or certainty with which category γ_i^* presents as pattern $\mathbf{x}$ or a set of patterns.

Equation (43) is taken here as the definition of a set of points in the feature space for category γ_i^*. Later, $p(\mathbf{x} \mid \gamma_i^*)$ will be redefined as a weight or probability density at point $\mathbf{x}$ in the feature space.

3-4-2-1 Commonality between Statistical Pattern Recognition and Artificial Intelligence

The set of points defined by Equation (43) is basic to *statistical pattern recognition and artificial intelligence* just as is the *Cartesian product space*

$$\mathcal{X}\boldsymbol{\gamma}: \text{ Cartesian product between feature space and category space.} \tag{44}$$

A category–feature relationship exists for *only classes, complex classes,* and classes. This is a fundamental structure in the knowledge base structure.

The event

$$(\mathbf{x}\gamma_i^*) \quad \text{or} \quad (\mathbf{x}, \gamma_i^*) \tag{45}$$

consists of the element **x** in the feature space and the element γ_i^* in the category space. *This event is one relationship in the category–feature relationship for category* γ_i^* and is a basic "piece" of knowledge characterizing category γ_i^*.

A basic question is, How, given some typical or atypical patterns from a category γ_i^*, can we "generate" patterns not previously seen? In **AI** this is accomplished by rules for inductive or deductive inference. In **SPR** it has been done traditionally by a heavily studied collection of functionals called category conditional probability density functions.

SPR has something to offer here which is not available in conventional **AI** studies; and that is knowledge obtained through examples (samples or repetition), an important source of knowledge for concept formation. The impact of using examples to learn regions of *insignificance* in the feature space of a category has only begun to be studied. But Pearson in 1894 was aware of it in his mathematical studies of evolution. Robbins (1948), Patrick (1965), Fralick (1967), Teicher (1960, 1963) Spragins (1966), Yakowitz (1969), and others began studying it in the 1960s as **SPR** studies.

Basic "pieces of knowledge" can be considered "chunks" in the feature space. To illustrate, let there be three categories γ_1^*, γ_2^*, and γ_3^*. For each category form a cross-product space consisting of patterns from the respective categories. Respective planes of patterns are illustrated in Figure 3.4 for the following.

$$\begin{aligned} &\mathfrak{X}\gamma_1\text{—Set of all points } (\mathbf{x}, \gamma_1^*) \\ &\mathfrak{X}\gamma_2\text{—Set of all points } (\mathbf{x}, \gamma_2^*) \\ &\mathfrak{X}\gamma_3\text{—Set of all points } (\mathbf{x}, \gamma_3^*). \end{aligned} \tag{46}$$

The planes illustrated are the domains of category–feature relationships for this example. When probability density is attached to points in the domain, a category–feature relationship is constructed, denoted $\mathcal{F}_i(\mathfrak{X}\gamma_i^*)$, an *i*th functional (**SPR**) set of relationships (**AI**). This is denoted $p(\mathbf{x}|\gamma_i^*)$ in **SPR.**

The pieces of knowledge $\mathcal{F}_i(\mathfrak{X}\gamma_i^*)$ for category γ_i^* reflect feature–feature relationships, feature–category relationships, and weight or probabilities through $\mathcal{F}_i$ (Figure 3.5). Inference rules have to be devised to estimate this knowledge from other knowledge when necessary.

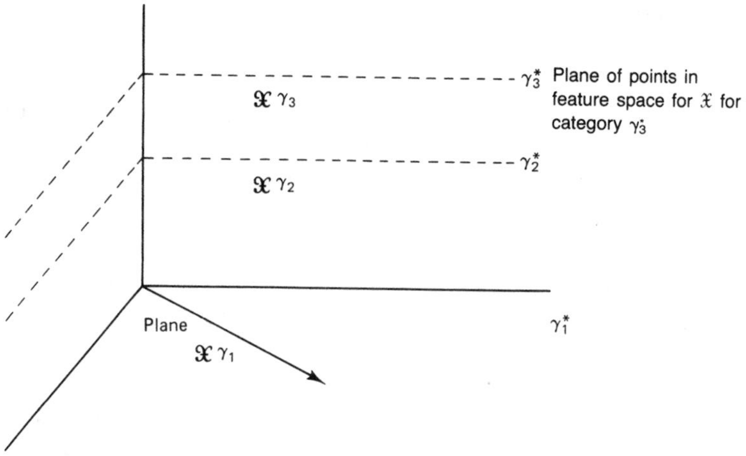

FIGURE 3.4. Cross-products of Category–feature space.

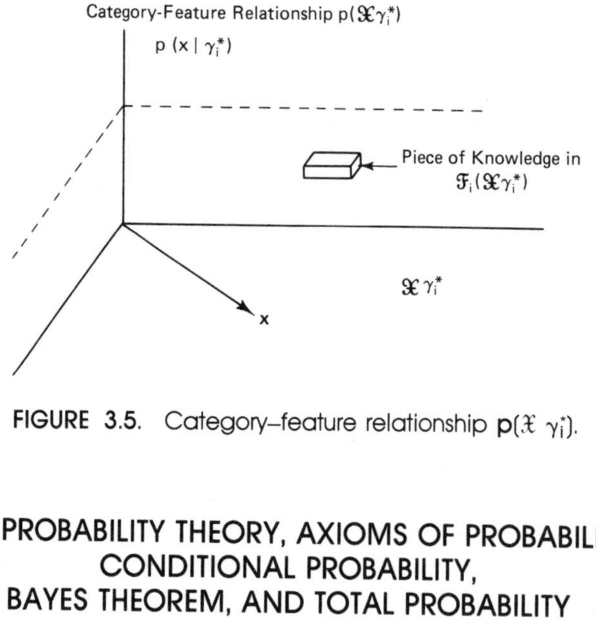

FIGURE 3.5. Category–feature relationship $p(\mathcal{X}\ \gamma_i^*)$.

3-5 PROBABILITY THEORY, AXIOMS OF PROBABILITY, CONDITIONAL PROBABILITY, BAYES THEOREM, AND TOTAL PROBABILITY

This section deals with the axiomatic approach to probability and results in a well-known form of inference called Bayes theorem. Then relative frequency is discussed which relates the axiomatic structure of Bayes theorem to one that can learn from examples (training records).

3-5-1 Axioms, Proposition, Theorem, and Theory

Let S, sets, and set operations be defined as in previous sections. What is an axiom? An *axiom* is defined as a "self-evident truth" or a "universally accepted principle or rule," or in logic as a "proposition that is accepted without proof for the sake of studying the consequences that follow from it." A *proposition* is "a plan proposed" or in logic "a statement affirming or denying something so that it can be characterized as true or false" or "a formal statement of a truth to be demonstrated." A *theorem* is "a theoretical proposition, statement, or formula embodying something to be proved from other propositions or formulas." A *corollary* is a "proposition that is incidentally proved in proving another proposition." A *theory* is a "coherent group of general propositions used as principles of explanation for a class of phenomena."

Bayes theorem will be derived entirely from the axioms of probability theory, a coherent group of self-evident truths. The theorem is proved accepting the axioms as true.

3-5-2 Probability Theory

The study of probability theory begins with three axioms of probability and a complementary relative frequency interpretation of probability. It includes definitions of conditional probability, total probability, statistically independent events, and a particular theorem known as Bayes theorem.

Based on the axioms and definitions, Bayes theorem follows—it is a proven proposition. The axioms of probability theory are reasonable and do not violate common sense. It follows then that Bayes theorem cannot violate common sense. But Bayes theorem is only one proposition. Another proposition to be proved is a theorem on a posteriori probability by Patrick. The proposition in the theorem by Patrick applies to a broader group of problems than does Bayes theorem.

3-5-2-1 Axioms of Probability

For two sets A and B in S, define a function $p(\ )$ such that

$$\begin{aligned} &P(A) \geq \emptyset \\ &P(S) = 1 \\ &\text{If } AB = \emptyset, \text{ then } P(A + B) = P(A) + P(B). \end{aligned} \tag{47}$$

A corollary to the above three axioms of probability is

$$P(A + B) = P(A) + P(B) - P(AB) \tag{48}$$

in general even if $AB = \emptyset$, which is easily proven starting with Eq. (47). (See a basic textbook on probability theory, e.g., Papoulis, 1965; Feller, 1957.)

3-5-2-2 Joint Probability

The product or intersection AB is a set and thus the axioms and corollaries of probability apply, resulting in

$$p(AB)\text{: Joint probability of } A \text{ and } B. \tag{49}$$

3-5-2-3 Conditional Probability

The probability of B given A is denoted

$$p(B|A)$$

and the definition of conditional probability is

$$p(B|A) \triangleq \frac{p(BA)}{p(A)}. \tag{50}$$

3-5-2-4 Bayes Theorem

Because (from Laws of Set Operations)

$$p(AB) = p(BA)$$

it follows using Eq. (50) that

$$p(B|A) = \frac{p(A|B)p(B)}{p(A)}, \tag{51}$$

which is Bayes theorem. At this point, Eq. (51), although proved based on axioms and definiton, has not been shown useful; it will be useful later when B is a category and A is a set of feature values. The function $p(A|B)$ will be a category-conditional probability density function which must be engineered using a knowledge base structure.

3-5-2-5 Total Probability

Let there be a set of categories $\gamma_1^*, \gamma_2^*, \ldots, \gamma_M^*$ which are mutually exclusive and exhaustive (S). These events can be used to partition another event such as $\mathbf{x}$ (a feature vector) into the sum of disjoint subsets:

$$\mathbf{x} = \mathbf{x}\,\gamma_1^* + \mathbf{x}\,\gamma_2^* + \ldots + \mathbf{x}\gamma_M^*. \tag{52}$$

By the third axiom in Eq. (47) and by Eq. (45),

$$p(\mathbf{x}) = \sum_{i=1}^{M} p(\mathbf{x}, \gamma_i^*) \tag{53}$$

which is an expression called total probability. Equation (52) was obtained from the following sequence of procedures,

$$\begin{aligned}\mathbf{x} &= (\mathbf{x}S) \\ &= \mathbf{x} \sum_{i=1}^{M} \gamma_i^* \\ &= \sum_{i=1}^{M} \mathbf{x}\, \gamma_i^*,\end{aligned}$$

where the latter follows from the Associative Law of the product.

3-6 RELATIVE FREQUENCY INTERPRETATION OR ANALYSIS

3-6-1 A Priori Probability Estimates

To be useful for decision making, probability theory must provide a "likelihood" of one category versus another category. It must provide a measure of how close features $\mathbf{x}$ for findings are to a category. We would like to be able to learn this closeness measure either using expert knowledge or hard data examples. Methods for determining closeness other than conventional distance measures are discussed in subsequent sections.

Up to this point in the discussion, probability theory has been introduced consisting of definitions, axioms, and Bayes theorem. Next the framework of probability theory will be used to embrace a likelihood or relative frequency or "vote" or experience. *Experience* has been defined as "the process of encountering or undergoing things as they occur in the course of time." A method of recording this experience is through trials.

The model considered consists of the previously defined feature space $\mathfrak{X}$ and category space $\boldsymbol{\gamma}$. An experiment is performed n times where each time one and only one category γ_i^* is observed. Define

$$n_{\gamma_i^*}$$

as the number of times out of n times that category γ_i^* is observed.

Define

$$\hat{P}(\gamma_i^*) \triangleq n_{\gamma_i^*}/n \qquad \text{(observing category space)} \tag{54}$$

as the relative frequency of category γ_i^*. Equation (54) is the definition of relative frequency. The experiment chosen provides that Eq. (54) is an estimate of the *a priori probability of category* γ_i^* given *supervised samples* (learning with a teacher).

3-6-2 Estimates of Category–Feature Relationship and Total Probability

Consider another experiment (or same experiment) performed n times, and each time a feature vector $\mathbf{x}$ is observed as is the joint event $(\mathbf{x}, \gamma_i^*)$. Define

$$\hat{P}(\mathbf{x}) \triangleq n_{\mathbf{x}}/n \qquad \text{(observing feature space)} \tag{55}$$

and

$$\hat{P}(\mathbf{x}, \gamma_i^*) \triangleq n_{(\mathbf{x},\, \gamma_i^*)}/n \ \text{(observing cross-product space)}, \tag{56}$$

where $n_{\mathbf{x}}$ is the number of times $\mathbf{x}$ occurred and $n_{(\mathbf{x},\, \gamma_i^*)}$ is the number of times $(\mathbf{x}, \gamma_i^*)$ occurred. Applying the definition of conditional probability, it follows that

$$\hat{p}(\mathbf{x}|\gamma_i^*) = \frac{n_{(\mathbf{x}|\gamma_i^*)}/\mathrm{n}}{n_{\mathbf{x}}/n} = \frac{n_{(\mathbf{x}|\gamma_i^*)}}{n_{\mathbf{x}}}, \tag{57}$$

which is the relative number of times feature $\mathbf{x}$ occurred with category γ_i^* compared with the number of times $\mathbf{x}$ occurred. This is *experience!* Experience results even if $n_{(\mathbf{x},\gamma_i^*)} = 1$ or $\emptyset$, whereby $\mathbf{x}$ is related to category γ_i^* only once or not at all.

3-7 RELATIVE FREQUENCY INTERPRETATION OF BAYES THEOREM

Substituting Eqs. (54), (55), and (57) into (56) results in

$$\hat{P}(\gamma_i^*|\mathbf{x}) = \frac{\hat{p}(\mathbf{x}|\gamma_i^*)}{\hat{p}(\mathbf{x})}\,\hat{P}(\gamma_i^*) \tag{58}$$

$$= \frac{n_{(\mathbf{x},\gamma_i^*)}/n_{\mathbf{x}}}{n_{\mathbf{x}}/n}\,(n_{\gamma_i^*}/n)\ ,\forall\ i \tag{59}$$

for any feature set $\mathbf{x}$. In practice it is natural to obtain experience as $\hat{p}(\mathbf{x}|\gamma_i^*)$. Furthermore, it is natural to study how to engineer the construction of $\hat{p}(\mathbf{x}|\gamma_i^*)$ from knowledge about γ_i^*. But such engineering is a departure from conventional probability theory, statistics, or even SPR. It is, however, the subject of this book. In practice, knowledge often is acquired about the feature set $\mathbf{x}$ given the category. This suggests calling $p(\mathbf{x}|\gamma_i^*)$ the category conditional probability density function (c.c.p.d.f.). Also, in practice, knowledge often is acquired about the category probability $P(\gamma_i^*)$. This results in knowledge as *a posteriori probability* expressed by the left-hand side of Eq. (58). A posteriori means "after the fact." The fact is the feature set $\mathbf{x}$. "Before the fact" knowedge is *a priori* and expressed as $\hat{p}(\gamma_i^*)$.

3-8 STATISTICALLY INDEPENDENT EVENTS

Two sets A and B are statistically independent if

$$P(AB) = P(A)P(B): \quad A \text{ and } B \text{ statistically independent} \qquad (60)$$

From the definition of conditional probability, Eq. 50, it follows that

$$P(B|A) = P(B): \quad \text{if A and B are statistically independent.} \qquad (61)$$

Extension to multiple sets $A_1, A_2, \ldots A_M$, which are statistically independent, include

$$P(A_{k_1}, A_{k_2}, \ldots, A_{k_r}) = P(A_{k_1})P(A_{k_2}) \ldots P(A_{k_r}) \qquad (62)$$

for any subset of the sets, indexed by k.

$$P(A_{k_i} + A_{k_j}) = P(A_{k_i}) + P(A_{k_j}) - P(A_{k_i})P(A_{k_j}) \qquad (63)$$

$$P(\bar{A}_{k_i} + \bar{A}_{k_j}) = P(\bar{A}_{k_i}) + P(\bar{A}_{k_j}) \qquad (64)$$

$$P((A_{k_i})(A_{k_j} + A_{k_l})) = P(A_{k_i})P(A_{k_j} + A_{k_l}). \qquad (65)$$

3-9 RANDOM VARIABLE, PROBABILITY DISTRIBUTION FUNCTION

3-9-1 Random Variable

Let S be a probability space consisting of a set of objects denoted by μ. To every μ, assign according to some rule a number $X(\mu)$, which is a *random variable*. Define now that μ is the *outcome* of an *experiment* and thus also is $X(\mu)$.

Given any real number x, we can observe the number of times in the experiment that

$$X(\mu) \leq x. \tag{66}$$

We define

$$X(\mu):\quad \text{Random variable}$$

$$x:\quad \text{Value of a random variable.} \tag{67}$$

3-9-2 Probability Distribution Function

Given a real number x, the set $\{X \leq x\}$ corresponds to a set of outcomes μ (the domain) such that $X(\mu) \leq x$. Define

$$p[X \leq x] \triangleq F_x(x), \qquad -\infty < x < \infty \tag{68}$$

probability distrbution function of the random variable X. If x has discrete values x_i on the real line, then

$$F_x(\mathrm{x}) = \sum_j p[X = x_j]$$

$$\forall j \ni x_j \leq x. \tag{69}$$

3-9-3 Probability Density Function (p.d.f.)

If X is a discrete random variable, then the probability density function (p.d.f.) is a set of numbers

$$p[X = x_j] = p_j, \qquad j = 1, 2, \ldots, V \tag{70}$$

with the constraint that

$$\sum_{j=1}^{V} p_j = 1 \,. \tag{71}$$

3-10 VECTOR SPACE AND LINEAR INDEPENDENCE

3-10-1 Vector

A vector is denoted $\mathbf{x}$ and is an ordered L-tuple of numbers written as a row, e.g., $\mathbf{x} = (x_1, x_2, \ldots, x_L)$ or as a column

$$x = \begin{bmatrix} x_1 \\ x_2 \\ \cdot \\ \cdot \\ \cdot \\ \cdot \\ x_L \end{bmatrix} \tag{72}$$

The latter is conveniently written $\mathbf{x} = [x_1, x_2, \ldots, x_L]$.

3-10-2 Unit Vectors

A unit vector denoted e_j is a vector with unity as the value of its jth component and with all other components zero:

$$\begin{aligned} e_1 &= [1, \emptyset, \ldots, \emptyset] \\ e_2 &= [\emptyset, 1, \ldots, \emptyset] \\ e_L &= [\emptyset, \emptyset, \ldots, 1] \end{aligned} \tag{73}$$

3-10-3 Linear Combinations

The linear combinations of L, L-component vectors $\mathbf{x}_1, \mathbf{x}_2, \ldots, \mathbf{x}_L$ is

$$\mathbf{x} = \sum_{j=1}^{L} a_j \mathbf{x}_j$$

where each a_j is constant. The unit vectors $e_1, e_2, \ldots e_L$ can be used to from a coordinate system of a vector space E^L where any vector $\mathbf{x}$ in E^L is

$$\mathbf{x} = \sum_{j=1}^{L} a_j e_j, \qquad \mathbf{x} \in E^L. \tag{74}$$

3-10-4 Linear Independence of Vectors

A set of vectors $\mathbf{x}_1, \mathbf{x}_2, \ldots, \mathbf{x}_L$ from E^L is said to be linearly dependent if there exist scalars a_j, not all zero such that

$$a_1\mathbf{x}_1 + a_2\mathbf{x}_2 + \ldots + a_L\mathbf{x}_L = \boldsymbol{\emptyset}, \tag{75}$$

where $\emptyset$ is a zero vector having all components zero.

If the only set of a_j for which Eq. (75) is true is $a_1 = a_2 = \ldots = a_L$

= Ø, then the vectors are *linearly independent.* Linear independence is an important and useful concept because a pattern cannot be completely represented unless all its independent components are present. An additional component would be redundant. Certainly, nonlinear expressions for a pattern in terms of a set of vectors are available. These expressions serve to provide dimensionality reduction reflecting problem knowledge (Patrick, 1972).

3-10-4-1 Basis or Spanning Set

A set of vectors $\mathbf{x}_1, \mathbf{x}_2, \ldots, \mathbf{x}_L$ from E^L is said to span or generate E^L if every vector $\mathbf{x}$ in E^L can be written as a linear combination of $\mathbf{x}_1, \mathbf{x}_2, \ldots, \mathbf{x}_L$.

3-10-4-2 Scalar Product or Inner Product

The scalar product (or inner product) of the L-component vector $\mathbf{x}$ and $\mathbf{y}$ is defined to be the scalar

$$\sum_{j=1}^{L} x_j y_j \triangleq (\mathbf{x}, \mathbf{y}) \tag{76}$$

In practice this represents a projection of $\mathbf{x}$ onto $\mathbf{y}$ and is useful to measure "how much of $\mathbf{y}$ is in $\mathbf{x}$." It can be used to determine the scalar coefficients a_j in Eq. (74) for representing pattern $\mathbf{x}$ as projection onto basis vectors.

3-10-4-3 Orthogonal, Orthonormal

Two vectors $\mathbf{x}$ and $\mathbf{y}$ have properties defined as follows:

$$(\mathbf{x}, \mathbf{y}) = \emptyset, \text{ assuming } \mathbf{x} \neq \emptyset, \mathbf{y} \neq \emptyset: \quad \textit{orthogonal} \tag{77a}$$

$$(\mathbf{x}, \mathbf{y}) = \emptyset, \text{ assuming } \mathbf{x} \neq \emptyset, \mathbf{y} = \emptyset: \quad \text{and}$$

$$(\mathbf{x}, \mathbf{x}) = 1: \quad \textit{orthonormal.} \tag{77b}$$

3-10-5 Linear Independence Compared with Statistical Independence

In decision making, *linear independence is a property of the feature space* $\mathfrak{X}$ and functions $d_j(\mathbf{x})$ used to represent vectors in the space. These functions need not be the unit vectors. These functions $d_j(\mathbf{x})$ are called *Basis functions.* For example, it may be possible to represent a complex class as a linear combination of the class–feature relationships of classes defining the complex class.

Statistical independence (if it applies) is a property of the category–feature relationship $p(\mathbf{x}|\gamma_i^*)$. For any two features x_j and x_k in the set of features $\mathbf{x}$, this property informs how the one feature x_j varies when feature x_k varies. In practice such variations must be learned and the construction or engineering of $p(\mathbf{x}\,|\gamma_i^*)$ provide for such knowledge. The variation may be *deterministic,* meaning that x_j always varies with x_k exactly the same way. On the other hand, x_j's variation may even be independent of x_k. For example, there may be narrow variations of x_j which do not affect x_k. When x_j has a large variation into another "quantum" (so to speak), x_k may then vary in a predictable way. Although this variation of x_k may be predicted, that prediction may itself only be to within some "quantum" of variation.

So, dependence among respective feature values is predictable but only with some certainty, relative frequencies, or weights. That is, the features are *statistically* dependent. *On the other hand, linear independence of all features is a statement that a pattern cannot be represented with any of the features missing.* The pattern representation is dependent on all the features being present. What we are dealing with, however, is a category of patterns. It may be that some pattern in the category does not need all the linearly independent features to uniquely identify the pattern. This suggests that there are subsets of patterns in a category. For a particular subset, patterns may be represented by a subset of the linearly independent basis vectors with no additional basis vector helping the representation. Particular patterns in the category subset may, however, be generated as a statistical act of one feature varying in a predictable way when another feature varies.

In summary, a category of patterns may consist of subsets of patterns, defined *Subcategories.* Patterns in one subcategory may not require the same basis vectors as patterns in another subcategory of the category. Moreover, statistical generation of patterns in one subcategory may be different from one in another subcategory.

Keep in mind that if the objective is to gather knowledge of categories and thus their patterns, then reasoning about this knowledge already has been accomplished in selecting the model for gathering the knowledge. Additional reasoning in forming conclusions also will follow given reasoning or decision rules.

Can knowledge about a category be outside the categories' space of basis functions and statistical variations? The answer is yes if the model is restricted to Bayes theorem. The theorem on a posteriori probability by Patrick allows for concept formation of new categories.

3-10-6 Distance Measure

A vector space includes the definition of distance from the vector (point) $\mathbf{x}$ to vector (point) $\mathbf{y}$:

$$d(\mathbf{x}, \mathbf{y}): \text{ Distance from } \mathbf{x} \text{ to } \mathbf{y}. \tag{78}$$

If the vector space is Euclidean, then

$$d(\mathbf{x}, \mathbf{y}) = \left[\sum_{j=1}^{L} (x_j - y_j)^2 \right]^{1/2}: \text{ Euclidean distance.} \tag{79}$$

A distance measure is used to express closeness of a vector $\mathbf{x}$ to vectors characterizing a category γ_i^*. For example, the category–feature relationship is itself closeness measure:

$$p(\mathbf{x}|\gamma_i^*): \quad \text{A closeness measure.} \tag{80}$$

But the Euclidean distance measure of Eq. (79) is too restrictive for a general classification system where a feature x_j can have values which cannot be ordered. One alternative is a closeness measure consisting of intersections and unions (SPR), i.e., conjunctions and disjunctions (AI), with probabilities (SPR), i.e., weights (AI). For example,

$$p(\mathbf{x}|\gamma_i^*) = (p_{11} \text{ if } x_1 = x_{11}, \, p_{12} \text{ if } x_2 = x_{12}, \ldots) * (p_{21} \text{ if } x_2 = x_{21}, \, p_{22} \text{ if } x_2 = x_{22}, \ldots.) * (\ldots.).$$

If the natural log is taken of the previous expression, then

$$\ln p(\mathbf{x}|\gamma_i^*) = \Sigma \ln [\text{weighted disjunctions}] \tag{81}$$

Properly stated, $p(\mathbf{x}|\gamma_i^*)$ and $\ln p(\mathbf{x}|\gamma_i^*)$ are inverse closeness measures because the closer $\mathbf{x}$ is to γ_i^* the larger the measure.

In Chapter 9 the **CONSULT-I®** closeness measure is presented for determining the closeness of a pattern $\mathbf{x}$ to a category γ_i^*. It is an engineered closeness measure designed not to violate the theory of this chapter but at the same time designed to incorporate capabilities for deduction and feature selection.

3-11 INFORMATION THEORY: DEFINITION OF INFORMATION

3-11-1 Background

Information theory (Kullback, 1959) and its companion, communication theory (Thomas, 1969), gave birth to modern artificial intelligence and statistical pattern recognition. They contribute insight to methods for feature value definition and feature selection. A brief review of information theory is found in Raeside (1976).

3-11-2 Information Conveyed in Observing a Feature, Given a Class

Let a feature x_j have values x_{j_v}, $v = 1, 2, \ldots, V$, and category conditional probability density function $p(x_j|\gamma_i^*)$ for category γ_i^*. The information conveyed when x_j is observed from category γ_i^* is

$$I_{x_j} = -\sum_{v=1}^{V} p(x_{j_v}|\gamma_i^*)\log_2[p(x_{j_v}|\gamma_i^*)]. \tag{82}$$

If $p(x_{j_v}|\gamma_i^*) = 1$, meaning that only one x_{j_v} can occur, then $I_{x_j} = \emptyset$, indicating that no information is conveyed by the experiment where x_j is observed.

In Eq. (82), $\{x_{j_v}\}$ is mutually exclusive. The information function associated with x_{j_v} is

$$I_{x_{j_v}} = -\log_2[p(x_{j_v}|\gamma\$058d2i)], \tag{83}$$

demonstrating that Eq. (82) is the expected information (average information) associated with feature x_j, given category γ_i^*.

3-12 FUZZY SET THEORY

3-12-1 Introduction

A theory of approximate reasoning (Zadah, 1965, 1979, 1982; Wechsler, 1976; Adlassnig, 1980; Tong, 1984; Negoita, 1985) provides useful mathematics for use in constructing models of feature values, category conditional probability density functions, and complex classes. This fuzzy set theory is not a substitute for the mathematics of probability theory or statistical pattern recognition. In fact, fuzzy set theory merges with statistical pattern recognition if the latter accounts for uncertain feature values and uncertain training of category conditional probability density functions. The relative frequency method of estimating or verifying probabilities is not replaced by fuzzy set theory.

3-12-2 Possibility Distribution

A universe of discourse U is a set of numbers. Each number u in U indexes a linguistic truth-value such as: very small, small, average, large, very large, etc. A set of values in U is denoted by F. For example, F may contain numbers indexing very small and small, respectively.

An observation or feature is denoted x, and this feature has some value u. For example, given that x is F where F "is" very small or small, what is the possiblity that $x = u$ where u is small? This possibility, also called the grade of membership of u in the fuzzy set F, is a number between Ø and 1. Let

$$\mu_F(u): \text{ Possibility that } x = u, \text{ given the fuzzy set } F \text{ where } u \text{ is one of the values of } F. \tag{84}$$

Formally

$$\text{Poss}\,\{x = u | x = F\} = \mu_F(u), \qquad u \in U.$$

This definition and rules to follow for fuzzy sets are axiomatic. Zadeh (1979) feels that "intuitively, possibility relates to our perception of the degree of feasibility or ease of attainment; whereas, probability is associated with the degree of belief, likelihood, frequency or proportion." This leaves room for considerable debate. The bottom line is that some knowledge is provided by people while some is provided by sampling. This brings up a very old argument of the axiomatic theory of probability versus the relative frequency concept of probability. Both are important. It is expected that after there is acceptance of using a priori or expert knowledge in decision making, there will be a shift toward verification (learning inferences) using samples from nature, as well as mathematical functions reflecting the physics/engineering of the problem.

3-13 A POSTERIORI CATEGORY PROBABILITY

Given category conditional probability density function

$$p(\mathbf{x}|\gamma_\xi^*),$$

the conventional a posteriori probability for category γ_i^* is expressed

$$\begin{aligned} p(\gamma_\xi^*|\mathbf{x}) &= \frac{p(\mathbf{x}|\gamma_\xi^*)P(\gamma_\xi^*)}{p(\mathbf{x})} \\ &= \frac{p(\mathbf{x}|\gamma_\xi^*)P(\gamma_\xi^*)}{\sum_{\alpha=1}^{M} p(\mathbf{x}|\gamma_\alpha^*)p\,(\gamma_\alpha^*)} \end{aligned} \tag{85}$$

when there is no concept formation, i.e., when Bayes theorem applies.

Anytime the categories are fixed *a priori* as in Bayes theorem or when the more general theorem on *a posteriori* probability by Patrick is not used, this a posteriori probability applies. It does not apply when concept (category) formation takes place according to the theorem on a posteriori probability by Patrick through statistical dependence among categories. A great deal is said about the calculation of $p(\mathbf{x}|\gamma_\xi^*)$ elsewhere in this book. Statistical pattern recognition is a discipline where models are carefully developed for $p(\mathbf{x}|\gamma_\xi^*)$. Artificial intelligence would use the rules discussed in Chapter 4 (without necessarily admitting to this) to engineer the constructon of $p(\mathbf{x}|\gamma_\xi^*)$.

The category conditional probability density function $p(\mathbf{x}|\gamma_\xi^*)$ is fundamental to all inference rules although many rules are approximations to it.

3-14 DECISION MAKING OR CONCLUDING RULES

3-14-1 Minimum Probability of Error Decision at a Focus

The minimum probability or error decision is made as follows:

$$\text{Decide category } \gamma_\xi^* \text{ if} \qquad (86)$$
$$p(\gamma_\xi^*|\mathbf{x}) = \max_\alpha \{p(\gamma_\alpha^*|\mathbf{x})\}, \qquad \forall\ \gamma_\alpha^* \in \boldsymbol{\gamma}'.$$

This requires that a sequence $\mathbf{x}$ of features be available. The decision space $\boldsymbol{\gamma}'$ is in the category space $\boldsymbol{\gamma}$ and suggests a differential diagnosis or focusing facility. That is, $\boldsymbol{\gamma}'$ contains a subset of categories. This decision rule will have to be modified when categories can be discovered through concept formation.

3-14-2 Differential Diagnosis: Focusing

The *differential diagosis* $\boldsymbol{\gamma}'$ thus consists of a presentation of the categories with the highest a posteriori probabilities. The presentation can be *only classes,* or *complex classes.*

3-14-3 Maximum Likelihood Decision

The maximum likelihood decision is made as follows:

$$\text{Decide category } \gamma_\xi^* \text{ if} \qquad (87)$$
$$p(\mathbf{x}|\gamma_\xi^*) = \max_\alpha \{p(\mathbf{x}\ |\gamma_\alpha^*)\}, \qquad \forall\ \gamma_\alpha^* \in \boldsymbol{\gamma}'$$

Whereas the minimum probability of error decision rule requires a priori category probabilities through Eq. (85), the maximum likelihood decision rule does not. Both rules provide that knowledge be stored in the category conditional probability density functions.

The maximum likelihood decision is the minimum probability of error decision where the a priori probabilities are assumed equal $(1/M)$.

3-14-4 Interpretation of A Posteriori Probabilities

The a posteriori probability

$$p(\gamma_i^*|\mathbf{x})$$

is an expression of the relative frequency that category γ_i^* presents as feature vector $\mathbf{x}$. This takes into account the a priori category probability $p(\gamma_i^*)$ and category conditional probability density $p(\mathbf{x}|\gamma_i^*)$. If $p(\mathbf{x}|\gamma_i^*)$ is relatively very large for category γ_i^*, then the a posteriori category probability relatively will not be influenced by the a priori probability $p(\gamma_i^*)$ unless $p(\gamma_i^*)$ is very, very small. Anyone making decisions should understand these concepts. There is evidence that some individuals make decisions without regard to the a priori probability while some even make decisions using a priori probabilities entirely without regard to $p(\mathbf{x}|\gamma_i^*)$.

One problem with presenting a posteriori probabilities to a user is that he may be unwilling or unable to handle a priori probabilities. Perhaps he wants to see the presentation as $p(\gamma_i^*|\mathbf{x})$, assuming equal a priori probabilities, along with a presentation of the a priori probabilities. This suggests a maximum likelihood decision approach.

3-14-5 Interpretation of Maximum Likelihood Decision

The likelihood of category γ_i^* is given by the equation for

$$\mathcal{L}_i = p(\mathbf{x}|\gamma_i^*),$$

which is identical to the a posteriori probability except for division by a number constant for all the categories and multiplication by the a priori probability. The likelihood reflects how much feature vector $\mathbf{x}$ matches a presentation (subcategory or subsubcategory) in the "hypercube" of category γ_i^* without regard to the relative frequency of the category in the whole population of categories.

The likelihood reflects how much $\mathbf{x}$ *looks like category* γ_i^*. Suppose that $\mathbf{x}$ looks like category γ_i^*, but a priori, category γ_i^* is "relatively not very likely." Does a user make a decision based on the likelihood, or does he weigh his decision by the a priori probability? What would compel a user to disregard or overrule a priori probability? One answer is, loss or risk.

3-15 INCORPORATING *LOSS*

Suppose L_i is the *loss* incurred in not deciding category γ_i^*. The information then important to the user includes these three numbers:

$$p(\mathbf{x}|\gamma_i^*),\ P_i,\ L_i.$$

The loss in not deciding category γ_i^* when it is true is

$$\frac{p(\mathbf{x}|\gamma_i^*)\ P_i L_i}{\sum_j\ p(\mathbf{x}|\gamma_i^*) P_j}. \tag{88}$$

We see that the factor $P_i L_i$ can result in high probable loss for a low a priori probability P_i if the loss L_i is high.

This gives the impression that the occurrence of $\mathbf{x}$ places "all bets off" concerning a priori probability. Not so, a priori probability still applies. Nature is not playing games by changing a priori probabilities. But the user still has to "play risk factors." For these reasons, it seems reasonable to present to the user

$$p(\mathbf{x}|\gamma_i^*),\ P_i,\ L_i,$$

and perhaps even

$$p(\gamma_i^*|\mathbf{x}).$$

A user educated in these aspects of decision making then will have more nearly complete information for making a decision. Using these concepts, it is possible to design intelligent decision rules which indicate likelihood along with population probability and loss.

There is a problem with presenting to the user a single decision (γ_i^*) corresponding to highest a posteriori probability or likelihood. That is, suppose the top categories in the differential diagnosis are close together in probability; then the user should want to know them all. An exception would be where the action to be taken (treatment in medical diagnosis) is identical for all categories in their differential diagnosis.

3-16 SUBCATEGORIES, COMPLEX CATEGORIES, AND STRUCTURED VERSUS ILL-STRUCTURED PROBLEMS

3-16-1 Subcategories

Mathematically, a subcategory is one of the *k*th columns of a category along with all minicolumns (minicolumn relative frequencies and set of independent probability density functions). A subcategory is a "hypercube" of the category. Some subcategories are identified with special names to distinguish them from the category as a whole.

A subcategory $\gamma_{i_k}^*$ "partitions" a category γ_i^* by the following defining equation:

$$p(\mathbf{x}|\gamma_i^*) = \sum_{k=1}^{K} p(\mathbf{x}|\gamma_{i_k}^*)\ p(\gamma_{i_k}^*|\gamma_i^*). \tag{89}$$

The subcategory conditional probability density function is

$$p(\mathbf{x}|\gamma_{i_k}^*) \tag{90}$$

with a mixing parameter (conditional a priori probability)

$$p(\gamma_{i_k}^*|\gamma_i^*). \tag{91}$$

When training samples are available for a category, estimation of the subcategory conditional probability density functions and/or mixing parameters can be an unsupervised estimation problem (learning without a teacher). Updating a category may require using metaknowledge (**AI**) to know that a new subcategory needs to be formed in order to achieve highest performance in keeping the category separated from other categories **(SPR).** This is a good example of where AI by itself is not sufficient but the construction of categories with intermixed subcategories **(SPR)** is essential.

3-16-2 Well-Structured versus Ill-Structured Problems

3-16-2-1 The Need for a Problem Model

Patrick *and others* (1972, 1974, 1975a, 1975b, 1979) observed that well-structured, recurring problems occur in medicine, where well structured means that there are a fixed number of features and a fixed number of categories. Such problems are named subsystems. To be useful, a subsystem should have recurring application and the knowledge base should be recurring. In this sense, a subspecialist trained at one medical center can transfer his expertise to another practice situation.

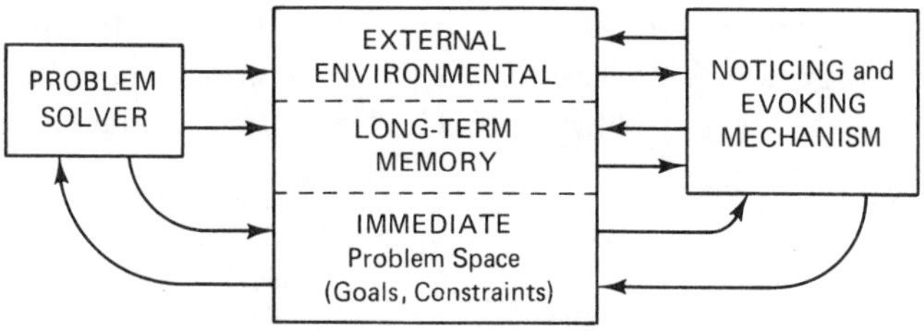

FIGURE 3.6. Simon's model for preparing a problem for solution. (Herbert A. Simon, "The Structure of Ill-Structured Problems," *Artificial Intelligence*, 4: 181–201, 1973. Used with permission.)

Simon (1973) suggested that "any problem solving process will appear ill structured if the problem solver is a machine that has access to a very large long-term memory of potentially relevant information."

He further suggests "there is merit to the claim that much problem-solving effort is directed to structuring problems; and only a fraction of it at solving problems once they are structured."

Further, "there may be nothing other than the size of the knowledge base to distinguish ISPs (Ill-Structured Problems) from WSPs (Well-Structured Problems)."

Patrick (1965, 1972) investigated conditions under which it is possible to learn (or estimate) without a teacher. In general, a certain sufficient amount of information is required about a problem before learning without a teacher is possible. In this sense, Patrick agrees with Simon's suggestion: "In general, problems presented to the problem solver by the world are best regarded as ISPs." They become WSPs only in the process of being prepared for the problem solvers. Simon (1973) suggested a model (Figure 3.6) which has many similarities to Patrick's Adaptive Estimation System (1969).

It is interesting that researchers developing a system named Caduceus, previously **INTERNIST** (Miller *and others,* 1982), claimed to set aside statistical pattern recognition and to be solving an ISP (Ill-Structured Problem) (Pople, 1982), and stating that medical diagnosis cannot be solved as a WSP (Well-Structured Problem). It is ironic (but expected) that the researcher's solution (see Chapter 12) is a closeness measure from statistical pattern recognition and is well structured.

3-16-2-2 Definition of a Well-Stuctured Problem

Simon (1973) suggested criteria for defining a WSP (Well-Structured Problem) but stresses that any definition of a WSP may not be complete. Using his definitions, we discuss **CONSULT-I®**. First, we define a *state* as a "condition with respect to structure or circumstances." A state may be one of the most often used but ill-defined terms in artificial intelligence. *The mere definition of a state implies structure.*

A well-structured problem in **CONSULT-I®** has:

1. *Initial States.* In **CONSULT-I®** this is the knowledge base consisting of categories, category–feature relationships, likelihood closeness measures, etc.
2. *Goal State.* Rank order of likelihood probabilities and/or rank-order a posteriori probabilities of categories existing a priori or formed during concept formation.
3. *Attainable State Changes.* Automatic in **CONSULT-I®** where columns are used to direct transitions, new complex classes are formed, or new subcategories formed.
4. *Knowledge (in Problem Spaces).* Category space, feature space, category conditional probability density functions, complex features, and so on.
5. *External World (Know How to Use It).* In **CONSULT-I®** the external world provides input through the interviewer and output through category probabilities and/or actions. In addition, the scientific method is used to evaluate decision-making performance and as a teacher to provide new training data.
6. *Practical Amount of Computation.* Microcomputers and future microcomputers or new alternative methods of computing.

Does nature play games changing complex classes, the feature space or category conditional probability density functions? To recognize this, a teacher is necessary to detect the difference between the model in **CONSULT-I®** and a new model to fit the new world. The General Problem Solver (GPS) requires, in addition to the ISP requirement:

1. Set of operators to change from one state to another state.
2. Set of differences to test for difference between pairs of states.
3. Table of Differences associated with the differences with one or more operators relevant to reducing or minimizing the difference.

3-16-2-3 Developing a CONSULT-I® Subsystem — A GPS (General Problem Solver)

We have observed the developer at work in developing a **CONSULT-I®** subsystem. He imposes steps 1, 2, and 3 of the GPS to bring about successive iterations of the **CONSULT-I®** subsystem.

Respective refinements of a **CONSULT-I®** subsystem involve adding and/or changing categories, adding and/or changing features (feature values), and correcting training of category conditional probability density functions.

The developer has access to the field of knowledge—textbooks, patients, experiments, etc. **CONSULT-I®** does not try to be a GPS, realizing that it does not have this field of knowledge.

3-16-3 Structuring an "Ill-Structured Problem"

3-16-3-1 Introduction

Let's look at rules discussed by Shortliffe (1983), for "ill-structured problems proposed for medical decision making" where "the conclusion and premise portions of a pertinent rule may not correspond clearly to disease and one of its manifestations." *In order to solve proposed "ill-structured" problems it is necessary to introduce the kind of structure in* **CONSULT-I®**.

a. *Definitional Rules.* If the patient is male, then he is not pregnant or lactating. In **CONSULT-I®** examples include **CAN'T** (cannot be) operations.

b. *Cause-to-Effect Rules.* If there is an elevation in parathyroid hormone levels and the patient has normal renal function, then anticipate that urinary calcium is depressed and phosphate is increased. This is analogous to a minicolumn in **CONSULT-I®**.

c. *Effect-to-Cause Rules.* If the patient has recurrent calcium oxalate kidney stones, then consider the diagnosis of hyperparathyroidism. In **CONSULT-I®** this is a complex feature or more generally a likelihood function for inference.

d. *Associational Rules.* If the patient has ______ and ______ then there is evidence that ______. Again, in **CONSULT-I®**, this is a complex feature or part of a column.

3-16-3-2 Relating Some "AI Rules" to A Posteriori Probability

The category conditional p.d.f. $p(\mathbf{x}|\gamma_i^*)$ is structured in Chapter 9 in terms of columns and minicolumns. With respect to the previous rules, a *definitional rule* is a column or minicolumns and specifically may be a **CAN'T** (see Chapter, Section 8-11) A *cause-to-effect* rule again is part of a column or is a minicolumn in **CONSULT-I®**. *The effect-to-cause rule* simply places a column or minicolumn with a class. The *associational rule* is a conjunction operation that may be a column or minicolumn or a complex feature (see Chapter 9). Thus, *these all are structures in the class conditional p.d.f.*

3-16-3-3 Global-Directed Reasoning

A focus of hypotheses can be established in **CONSULT-I®** to include categories, subcategories (columns), subsubcategories (minicolumns), complex features, or even features (primitives). The interviewer then can ask only questions related to this focus. *The ability to establish a focus, called Goal-Directed Reasoning* (Shortliffe, 1983), thus requires structure. The focus is directed by goals established a priori.

3-16-3-4 Data-Driven Reasoning

Data-Driven reasoning or "forward-chained" control operates without a focus (goals) (Shortliffe, 1983). In **CONSULT-I®** this is analogous to processing all categories and computing all relative a posteriori probabilities.

3-16-3-5 Hypothesis-Directed Reasoning

This is said to include properties of goal-directed reasoning and data-driven reasoning *because a focus is determined from the data rather than by goals established a priori.* For discussion of Hypothesis Directed Reasoning see Wolf and others, 1985 and Eddy and Clanton, 1982. Actually, the a priori method of determining the focus is a form of goal direction. In **CONSULT-I®** this can be accomplished by ways as in feature selection and activation rules.

3-16-3-6 Comments on Structure of Reasoning in CONSULT-I®

The three types of reasoning just described required structure. It appears that some researchers build their models in a computer and avoid detailed model description. The underlying structures for all three methods are at least a part of that in **CONSULT-I®**.

3-16-4 Different Methods of Reasoning Look Different to the User

The three methods of reasoning appear different to the user. Hypothesis-directed reasoning would appear the most conversational-like with humanlike behavior to the user. That could be an advantage of user friendliness for some uses, but would be unnecessarily time consuming to other more sophistcated users. *Goal-Directed Reasoning unstructures the previously structured categories for the sake of appearing intelligent and can be cumbersome. In any case, structuring must be carefully done as in **CONSULT-I®** before any reasoning procedure can achieve optimum performance.*

The theorem on a posteriori probability (Patrick) allows for concept formation during learning. These concepts are new categories not previously described in the knowledge base. Is this solving an unstructured problem? It is unstructured in that the structure of the categories did not exist before they were formed. It is structured in that the structure existed in the first place to form the new concepts (categories).

4

Methods Studied in Artificial Intelligence Applied to Classification Systems

4-1 INTRODUCTION

Optimum decision rules have been studied in **SPR.** Beginning in Chapter 5, optimum decision rules are developed. Additional or alternative philosophies or theorems for optimum decision rules are not contributed by **AI.** Rather, **AI** contributes procedures for making the knowledge base structure accessible to the inference function of SPR and certain bookkeeping operations such as categories processed, focus for a differential diagnosis, branches in feature selection, and certain search procedures.

For example, production rule approaches are an alternative method for developing a modular knowledge base structure used to implement an inference function. The inference function can be described by the column with or without minicolumn modification of **CONSULT-I®**. *In production rule approaches, a control strategy is used to assemble the modular production rules to construct the inference function.* This assembly can involve feature selection. From the **SPR** viewpoint this "boils down" to search procedures for a **SPR** solution but **SPR** does not do it "in the blind" as production rule approaches may.

Controlled search techniques from AI can be useful in implementing a **SPR** inference but should not be implemented without guidance from **SPR.**

AI contributes important viewpoints such as induction, deduction, logical constructions, a basic understanding of heuristics or rules, and definitions of types of learning. Most of these are present in **SPR,** and **AI** sharpens awareness about them to assist in implementation.

This chapter begins with **AI** notation (Patrick, 1972; Barr and Feigenbaum, 1981; Nilsson, 1980; Winston, 1977; Rich, 1983; Brodie *and others,* 1984), different from **SPR** mostly in symbolic form than in meaning. Predicate calculus and axiomatic formulation are presented and also used in **SPR.** Semantic networks and causal networks are discussed. Material in Chapter 3 helps us to understand uses for these networks. First, nodes in a network can be feature values, complex feature values, categories, and classes. Links in a network are constructions in the category–feature relationship. Thus causal networks provide a complementary description of the category–feature relationship but without the details. Causal networks are surrogates of a **SPR** logical inference function as a category conditional probability density function just as production rule approaches are surrogates of a column inference in the category conditional probability density function.

Blind and guided and/or graph search techniques are discussed. What are they used for? Well, if an inference function is being constructed from modular knowledge in the form of production rules, the modules must be put together to form the inference. Criteria for putting the rules together are implemented to achieve previously defined goals. Goals guide the search but a particular sequence of appending modules is a branch through the graph.

CONSULT-I® uses an organized approach to construct the inference function, called column direction. The goal precisely is construction of a likelihood function. The guidance is column directed.

Section 4-16 deals with heuristics or rules used in forming new knowledge from existing knowledge. Relationships of these heuristics to SPR construction are provided.

4-2 LOGIC

4-2-1 Propositional Calculus

In propositional calculus, *connectives* are:

And	$\wedge$
Or	$\vee$
Not	$\neg$
Implies	$\rightarrow$
Equivalent	$\equiv$

Given two *propositions* X and Y, possible considerations are:

$X \wedge Y$ is TRUE if X is TRUE and Y is TRUE.

$X \vee Y$ is TRUE if either X is TRUE or Y is TRUE or both.

$\neg X$ is TRUE if X is FALSE and FALSE if X is TRUE.

$X \rightarrow Y$ the TRUTH of X implies the TRUTH of Y: INFERENCE.

$X \equiv Y$ is TRUE if both X and Y are TRUE or both X and Y are FALSE.

Sentences of propositional logic are defined through a combination of variables and connectives. The rules for combination constitute the *syntax.* A typical sentence is

$$((X \rightarrow Y \wedge Z)) \equiv ((X \rightarrow Y) \wedge (X \rightarrow Z)),$$

which states that "saying X implies Y and Z is the same as saying X implies Y and X implies Z."

A more important sentence is the well-known *inference* rule:

$$(X \wedge (X \rightarrow Y)) \rightarrow Y,$$

which states that if sentence X is true and sentence $X \rightarrow Y$ is true, then we *infer* that sentence Y is true. This is the Major Premise and Minor Premise of classical logic, also called *Modus Ponens.*

These are simple but basic rules of inference. For example, the **CONSULT-I®** closeness measure is constructed from much more complex rules of inference.

4-3 PREDICATE CALCULUS

Often referred to in AI literature, predicate calculus is now discussed. A predicate is a statement applied to one or more arguments and has a value of either TRUE or FALSE. For example, in terms of classification systems, we can take the following SPR viewpoints: A *predicate*

( ) is a category with nonzero probability

can be applied to category ω_i^*, with the value either TRUE or FALSE. An example of a two-argument predicate is

category ( ) has a posteriori probability greater than category ( ) applied to category ω_i^* and category ω_j^*.

In these examples, ω_i^* and ω_j^* are *variables*.

Quantifiers are simple concepts from mathematics:

$\forall$ For all
$\exists$ There exists.

For example,

$\forall$ Probability $(P) \rightarrow$ Less than or equal to one (P),

which means that "for all variables P, if P is a probability, then $P \leq 1$." This example and more complicated sentences are called *Well-Formed Formulas* (W.F.F.s). The sentence of predicate calculus thus is a syntactically allowed combination of connectives, predicates, variables, constants, and quantifiers. The connectives are the same as those for propositional calculus.

The previous example of a well-formed formula can be compared with two of the axioms of probability theory in Chapter 3. Again we see the relationship between **AI** and **SPR**.

4-4 FIRST-ORDER LOGIC

A *function* F ( ) is an operation on one or more arguments which "returns" an object. For example, a complex class function

$$\Omega_{12}^* = \text{complex class}(\omega_1, \omega_2), \quad \omega_1\text{: Cardiomegaly}, \quad \omega_2\text{: Pleural effusion}$$

returns the complex class

$$\Omega_{12}^* = \text{Congestive heart failure.}$$

The predicate *equals* is defined by $X = Y$ if and only if for all predicates P, $P(X) \equiv P(Y)$ and for all functions F, $F(X) \equiv F(Y)$.

This First-Order Logic extends predicate calculus through definitions of *function* which return objects and predicate *equals*. We see in this example of first-order logic that the first-order logic in **AI** is an example of a set theory operation in **SPR** in Chapter 3.

4-5 AXIOMATIC FORMULATION

Problem solving utilizing the methods just presented is accomplished by:

Specifying vocabulary:	Constants, variables, predicates, functions.
Defining axioms:	Expressions of relationships among objects in vocabulary
Example:	Minimizing probability of error.

An important but elementary example from statistical pattern recognition is where objects are a posteriori category probabilities and the decision space consists of all the categories. Define the predicate Larger

$$\forall\ \gamma_1^*, \gamma_2^*, \ldots, \gamma_M^*\ \text{Larger}\ (\gamma_1^*, \gamma_2^*) = a_1 \wedge \text{Larger}\ (a_1 \gamma_3^*) = a_2 \wedge$$
$$\ldots\ \text{Larger}\ (a_{M-1}, \gamma_M^*) \rightarrow$$
$$\text{Larger}\ (\gamma_1^* \gamma_2^* \ldots \gamma_M^*) \equiv \gamma_{\text{Max}}^*.$$

The category γ_{Max}^* is the category with the largest a posteriori probability so that announcing category γ_{Max}^* results in probability of error:

$$\sum_{\gamma_i^* \neq \gamma_{\text{Max}}^*} p(\gamma_i^* | \mathbf{x}).$$

This, an example using methods from artificial intelligence, is simply a restatement of the minimum probability of error decision rule of **SPR** (in Chapter 3). This **AI** restatement is, however, closer to the language of digital computer programming or how a machine is brought about to formulate the problem than would be the **SPR** statement.

4-6 SEMANTIC NETWORKS AND CAUSAL NETWORKS

A semantic network consists of *nodes* (drawn as dots, circles, or boxes in illustrations) and *arcs* (or *links,* drawn as arrows). Nodes represent *objects, concepts,* or *situations.* Arcs represent *relations* between nodes.

This structure is useful for representing *inheritance hierarchies, property hierarchies.* As such, it is useful for representing *category–feature relationships, complex class–feature* relationships, etc., as suggested by Ledley and Lusted (1959) and Patrick (1972, 1979).

A semantic network is presumed to have no *formal semantics* and thus there is no logic. Nodes may "own" other nodes and thus are *associative;* but there is no *cause and effect* between nodes.

A semantic network is useful for defining category–feature relationships but does not contain the logic structure for computing likelihood, scores, promise, belief, or disbelief as needs to be done by classification systems in artificial intelligence or statistical pattern recognition.

4-6-1 Control Strategy

The choice of operators and the sequence in which they are used is determined by a control strategy. For example, in **CONSULT-I®** there is both a control strategy at different local levels as well as a global control strategy. Locally, **CONSULT-I®** has a control strategy to compute a category conditional probability density value for each of several subcategories. However, when local dependencies exist within a subcategory, **CONSULT-I®** activates a local control strategy to compute a probability density value involving the local dependence. For each category, the maximum probability density value is found over all subcategories, corresponding to different statistical presentations of the category.

A global control strategy in **CONSULT-I®** provides for ranking likelihoods of the categories after the local control strategies have been applied. This results in a mechanism for parallel processing to reduce computation time.

For each category, individual feature likelihoods are computed later to be used in explanations and feature selection.

4-7 SEARCH PROCEDURES FOR PROBLEM SOLVING

4-7-1 Introduction

Solving sets of equations, either linear or nonlinear is a well-established problem in engineering and mathematics. Such problem solution has been given special attention in artificial intelligence where the status of the solution is called a *state*. Definition of the problem and its solution has three components:

4-7-1-1 Data Base

The data base in a search procedure consists of data structures including arrays, lists, sets of predicate calculus sentences and/or semantic networks. The latter, semantic networks, is an interpretation of category–feature relationships, complex class–feature relationships, and so on. The data base is not static but changes during problem solution corresponding to different states. The data base also can include causal networks.

4-7-1-2 Operators

Operators are rules of inference which are sentences from propositional calculus, predicate calculus or first-order calculus which modify the data base and thus cause a new state. If the data base includes causal networks, then the nodes and arcs of the causal network can be changed by operators. In **CONSULT-I®** there are operations for deductions which can generate category presentations not previously seen.

4-8 BLIND AND/OR GRAPH SEARCH

Consider a graph shown in Figure 4.1 which consists of OR nodes and AND nodes. Node 1 is a *starting* node and nodes 8, 9, 10, and 11 are terminal nodes. A node represents a goal or problem description. The successors of an OR node represent *subproblems,* only one of which need be solved in order to reach a terminal goal.

The successors of AND nodes represent subproblems, all of which must be solved in order to reach a terminal goal. The subproblems which are successors of an AND node represent the decomposition of a problem into subproblems, each of which is easier to solve than the original problem. This decomposition is called *Reasoning Backwards,* goal directed or top-down. The application of an operator at a node in Figure 4.1 to obtain a new node (state) is called *Reasoning Forward,* data driven or bottom-up.

Two methods of searching AND/OR graphs are described next.

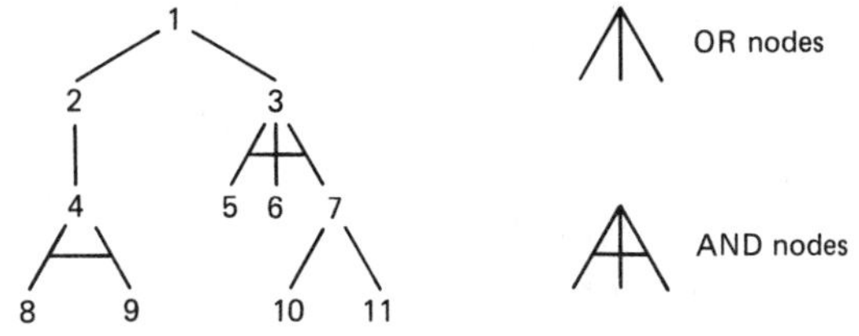

FIGURE 4.1. AND/OR graph concepts.

4-9 BREADTH-FIRST SEARCH OF AN AND/OR TREE

In breadth-first search, the process begins at a *start node n* which is expanded to generate *m* successor nodes to this node *n*. For each of these *m* successors with more than one successor (subproblem), these subproblems (or successors) are generated *but not immediately processed.* This is analogous in **CONSULT-I®** to activating multiple categories for processing. In the terminology of **CONSULT-I®**, a first subset of features is one of the *m* successors to node *n*. Successors to the *m* successors of node *n* could represent other subsets of features to be processed for that event, but they are not immediately processed. This is contrasted with depth-first immediate processes. Another example of breadth-first search *in* **CONSULT-I®** *is the activation of subsystems for initial processing. This is a focusing technique.* This is contrasted with depth-first search described below where, for the first example cited, each event would be processed prior to going on to the next event.

4-10 DEPTH-FIRST SEARCH OF AN AND/OR TREE

In this method, all *m* immediate successors of node *n* are generated and for each of these, successors are generated. All second-level successors are immediately processed and further expansion takes place at the first level.

These two methods of search are considered *blind search,* which can result in a *combinatorial explosion* well known in artificial intelligence. This is because the order of expanding the nodes is purely arbitrary and does not use problem knowledge to direct the processing. In **CONSULT-I®,** the processing is *column directed,* i.e., a view of the processing route through the graph is had at the starting node where appropriate.

Again, we interrupt to indicate that no new decision-making theory is being developed. The decision theory expressed by the theory on a posteriori probability by Patrick and methods for constructing category conditional probability density functions is optimum. However, we are developing an understanding of basic search techniques in artificial intelligence to show how they might be used in constructing probability density functions, activating subsystems, and developing hierarchies of primitives, classes, only classes, and complex classes. Patrick's theorem discussed elsewhere provides for concept formation of complex classes based on a priori knowledge, avoiding blind search, and combinatorial explosion.

4-11 HEURISTIC STATE-SPACE SEARCH AND ORDERED STATE-SPACE SEARCH

A heuristic state-space search is usually a variation of blind search where some problem knowledge is utilized in the former. For example, the successor node which has greatest *promise* is picked, and the successor node need not be immediate to the first node. In **CONSULT-I®**, such might be viewed as interactive feature selection, flags to trigger minicolumns, and recognition of insignificant features to allow "jumping over nodes." In this regard, **CONSULT-I®** uses *ordered state-space search* where direction is provided by columns and/or promise corresponding to feature selection. *In* **CONSULT-I®**, *known relationships between classes, only classes, and complex classes provide enormous order for eliminating unnecessary search.* This is achieved through the concept formation from the theorem on a posteriori probability by Patrick.

4-12 PRODUCTION SYSTEMS

A production system consists of the following three components:

1. Production Rules. A production rule is a condition–action pair:

If (condition) then (action).

Production rules are part of the system's data base. They are "independent pieces of knowledge" and as such can be individually changed or updated. This can be referred to as *modularity,* a desirable property. The production rules are a form of *knowledge representation* which can be referred to as *uniform* because it is used "throughout" the system. This is considered an advantage because people can understand it better.

2. Context Data Structure. The condition part of a production rule must be present in the context data structure for the production rule to take action. The action of a production rule can change the context data structure so that other production rules may have their conditions satisfied. The context data structure can consist of lists, arrays, strings, or special structures.

3. Interpreter. The interpreter in a production system is a program that decides which production to process next. It resolves conflicts by choosing one production rule when multiple rules are active at a particular stage. Such conflict resolution can be viewed as attention focusing. The interpreter examines production rules in *cycles* to determine which ones may be active. Consistent with the previous discussion, there are three phases of each cycle: *matching, conflict resolution,* and *action.* A disadvantage is *inefficiency.*

Production systems are considered to have some disadvantages as implied above. First, they do not efficiently utilize predetermined sequences (columns as in **CONSULT-I®**). The most serious consequence of this is decreased performance from the standpoint of statistical pattern recognition because *nonlocal statistical dependencies are not part of the knowledge representation.* Another consequence is high overhead in terms of inefficient program execution, and other disadvantages are *Opaqueness* and *Lack of Direction.*

Production systems are considered to be *opaque* in that *flow of control is difficult to follow.* This prompts developers of production systems to stress importance of "exploring reasoning used by the system." Rather than an advantage, this is a serious disadvantage because "explaining reasoning" is a necessity inherent to the system because of lack of direction.

4-13 INTRODUCTION TO KNOWLEDGE AND KNOWLEDGE REPRESENTATION

Decision making whereby events in the decision space are rank-ordered with respect to likelihoods or a posteriori probabilities utilizes knowledge about the events. But, what is knowledge? Aspects of this knowledge are as follows:

1. Features. A category is characterized by all possible sets of feature values (patterns) for an established set of features. One possible set of feature values is called a feature vector. In medical classification systems, features correspond to signs, symptoms, and laboratory tests.

2. Category. Categories in the decision space in, for example, a breast disease subsystem include the only class breast cancer; the only class breast cyst; the complex class breast cancer and breast cyst.

3. Category–Feature Relationship. The category–feature relationship described by $p(\mathbf{x}|\omega_i^*)$ or $p(\mathbf{x}|\Omega_\xi^*)$ is the set of all possible feature vectors for the category, with some indication of their relative frequency of occurrence.

An artificial intelligence system that ignores relative frequencies is ignoring a vast amount of knowledge useful for evaluating confidence and variance and for predicting. Certainly, some artificial intelligence applications may be deterministic, for which relative frequencies are not needed. An application where they are essential is medical diagnosis.

So far, we have described knowledge present in a learning system or an estimation system. Patrick (1969) described the concept of an adaptive estimation system which suggests two additional properties of knowledge: performance and meta-knowledge.

4. Performance and Adaptation. A decision-making system utilizing learning or estimation can be evaluated by an observer external to the system. Through the scientific method, this can lead to changing the knowledge in the system in the quest for better performance.

5. Meta-Knowledge. A system's meta-knowledge is what it knows about its knowledge. In a decision-making system having the goal of ranking category probabilities, there are various ways to incorporate meta-knowledge. However, a warning is in order—a system learning what it does not know can involve learning without a teacher (Patrick, 1965, 1968, 1972). Often, a teacher is provided by the environment so that the problem is an adaptive estimation problem.

A system can know:

a. When a decision cannot be made because of too little information.
b. When the probability density distribution of a feature is too "fuzzy."
c. When there probably is a complex class.
d. When more features are needed to achieve a certain performance.
e. When two categories are similar.

4-14 REASONING

A system is said to reason if it can do something it has not been explicitly told how to do. Data retrieval is not reasoning. On the other hand, if a presentation of a category which previously was not in the system's data base can be generated by the system, then reasoning has taken place. In this regard production systems may be very misleading because:

1. All possible productions in a production system exist even though they are not part of the data base.
2. All possible searches exist in an AND/OR graph even though they are not part of the data base.
3. All possible states exist in a Causal Network even though they are not part of the data base.

By definition, these systems can reason but they are still limited. Perhaps reasoning is in the eye of the beholder. A child outperforms any existing robot in terms of certain classification problems but is considered by many unable to reason. Is there a threshold of activity before there is reasoning?

4-15 HIERARCHICAL REPRESENTATION OF KNOWLEDGE

4-15-1 Introduction

Researchers have been interested in describing the reasoning process of decision making using definitions and constructions not directly based on a mathematical model. At some point such ideas should be placed in context of a model which can be examined and, if useful, tested. This section begins with a question: What facility is needed in addition to features with feature values, *only classes, complex classes,* classes, and category–feature relationships, including columns and minicolumns and intermediate classes (or categories)?

A method of *cause and effect* or inference is brought into the hierarchical representation of knowledge. *Is cause and effect inherent to a class–feature relationship or category–feature relationship?* The answer is yes as shown by the ability to perform concept formation in the theorem on a posteriori probability by Patrick.

4-15-2 Cause and Effect in *CONSULT-I*®

A medical diagnostician observes *feature values* which are *effects* of a *cause,* namely, diseases (categories). Other effects of the causes are only classes and complex classes. Categories are conclusions or summaries of interest while classes are internal and may be either cause or effect. This implies a feedback system where an effect of one cause may be a cause of another effect. The theorem on a posteriori probability (Patrick) is the theoretical framework for such a feedback system.

For example, a category may develop through a training session which initially, as an *only class,* is the only category in the decision space. This category may be a feature value for a complex class higher in the hierarchy, and is called a cause of that complex class.

4-15-3 Artificial Intelligence Viewpoint

A viewpoint of cause and effect has been described by several investigators.

We now present some of these viewpoints and compare or integrate them with similar viewpoints from the theorem on a posteriori probability by Patrick.

Hierarchical representation of knowledge is at *levels* and *each level involves a semantic network.* These levels in the theorem by Patrick would "own" classes, categories, complex classes, etc. Nodes in a network are category–feature relationships, class–feature relationships, . . . , or portions thereof.

Categorical knowledge, a term used in **AI,** is at a lowest level and would seem to be complex features or even feature values themselves. At a higher level is *syndrome knowledge,* which would seem to be categories.

A *primitive node* does not contain internal structure and would seem to be a feature value (Primitive in **CONSULT-I®**) or a class. A *composite node* would seem to be an only class or complex class. A *primitive node* may have *components* which are other primitive nodes. This seems to suggest that a primitive node is a class or a complex feature (Patrick, 1979). *Components* involve *component summation* and *component decomposition.*

Component Summation would seem to be formation of a class from features or of a complex class from classes. *Component Decomposition* would seem to be the decomposition of a complex class into classes or a class into feature values. Then Component Decomposition looks for unaccounted components or feature values. Great emphasis is placed on multivariate relationships suggesting a class–feature relationship. **CONSULT-I®** inherently utilizes class–feature relationships with multidimensional relationships. On the other hand, **INTERNIST** (Miller *and others,* 1982), **PIP** (Patil *and others,* 1981), and **MYCIN** (Shortliffe and Buchanan, 1975) do not.

Apparently, classes and feature values are considered *mutually complementary* while alternative high-level categories or sequences are considered mutually exclusive or competing.

4-15-4 Problem Solving from the Artificial Intelligence Viewpoint

Problem solving from the viewpoint of AI is *initial formulation,* which would seem to be classes and only classes. Additional feature values would seem to be collected through *aggregation and elaboration.* Reasoning would seem to be the formation of complex classes and possibly sequences. A final concept of *Projection* would seem to be a decomposition into components for the purpose of explanation.

4-16 HEURISTICS OR RULES FROM ARTIFICIAL INTELLIGENCE

4-16-1 Introduction

Construction of the category conditional probability density function is central to artificial intelligence with statistical pattern recognition. This construction involves computer learning by instruction, learning from examples, and may involve learning by discovery. It is desirable to perform as much learning by discovery "off line" as possible.

Certain rules or heuristics studied in artificial intelligence have structures similar in part to those used in **CONSULT-I®**. **CONSULT-I®** is more complex because learning includes an accounting of relative frequency of patterns, subcategories, or categories. This relative frequency is important knowledge.

We will now present certain rules using (for consistency) the same notation as in *Machine Learning* (Michalski *and others,* 1983).

4-16-2 Constraints in the Feature Space

Consider a set of features where one of the features specifies a complex feature while the other features characterize the state. For example, if the complex feature is chest pain, the absence of chest pain suppresses the need to obtain values for other features in the complex which characterize the chest pain. This is an example of a Type 1 feature discussed elsewhere. Using a combination of notation from artificial intelligence and statistical pattern recognition, an appropriate rule is

$$[\text{complex}(x_{i_j}) = \text{FALSE}] \Rightarrow [\text{complex}(x_i) = NA], \qquad (1)$$

where NA (not applicable) is a special value for the complex feature.

This describes in part the missing feature operation discussed elsewhere but does not specify how to project relative frequencies.

More generally, rules can be used to describe relations between features in a subset of features. These relations can be reflexive, symmetric, transitive, etc. Other interrelationships among features in a subset of features include product, ratio, sum of squares, simultaneous equations, etc. Learning which relationship applies is achieved by learning from examples.

4-16-3 Dropping Condition Rule

The rule

$$A \,\&\, S :::> K \quad |< \quad A :::> K \qquad (2)$$

states that a concept description can be generalized by simply removing a conjunctively linked expression (S). If the concept is a pattern, then this rule generates a whole class of patterns from one typical pattern (*Induction*). This is the underlying logic or heuristic behind the missing feature operation in **CONSULT-I®** discussed in Chapter 8. However, because relative frequency is projected, *the rules provide deduction if a new pattern is tested for a measure of class membership.*

4-16-4 Adding Alternative Rule

The rule

$$A :::> K \quad |< \quad A \vee B :::> K \qquad (3)$$

uses logical disjunction (OR) $\vee$ to provide the alternative concept $A \vee B$ to concept A. This rule applies extensively to Type Ø features in **CONSULT-I®**, **The OUTCOME ADVISOR®**, and **CONSULT LEARNING SYSTEM®**. It is related to the concept of equivalence in statistics where there also is relative frequency.

4-16-5 Extending Reference Rule

In **CONSULT-I®** there are features for a total system, most of which are insignificant for any category in a subsystem. Although the following rule from artificial intelligence does not provide for weights or probabilities, it helps us understand the integration of artificial intelligence with statistical pattern recognition.

The rule is, that if $R_1 \subseteq R_2 \subseteq$ DOM (L) and DOM (L) denotes the domain of L, then

$$A \ \& \ [L - R_1] \ :::> K \quad |< \quad A \ \& \ [L - R_2] \ :::> K. \tag{4}$$

Considering **CONSULT-I®**, $R_2 - R_1$ might be *insignificant features,* and utilizing these features should not prevent result K. The extended reference rule of AI is part of the insignificant feature concept in **CONSULT-I®**. Again, in **CONSULT-I®**, probabilities are utilized to indicate degree of insignificance providing additional "power."

4-16-6 Closing Interval Rule

The closing interval rule is like a fuzzy set operation used in a **CONSULT-I®** Type Ø feature. Suppose that L is a Type Ø feature and a and b are two specific values; then

$$\left.\begin{array}{l} A \ \& \ [L = a] \ :::> K \\ A \ \& \ [L = b] \ :::> K \end{array}\right| < A \ \& \ [L = a \vee b] \ :::> K \tag{5}$$

is a rule stating the concept that if feature L has value equal to either a or b then result K follows.

4-16-7 Climbing Generalization Tree Rule

This rule would indicate, for example, that if only class ω_i^* occurred, then class ω_i is at a lower level in that hierarchy. Let $a,b, \ldots ,i$ be nodes in a hierarchy as s represents the lowest parent node to the other node. Then the rule

$$\left.\begin{array}{l} A \ \& \ [L = a] \ :::> K \\ A \ \& \ [L = b] \ :::> K \\ \cdot \\ \cdot \\ \cdot \\ A \ \& \ [L = i] \ :::> K \end{array}\right| < \quad A \ \& \ [L = s\ ] \ :::> K. \tag{6}$$

A special case is a path along nodes in a network.

4-16-8 Turning Constraints into Variable Rule

Let $F(v)$ stand for some descriptive dependence on feature v, and let this description hold for $v = a,b, \ldots$, and so on. Then a generalization is that the rule holds for all v. This is said to be a common rule used in inductive inference. Patrick (1972) proposed such rules for statistical dimensionality reduction in statistical pattern recognition. For example, let $v = (x_1 | x_2)$ the ratio of two features. If a functional $F(v)$ can be found whose domain is an important attribute for a class (category), then $F(v)$ is a *significant feature* for the category (see Patrick, 1972, 1979). In particular, $F(v)$ is a complex feature because it is a function of two features.

To determine that such a rule applies requires learning by induction, in particular learning by example. A straight-line fit of a linear regression line is an example of the rule.

4-16-9 Turning Conjunction into Disjunction Rule

Define the rule

$$F_1 \ \& \ F_2 \ ::: > K \quad | < \quad F_1 \vee F_2 \ ::: > K, \tag{7}$$

which states that iff F_1 & F_2 implies K then F_1 or F_2 implies K. This is an interesting rule, one interpretation of which is that F_2 is dependent on or correlated with F_1. If we know F_1 is true, we know F_2 is true. Again, the application of this rule can be inductively learned by example (statistics). It can be an important rule applied to embedded features in a Type 1 feature (in **CONSULT-I®**).

4-16-10 Extending the Quantification Domain Rule

The rule

$$\forall \ x, \quad F(x): \ ::: > K \quad | < \quad \exists \quad v, F(v) \ ::: > K \tag{8}$$

states that if for all x, $F(x)$ implies K then there exists a v for which $F(x)$ generalizes to K.

4-16-11 Inductive Resolution Rule

Consider a predicate P and F_1 and F_2 arbitrary formulas for a rule

$$(P \Rightarrow F_1) \ \& \ (\sim P \Rightarrow F_2) \quad | > \quad F_1 \vee F_2, \tag{9a}$$

which reformulates to

$$\left. \begin{array}{l} P \ \& \ F_1 \ ::: > K \\ \sim P \ \& \ F_2 \ ::: > K \end{array} \right| < \quad F_1 \vee F_2 \ ::: > K \tag{9b}$$

applying this to the new theorem on a posteriori probability by Patrick, in particular Chapter 5,

$$(x_{s_i} \rightarrow \omega_i) \;\&\; (x_{I_i} = x_{s_j} \rightarrow \omega_j) \quad |< \quad \omega_i \text{ or } \omega_j \tag{10a}$$

$$\left.\begin{array}{r} x_{s_i} \;\&\; \omega_i \;:::>\; \Omega^*_{ij} \\ (x_{I_i} = x_{s_j}) \;\&\; \omega_{j_i} \;:::>\; \Omega^*_{ij} \end{array}\right| < \quad \omega_i \text{ or } \omega_j \;:::>\; \Omega^*_{i_j}. \tag{10b}$$

4-16-12 Extension against Rule

Let R_1 and R_2 be disjoint sets and define the rule

$$\left.\begin{array}{l} A \;\&\; [L = R_1] \;:::>\; K \\ A \;\&\; [L = R_2] \;:::>\sim K \end{array}\right| < \quad A \;\&\; [L \neq R_2] \;:::>\; K, \tag{11}$$

where the first term on the left is a description of a pattern belonging to class K and the second term on the left is descriptive of a pattern not belonging to class K. The generalization is a discriminant function for class K.

For example, R_2 is a *rule out feature value* for class K and a *rule in feature value* for class $\sim K$. If R_2 does not occur then there is no Can't operation and class K is possible (in this example it is ruled in).

4-16-13 Constructive Generalization Rules

4-16-13-1 Generalization by Applying Knowledge of Relationships between Concepts

Let F_1 be a feature value such as high blood pressure, which proceeding upward in a knowledge hierarchy, also is a class Hypertension denoted by F_2. Let A denote another class. Now consider the rule

$$\left.\begin{array}{l} A \;\&\; F_1 \;:::>\; K \\ F_1 \;:::>\; F_2 \end{array}\right| < \quad A \;\&\; F_2 \;:::>\; K, \tag{12}$$

which states that class A and high blood pressure imply the complex class K extends to class A and class Hypertension (F_2) implies complex class K because high blood pressure (F_1) implies hypertension (F_2).

This generalization rule can, for example, be applied to concepts in a knowledge base structure to obtain the next highest level. The rule can be used in constructing models for generating complex classes from only classes.

The rule also has certain similarities to the fuzzy set "or operation." For example, the inference of any subcategory of a category implies the category.

4-16-13-2 Counting Arguments Rule

This rule simply is a complex feature such as a Type 1 feature, which counts the number of features that are true.

4-16-14 Frames

A *frame,* introduced by Minsky in 1975, provides instruction within which other knowledge is interpreted. The other knowledge is represented in *slots.* The structure of a frame is similar to that of a complex feature introduced in 1972 by Patrick and in 1975 by Patrick and Shen. An example of a complex feature is the Type 1 feature used throughout this book, where the "slots" are binary choice features.

A frame is used to describe a class of objects and as such is a concept. A slot in the frame can be used to bring about ("trigger") a conditional branch to another frame. For example, this represents a common sense approach to constructing an interviewer.

The complex feature is the framework for a class conditional probability density function and as such carries probabilities for the various regions or patterns in its domain. Thus, the complex feature can learn by example where a pure frame cannot.

4-17 CLASS CONDITIONAL FUNCTION USING AI CONCEPTS

4-17-1 Introduction

Integration of **AI** and statistical pattern recognition requires knowing similarities and differences. The objective is a methodology more powerful than either **AI** or statistical pattern recognition alone. A similarity is that **AI** uses a structure similar to statistical pattern recognition between features (facts) and classes (hypotheses), i.e. $F \rightarrow H$ relationships. Further, **AI** has feature-to-feature relationships, i.e. $F \rightarrow F$ relationships, analogous to complex features and dependencies in statistical pattern recognition. Going further, **AI** considers relationships between class and class (between hypothesis and hypothesis), i.e. $H \rightarrow H$ relationships. In statistical pattern recognition the traditional Bayes theorem does not provide for this relationship. On the other hand, the theorem on a posteriori probability by Patrick defines classes and categories (only classes and complex classes). This new theorem provides for relationships class → category. Then there is a category → category relationship involving both space (features) and time (examples or samples). The new theorem on a posteriori probability by Patrick captures the hypothesis → hypothesis relationship of **AI** and provides for examples (as probability or statistics) so that ultimately a posteriori probabilities are computed.

4-17-2 AI Notation

Let

$$F\text{: observational statement (facts)} \tag{13a}$$

in AI be analogous to a feature vector in **SPR.**

Analogous to a category feature relationship domain structure of **SPR,** let

$$H \quad |> \quad F \quad \text{(read: } H \text{ specializes to } F\text{)}, \tag{13b}$$

where H is an hypothesis (class in SPR) and $|>$ is called the *specialization symbol.* Using the *generalization symbol* $|<$ obtain

$$F \quad |< \quad H \quad \text{(read: } F \text{ generalizes to } H\text{)} \tag{13c}$$

Deriving F from H is a form of *deductive inference* while deriving H from F is a form of *inductive inference.*

4-17-3 A Problem with Inductive Inference

A problem with inductive inference to construct a hypothesis is well illustrated by the following statement (Michalski *and others,* 1983): *"For any given set of facts, a potentially infinite number of hypotheses can be generated that implies these facts. Background knowledge is therefore necessary to provide the constraints and a preference criterion for reducing the infinite choice to one hypothesis or a few most preferable ones."* Elsewhere we have discussed this problem with regard to production systems where sets of production rules are operated upon in sequence guided by separate rules of direction. It is difficult to organize sufficient background knowledge for a hypothesis (class or category) using this approach. Patrick's theorem provides for introducing a priori knowledge to make possible concept formation of complex classes.

In **CONSULT-I®** there is a precise procedure for introducing background knowledge and a preference criterion. This procedure is that of columns with appended minicolumns which describe a typical or atypical inference $F \rightarrow H$. This inference may be statistical or uncertain such that a "hypercube" of inference structure is provided in $F \rightarrow H$. This statistical departure from pure **AI** is another example of integrating statistical pattern recognition with **AI**.

4-17-4 Concept Acquisition and Descriptive Generalization

A useful distinction has been made between concept acquisition and descriptive generalization (Michalski *and others,* 1983). Here we present these in terms of classes and features.

4-17-4-1 Concept Acquisition

a. Learning a characteristic description of a class (category) of patterns (objects, cases).
b. Learning a discriminant descriptive of a class that distinguishes the given class from a *limited number of other classes.*
c. Inferring sequence extrapolation rule.

Importance of a limited number of classes is noted as this is analogous to the focus concept and subsystem concept. An illustration of the inferring sequence extrapolation rule is given shortly.

4-17-4-2 Descriptive Generalization

a. Formulating a theory characterizing a collection of entities.
b. Discovering classes or categories in observational data.
c. Determining a taxonomic description (classification) of a collection of patterns.

Whereas Concept Acquisition is associated with decision making using a structure (subsystem) of classes, categories, features, $F \rightarrow H$ rules, $F \rightarrow F$ rules, and $H \rightarrow H$ rules, Descriptive Generalization concerns *learning* $F \rightarrow H$ rules, $F \rightarrow F$ rules, and $H \rightarrow H$ rules.

CONSULT-T® involves Concept Acquisition utilizing knowledge obtained by Descriptive Generalization in **CONSULT LEARNING SYSTEM®**.

These distinctions are not to be taken as pure, but indeed they are two very important procedures which are very different.

4-18 THE LIKELIHOOD FUNCTION AS INDUCTIVE INFERENCE WITH LOCAL CONCEPT FORMATION

4-18-1 Introduction

In this section we address the question as to whether, in a classification system, it is necessary to form second-level concept formation or is the alternative integrating Type Ø and Type 1 features into a likelihood function sufficient. Following the notation by Michalski *and others,* 1983), let $E_1, E_2, \ldots$ be facts or feature values, G_1 a conjunctive generalization of E_1 and E_2, and so on, as shown in Figure 4.2.

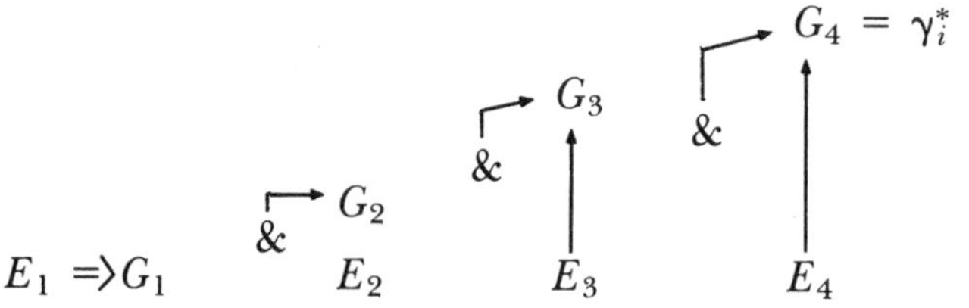

FIGURE 4.2. Illustration of Induction.

With the likelihood function concept, some highest-level category $\gamma_i^* = G_4$ is iteratively expressed by

$$\begin{aligned} p(G_2|E_1,E_2) &= p(G_2,G_1|E_1E_2) = p(G_2|G_1\not{E}_1E_2)\; p(G_1|E_1\not{E}_2) \\ &= p(G_2|G_1,E_2)p(G_1|\,E_1) \end{aligned} \tag{14}$$

$$\begin{aligned} p(G_3|E_1E_2E_3) &= p(G_3,G_2,G_1|E_1E_2E_3) \\ &= p(G_3|G_2G_1\not{E}_1\not{E}_2E_3)\; p(G_1G_2|E_1E_2E_3) \\ &= p(G_3|G_2G_1E_3)p(G_2|G_1,\not{E}_1,E_2\not{E}_3)p(G_1|E_1\not{E}_2\not{E}_3) \\ &= p(G_3|G_2G_1E_3)p(G_2|G_1E_2)p(G_1|E_1). \end{aligned} \tag{15}$$

Likewise

$$\begin{aligned} p(\gamma_i^* = G_4|E_1E_2E_3) &= p(G_4|G_3,G_2,G_1,E_4)\; p(G_3|G_2,G_1,E_3) \\ &\quad p(G_2|G_1,E_2)p(G_1|E_1). \end{aligned} \tag{16}$$

In **CONSULT-I®**, column direction of uncertain concepts allows for designing concepts G_1, G_2, G_3, G_4, and so on, into an uncertain likelihood function consisting of a hierarchical conjunction of uncertain concepts. These concepts are formed and visualized by the developer in terms of the real world features $E_1E_2, \ldots$. A particular feature can be a complex feature such as a Type 1 feature where multiple features are embedded. Ultimate performance in classifying category γ_i^* does not require "calling out" formed concepts $G_1, G_2, \ldots$ as they occur. Artificial intelligence and statistical pattern recognition are thus naturally integrated in **CONSULT-I®**.

5

Theorem on A Posteriori Probability (Patrick)

5-1 INTRODUCTION

A theorem on a posteriori probability (Patrick) was presented in 1983 at MEDINFO '83 with elaboration in October 1983 at the Symposium for Computer Applications in Medical Care (Fattu and Patrick, 1983) and in November 1984 and 1985 at the Symposium for Computer Applications in Medical Care (Patrick and Fattu, 1984, 1985). In this chapter the theorem is derived from axiomatic probability theory. A proposition dealing with the likelihood function (Patrick) corresponding to the theorem on a posteriori probability is presented.

The theorem by Patrick provides for concept formation through a statistical dependence among categories which goes far beyond the capabilities of the Bayes model. Several propositions are presented concerning the significance and application of this statistical dependence.

Models are presented for the concept formation of a complex class category(ies) which utilizes in part this statistical dependence.

Complex class models allow for deducing what a pattern should look like for a complex class even though previously it (patterns from the complex class) never was seen. In Section 5-6-4-2 the c.c.p.d.f. for a complex class is expressed in terms of c.c.p.d.f.'s for the respective significant feature of only classes. The result is extended in Section 5-6-4-5. An interesting result is that for a two-class problem,† *a complex class can exist (given findings) with highest probability if the significance in the feature space of each* only class *is greater than the insignificance of the other* only class (Sections 5-6-3 and 5-6-5).

In Section 5-8 a model for generating a complex class is presented based upon the number of features *like* one class and the number *like*

†With two classes as the building blocks there can be two *only classes* and one *complex class.*

another class. In Section 5-9 a generalization of this approach is presented.

An instructive approach for complex class generation presented in Section 5-16-2 is where features for each class are assumed statistically independent while classes are independently involved in forming a complex class. This is used to obtain further insight into a feedback interpretation of the theorem on a posteriori probability by Patrick.

In Section 5-18 complex class categories are formed by concept formation which requires a functional relationship between the complex category and previously learned only classes.

Later, in Chapter 7 (Section 7-6-3), another look at complex class formation is presented where classes occur independently but the complex class depends on the classes.

In Chapter 9 an important and basic model for complex class generation is presented. Section 9-13 deals with constructing a complex class hypercube using previously learned knowledge about only class hypercubes.

5-2 PRELIMINARIES

As defined before, the category space $\boldsymbol{\gamma}$ consists of M mutually exclusive and exhaustive categories $\gamma_1^*, \gamma_2^*, \ldots, \gamma_M^*$. In addition, define a feature space $\mathfrak{X}$ with $\mathbf{x} \in \mathfrak{X}$. As before, there exist category–feature relationships $p(\mathbf{x}|\gamma_i^*) \in \mathcal{F}_i \; \forall_i$ satisfying the axioms and laws of probability theory. Definitions are the same as for Bayes theorem.

A departure from Bayes now begins with the definition of a class space $\mathcal{C}$:

$$\mathcal{C}\colon \omega_1, \omega_2, \ldots, \omega_{M_1}. \tag{1}$$

The category space $\boldsymbol{\gamma}$ and class space $\mathcal{C}$ must be considered separate, although there will be components which are the same. For example, the two spaces will have certain features in common. As another example, a class in $\mathcal{C}$ is the logical union of all categories in $\boldsymbol{\gamma}$ which "contain" the class. Even more important are certain properties of categories in $\boldsymbol{\gamma}$ which exist for Patrick's theorem but not for Bayes theorem. For Patrick's theorem, categories $\gamma_1^*, \gamma_2^*, \ldots,$ in $\boldsymbol{\gamma}$ are mutually exclusive but there can exist relationships among the category conditional probability density functions. These relationships constitute knowledge in terms of *significant and insignificant features of each category. Significance or insignificance is defined in terms of probability or relative fre-*

quency. This relative frequency itself becomes part of the knowledge base. It is used to provide knowledge which relates some of the category conditional probability density functions. The models relating certain category conditional probability density functions may be considered in another space, say $\mathfrak{M}$, distinct from the class space $\mathscr{C}$, category space $\mathcal{Y}$, feature space $\mathscr{F}$, or cross-product spaces $\mathscr{C} \times \mathscr{F}$ and $\mathcal{Y} \times \mathscr{F}$. The space $\mathfrak{M}$, called the Model Space, contains the "glue" relating classes, only classes, and complex classes. This "glue" can be functional relationships, logical relationships, logical relationships involving probability weights, and so on.

Also, there exist *class–feature relationships* denoted

$$p(\mathbf{x}|\omega_i), \qquad i = 1, 2, \ldots, M_1$$

for the cross-product space $\mathscr{C}\ \mathfrak{X}$. Recall that the *category–feature relationships* are for a cross-product space $\mathcal{Y}\ \mathfrak{X}$. So, with Patrick's theorem on a posteriori probability we have two "kinds" of conditional probability density functions with which to deal (to engineer).

Proceeding forward we develop categories using the primitive classes in the class space $\mathscr{C}$. Starting with the classes (which are primitive sets) in $\mathscr{C}$, form new sets and name them as follows:

$$\omega_1^* = \omega_1\bar{\omega}_2\bar{\omega}_3 \ldots \bar{\omega}_M : \quad \textit{only class } \omega_1$$

$$\vdots$$

$$\omega_i^* = \bar{\omega}_1\bar{\omega}_2 \ldots \bar{\omega}_{i-1}\omega_i\bar{\omega}_{i+1} \cdots : \quad \textit{only class } \omega_i \tag{2}$$

$$\Omega_{abc\ldots}^* = \omega_a\omega_b\omega_c \cdots \cap \quad \text{(all class complements not to the left of } \cap\text{)}.$$

The last set† is named a *complex class.* In general a complex class is denoted Ω_ξ^*:

$$\begin{aligned} \Omega_\xi^*&: \text{ set containing classes } \omega_{\xi_1}, \omega_{\xi_2}, \ldots \\ &: \text{ complex class.} \end{aligned} \tag{3}$$

A complex class consisting entirely of primitive classes ω_i and ω_j is denoted Ω_{ij}^*. In studying complex classes, it sometimes is convenient to limit discussion to a model where there are two primitive classes ω_i and ω_j so that notation is simpler.

†The class complement of ω_a is $\bar{\omega}_a$.

5-3 THEOREM ON A POSTERIORI PROBABILITY (PATRICK) AND LIKELIHOOD (PATRICK)

Propositon 1: Sets $\omega_i^*, \Omega_{ij}^*, \ldots, \Omega_\xi^*$

are mutually exclusive.

$$\text{Proof: } \omega_i^* = \omega_i \cap \bar{\omega}_j$$

$$\Omega_{ij}^* = \omega_i \omega_j \tag{4}$$

$$\vdots$$

$$\Omega_\xi^* = \Omega_\xi \cap \bar{\Omega}_\xi.$$

The first element ω_i^* in the series (set) is mutually exclusive of successive elements by construction. The general element Ω_ξ^* is mutually exclusive of previous elements and successive elements in the series by construction; the proof follows by induction.

The category space now formally is defined as the collection of sets on the left-hand side of Eq. (4).

Proposition 2: $$p(\omega_i) = p(\omega_i^*) + \sum_{\forall \Omega_\xi^* \ni \omega_i \in \Omega_\xi^*} p(\Omega_\xi^*). \tag{5}$$

(reads: for all Ω_ξ^* such that ω_i is in Ω_ξ^*)

Proof: The set of categories $\omega_i^*, \Omega_1^*, \Omega_2^*, \ldots$ are mutually exclusive and constitute all events containing ω_i. Applying Total Probability, Eq. (5) follows.

Equation (5) is a relationship between a class in the class space $\mathscr{C}$ and categories in the category space γ. This relationship is unique to the model used in Patrick's theorem and does not exist in Bayes theorem.

Proposition 3: $$p(\omega_i, \mathbf{x}) = p(\omega_i^*, \mathbf{x}) + \sum_{\omega_i \in \Omega_\xi^*} p(\Omega_\xi^*, \mathbf{x}). \tag{6}$$

Proof: Application of Total Probability and Joint Probability.

Proposition 4: $$p(\omega_i|\mathbf{x}) = p(\omega_i^*|\mathbf{x}) + \sum_{\omega_i \in \Omega_\xi^*} p(\Omega_\xi^*|\mathbf{x}). \tag{7}$$

Proof: Follows from Proposition 3 and definition of conditional probability.

Proposition 4 is an expression for an inference function in class space $\mathscr{C}$ in terms of inference functions in the category space $\boldsymbol{\gamma}$.

Proposition 5: Likelihood (Patrick)

$$p(\mathbf{x}|\omega_i) = p(\mathbf{x}|\omega_i^*) \frac{p(\omega_i^*)}{p(\omega_i)} + \sum_{\omega_i \, \varepsilon \, \Omega_\xi^*} p(\mathbf{x}|\Omega_\xi^*) \frac{p(\Omega_\xi^*)}{p(\omega_i)}. \tag{8}$$

Proof: Follows from Proposition 3 and definition of conditional probability.

Theorem on A Posteriori Class Probability (Patrick)

$$p(\omega_i|\mathbf{x}) = \frac{p(\mathbf{x}|\omega_i^*)p(\omega_i^*) + \sum_{\omega_i \, \varepsilon \, \Omega_\xi^*} p(\mathbf{x}|\Omega_\xi^*)p(\Omega_\xi^*)}{p(\mathbf{x})}, \; i = 1, 2, \ldots, M_1 \tag{9}$$

M_2 equations $p(\mathbf{x}|\Omega_\xi^*)$, $\xi = 1, 2, \ldots, M_2$

Proof: Follows from Proposition 4.

The theorem on a posteriori probability by Patrick is a set of M_1 equations (each of the form in Eq. 9) for $i = 1, 2, \ldots, M_1$. These equations are axiomatic. It isn't too early to point out that there are M_2 equations $p(\mathbf{x}|\Omega_\xi^*)$, $\xi = 1, 2, \ldots, M_2$ [from (3)].

Thus, with $M = M_1 + M_2$ equations, we anticipate solving for M unknowns. Indeed, there are M category conditional probability density functions to learn about.

Especially in Section 5-18, learning the M category conditional probability density functions using sequential samples is developed. *This involves a new form of learning without a teacher where categories are statistically dependent during learning.* All of this embodies Patrick's theorem on a posteriori probability.

The new theorem by Patrick provides an important link between **AI** and **SPR.** Previous ideas of concept formation and learning without a teacher are now formally developed using **SPR.** This method of learning without a teacher in **AI** (called Type 2 Learning Without a Teacher) is quite different from conventional learning without a teacher (Type 1 Learning without a Teacher) involving Bayes theorem.

5-4 EXTENSION

5-4-1 Corollaries to the Theorem (Patrick)

In like manner, it follows that

$$p(\omega_i^*|\mathbf{x}) = \frac{p(\mathbf{x}|\omega_i)P(\omega_i) - \sum_{\omega_i \in \Omega_\xi^*} p(\mathbf{x}|\Omega_\xi^*)P(\Omega_\xi^*)}{p(\mathbf{x})} \tag{10a}$$

$$p(\Omega_\xi^*|\mathbf{x}) = \frac{p(\mathbf{x}|\omega_i)P(\omega_i) - p(\mathbf{x}|\omega_i^*)P(\omega_i^*)}{p(\mathbf{x})} \text{ (two classes).} \tag{10b}$$

Further insight is obtained when training samples $\mathbf{x}_1, \mathbf{x}_2, \ldots, \mathbf{x}_n$ are used to iterate (10a) or (10b). This iteration in the theorem by Patrick parallels iteration in Bayes theorem. The iteration is a basic inference by learning. In Patrick we will see that categories are statistically dependent during learning although that does not hold for Bayes.

5-4-2 Learning Using the Theorem by Patrick

The theorem by Patrick is not fully developed until inference is conditioned on samples since the characterization of *all* concepts is unknown. Let $\mathbf{x}_1, \mathbf{x}_2, \ldots, \mathbf{x}_n$ be a set of training samples. The objective is to obtain

$$p(\omega_i^*|\mathbf{x}, \mathbf{x}_1, \ldots, \mathbf{x}_n) \quad \forall \quad \omega_i^*$$

$$p(\Omega_\xi^*|\mathbf{x}, \mathbf{x}_1, \ldots, \mathbf{x}_n) \quad \forall \quad \Omega_\xi^*$$

where $\mathbf{x}$ is to be categorized, and learning has been progressing using a set of n learning samples (records)

$$\dot{\mathbf{x}}_n \triangleq \mathbf{x}_1, \mathbf{x}_2, \ldots, \mathbf{x}_n.$$

It is possible that all potential† Ω_ξ^* may not exist in nature. Still, we can infer what they could look like. This is not to suggest that all potential $p(\Omega_\xi^*|\mathbf{x}, \mathbf{x}_1, \ldots, \mathbf{x}_n)$ should be calculated. For example, a method for deciding if calculation should proceed is: If the probability that the complex class exists exceeds some threshold, based on the only classes; or if the leading only class a posteriori probability is below some

†A potential category is one that theoretically can be constructed from classes.

threshold. Networking can be used to reduce complexity for automatic formation of complex classes when they exist. Such methods or rules for deciding if calculations should proceed are part of the knowledge base, an **AI** concept. These are search procedures for the "optimum" solution. Optimum here means the identification of the true (existing) categories with subsequent inference of these categories with lowest probability of error.

Do not confuse the true set of knowledge (categories and the category feature relationships) with the methods used to search for this knowledge. Also, realize that *relative frequency itself is knowledge* that must be used in the search for new knowledge.

5-4-3 Considerations for Learning in the Theorem by Patrick

Now, there are these considerations:

1. Are the samples (records) $\mathbf{x}_1, \mathbf{x}_2, \ldots, \mathbf{x}_n$ supervised; i.e., are they of known category?
2. Are there training sessions—some samples from, say ω_i^*, then some from ω_j^*, and so on?
3. Is training for only classes or classes? That is, are the samples from ω_i^*, ω_j^*, . . . or are they from ω_i, ω_j, . . .?

In medical diagnostic systems the problem is likely one of training with samples from only classes $\omega_1^*, \omega_2^*, \ldots, \omega_{M_1}^*$, and not all complex classes are trained a priori. Thus, concept formation is for complex classes with class formation an intermediate step. It is possible to form concepts of only classes where complex classes have been known a priori. Then initial training may be for some only classes and some complex classes. New only classes and complex classes are created by concept formation.

5-4-4 Forming Complex Classes as Concepts with Classes as Intermediate Concepts

One reasonable approach then is to consider that the existence of complex classes is not known a priori. There exists a mixture for the p.d.f. of the feature vector $\mathbf{x}$,

$$p(\mathbf{x}) = \sum_{i=1}^{M_1} p(\mathbf{x}|\omega_i^*)P(\omega_i^*) + \sum_{\xi=1}^{M_2} p(\mathbf{x}|\Omega_\xi^*)P(\Omega_\xi^*), \tag{11}$$

where the M_1 only classes are trained (first term on the right-hand side of Eq. (11)) but the second term is a mixture which needs to be resolved. *This is learning without a teacher but there is inherent knowledge about the* Ω_ξ^* *in terms of the only classes.* For a particular complex class Ω_ξ^* we seek to compute

$$p(\mathbf{x}|\Omega_i^*, \mathbf{x}_1, \mathbf{x}_2, \ldots, \mathbf{x}_n),$$

a consideration revisited throughout this chapter.

5-5 ASPECTS OF THE THEOREM ON A POSTERIORI PROBABILITY (PATRICK)

5-5-1 Introduction

How does the theorem on a posteriori probability by Patrick differ from Bayes theorem? Should we train the classes or only classes? Is learning with a teacher involved? These are important considerations discussed in this section. It is assumed in this section that there are two classes, ω_i and ω_j, and thus only one complex class (i.e., $M_1 = 2, M_2 = 1, M = 3$).

5-5-2 Training by Classes without a Complex Class Model

Suppose that training samples are available for two classes ω_i and ω_j and thus $p(\omega_i, \mathbf{x})$ and $p(\omega_j, \mathbf{x})$ are learned by example (with a teacher). Some samples are from both ω_i and ω_j. *The events* $(\omega_i, \mathbf{x})$ *and* $(\omega_j, \mathbf{x})$ *are not mutually exclusive as required by Bayes theorem because there are samples* $\mathbf{x}$ *for which both* ω_i *and* ω_j *occur for the same sample.* This situation arises in practice where the developer designs a subsystem with two classes to find that the two classes are not mutually exclusive and Bayes theorem cannot be applied. Using the theorem on a posteriori by Patrick we know that

$$p(\omega_i,\mathbf{x}) = p(\omega_i^*,\mathbf{x}) + p(\Omega_{ij}^*,\mathbf{x})$$
$$p(\omega_j,\mathbf{x}) = p(\omega_j^*,\mathbf{x}) + p(\Omega_{ij}^*,\mathbf{x}),$$

where the left-hand sides of both equations are learned by example (our earlier assumption).

Now request learning by example of either $p(\omega_i^*,\mathbf{x})$ or $p(\omega_j^*,\mathbf{x})$, but presume to start with the former. From the first equation,

$$p(\Omega_{ij}^*,\mathbf{x}) = p(\omega_i,\mathbf{x}) - p(\omega_i^*,\mathbf{x}) \qquad (12)$$

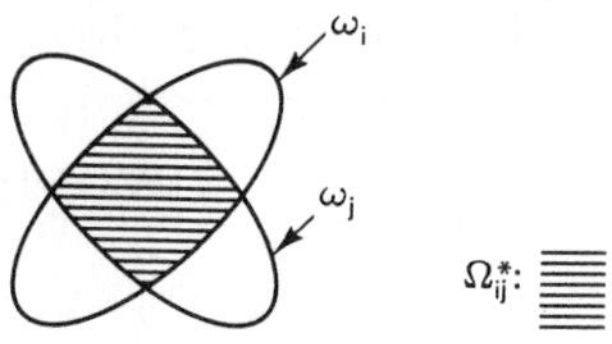

FIGURE 5.1. Regions in the feature space for inductive learning of two classes ω_i and ω_j.

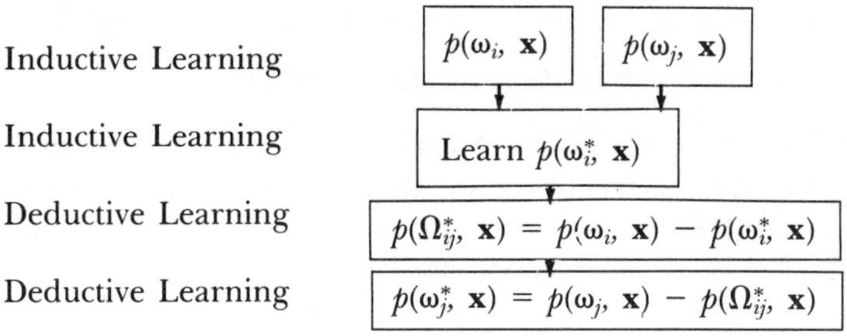

FIGURE 5.2. Graph of sequence of three sessions of inductive learning followed by deductive learning.

and *we learn by deduction about the complex class Ω_{ij}^* since the right-hand side terms both have been learned by induction;* and then from the second equation we learn about ω_j^* by deduction,

$$p(\omega_j^*,\mathbf{x}) = p(\omega_j,\mathbf{x}) - p(\Omega_{ij}^*,\mathbf{x}), \tag{13}$$

since both terms on the right-hand side are known.

Regions in the feature space for the two classes are shown in Figure 5.1 and a graph of the sequential learning process is shown in Figure 5.2.

We note that three inductive learning sessions are required to learn (by deduction) about three categories, ω_i^*, ω_j^*, and Ω_{ij}^*; and one could ask, Why not have three inductive learning sessions to learn ω_i^*, ω_j^*, and Ω_{ij}^* in the first place?† Why not? The problem presented required learning by discovery as illustrated in Figure 5.2. The latter problem was not the problem presentation.

5-5-3 Training by Classes with a Category Model

Figure 5.1 suggests that learning regions of insignificance in the feature space for categories is possible. In particular, regions of in-

†As would have been done in an ordinary Bayes formulation.

significance for category Ω_{ij}^* are where either class ω_i or ω_j and both classes do not occur. The complement region of significance for category Ω_{ij}^* is a candidate region for patterns from that complex class. Denote this region by $\mathfrak{X}_{ij}$,

$$\mathfrak{X}_{ij} = g(x_i, x_j), \tag{14}$$

where x_i and x_j are in regions of the feature space where respective classes ω_i and ω_j occur. These regions will be learned to some degree of certainty expressible by probabilities. Then,

$$p(\Omega_{ij}^*,\mathbf{x}) = h(p(\omega_i,\mathbf{x}), p(\omega_j,\mathbf{x})) \tag{15}$$

is an expression for the complex class p.d.f. computed using region $\mathfrak{X}_{ij}$, the certainty for this region, and the training samples from classes ω_i and ω_j. These training samples are in two sets, one from class ω_i and one from class ω_j. *But some of the samples are from both classes. The important point is that there are only two sets of training samples and thus two inductive learning sessions. Samples from both classes ω_i and ω_j are deduced and characterize Ω_{ij}^*. A third inductive learning session is not required.*

Thus we have two inductive learning sessions to learn $p(\omega_i,\mathbf{x})$ and $p(\omega_j,\mathbf{x})$ and then learn $p(\Omega_{ij}^*,\mathbf{x})$ by deduction using Eq. (15). Then by deduction and the new theorem on a posteriori probability,

$$p(\omega_i^*,\mathbf{x}) = p(\omega_i,\mathbf{x}) - p(\Omega_{ij}^*,\mathbf{x}) \tag{16a}$$

$$p(\omega_j^*,\mathbf{x}) = p(\omega_j,\mathbf{x}) - p(\Omega_{ij}^*,\mathbf{x}). \tag{16b}$$

The two sessions of inductive learning followed by deductive learning are illustrated in the graph of Figure 5.3. *The use of a model for the complex class has reduced the required number of inductive learning sessions from three to two.* (Patrick's theorem applied.)

Inductive learning takes place over time and space. In a practical decision-making system it may be best to perform inductive learning off line.

To formulate the problem as starting by training *classes* as just accomplished is not appropriate in practice. Rather, training only classes is appropriate in practice as discussed in the next section.

5-5-4 Training by Only Classes

In developing expert systems for medical diagnosis it has been found convenient to use inductive learning to obtain $p(\mathbf{x}|\omega_i^*)$ and $p(\mathbf{x}|\omega_j^*)$. It is natural to know about single diseases (only classes). Perhaps as knowledge bases become more accurate we will find that some of these only classes are not pure.

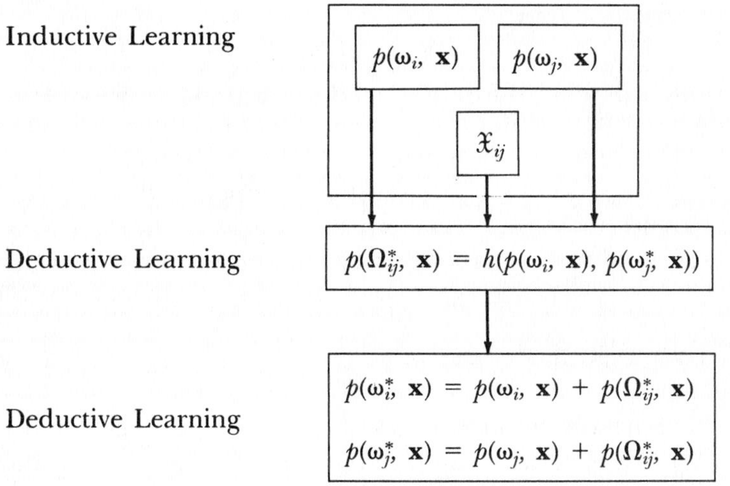

FIGURE 5.3. Graph showing inductive learning (two sessions shown in top box) followed by deductive learning.

Given that knowledge or training is available for only classes, we must then learn about complex classes. This requires creating a model for deducing a complex class from only classes.

5-6 COMPLEX CLASS MODEL BASED ON INSIGNIFICANCE AND DEDUCTION

5-6-1 Introduction

A "class-feature" event $(\omega_i, \mathbf{x})$ is related to that of an only class and complex class by the equation

$$(\omega_i,\mathbf{x}) = (\omega^*_i,\mathbf{x}) + (\Omega^*_{ij},\mathbf{x}) \tag{17}$$

for a two-class ($M_1 = 2$) model. Recall that†

$$\omega^*_i = \omega_i\bar{\omega}_j$$
$$\omega^*_j = \omega_j\bar{\omega}_i$$
$$\Omega^*_{ij} = \omega_i\omega_j.$$

†The intersection of two events A and B is denoted with a comma (A, B) or without a comma $(A\ B)$.

5-6-2 Cross-Learning

Equation (17) suggests that *cross-learning* is possible, a construction where knowledge of an only class can provide knowledge about a complex class or another only class. On the other hand, Eq. (17) is the equation for a mixture suggesting unsupervised learning (*learning without a teacher-Type 2*). A certain sufficient amount of a priori knowledge will have to be introduced for successful resolution of the mixture.

5-6-3 Two Induction Sessions

Suppose that supervised samples $\mathbf{x}_1, \mathbf{x}_2, \ldots, \mathbf{x}_n$ are used to learn about ω_i^* and ω_j^*. Learning results in knowledge about significant and insignificant features† and feature values of $\mathbf{x}$ for categories (only classes). This results in a model for the complex class which can be used for deduction.

Humans currently are more efficient than computers at off-line induction for creating certain models. Therefore, "using humans" to create models by off-line induction may be desirable.

5-6-4 On-Line Deduction

The complex class model obtained during inductive learning sessions can be used to *deduce* or generate a complex class presentation at recognition time, just as a presentation with a missing feature can be deduced or generated using a projection operation.

5-6-4-1 Feature Space Constraints (the Teacher)

Previously in Section 3-4-2 the concept of *insignificant features* was discussed. Assume that a procedure is available to use training samples to identify the insignificant features and feature values of ω_i^* and ω_j^*, respectively. Let, for category ω_i^*,

$$\omega_i^*: \quad \mathbf{x} = \mathbf{x}_{s_i} + \mathbf{x}_{I_i} \tag{18}$$

where $\mathbf{x}_{s_i}$ and $\mathbf{x}_{I_i}$ are *significant* and *insignificant* feature subsets for only class ω_i^*. Likewise,

$$\omega_j^*: \quad \mathbf{x} = \mathbf{x}_{s_j} + \mathbf{x}_{I_j}. \tag{19}$$

†An insignificant feature for a category is one for which all feature values are equally likely or are "normal"; the feature values have the same probability as for all other categories for which the feature is insignificant.

Identification of insignificant features for respective categories (only classes in this case) is very important a priori knowledge for resolving learning without a teacher-Type 2. Learning without a teacher-Type 2 then becomes possible by deduction. A relatively simplifed but important and revealing complex class model is,

$$\Omega_{ij}^{*}: \quad \mathbf{x} = \mathbf{x}_{s_i} + \mathbf{x}_{s_j}, \tag{20}$$

which presumes that

$$\mathbf{x}_{s_j} = \mathbf{x}_{I_i}$$

$$\mathbf{x}_{s_i} = \mathbf{x}_{I_j}.$$

This is an ideal model where significant features for one only class are insignificant for another only class.

5-6-4-2 Category Models

Using the previous preliminaries, models for category conditional probability density functions are constructed as follows:

$$p(\omega_i^*, \mathbf{x}) = p(\omega_i^*, \mathbf{x}_{s_i})p(\omega_i^*, \mathbf{x}_{I_i}) \tag{21a}$$

$$p(\omega_j^*, \mathbf{x}) = p(\omega_j^*, \mathbf{x}_{s_j})p(\omega_j^*, \mathbf{x}_{I_j}) \tag{21b}$$

$$p(\Omega_{ij}^*, \mathbf{x}) = p(\omega_i^*, \mathbf{x}_{s_i})p(\omega_j^*, \mathbf{x}_{s_j}) \tag{21c}$$

These three models (equations) were constructed such that for only classes ω_i^* and ω_j^* there are both signifcant and insignificant features whereas for complex class Ω_{ij}^* there are only significant features. Equations (21a) and (21b) are without loss of generality whereas Eq. (21c) presumes the model of Eq. (20).

At recognition time, a pattern $\mathbf{x}$ from category ω_i^* will produce a relatively large value for $p(\omega_i^*,\mathbf{x})$ because the probability is not affected by insignificant features (see Section 9-9 on insignificant features). Likewise, a pattern from Ω_{ij}^* will produce a relatively large value for $p(\Omega_{ij}^*,\mathbf{x})$ because there are no insignificant features for this complex class and all features for the pattern from Ω_{ij}^* would be significant (high value of marginal likelihood measure).

Equation (21c) demonstrates a "cross-learning" where, after inductive learning about only classes ω_i^* and ω_j^*, deductive learning takes place about complex class Ω_{ij}^*.

Note particularly that Eq. (21c) is not just the product of the respective p.d.f.'s of ω_i^* and ω_j^*. Instead, it is the product of two interrelated p.d.f.'s with the interrelationship† *in the feature space.* This will be a characteristic of mod-

---

†In Eq. (21b) for example, the insignificant features have values independent of the significant features.

els for generating complex classes—that there be an interrelationship in the feature space involving the appropriate only classes. Note for this example that direct computation of $p(\mathbf{x},\omega_i)$ or $p(\mathbf{x},\omega_j)$ was not needed. These classes were involved indirectly from the model of Eq. (17) used in arriving at Eqs. (21).

5-6-4-3 Expressions for the Classes

We do not need to know directly about classes ω_i and ω_j for this problem; but that knowledge can be obtained. Substituting Eqs. (21a) and (21b), respectively, into model Eq. (17) results in

$$p(\omega_i,\mathbf{x}) = p(\omega_i^*,\mathbf{x}_{s_i})\,[p(\omega_i^*,\mathbf{x}_{\mathrm{I}_i}) + p(\omega_j^*,\mathbf{x}_{s_j})] \tag{22a}$$

$$p(\omega_j,\mathbf{x}) = p(\omega_j^*,\mathbf{x}_{s_j})\,[p(\omega_j^*,\mathbf{x}_{\mathrm{I}_j}) + p(\omega_i^*,\mathbf{x}_{s_i})] \tag{22b}$$

Equation (22a) demonstrates how knowledge about class ω_i is deduced from ω_i^* and ω_j^* with an intermediate deduction about complex class Ω_{ij}^*. Knowledge about ω_i^* and ω_j^* is induced during off-line learning.

Although class ω_i is not in the decision space, it is an event that could be recognized using the p.d.f. of Eq. (22).

5-6-4-4 Differences from Bayes Theorem

The problem formulation began presuming inductive learning about only classes. The theorem on a posteriori probability by Patrick provides for *cross-learning* because although categories ω_i^*, ω_j^*, and Ω_{ij}^* are mutally exclusive from the statistical viewpoint, there is a relationship between Ω_{ij}^* and ω_i^*, ω_j^*. *Equation (21c) does not exist for Bayes theorem since the internal structure does not exist to define classes ω_i and ω_j which are not in the decision space.* Elsewhere in this book, cross-learning takes the form of a statistical dependence during concept formation of a posteriori probability (Patrick). With the theorem on a posteriori probability (Patrick), it is possible to have a posteriori knowledge about classes ω_i and ω_j without really knowing about categories in the decision space. For example, inductive off-line learning about ω_i and ω_j could take place but these classes are not mutually exclusive. The theorem (Patrick) provides the model through which one should determine categories ω_i^*, ω_j^*, and Ω_{ij}^* which are mutually exclusive. Nowhere does Bayes theorem provide this facility.

5-6-4-5 Extensions

Equations (18), (19), and (20) presume strict separation of insignificant and significant features for a category. In practice the strict separation can be relaxed. Extensions are possible.

For example:

1. The same feature(s) can be significant for more than one class.
2. The same feature(s) can be insignificant for more than one class.
3. There can be degrees of feature significance for a class.
4. Significance or insignificance of features for a class can involve complex constraints on the feature space. Resulting domains or covers can have different probabilities.
5. The complex class model may not be as simplistic as Equation (21c) but can have significant features of one class ω_i^* dependent on significant features of another class.
6. A complex class model can have a feature independent of any of the involved only classes.

To implement these properties, let

$$\begin{aligned} \mathbf{x}(S_i),\ S_i &= 1, 2, \ldots \\ \mathbf{x}(I_i),\ I_i &= 1, 2, \ldots \end{aligned} \tag{23}$$

be subsets of features for only class ω_i^* which are significant and insignificant, respectively (presume also for only class ω_j^*). Then, analogous to Eqs. (18), (19), and (20),

$$\omega_i^*: \quad \mathbf{x} = \sum_{S_i} \mathbf{x}(S_i) + \sum_{I_i} \mathbf{x}(I_i) \tag{24}$$

$$\omega_j^*: \quad \mathbf{x} = \sum_{S_j} \mathbf{x}(S_j) + \sum_{I_j} \mathbf{x}(I_j). \tag{25}$$

Also,

$$\Omega_{ij}^*: \quad \mathbf{x} = \sum_{S_{ij}} \mathbf{x}(S_{ij}) + \sum_{I_{ij}} \mathbf{x}(I_{ij}), \tag{26}$$

where

$$\mathbf{x}(S_{ij})$$
$$\mathbf{x}(I_{ij})$$

are subsets of features for complex class Ω_{ij}^* which are significant and insignificant, respectively. The number of possible relationships between Eq. (26) and Eqs. (24) and (25) is very large. Analogous to Eq. (21),

$$p(\omega_i^*,\mathbf{x}) = p(\omega_i^*,\{\mathbf{x}_{S_i}\})\ p(\omega_i^*,\{\mathbf{x}_{I_i}\}) \tag{27a}$$

$$p(\omega_j^*,\mathbf{x}) = p(\omega_j^*,\{\mathbf{x}_{S_j}\})\, p(\omega_j^*,\{\mathbf{x}_{I_j}\}) \tag{27b}$$

an expression for $p(\Omega_{ij}^*,\mathbf{x})$ in terms of Eqs. (24) and (25) can be constructed after additional a priori knowledge is specified; and a reasonable model for the complex class p.d.f. is

$$p(\Omega_{ij}^*,\mathbf{x}) = p(\omega_i^*, \{\mathbf{x}_{S_i}\})\, p(\omega_j^*, \{\mathbf{x}_{S_j}\}|\{\mathbf{x}_{S_i}\})C.$$

Assuming that dependence is handled through the column approach (see Section 9-7) then the above equation simplifies to

$$p(\Omega_{ij}^*,\mathbf{x}) = \prod_{S_i} p(\omega_i^*,\mathbf{x}_{S_i}) \prod_{S_j} p(\omega_j^*,\mathbf{x}_{S_j})C. \tag{27c}$$

C is normalizing constant for insignificant features for the complex class.

5-6-5 Decision to Process for Complex Classes

In practice, only classes can be processed first. *For a single column, Eqs. (27) can be used to determine when to process for complex classes.* The decision to process can be based on the probabilities of insignificance. For two only classes ω_i^* and ω_j^*, respective probabilities of insignificance are

$$\mathcal{S}(\omega_i^*) \triangleq \prod_{I_i} p(\omega_i^*,\mathbf{x}_{I_i}) \tag{28a}$$

$$\mathcal{S}(\omega_j^*) \triangleq \prod_{I_j} p(\omega_j^*,\mathbf{x}_{I_j}) \tag{28b}$$

and respective probabilities of significance are

$$S(\omega_i^*) \triangleq \prod_{S_i} p(\omega_i^*,\mathbf{x}_{S_i}) \tag{29a}$$

$$S(\omega_j^*) \triangleq \prod_{S_j} p(\omega_j^*,\mathbf{x}_{S_j}) \tag{29b}$$

Compare the complex class probability

$$S(\omega_i^*)S(\omega_j^*)$$

with

$$S(\omega_i^*)\ \mathcal{S}(\omega_j^*)$$

and

$$\mathfrak{S}(\omega_i^*)S(\omega_j^*).$$

For a complex class to have higher probability than an only class it is sufficient that

$$S(\omega_j^*) > \mathfrak{S}(\omega_j^*) \tag{30a}$$

or

$$S(\omega_i^*) > \mathfrak{S}(\omega_i^*). \tag{30b}$$

5-6-5-1 Proposition 1 for Complex Class Occurrence

For this model we conclude that for class ω_i to occur with higher probability as a complex class with class ω_j than as an only class it is sufficient that significance of ω_i^* be greater than insignificance of ω_i^* or significance of $\bar{\omega}_j^*$ be greater than insignificance of ω_j^*.

5-6-5-2 Proposition 2 for Complex Class Occurrence

Another result is that for ω_i and ω_j to have *higher probability as a complex class than as only classes it is sufficient that significance of* ω_i^* *be greater than insignificance of* ω_i^* *and significance of* ω_j^* *be greater than insignificance of* ω_j^*.

The latter result appeals to common sense because either ω_i^*, ω_j^*, or Ω_{ij}^* occurs; only one occurs since they are mutually exclusive.

A single probability expression is not sufficient for this model. Rather, the structure of the feature space must be considered because it is the *feature space structure (levels of significance and insignificance) of one only class relative to the feature space structure of another only class wherein "lies the teacher"* for resolving the mixture problem (and concept formation) in this Learning Without a Teacher-Type 2. That is, if

$$p(\mathbf{x}\omega_i^*, \mathbf{x}\bar{\omega}_j^*) > p(\mathbf{x}\omega_i^*, \mathbf{x}\omega_j^*) \tag{31a}$$

and

$$p(\mathbf{x}\omega_j^*, \mathbf{x}\bar{\omega}_i^*) > p(\mathbf{x}\omega_j^*, \mathbf{x}\omega_i^*), \tag{31b}$$

then a complex class is more likely than either only class. This is illustrated in Figure 5.4. For the example in Figure 5.4, the above equations for a complex class translate into

$p(|||) > p($ $)$ (32a)

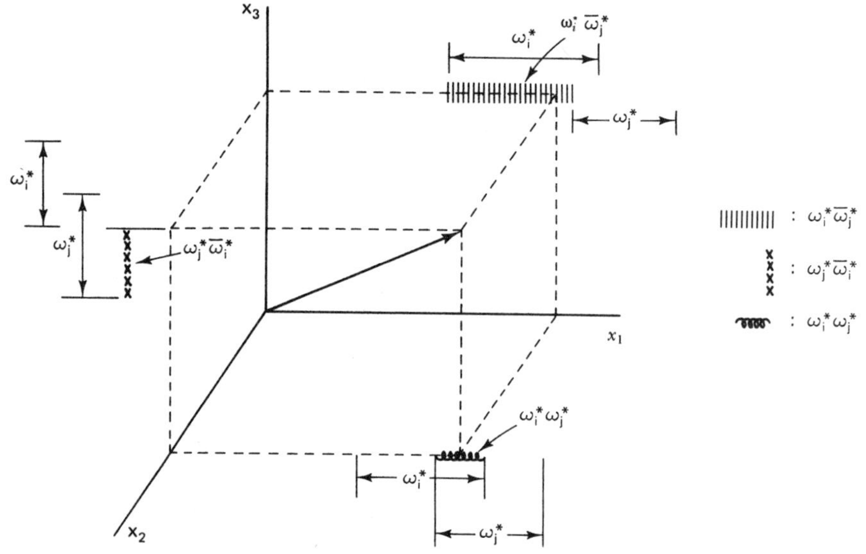

FIGURE 5.4. Illustration of Regions of Significance for events $\omega_i^*\bar{\omega}_j^*$, $\omega_j^*\bar{\omega}_i^*$, and $\omega_i^*\omega_j^*$.

and

$$p(\times\times\times) > p(\wr). \tag{32b}$$

Figure 5.4 is meant to *illustrate* all the probability "mass" for the only classes and complex class. Further illustrated is that it is necessary to have regions in the feature space for events such as $\omega_i^*\bar{\omega}_j^*$. These are strong requirements.

The requirements can be loosened by using

$$p(\mathbf{x}\omega_i^*)p(\mathbf{x}\bar{\omega}_j^*) > p(\mathbf{x}\omega_i^*)p(\mathbf{x}\omega_j^*)$$

and

$$p(\mathbf{x}\omega_j^*)p(\mathbf{x}\bar{\omega}_i^*) > p(\mathbf{x}\omega_j^*)p(\mathbf{x}\omega_i^*),$$

which is equivalent to

$$p(\mathbf{x}\omega_j^*) < 1/2$$

and

$$p(\mathbf{x}\omega_i^*) < 1/2.$$

5-7 EXAMPLE OF LEARNING VERSUS RECOGNITION AND FEEDBACK IN THE THEOREM BY PATRICK

5-7-1 Example of Feedback for Learning by Deduction

Consider a two-class model where Ω_ξ^* has the form

$$\Omega_\xi^* = \Omega_{ij}^*, \qquad \text{since } M_1 = 2;$$

i.e., there are two classes in the complex class. Then

$$p(\omega_i) = p(\omega_i^*) + p(\omega_i, \omega_j) \tag{33a}$$

and

$$p(\omega_j) = p(\omega_j^*) + p(\omega_i, \omega_j) \tag{33b}$$

or

$$p(\omega_i|\mathbf{x}) = p(\omega_i^*|\mathbf{x}) + p(\Omega_{ij}^*|\mathbf{x}) \tag{34}$$

$$p(\omega_j|\mathbf{x}) = p(\omega_j^*|\mathbf{x}) + p(\Omega_{ij}^*|\mathbf{x}) \tag{35}$$

These equations suggest that x affects $(\Omega_{i\xi}^*|\mathbf{x})$ and in turn affects the probability of the class ω_i. Or, an increased probability of class ω_i because of an increase in $p(\omega_i^*|\mathbf{x})$ increases the probability of any complex class $\Omega_{i\xi}^*$ containing class ω_i, not previously influenced by this increased probability. (A feedback system interpretation will be presented.)

Further,

$$p(\mathbf{x}|\omega_i) = p(\mathbf{x}|\omega_i^*)\frac{p(\omega_i^*)}{p(\omega_i)} + p(\mathbf{x}|\Omega_{ij}^*)\frac{p(\Omega_{ij}^*)}{p(\omega_i)} \tag{36a}$$

$$p(\mathbf{x}|\omega_j) = p(\mathbf{x}|\omega_j^*)\frac{p(\omega_j^*)}{p(\omega_j)} + p(\mathbf{x}|\Omega_{ij}^*)\frac{p(\Omega_{ij}^*)}{p(\omega_j)} \tag{36b}$$

5-7-1-1 Learning versus Recognition

It is important to distinguish between learning and recognition. Learning involves processing training samples $\mathbf{x}_1, \mathbf{x}_2, \ldots, \mathbf{x}_n$ to estimate conditional probability density functions. Recognition is determination of

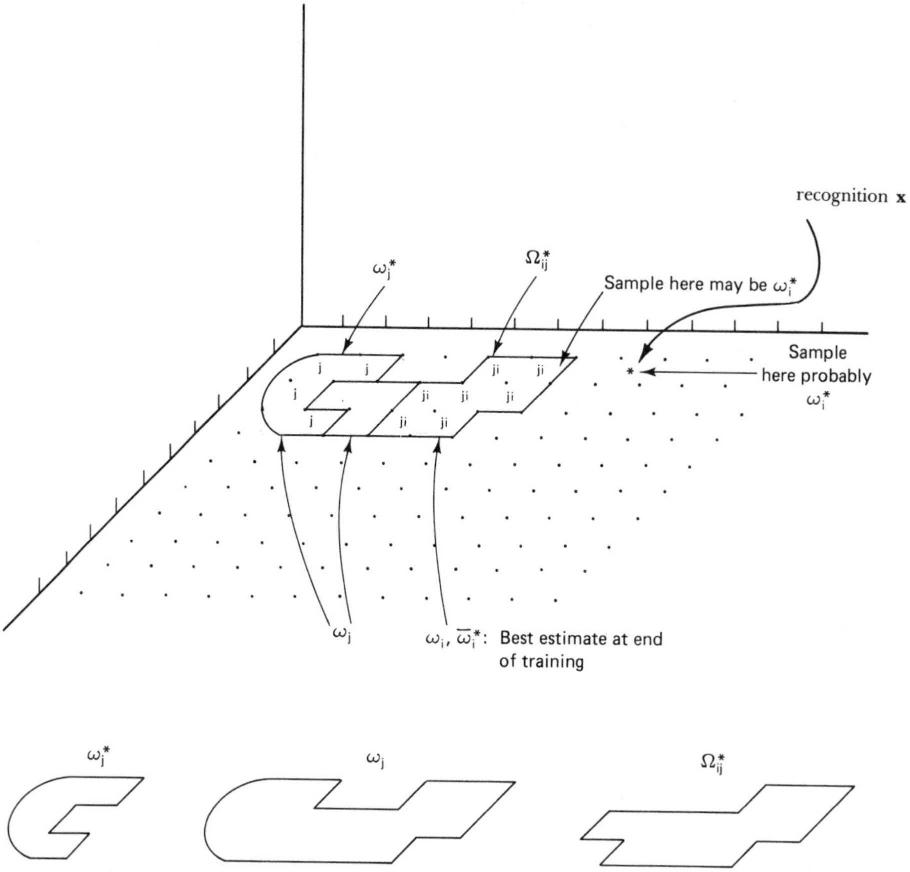

FIGURE 5.5. Illustration of learning versus recognition.

likelihood function values using already established conditional probability density functions.

Consider Eq. (36a) with $p(\mathbf{x}|\Omega_{ij}^*)$ eliminated using Eq. (36b)

$$p(\mathbf{x}|\omega_i^*) = \frac{p(\omega_i)}{p(\omega_i^*)}\, p(\mathbf{x}|\omega_i) - \left[\frac{p(\omega_j)}{p(\omega_i^*)}\, p(\mathbf{x}|\omega_j) - \frac{p(\omega_j^*)}{p(\omega_i^*)}\, p(\mathbf{x}|\omega_j^*)\right]. \quad (37)$$

Continuing this example, suppose that samples are available to estimate as follows:

$p(\mathbf{x}|\omega_j^*)$: estimated from training (see Figure 5.5)

and other samples are available to estimate:

$p(\mathbf{x}|\Omega_{ij}^*)$: estimated from training (see Figure 5.5).

Assuming a priori probabilities known or equally likely, from Eq. (36b):

$p(\mathbf{x}|\omega_j)$: by deduction (see shaded area in Figure 5.5).

A sample from ω_i^* has not been observed but samples from ω_i have been observed through Eq. (37) because samples from ω_i^* were abnormal. Using the fact that

$$\omega_i = (\omega_i, \bar{\omega}_i^*) + (\omega_i, \omega_i^*), \tag{38}$$

the term in the bracket on the right-hand side of Eq. (37) is manipulated to obtain

$$p(\mathbf{x}|\omega_i, \bar{\omega}_i^*) = \left[\frac{p(\omega_j)}{p(\omega_i)} p(\mathbf{x}|\omega_j) - \frac{p(\omega_j^*)}{p(\omega_i)} p(\mathbf{x}|\omega_j^*) \right]. \tag{39}$$

So we now have feedback about the conditional probability density function of class ω_i excluding only class ω_i^*. This is illustrated in Figure 5.5. Samples from ω_j^* and Ω_{ij}^* are informing us about class ω_i. Of course, this information is primarily from Ω_{ij}^* but the accounting had to be kept straight.

In Figure 5.5 the areas for ω_j, ω_j^*, Ω_{ij}^*, and $(\omega_i, \bar{\omega}_i^*)$ are illustrated. With this training, *we now turn to a recognition mode* and observe an additional sample, **x**.

Could this sample be from ω_i^*? Have we learned anything about ω_i^* during training where there were samples from $\bar{\omega}_i^*$? The answer requires a model (Patrick, 1965, 1968, 1969, 1972).

It is reasonable that a sample falling where Ω_{ij}^* exists could be from ω_i^*, as illustrated in Figure 5.5. Likewise, a recognition sample in $\mathfrak{S}$ where there were no training samples could be from ω_i^*, as illustrated in Figure 5.5.

At this point, the Scientific Method is applied. Can we discover anything from the problem to suggest the difference between ω_i^* and Ω_{ij}^*? This is unsupervised learning. *A necessary and sufficient a priori condition is that $p(\mathbf{x}|\omega_i^*)$ and $p(\mathbf{x}|\Omega_{ij}^*)$ be linearly independent* (Patrick, 1972).

Linear independence can be achieved when a feature for Ω_{ij}^* has values different from those for ω_i^*, a reasonable model. Once postulated, this model needs to be verified by the scientific method.

5-7-2 Discovering a Complex Class—Induction

The inductive process of discovering $p(\mathbf{x}|\Omega_{ij}^*)$, given samples from ω_i^* and ω_j^*, is considered again. First, observe that

$$\omega_i^* + \omega_j^* + \Omega_{ij}^* = \mathfrak{S}, \tag{40}$$

where $\mathfrak{S}$ is the complete decision space. Samples from ω_i^* and ω_j^* give us knowledge of $(\mathfrak{S}, \bar{\Omega}_{ij}^*)$, where

$$\mathfrak{S} = (\mathfrak{S}, \bar{\Omega}_{ij}^*) + (\mathfrak{S}, \Omega_{ij}^*). \tag{41}$$

A model is needed to infer knowledge about Ω_{ij}^*. given knowledge about $(\mathfrak{S}, \bar{\Omega}_{ij}^*)$. This inductive problem can be more difficult than the previous one of decomposition or deduction.

If new recognition samples are observed in $(\mathfrak{S}, \Omega_{ij}^*)$ but they look like ω_i^* and like ω_j^* to some extent, then they could be from Ω_{ij}^*. A Model from Ω_{ij}^* is suggested as follows:

Model for Ω_{ij}^*:

1. $\mathbf{x}$ not in $(\mathfrak{S}, \bar{\Omega}_{ij}^*)$.
2. Ω_{ij}^* has primitives† (in $\mathbf{x}$) found in ω_i^*. (42)
3. Ω_{ij}^* has primitives (in $\mathbf{x}$) found in ω_j^*.

Expression (42) is important. To discover Ω_{ij}^*, we must know something about its primitives. By first learning about ω_i^* and ω_j^*, we have learned that one place to look for Ω_{ij}^* is from knowledge of $(\mathfrak{S}, \bar{\Omega}_{ij}^*)$. Also, we have learned about primitives that can be tried for Ω_{ij}^*.

Training at this point for Ω_{ij}^* can be supervised (i.e., a nonrecognition mode). The model of (42) could be a framework for processing the training data.

5-8 RULES DEFINING COMPLEX CLASSES FROM ONLY CLASSES BASED ON LIKENESS AND UNLIKENESS

5-8-1 Introduction

Consider again two only classes ω_1^* and ω_2^* and a complex class Ω_{12}^* involving classes ω_1 and ω_2. There exists probability density functions $p(\mathbf{x}|\omega_1^*)$, $p(\mathbf{x}|\omega_2^*)$, and $p(\mathbf{x}|\Omega_{12}^*)$. Given $p(\mathbf{x}|\omega_1^*)$ and $p(\mathbf{x}|\omega_2^*)$, how can $p(\mathbf{x}|\Omega_{12}^*)$ be obtained? Various approaches are considered where $p(x_j|\omega_i^*)$ for each feature x_j can be used. It is presumed that at this stage of learning, knowledge about ω_i^* is limited to ω_i.

†Primitive is used here to mean a feature primitive, i.e., specific feature values.

5-8-2 Complex Class Rules (CC Rules)

It is convenient to define condition strings for use in "Complex Class Rules" (CC Rules) as follows:

Like (ω_i^*): Probably like class ω_i (a threshold is involved).

n_i Like (ω_i^*): There exists n_i features x_j for which $p(x_j|\omega_i^*) > T$, T = Threshold.

n_{ij} with n_i Like ω_i and n_j Like ω_j

of m_i Like $\omega_i^* \ni m_{ij}$ Unlike ω_j.

No Can't (Ω_{12}^*): There exists no Can't on the complex class Ω_{12}^*.

A complex class rule requiring multidimensional probability density functions is

$$\text{If } \langle n_i \text{ Like } (\omega_i^*)\rangle \text{ and } \langle n_j \text{ Like } (\omega_j^*)\rangle \text{ and } \langle \text{no Can't } \Omega_{ij}^*\rangle \rightarrow \Omega_{ij}^*. \tag{43}$$

The probability of Ω_{ij}^* can be taken as the minimum of the respective class probabilities. There are many hidden assumptions implied in this CC Rule concerning statistical independence or linear independence.

A CC Rule clearly requiring that **x** have features "like ω_i" and features "like ω_j which are unlike ω_i" is as follows:

$$\begin{aligned}
&\text{If } \langle n_{ij} \text{ with } n_i \text{ Like } \omega_i^* \text{ and } n_j \text{ Like } \omega_j^*\rangle\\
&\text{And } \langle\langle \text{of } m_i \text{ Like } \omega_i^* \ni m_{ij} \text{ Unlike } \omega_j^*\rangle\\
&\text{Or } \langle \text{of } m_j \text{ Like } \omega_i^* \ni m_{ji} \text{ Unlike } \omega_i^*\rangle\rangle\\
&\text{And } \langle \text{No Can't } (\Omega_{ij}^*)\rangle \rightarrow \Omega_{ij}^*,\ \rho(\Omega_{ij}^*|\mathbf{x}).
\end{aligned} \tag{44a}$$

A corresponding c.c.p.d.f. for Ω_{ij}^* can be expressed:

$$p(\mathbf{x}|\Omega_{ij}^*) \triangleq \left[\prod_{m_i \text{ Like } \omega_i} p(x_k|\omega_i^*)\right]\left[\prod_{m_{ji} \text{ Like } \omega_j \text{ But Unlike } \omega_i} p(x_k|\omega_j^*)\right]. \tag{44b}$$

An assumption in Eq. (44b) [but not Eq. (44a)] is that the features are statistically independent. Another assumption is that there are m_{ji} features for class ω_j^* which are linearly independent of class ω_i^*.

5-8-3 Discussion of Linear Independence when Describing Likeness

The probability density functions used in Eq. (44b) for a particular only class must not "jump across" columns or minicolumns (different presentations) of an only class. But the probability density functions can be for any presentation of an only class. This requirement is not difficult to implement. The requirement of linearly independent features is a strong requirement. *Alternatively, if two classes can affect the same feature,* then the probability density function of that feature for the complex class of the two classes needs to be known. Given a complex class, the ways a feature probability density function can differ from the respective feature probability density functions of the classes is discussed next.

5-8-4 Complex Class-Conditional Probability Density Function of a Feature

Suppose that the class-conditional probability density function of feature x_j for only class ω_i^* is

$$g(x_j = x_{j_v} | \omega_i^*), \qquad v = 1,2, \ldots, V. \tag{45}$$

The simplest effect of class ω_j complexed with class ω_i is a transformation of the random variable X_j. Examples are

$$Y_j = a_j X_j + m_j \tag{46a}$$

$$Y_j = a_j (X_j)^2, \tag{46b}$$

where Y_j is a random variable having probability density function

$$p(y_j = y_{j_v} | \Omega_{ij}^*), \qquad v = 1,2, \ldots, V. \tag{47}$$

Using well-known transformation techniques, Eq. (47) can be obtained in terms of Eq. (45) as

$$p(y_j = y_{j_v} | \Omega_{ij}^*) = g\left(\frac{y_j - m_j}{a_j} = y_{j_v} | \omega_i^* \right). \tag{48a}$$

For $Y_j = a_j X_j = m_j$,

$$p(y_j = y_{j_v} | \Omega_{ij}^*) = g\left(\frac{\sqrt{y_j - m_j}}{a_j} = y_{j_v} | \omega_i^* \right). \tag{48b}$$

Letting y_j denote those features in $\mathbf{x}$ for which Eq. (48a) applies, we utilize Eq. (44a) for the other features in conjunction with Eq. (48a) for features y_j to obtain

$$p(\mathbf{x}|\Omega_{ij}^*) = \prod_{m_i \text{ Like } \omega_i} p(x_k|\omega_i^*) \prod_{m_{ji} \text{ Like } \omega_j} p(\mathbf{x}_k|\omega_j^*) \quad g\left(\frac{y_k - m_k}{a_k} |\omega_i^*\right), \tag{49}$$

where

y_k: a feature obeying Eq. (46a) under complex.

5-8-5 Direct Complex Class Knowledge

Of course, conditions more complicated than Eqs. (46a) or (46b) can be imposed such as conditions over multiple features. Some point is reached where the knowledge about a complex class *is "sufficiently complicated" to merit direct training of column(s) and/or minicolumns for that complex class.*

5-9 GENERALIZED COMPLEX CLASS MODEL

The building blocks of a generalized complex class model include the feature values and probabilities of all classes or only classes that contribute to an understanding of the complex class. The respective probabilities are

$$p_{j_v}^c, \; c = {}^*i, {}^*k, i, k, \tag{50}$$

where $^*i$ indicates the ith only class ω_i^*, i the ith class ω_i.

Example $M_1 = 2$

For $M_1 = 2$,

$$p_{j_v}^c = g(p_{j_v}^{*i}, p_{j_v}^{*k}, p_{j_v}^i, p_{j_v}^k) \tag{51}$$

where g is a function to be defined. Possible g's are:

$$p_{j_v}^c = \alpha_{j_i} p_{j_v}^{*i} + b_{j_k} p_{j_v}^{*k} \tag{52a}$$

or

$$p_{j_v}^c = \alpha_{j_i} p_{j_v}^i + b_{j_k} p_{j_v}^k. \tag{52b}$$

Equation (52a) suggests that the complex class probability is a linear combination of respective only class probabilities where, of course, appropriate normalization is achieved by the coefficients. There are applications for which this model can be expected to hold.

5-10 SUSPECTING A COMPLEX CLASS FROM ONLY CLASS KNOWLEDGE

Replace Eq. (52a) by

$$p(x_j = x_{j_v}|\Omega^*_{jk}) = \alpha_{j_i}\, p(x_j = x_{j_v}\,|\omega^*_i) + b_{j_k}\, p(x_j = x_{j_v}|\omega^*_k). \tag{53}$$

Then examine

$$p(\mathbf{x}|\omega^*_i) \quad \text{and} \quad p(\mathbf{x}|\omega^*_k).$$

Define a threshold T_1 such that if

$$p(\mathbf{x}|\omega^*_i) - p(\mathbf{x}|\omega^*_k) > T_1$$

and

$$p(x_j = x_v|\omega^*_i) < T_2$$

$$p(x_j = x_{j_v}|\omega^*_k) > T_2$$

then set

$$\alpha_{j_i} = \emptyset$$

$$b_{j_k} = 1 \tag{54}$$

to form a p.d. at x_{j_v} for the complex class. This indicates that although $\mathbf{x}$ looks like ω^*_i, feature x_j looks like ω^*_k. The alternative that $\mathbf{x}$ looks like ω^*_k but x_j looks more like ω^*_i is also defined.

Let

$$N(\alpha_{j_k}) = \text{Number of } \alpha_{j_k} = 1$$

$$N(b_{j_k}) = \text{Number of } b_{j_k} = 1. \tag{55}$$

A complex class Ω^*_{ik} is suspected to exist if

$$N(\alpha_{j_k}) > N_0 \quad \text{and} \quad N(b_{j_k}) > N_0 \tag{56}$$

for some threshold N_0.

This model for a complex class is one where the feature vector $\mathbf{x}$ looks like only class ω^*_1 with threshold above T_1 but with feature(s) that look like ω^*_2, while at the same time the feature vector $\mathbf{x}$ looks like only class ω^*_2 with threshold above T_2 but with feature(s) that look like ω^*_1.

This model has promise for complex classes where some features are characteristic of ω_1^* while others are characteristic of ω_2^*. Here training only classes can provide information about a complex class without training directly for the complex class.

If Eq. (52b) had been used, then training the classes would provide the knowledge about the complex class. This implies that experience with other complex classes (other than Ω_{ik}^*) which contain ω_i and ω_k is available.

5-11 SUSPECTING AN ONLY CLASS FROM COMPLEX CLASS KNOWLEDGE

Let

$$p(x_j = x_{j_v}|\omega_k^*) = \alpha_{j_c}\, p(x_j = x_{j_v}|\Omega_{ik}^*) + b_{j_i}\, p(x_j + x_{j_v}|\omega_i^*),$$

which is analogous to Eq. (53) and presumes that training is available about a complex class Ω_{ik}^* and an only class ω_i^*. Then examine

$$p(\mathbf{x}|\omega_i^*) \quad \text{and} \quad p(\mathbf{x}|\Omega_{ik}^*).$$

Define a threshold T_1 such that if

$$p(\Omega_{ik}^*|\mathbf{x}) - p(\omega_i^*|\mathbf{x}) > T_1 \tag{57}$$

and

$$p(x_j = x_{j_v}|\omega_i^*) < T_2$$
$$p(x_j = x_{j_v}|\Omega_{ik}^*) > T_2.$$

Then

$$\alpha_{j_c} = 1$$
$$b_{j_c} = \emptyset.$$

This indicates that although $\mathbf{x}$ looks like Ω_{ik}^*, feature x_j does not.

Let

$$N(\alpha_{j_k}) = \text{Number of } \alpha_{j_k} = 1.$$

An only class ω_j^* is suspected to exist if

$$N(\alpha_{j_k}) > N_0$$

for some threshold N_0.

5-11-1 Desirable and Undesirable Feature Sensitivity

Feature sensitivity is a feature property reflecting to what extent a value for that feature can influence the a posteriori category probability. It is motivated by the experimental observation that some features can have "unreasonable" influence.

High Feature Sensitivity is a desirable property when that feature is not correlated with other features. For example, Sex = M, F can sort out two separate presentations of the category. If Sex is not correlated with other features, then this possibly high feature sensitivity is desirable.

Alternately, if a sensitive feature is correlated with one or more other features, then providing for this dependence in a column or minicolumn (see Section 9-15) can properly utilize the feature sensitivity to advantage.

To decrease the sensitivity of a sensitive feature is an alternative which, in effect, is a *smoothing operation.* Errors will be decreased by decreasing feature sensitivity when there is uncorrelated use† of the sensitive feature. Unreasonable fluctuations in the likelihood function will be reduced. Decreasing Feature Sensitivity gives protection against incorrect feature values but can prevent identification of a category with high likelihood.

Feature sensitivity should not be reduced for individual features because of the product effect in the likelihood function. *Rather, reducing feature sensitivity is a property of dependencies among features.* For example, if a pattern looks like a category based on, say, certain primitives being true but then another (other) primitive (Patrick, 1965) is not true, the sensitivity of the primitive(s) not being true could be reduced. Functionals can be defined to adjust a particular feature's sensitivity as a function of other feature likelihoods for the category concerned. *Thus, feature sensitivity is with respect to a particular category and is affected by likelihoods of other features for that category.*

5-12 BINARY CHOICE FORMULATION

Consider an approach where the category space consists of

$$\{\omega_i^*\}_{i=1}^{M}$$

†By uncorrelated use of a sensitive feature we mean that in the presence of actual correlation, the correlation was not engineered into the c.c.p.d.f.

and the objective is to decide ω_i^* vs. $\bar{\omega}_i^*$:

$$\omega_i^* \text{ vs. } \bar{\omega}_i^*: \quad \text{Binary Choice.} \tag{58}$$

This binary choice formulation (see Ben-Bassat *and others,* 1980) is aimed in part at the problem of complex classes. The idea is to focus on ω_i^* and then all other categories.

It is well known that constructing the c.c.p.d.f. of $\bar{\omega}_i^*$ requires knowledge of c.c.p.d.f. for all categories in $\bar{\omega}_i^*$. It is not possible to escape the model of Bayes (without Concept formation) or the model of Patrick (with Concept formation). To learn $\bar{\omega}_i^*$ requires learning about all categories in $\bar{\omega}_i^*$ whether present a priori or by concept formation.

For the binary choice formulation,

$$p(\omega_i^*|\mathbf{x}) = \frac{p(\mathbf{x}|\omega_i^*)\, p(\omega_i^*)}{p(\mathbf{x})}, \tag{59}$$

where

$$p(\mathbf{x}) = p(\mathbf{x}|\omega_i^*)p(\omega_i^*) + p(\mathbf{x}|\bar{\omega}_i^*)p(\bar{\omega}_i^*). \tag{60}$$

The binary mixture (60) is an oversimplication as discussed above.

The binary choice approach was attempted to handle the complex class problem with the idea that it could provide for active multiple classes. The idea was to sort or sift out only class ω_i^* from the "clutter." The normalization constant $p(\mathbf{x})$ in Eq. (60) demonstrates that.

This is presented to emphasize that a "binary choice" formulation does not handle complex classes. Furthermore, we stress that by considering $\bar{\omega}_i^*$, complexity has not been avoided because the function $p(\mathbf{x}|\bar{\omega}_i^*)$ must be considered in terms of conditional probability density functions for all *only classes* in $\bar{\omega}_i^*$, which number $(M_1 - 1)$.

5-13 STRUCTURED MODEL FOR COMPLEX CLASSES

Complex classes were recognized by Habbema in 1976, who limited considerations to features with two values (Binary Features). In the model there are M classes

$$\{\omega_i\}_{i=1}^{M}$$

and L features. Because each feature has two values, there are

$$2^{(M+L)}$$

probabilities to estimate. We will reformulate the work in terms of concepts and notations used in this book. Habbema (1976) proposes a simplifying model where, for class ω_i in the complex class Ω,

$$p(x_j = T|\omega_i, \varepsilon \text{ Complex class}) = p(x_j|\omega_i) \triangleq \Pi_{ji},$$

which provides simplification in that dependence of ω_1 on the complex class is eliminated.

The probability that no class ω_t, $t = 1, 2, \ldots, k$ has feature value x_{j_t}, an event denoted $\bar{x}_{j_t}$, is

$$p(\bar{x}_{j_t}|\Omega^*) = (1 - \Pi_{j_\emptyset}) \prod_{t=1}^{k} (1 - \Pi_{j_t})^{\eta_t}, \tag{61}$$

where

$$\begin{aligned} \eta_t &= 1 \qquad \text{if } \omega_t \ \varepsilon \ \Omega_i \ldots \\ &= \emptyset \qquad \text{otherwise} \end{aligned} \tag{62}$$

and

$$\Pi_{j_\emptyset} = \text{probability of } x_j = T \text{ with no disease.}$$

The term $\Pi_{j_\emptyset}$ in effect adds another class called no disease.† Presumed here is that one class has a feature value for x_j, independent of other classes.

The sought-after result is

$$\begin{aligned} p(x_j = T|\Omega^*) &= 1 - p(\bar{x}_{j_T}|\Omega^*_{i\ldots}) \\ &= 1 - [(1 - \Pi_{j_\emptyset}) \prod_{t=1}^{k} (1 - \Pi_{j_t})^{\eta_t}], \end{aligned} \tag{63}$$

which is the probability for the one remaining class ω_i having feature $x_j = T$. A special case is where the complex class is Ω^*_{123}. Then

$$p(x_j = T|\Omega^*_{123}) = 1 - [(1 - \Pi_{j_\emptyset})(1 - \Pi_{j_1})(1 - \Pi_{j_2})], \tag{64}$$

which is the probability that feature x_j is True given a complex class consisting of ω_1 and ω_2 and the feature is true for class ω_3. This assumes that class ω_3, initially without feature $x_j = T$, acquires $x_j = T$ with probability independent of other classes in the complex.

For L sets of features [all Type 1 (see Section 8-8)] and complex class Ω_{123}, and assuming statistically independent features, we extend Eq. (64) to obtain

---

†If this were an example from medical diagnosis.

$$p(\mathbf{x}|\Omega^*_{123}) = \prod_{j=1}^{L} g(x_j, [(1 - \Pi_{j_\emptyset})(1 - \Pi_{j_1})(1 - \Pi_{j_2})]), \qquad (65)$$

where

$$\begin{aligned} g([\ ]) &= 1 - [\ ], \; x_j = T \\ &= [\ ] \qquad x_j = F. \end{aligned}$$

The careful reader will note similarities between Eq. (65) and the expression with statistically independent classes (Section 5-16-2), Eqs. (77) and (79). The result in Eqs. (77) and (79) is for a complex class model where classes occur independently, with the complex class dependent on both classes, and the features are statistically independent within each class. Presumed is that the binary featue $x_j = T$ is due to only one class in the complex.

A model of this sort can be extended to where various classes in the complex are identified with affecting various features. Effects on features by two or more classes could be identified as *additive,* product, exponential, combinations of these three, etc. An inductive process of forming a complex class model from only class–feature relationships can be postulated. Various induced complex classes can then be tested for their closeness to a recognition sample (likelihood function) with the closest one decided. There is no reason to expect unique generation of complex classes to explain a recognition sample. Certain generated complex classes should be made unacceptable by a priori criteria such as impossible combinations of classes, features not having additive or multiplicative values, possibly by classes. *Complex class packets* can be defined where:

1. Two feature values x_{j_v}, x_{ξ_v} are coupled to two classes.
2. Feature value x_{j_v} cannot be explained by any existing class.
3. Two feature values x_{j_v}, x_{ξ_v} can be explained by no existing class.
4. Classes ω_i and ω_j as a complex class affect pairs of features (x_j, x_k) in a way ( ).

The optimum extension of this last rule is that:

5. Classes ω_i and ω_j as a complex class can affect features $(x_1, x_2, \ldots, x_L)$ in ways (. . .); i.e., form the complex class conditional probability density function $p(\mathbf{x}|\Omega^*_{12})$,

which adds relative frequencies to the ways the features are affected.

5-14 RELATIVE FREQUENCY INTERPRETATION OF THEOREM ON A POSTERIORI PROBABILITY (PATRICK)

5-14-1 Relative Frequency Model

Consider an experiment performed n times; and each time a feature vector $\mathbf{x}$ is observed as are the joint events . . . $(\mathbf{x}, \omega_i^*)$, . . . $(\mathbf{x}, \Omega_\xi^*)$, $\xi = 1, 2, \ldots$. Define

$$\begin{aligned} \hat{P}_{\omega_i^*} &= n_{\omega_i^*}/n \\ \hat{P}_{\Omega_\xi^*} &= n_{\Omega_\xi^*}/n \\ \hat{p}(\mathbf{x}) &= n_{\mathbf{x}}/n \\ \hat{p}(\mathbf{x}, \Omega_\xi^*) &= n_{(\mathbf{x},\, \Omega_\xi^*)}/n \\ \hat{p}(\mathbf{x}, \omega_i^*) &= n_{(\mathbf{x},\, \omega_i^*)}/n. \end{aligned} \tag{66}$$

Then, the likelihood (Patrick), Eq. (8), can be rewritten

$$\hat{P}(\mathbf{x}|\omega_i) = \frac{n_{(\mathbf{x},\omega_i^*)}/n}{\hat{P}(\omega_i)} + \sum_{\omega_i \,\varepsilon\, \Omega_\xi^*} \frac{n_{(\mathbf{x},\Omega_\xi^*)}/n}{\hat{P}(\omega_i^*)} \tag{67}$$

or from Eq. (5)

$$\hat{P}(\omega_i) = n_{\omega_i}^*/n + \sum_{\omega_i \,\varepsilon\, \Omega_\xi^*} n_{\Omega_\xi}^*/n.$$

Equation (67) can be rewritten

$$\hat{p}(\mathbf{x}|\omega_i) = \frac{n_{(\mathbf{x},\, \omega_i^*)} + \sum\limits_{\omega_i \,\varepsilon\, \Omega_\xi^*} n_{(\mathbf{x},\, \Omega_\xi^*)}}{n_{\omega_i^*} + \sum\limits_{\omega_i \,\varepsilon\, \Omega_\xi^*} n_{\Omega_\xi}^*} \tag{68}$$

$$= \frac{\text{Number of times } \mathbf{x} \text{ occurred with } \omega_i^* \text{ or any } \Omega_\xi^* \text{ containing } \omega_i^*}{\text{Number of times } \omega_i^* \text{ occurred or any } \Omega_\xi^* \text{ containing } \omega_i \text{ occurred.}}$$

Various "machines" can be devised to implement such an equation. Various approaches can be taken which include causal networks where "feedback" from "states" affect a class. Equation (68) is an organized way to explain feedback from "states" or "nodes."

5-14-2 Practical Consideration

Considerable attention over the last several decades of decision-making research has been given to what we now can understand as the terms:

$$n_{(\mathbf{x},\omega_i^*)} \text{ and } n_{\omega_i^*}$$

Indeed, the *complex classes* Ω_ξ^* with nonzero relative frequencies $n_{(\mathbf{x},\Omega_\xi^*)}$ may not be known in practice. This suggests the need for ways to obtain $n_{(\mathbf{x},\Omega_\xi^*)}$ indirectly for use in Eq. (68), i.e., not necessarily directly from experiment. A way is to devise models, for example, where $n_{(\mathbf{x},\ \Omega_\xi^*)}$ is a function of relative frequencies for only classes or classes themselves. This will require a new definition of relative frequency to reflect a correlation level because much of the information is in the feature space.

Using the relationship

$$\hat{P}(\mathbf{x},\Omega_\xi^*) = n_{(\mathbf{x},\Omega_;^*} \text{gj)}/n$$

define

$$\hat{p}(\mathbf{x},c_i) = \sum_{\omega_i\ \varepsilon\Omega_\xi^*} \hat{p}(\mathbf{x},\Omega_\xi^*) = \frac{1}{n} \sum_{\omega_i\ \varepsilon\Omega_\xi^*} n_{(\mathbf{x},\Omega_\xi^*)},$$

where c_i is an event of any complex class containing class ω_i.

Assuming that the combined relative frequency of all *complex classes* containing ω_i is equal to the relative frequency of *only* class ω_i^*, Eq. (67) becomes

$$\hat{p}(\mathbf{x}|\omega_i) = \frac{2n_{(\mathbf{x},\omega_i^*)}/n}{\hat{P}(\omega_i)}$$

where

$$\hat{p}(\mathbf{x}_i) = \frac{2n_{\omega_i^*}}{n}$$

This is a special and restrictive example to assist with the relative frequency interpretation of the Likelihood (Patrick). An interpretation is that the feature vector $\mathbf{x}$ updates the class conditional probability density function of a class ω_i whether that sample came from an *only class* ω_i^* or a complex class Ω_ξ^* which contains class ω_i. If that sample came from ω_i^* and a model exists relating a complex class to ω_i, then that complex class also is updated.

Combining the above two equations results in

$$p(\mathbf{x}|\omega_i) = \frac{n_{(\mathbf{x},\omega_i^*)}}{n_{\omega_i^*}}$$

for the special example under consideration.

5-14-3 Partitioning the Feature Vector

Let the feature vector $\mathbf{x}$ consist of three mutually exclusive sets:

$$\mathbf{x} = [\mathbf{x}_A, \mathbf{x}_B, \mathbf{x}_C].$$

Suppose that, in Eq. (67)

$$n_{(\mathbf{x},\omega_i^*)} = n_{(\mathbf{x}_A,.,\ \mathbf{x}_C,\ \omega_i^*)}$$

$$n_{(\mathbf{x},\Omega_\xi^*)} = n_{(.,\ \mathbf{x}_B,\ \mathbf{x}_C,\ \omega_i^*)},$$

where the (.) indicates insignificant features. Insignificant samples are not available for observation.

First, we process samples for ω_i^* obtaining from Eq. (68)

$$\hat{p}(\mathbf{x}|\omega_i) = \frac{n_{(\mathbf{x}_A,\ .\ ,\ \mathbf{x}_C,\ \omega_i^*)}}{n_{\omega_i^*}}$$

because at this time or location, there are no other samples. The a priori probabilities for all complex classes, $p(\Omega_\xi^*)$, are zero at this time or location. The above estimate is the best estimate of the conditional probability density functions for class ω_i and *only class* ω_i^*.

Next, at another time or location, the a priori probabilities of only classes, $p(\omega_i^*)$ are zero; but a priori probability for complex class Ω_ξ^*, $p(\Omega_\xi^*)$, is nonzero. Now, from Eq. (8)

$$p(\mathbf{x}|\omega_i) = p(\mathbf{x}|\Omega_\xi^*)\ \frac{p(\Omega_\xi^*)}{p(\omega_i)}$$

$$= p(\mathbf{x}|\Omega_\xi^*)$$

because of the assumption. Using the above estimate,

$$p(\mathbf{x}|\Omega_\xi^*) = \frac{n_{(\mathbf{x}_A.\ 2.\ .\ \mathbf{x}_C,\ \omega_i^*)}}{n_{\omega_i^*}}$$

or

$$n_{(.,\ \mathbf{x}_B,\ \mathbf{x}_C,\ \omega_i^*)} = n_{(\mathbf{x}_A,\ .\ ,\ \mathbf{x}_C,\ \omega_i^*)}.$$

Previous samples of an only class used to update a class now are being used to update a complex class. The assumptions are:

1. Certain samples are significant for the only class, certain samples for the complex class, and certain samples for both.
2. There is a time or location separation for observing the only class versus the complex class.

In effect, a priori probabilities are being turned on and off, which means the problem is time varying or a feature is carrying a signal for affecting the a priori probabilities.

5-14-3-1 A Priori Category Probabilities that Depend on Feature Values

Consider the special case of the Theorem on A Posteriori Probability (Patrick) when there are no complex classes, i.e., Bayes theorem.

$$p(\omega_i|\mathbf{x}) = \frac{p(\mathbf{x}|\omega_i)p(\omega_i)}{p(\mathbf{x})}, \quad \omega_i = \omega_i^*.$$

Let

$$\mathbf{x} = [\mathbf{x}_A, \mathbf{x}_p],$$

where we name the features in the set $\mathbf{x}_p$ as the population features. Then

$$p(\mathbf{x}|\omega_i) = p(\mathbf{x}_A|\mathbf{x}_p, \omega_i)p(\mathbf{x}_p|\omega_i)$$

and Bayes theorem becomes

$$p(\omega_i|\mathbf{x}) = \frac{p(\mathbf{x}_A|\mathbf{x}_p, \omega_i)}{p(\mathbf{x})} [p(\mathbf{x}_p|\omega_i)p(\omega_i)],$$

where we define

$$p(\omega_i) = p(\mathbf{x}_p|\omega_i)p(\omega_i)$$

as the *population a priori probability.*

The population a priori probability might involve such features in $\mathbf{x}_p$ as:

1. Age
2. Sex

5-14-3-2 Features Not Dependent on Any Other Feature

A population feature does not depend upon another feature. That is, the category presentation does not vary with age, sex, or any other population feature. For example, a category can have a presentation for one age group and a different presentation for another age group.

When features are indeed population features, separating them to form the population probability $P(\omega_i)$ can provide considerable convenience. For example, likelihood can be viewed separately from population probability.

If $\mathbf{x}_p$ *contains appropriate signals, the population probability can be the vehicle for turning on and off a priori probabilities* in the Theorem on A Posteriori Probability (Patrick). Using this procedure, the adaptive nature of time variation is directly incorporated into nature, which is providing the samples.

5-14-4 Complex Class Relative Frequency in Terms of Only-Class Relative Frequency—A Proposition

Suppose that classes ω_i and ω_j have nonzero values for $\hat{P}(\mathbf{x}, \omega_i)$ and $\hat{P}(\mathbf{x}, \omega_j)$, and we assume it just as likely that a complex class exists as not. From construction, it follows that for feature vector $\mathbf{x}$

$$\hat{P}(\mathbf{x},\Omega_{ij}^*) \geq \{\hat{P}(\mathbf{x},\omega_i^*),\ \hat{P}(\mathbf{x},\omega_j^*)\}$$

or

$$\frac{n_{(\mathbf{x},\Omega_{ij}^*)}}{n} \geq \left\{\frac{n_{(\mathbf{x},\ \omega_i^*)}}{n},\ \frac{n_{(\mathbf{x},\ \omega_j^*)}}{n}\right\}$$

This suggests replacing $\geq$ by minimum.

Proposition: If the relative frequency of $\mathbf{x}$ with all *complex classes* Ω_ξ^* containing ω_i equals the relative frequency of $\mathbf{x}$ with ω_i^*, then

$$\hat{p}(\mathbf{x}|\omega_i) = \frac{n_{(\mathbf{x},\omega_i^*)}}{n}$$

and

$$\hat{p}(\mathbf{x}|\Omega_{ij}^*) \geq \left\{\frac{n_{(\mathbf{x},\ \omega_i^*)}}{n},\ \frac{n_{(\mathbf{x},\ \omega_j^*)}}{n}\right\}.$$

5-15 LEARNING A POSTERIORI PROBABILITY IN THE THEOREM (PATRICK)

Equation (9) in Section 5-3 for a posteriori probability of class ω_i is axiomatic, i.e., derived using axioms of probability theory. Learning theory, estimation theory, or statistical pattern recognition has involved the study of probabilities when there are fixed but unknown parameters. In that regard, define:

$\mathbf{b}_i^*$: Set of fixed but unknown parameters characterizing $p(\mathbf{x}|\omega_i^*)$.

$\mathbf{B}_\xi^*$: Set of fixed but unknown parameters characterizing $p(\mathbf{x}|\Omega_\xi^*)$.

The a priori probabilities $p(\omega_i^*)$ and $p(\Omega_\xi^*)$ also are fixed but unknown parameters.

First observe that, if

$$\mathbf{b} = [\{\mathbf{b}_i^*, p(\omega_i^*)\}, \{\mathbf{B}_\xi^*, p(\Omega_\xi^*)\}] \tag{69}$$

is the set of all fixed but unknown parameters, then

$$p(\mathbf{x}|\omega_i,\mathbf{b})$$

is a known† functional, whereas $p(\mathbf{x}\,|\omega_i)$ is unknown unless all parameters characterizing it are known. Let $\mathbf{y}_1, \mathbf{y}_2, \ldots, \mathbf{y}_n = \dot{\mathbf{y}}_n$ be a set of statistically independent vector samples from $p(\mathbf{x}|\omega_i)$. Then we note the following theorem

Learning Theorem (Patrick) for Class Conditional Probability Density

$$p(\mathbf{x}|\omega_i\dot{\mathbf{y}}_n) = \int p(\mathbf{x}|\omega_i,\mathbf{b})p(\mathbf{b}|\dot{\mathbf{y}}_n)\, d\mathbf{b}. \tag{70}$$

Proof:

1. $p(\mathbf{x}|\omega_i,\dot{\mathbf{y}}_n) = \int p(\mathbf{x},\mathbf{b}|\omega_i,\dot{\mathbf{y}}_n)d\mathbf{b}$
   because **b** is a vector introduced and then integrated out, a mathematical manipulation.
2. $p(\mathbf{x},\mathbf{b}|\omega_i,\dot{\mathbf{y}}_n) = p(\mathbf{x}|\mathbf{b},\omega_i,\dot{\mathbf{y}}_n)\, p(\mathbf{b}|\dot{\mathbf{y}}_n)$
   follows from conditional probability.
3. $p(\mathbf{x}|,\mathbf{b},\omega_i,\dot{\mathbf{y}}_n) = p(\mathbf{x}|\mathbf{b},\omega_i)$
   because by definition $p(\mathbf{x}|\omega_i)$ is completely characterized by **b**.

The theorem is proven.

---

†When we write $p(\mathbf{x}|\omega_i)$ we must realize that it is characterized by parameters in **b**. If **b** is not known, it must be learned.

Applying Eq. (70) to the expression for the Likelihood (Patrick) [Eq. (8)], there results

$$p(\mathbf{x}|\omega_i,\dot{\mathbf{y}}_n) =$$

$$\left[\int p(\mathbf{x}|\mathbf{b}_i^*)\ p(\omega_i^*)\ p(\mathbf{b}|\dot{\mathbf{y}}_n)d\mathbf{b}\right] * \frac{1}{p(\omega_i)} +$$

$$\left[\sum_{\omega_i \in \Omega_\xi} \int p(\mathbf{x}|\mathbf{B}_\xi^*,\Omega_\xi^*)\ p(\Omega_\xi^*)\ p(\mathbf{b}|\dot{\mathbf{y}}_n)d\mathbf{b}\right] * \frac{1}{p(\omega_i)}. \tag{71}$$

The vector samples $\mathbf{y}_1, \mathbf{y}_2, \ldots, \mathbf{y}_n$ are assumed statistically independent and identically distributed from probability density function $p(\mathbf{x}|\omega_i)$. From the Likelihood (Patrick) we see that some of these samples can be from only class ω_i^* while others are from complex classes. The occurrence of the mix of samples depends upon the mixing parameters $p(\omega_i^*)$ and $\{p(\Omega_\xi^*)\}$. At stage n, the class conditional probability density function $p(\mathbf{x}|\omega_i)$ is at some stage of learning.

It is inescapable that some models have been used for the families of probability density functions, those for complex classes being different from those for only classes. These models correspond to probability density functions that can be characterized by parameters.

Suppose that at stage n supervised training has led to estimation of the class conditional probability density function for an only class ω_i^* and thus likewise for ω_i, through Eq.(8) with no complex classes active. Then suppose that we are able to determine that estimation of $p(\mathbf{x}|\omega_i)$ begins to differ after stage n. With the constraint that all additional training samples are from class ω_i, it follows that

$$p(\mathbf{x}|\omega_i,\mathbf{y}_{n+n_i}) - p(\mathbf{x}|\omega_i,\mathbf{y}_n)$$

is an estimate for the conditional probability density function of the complex classes, where n_i is the number of additional samples. This is stated loosely in the following proposition.

Proposition: Samples supervised from an only class used to estimate the conditional probability density function of a class provide the template against which to compare the later stage estimate of conditional probability density function of the class. The difference between the template and later stage estimate is an estimate of the conditional probability of complex classes. In general, the conditional probability density function of complex classes is a mixture to which the techniques of unsupervised estimation must be applied.

Proposition: A mixture of complex classes can be unmixed by the method of the above proposition.

The changing sample presentations with time (stages) provides a teacher with which to apply the scientific method to solve unsupervised learning problems. Without a teacher or otherwise sufficient a priori knowledge, the solution is impossible.

5-16 CONSULT-I® LIKELIHOOD FUNCTION FEEDBACK SYSTEM

5-16-1 Interpretation for a Special Example

The theorem on a posteriori probability (by Patrick) where the decision space consists of *only classes* and complex classes states that

$$p(\omega_i|\mathbf{x}) = p(\omega_i^*|\mathbf{x}) + \sum_{\omega_i \varepsilon \Omega_\xi} p(\Omega_\xi^*|\mathbf{x}). \tag{72}$$

Because

$$p(\mathbf{x},\omega_i) = p(\mathbf{x},\omega_i^*) + \sum_{\Omega_\xi^* \ni \omega_i \varepsilon \Omega_\xi^*} p(\mathbf{x},\Omega_\xi^*),$$

it follows that

$$p(\mathbf{x}|\omega_i) = p(\mathbf{x}|\omega_i^*)\,\frac{p(\omega_i^*)}{p(\omega_i)} + \sum_{\omega_i\,\varepsilon\Omega_\xi^*} \frac{P(\Omega_\xi^*)}{P(\omega_i)}. \tag{73}$$

In practice, training usually is available to construct or estimate $p(\mathbf{x}|\omega_i^*)$. The conditional probability density function for complex classes $p(\mathbf{x}|\Omega_\xi^*)$ must be estimated directly, formed through an inductive learning session, obtained deductively through a model. We will utilize the latter approach to develop a feedback interpretation of Eq.(73) from the engineering standpoint.

5-16-2 Features Statistically Independent for a Class and Classes Independent for *Complex Class*

Denote the classes in *complex class* Ω_ξ^* as

$$\{\omega_{\xi_w}\}_{w=1}^{N(\xi)}, \tag{74}$$

where $N(\xi)$ is the number of classes in complex class Ω_{ξ_w}. Define

$$\begin{aligned} \delta_{j_{\xi_w}}(y) &= y, \qquad \text{feature } j \text{ significant for class } \omega_{\xi_w} \\ &= 1, \qquad \text{otherwise.} \end{aligned} \tag{75}$$

Then the class conditional probability density function for class ω_{ξ_w} is

$$p(\mathbf{x}|\omega_{\xi_w}) = \prod_{j=1}^{L} \delta_{j_{\xi_w}}(p(x_j|\omega_{\xi_w})), \tag{76}$$

where the features $\{x_j\}$ are assumed statistically independent for class ω_{ξ_w} (not a necessary assumption). *Invoking an assumption that functions* $p(\mathbf{x}|\omega_{\xi_w})$ *are multiplied together for respective classes* $\{\omega_{\xi_w}\}$ *in complex class* Ω_ξ^* *to produce the complex class* Ω_ξ^* *we obtain*

$$p(\mathbf{x}|\Omega_\xi^*) = \prod_{\omega_{\xi_w} \varepsilon \Omega_\xi^*} \prod \delta_{j_{\xi_w}}(p(x_j|\omega_{\xi_w})). \tag{77}$$

Although this is a specific model and may appear restrictive, the result will aid in understanding other models. This model presumes that events $(\mathbf{x}, \omega_{\xi_w})$ are statistically independent in forming the complex class.

The model becomes precise when each feature x_j is significant for only one class.

Next denote by

$$\{\Omega_{i_\xi}^*\}_{\xi=1}^{E(i)} \tag{78}$$

all *complex classes* containing class ω_i, where $E(i)$ is the number of such complex classes. It is convenient to extract $p(\mathbf{x}|\omega_i)$ from Eq. (77) for ξ and i_ξ to obtain

$$p(\mathbf{x}|\Omega_{i_\xi}^*) = \left[\prod_{\omega_{\xi_w} \varepsilon [\Omega_{i_\xi}^* - \omega_i]} \prod_{j=1}^{L} \delta_{j_{\xi_w}}(p(x_j|\omega_{\xi_w})) \right] p(\mathbf{x}|\omega_i) \tag{79}$$

$$\triangleq C(i_\xi, i) p(\mathbf{x}|\omega_i) \frac{P(\omega_i)}{p(\Omega_\xi^*)}, \tag{80}$$

where

$$C(i, i) = \quad [\;] \frac{P(\Omega_\xi^*)}{P(\omega_i)} .$$

Equation (79) or (80) is the *complex class* conditional probability density function for the ξth complex class containing ω_i, $\Omega^*_{i_\xi}$ under the assumption stated, and

$$C(i_\xi, i) = \left[\prod_{\omega_{\xi_w} \varepsilon [\Omega^*_{i_\xi - \omega i}]} \prod_{j=1}^{L} \delta_{j_{\xi_w}} (p(x_j|\omega_{\xi_w}) \right] \frac{p(\Omega^*_\xi)}{p(\omega_i)} \cdot \qquad (81)$$

Define

$$C(i, i) \triangleq \frac{p(\omega^*_i)}{p(\omega_i)}$$

for the coupling of only class ω^*_i to $p(\mathbf{x}|\Omega^*_{i_\xi})$.

5-16-3 Feedback System Interpretation

Substituting Eq. (78) and the definities $C(i, i)$ into Eq. (73) results in

$$p(\mathbf{x}|\omega_i) = C(i, i)p(\mathbf{x}|\omega^*_i) + \sum_{\omega_i \, \varepsilon \, \Omega^*_{i_\xi}} C(i_\xi, i)p(\mathbf{x}|\omega_i). \qquad (82)$$

Rearranging terms in Eq. (82) gives

$$p(\mathbf{x}|\omega_i) = \frac{C(i, i)p(\mathbf{x}|\omega^*_i)}{\left[1 - \sum_{\omega_i \, \varepsilon \, \Omega^*_{i_\xi}} C(i_\xi, i) \right]} \cdot \qquad (83)$$

Note from Eq. (80) that $C(i_\xi, i)$ is calculated from sets of

$$\{p(\mathbf{x}|\omega_{\xi_w})\}_{\omega_{\xi_w} \varepsilon \Omega^*_{i_\xi}}.$$

There are $i = 1, 2, \ldots, M_1$ feedback systems of the form Eq. (83) with interconnecting of the outputs to the terms in $C(i_\xi, i)$. This is diagrammed in Figure 5.6.

An expression for $p(\mathbf{x}|\Omega^*_\xi)$ is obtained after substituting Eq. (83) into Eq. (77).

Thus, starting with the *only class* conditional probability density functions $\{p(\mathbf{x}|\omega^*_i)\}$, the *complex class* conditional probability density functions $\{p(\mathbf{x}|\Omega^*_\xi)\}$ are generated, with the class conditional probability density functions $p(\mathbf{x}|\omega_i)$ generated as an intermediate step.

The practical limitations of this result are that features are assumed statistically independent in Eq. (76) and the complex class model is a product as in Eq. (77). This does not provide for complex

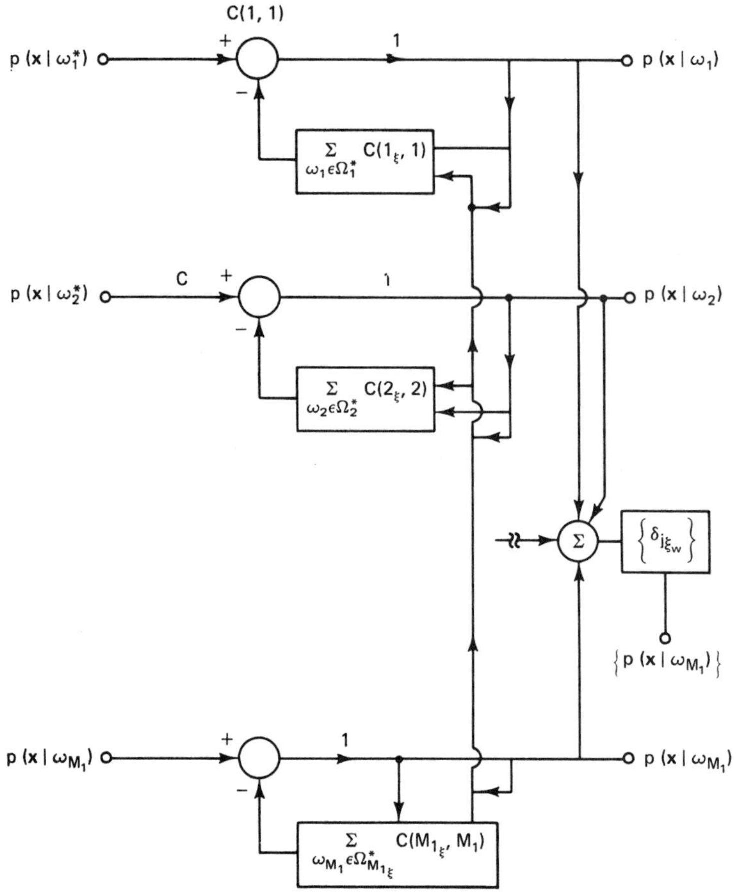

FIGURE 5.6. Generation of classes and *complex classes* from *only classes.*

class formation through statistical dependence among only classes and does not provide for a complex class of likeness or unlikeness to only classes. However, theoretically it shows feedback from complex classes in determining those classes which form complex classes.

This is not concept formation by example but is learning concepts by deduction using models. The model does not involve regions of significance and insignificance in the feature space of only classes as is done elsewhere in this book, resulting in practical complex class generation.

5-16-4 State Interpretation

Depending on the method of processing, the system in Figure 5.6 is at a particular state. The final state is achieved where the $\{p(\mathbf{x}|\omega_i^*)\}_{i=1}^{M_1}$ are all available and input to the system. Otherwise, the system is at some other state based on incomplete information.

5-16-5 Iterative Feedback Interpretation

Given a next feature x_r where $\mathbf{x}_{r-1}$ has been previously processed, the class conditional probability density function for class ω_i is

$$p(\mathbf{x}|\omega_i) = p(x_r|\mathbf{x}_{r-1}, \omega_i)p(\mathbf{x}_{r-1}|\omega_i) = p(x_r|\omega_i)p(\mathbf{x}_{r-1}|\omega_i) \tag{84}$$

$$= p(x_r|\omega_i^*)p(\mathbf{x}_{r-1}|\omega^*_i)\frac{p(\omega_i^*)}{p(\omega_i)} + \sum_{\omega_i \in \Omega_\xi^*} p(x_r|\Omega_\xi^*)$$

$$p(\mathbf{x}_{r-1}|\Omega_\xi^*)\frac{p(\Omega_\xi^*)}{p(\omega_i)} \tag{85}$$

For class ω_{ξ_w} in complex class Ω_ξ^*, invoke again the model assuming features statistically independent for a class:

$$p(\mathbf{x}_r|\omega_{\xi_w}) = \prod_{j=1}^{L} \delta_{j_{\xi_w}} (p(x_r|\omega_{\xi_w})p(\mathbf{x}_{r-1}| \omega_{\xi_w})). \tag{86}$$

The *complex class* conditional probability density function for Ω_ξ^* is

$$p(\mathbf{x}_r|\Omega_\xi^*) = \prod_{\omega_{\xi_w} \in \Omega_\xi^*} \prod_{j=1}^{r} \delta_{j_{\xi_w}} (p(x_j|\omega_{\xi_w})) =$$

$$\left[\prod_{\omega_{\xi_w} \in [\Omega_{i_\xi}^* - \omega_i]} \prod_{j=1}^{r} \delta_{j_{\xi_w}} (p(x_j|\omega_{\xi_w})) \right] p(x_r|\omega_i)p(\mathbf{x}_{r-1}|\omega_r)$$

$$\triangleq \left[C(i_\xi, i; \mathbf{x}_{r-1}) \prod_{\omega_{\xi_w} \in [\Omega_{i_\xi}^* - \omega_i]} \delta_{r_{\xi_w}} (p(x_r|\omega_{\xi_w})) \right] p(x_r|\omega_i)p(\mathbf{x}_r - 1|\omega_i)$$

$$= [C(i_\xi, i; \mathbf{x}_{r-1})p(\mathbf{x}_{r-1}|\omega_i)]\ [C(i_\xi, i; x_r)p(x_r|\omega_i)]. \tag{87}$$

Thus,

$$p(\mathbf{x}_r|\omega_i) = p(x_r|\omega_i)p(\mathbf{x}_{r-1}|\omega_i) =$$
$$C(i, i)p(\mathbf{x}_{r-1}|\omega_i^*)\ p(x_r|\omega_i) +$$
$$\sum_{\omega_i \in \Omega_\xi^*} [C(i_\xi, i; \mathbf{x}_{r-1})p(\mathbf{x}_{r-1}|\omega_i)]\ [C(i_\xi, i; x_r)p(x_r|\omega_i)] \tag{88}$$

or, rearranging terms,

$$p(x_r|\omega_i)p(\mathbf{x}_{r-1}|\omega_i)\left[1 - \sum_{\omega_i \in \Omega_\xi^*} C(i_\xi, i; \mathbf{x}_{r-1})C(i_\xi, \text{i}; x_r)\right]$$
$$= C(i, i)p(\mathbf{x}_r|\omega_i^*)\ p(\mathbf{x}_{r-1}|\omega_i^*) \tag{89}$$

such that

$$p(x_r|\omega_i)p(\mathbf{x}_{r-1}|\omega_i) = \frac{C(i, i)p(x_r|\omega_i^*)\ p(\mathbf{x}_{r-1}|\omega_i^*)}{\left[1 - \sum_{\omega_i \in \Omega_\xi^*} C(i_\xi, i; \mathbf{x}_{r-1})C(i_\xi, i; x_r)\right]} \tag{90}$$

Presuming that $p(x_{r-1}|\omega_i^*)$ and $\{C(i_\xi, i; \mathbf{x}_{r-1})\}$ $\omega_i \in \Omega_\xi^*$ have been computed and stored at stage $r - 1$, updating utilizing feature value x_r can be achieved as illustrated in Figure 5.7, utilizing $p(\mathbf{x}_r|\omega_i^*)$ and $\{C(i_\xi, i; x_r)\}$.

Stored at Stage $r-1$:
$p(\mathbf{x}_{r-1}|\omega_i^*)$
$\{C(i_\xi, i; \mathbf{x}_{r-1})\}$
At Stage r:
$\{C(i_\xi, i; x_r)\}$ obtained from feedback systems $\{i_\xi\}$.

5-17 FIRST-ORDER PRODUCT MODEL FOR COMPLEX CATEGORY

Remove one complex category Ω_ξ^* from the Σ in Eq. (72) and rewrite Eq. (72) as follows:

$$p(\mathbf{x}, \omega_i) = p(\mathbf{x}, \omega_i^*) + \sum_{\omega_i \in \Omega_\xi} p(\mathbf{x}, \Omega_\xi^*)$$
$$= p(\mathbf{x}, \omega_i^*) + \sum_{\substack{\omega_i \in \Omega_\xi^* \\ \Omega_\xi^* \neq \Omega_\eta^*}} p(\mathbf{x}, \Omega_\xi^*) + p(\mathbf{x}, \Omega_\eta^*) \tag{91}$$

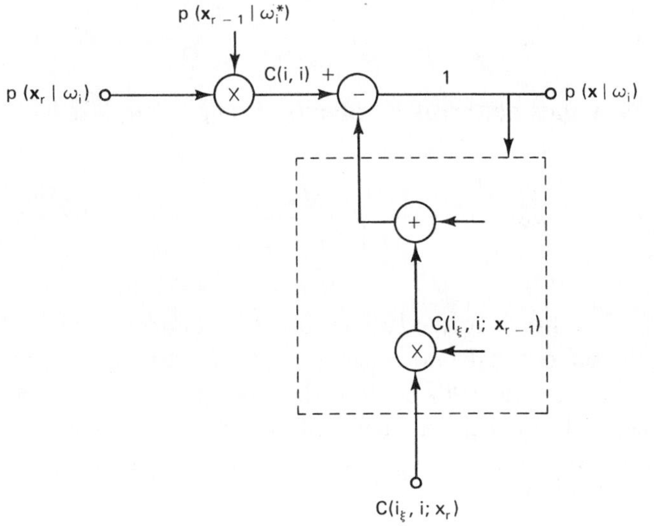

FIGURE 5.7. Iterative feedback interpretation.

Note that

$$p(\mathbf{x}, \Omega^*_\mu) = p(\mathbf{x}, \Omega^*_\eta\ \bar{\omega}_i) \tag{92a}$$

$$p(\mathbf{x}, \Omega^*_\eta) = p(\mathbf{x}, \Omega^*_\mu, \omega_i), \tag{92b}$$

where Ω^*_η is the removed complex class and Ω^*_μ is that complex class modified not to contain class ω_i. Assume a model

$$p(\mathbf{x}, \Omega^*_\eta) = p(\mathbf{x}, \omega_i)p(\mathbf{x}, \Omega^*_\mu). \tag{93}$$

This model imposes the single assumption that class ω_i affects the complex class event $(\mathbf{x}, \Omega^*_\eta)$ in a statistically independent manner. Substituting Eq. (93) in Eq. (91) and gathering terms involving $p(\mathbf{x}, \omega_i)$ to the left-hand side results in

$$p(\mathbf{x}, \omega_i)[1 - p(\mathbf{x}, \Omega^*_\mu)] = p(\mathbf{x}, \omega^*_i) + \sum_{\substack{\omega_i \in \Omega^*_\xi \\ \Omega^*_\xi \neq \Omega^*_\eta}} p(\mathbf{x}, \Omega^*_\xi)$$

or

$$p(\mathbf{x}, \omega_i) = \frac{p(\mathbf{x}, \omega^*_i) + \sum\limits_{\substack{\omega_i \in \Omega^*_\xi \\ \Omega^*_\xi \neq \Omega^*_\eta}} p(\mathbf{x}, \Omega^*_\xi)}{[1 - p(\mathbf{x}, \Omega^*_\mu)]} \tag{94}$$

Let

$$p(\mathbf{x}, \Omega^*_{\eta e}) = p(\mathbf{x}\ \omega_i)p(\mathbf{x}, \Omega^*_{\mu_e})$$

and repeatedly gather terms involving $p(\mathbf{x}\omega_i^*)$ to the left-hand side, obtaining

$$p(\mathbf{x}, \omega_i) = \frac{p(\mathbf{x}, \omega_i^*)}{\prod_e [1 - p(\mathbf{x}, \Omega^*_{\mu_e})]} \tag{95}$$

Equation (95) is the sought-after result. For a two-class example below the category space consists of ω_1^*, ω_2^*, and Ω^*_{ij} and Eq. (95) simplifies to the two Eqs. (96a) and (96b). Note that as $p(\mathbf{x}, \omega_j)$ increases, then $p(\mathbf{x}, \omega_i)$ decreases. Given training for only classes ω_i^* and ω_j^*, the equation can be solved for $p(\mathbf{x}, \omega_i)$ and $p(\mathbf{x}, \omega_j)$. In turn, $p(\mathbf{x}, \Omega^*_{ij}) = p(\mathbf{x}, \omega_i)p(\mathbf{x}, \omega_j)$ according to Eq. (93).

Example:

$$M_1 = 2$$

$$p(\mathbf{x}, \omega_i) = \frac{p(\mathbf{x}, \omega_i^*)}{[1 - p(\mathbf{x}, \omega_j)]} \tag{96a}$$

$$p(\mathbf{x}, \omega_j) = \frac{p(\mathbf{x}, \omega_j^*)}{[1 - p(\mathbf{x}, \omega_i)]} \tag{96b}$$

and from Eq. (83)

$$p(\mathbf{x}, \Omega^*_{ij}) = p(\mathbf{x}, \omega_i)p(\mathbf{x}, \omega_j). \tag{96c}$$

5-18 THEOREM ON A POSTERIORI PROBABILITY (PATRICK) WITH CONCEPT FORMATION THROUGH STATISTICALLY DEPENDENT CATEGORIES

5-18-1 Mixtures and Bayes Inference for Learning without a Teacher

Previous work in concept formation involved Bayes inference (Patrick, 1965; Fralick, 1967; Patrick *and others,* 1967, 1970, 1974, 1975) based on mixtures also studied by Robbins (1948), Teicher (1960, 1963), Yakowitz (1969), and Spragins (1966).

Patrick (1972) developed the parameter conditional mixture

$$p(\mathbf{x}|\mathbf{b}) = \sum_{i=1}^{M_1} p(\mathbf{x}|\omega_i^*, \mathbf{b}_i)P_i, \tag{97a}$$

where categories $\{\omega_i^*\}$ are mutually exclusive, category ω_i^* is characterized by $\mathbf{b}_i$ and mixing parameter P_i, and

$$\mathbf{b} \triangleq [\mathbf{b}_1, \mathbf{b}_2, \ldots, \mathbf{b}_{M_1}, P_1, P_2, \ldots, P_{M_1}]. \tag{97b}$$

Given samples $\mathbf{x}_1, \mathbf{x}_2, \ldots, \mathbf{x}_n$, when can Eq. (97a) be uniquely resolved solving for the terms in $\mathbf{b}$? The answer is that it can when the family of c.c.p.d.f.'s are linearly independent.

An iterative form for learning $\mathbf{b}$ is

$$p(\mathbf{b}|\mathbf{x}_1, \mathbf{x}_2, \ldots, \mathbf{x}_n) = \frac{\sum_{i=1}^{M_1} p(\mathbf{x}_n|\omega_i^*, \mathbf{b}_i)P_i}{p(\mathbf{x}_n|\mathbf{x}_1, \mathbf{x}_2, \ldots, \mathbf{x}_{n-1})} p(\mathbf{b}|\mathbf{x}_1, \mathbf{x}_2, \ldots, \mathbf{x}_{n-1}) \tag{97c}$$

The term in the numerator in the right-hand side of Eq. (97c) is the conventional mixture. There is no provision in this Bayes inference for forming new categories Ω_ξ^*, which are in some way like or dislike the categories

$$\omega_1^*, \omega_2^*, \ldots, \omega_{M_1}^*.$$

5-18-2 Concept Formation Using the Theorem on A Posteriori Probability (Patrick)

The theorem on a posteriori probability by Patrick provides for more extensive inference than does Bayes theorem.

The mixture in the theorem by Patrick has the form,

$$p(\mathbf{x}|\mathbf{b}) = \sum_{i=1}^{M_1} p(\mathbf{x}|\omega_i^*, \mathbf{b})P_i + \sum_{\xi=1}^{M_2} p(\mathbf{x}|\Omega_\xi^*, \mathbf{b}_\xi)P_\xi, \tag{98a}$$

as compared with Eq. (97a) for Bayes.

For the theorem by Patrick, parameters in $\mathbf{b}$ are

$$\begin{aligned}\mathbf{b} = [&\mathbf{b}_1, \mathbf{b}_2, \ldots, \mathbf{b}_{M_1}; \mathbf{b}_{M_1+1}, \ldots, \mathbf{b}_{M_1+M2};\\ &P_1, \ldots, P_{M_1}; P_{M_1+1}, \ldots, P_{M_1+M_2}]\end{aligned} \tag{98b}$$

The inference function for **b** using the theorem by Patrick is

$$p(\mathbf{b}|\mathbf{x}_1,\ldots,\mathbf{x}_n) = \left[\frac{\sum_{i=1}^{M_1} p(\mathbf{x}|\omega_i^*,\mathbf{b}_i)P_i + \sum_{\xi=1}^{M_2} p(\mathbf{x}|\Omega_\xi^*,\mathbf{b}_\xi)P_\xi,}{p(\mathbf{x}_n|\mathbf{x}_1,\ldots,x_{n-1})}\right] p(\mathbf{b}|\mathbf{x}_1,\ldots,\mathbf{x}_{i-1}). \tag{98c}$$

In the theorem by Patrick there are additional expressions to be used with Eq. (98c). At stage $(n - 1)$ there exists the iterative expression

$$p(\mathbf{x}_n, \Omega_\xi^*|\mathbf{b}_\xi, \mathbf{x}_1,\ldots,\mathbf{x}_{n-1}) = g_\xi(\{p(\mathbf{x},\omega_i|\mathbf{x}_1,\ldots,\mathbf{x}_{n-2},\mathbf{b})\}_{i=1}^{M_1}) \tag{98d}$$

for the complex class Ω_ξ^*.

Inserting Eq.(98d) into Eq. (98a) and letting **x** be $\mathbf{x}_n$, we get

$$p(\mathbf{x}_\mathrm{n}|\mathbf{b}), \mathbf{x}_1,\ldots,\mathbf{x}_{\,\mathrm{n}-1}) = \sum_{i=1}^{M_1} p(\mathbf{x}_n|\omega_i^*, \mathbf{b}_i, \mathbf{x}_1,\ldots,\mathbf{x}_{n-1})P_i + \sum_{\xi=1}^{M_2} g_\xi\,(\{p(\mathbf{x},\omega_i|\mathbf{x}_1,\ldots,\mathbf{x}_{n-2},\mathbf{b}\}_{i=1}^{M_2})P_\xi. \tag{99}$$

Substituting Eq. (98d) into Eq. (98c) results in

$$p(\mathbf{b}|\mathbf{x}_1,\ldots,\mathbf{x}_n) = \left[\sum_{i=1}^{M_1} p(\mathbf{x}_n|\omega_i^*,\mathbf{b}_i)P_i + \sum_{\xi=1}^{M_2} g_\xi(p(\mathbf{x}_n, \omega_i|\mathbf{x}_1,\ldots,\mathbf{x}_{n-2})_{i=1}^{M_1})P_\xi\right] * \frac{p(\mathbf{b}|\mathbf{x}_1,\ldots,\mathbf{x}_{n-1})}{p(\mathbf{x}_n|\mathbf{x}_1,\ldots,\mathbf{x}_{n-1})} \tag{100}$$

Equation (98d) illustrates the dynamic concept formation in the theorem on a posteriori probability by Patrick. This concept formation does not exist in the theorem by Bayes.

Equation (100) is the interactive expression for learning parameters in **b**. The numerator on the right-hand side of Eq. (100) involves the c.c.p.d.f.'s for only classes $\{\omega_i^*\}$ and complex classes $\{\Omega_\xi^*\}$. The c.c.p.d.f.'s for the complex classes $\{\Omega_\xi^*\}$ at stage n have a *family structure* determined at stage $n-1$. This construction of changing a family structure during iteration exists in the theorem by Patrick but not in the theorem by Bayes.

In Eq. (100), there are sets of learning sessions prior to stage n. A particular special case is where supervised training sessions (learning with a teacher) are used during the iteration to learn the c.c.p.d.f.s of only classes. The c.c.p.d.f.'s for complex classes are constructed through functions g_ξ. After this, Eq. (100) could be used with unsupervised samples for learning or recognition.

This illustrates how a certain amount of a priori knowledge must be introduced in order to learn without a teacher. Supervised training sessions are used in the theorem by Patrick to learn about only classes prior to forming more complex concepts.

6

Engineering Hierarchical Knowledge Structures

6-1 INTRODUCTION

For classification problems about which this book deals, the highest level of inference are categories (or actions appropriate for the categories or subcategories) in a system. The goal is to be able to recognize a category given its feature values and take an appropriate action. The lowest level in the hierarchical structure are the features (with feature values). Because of possible uncertainties, the goal is redefined as computing the a posteriori probabilities or likelihoods of the categories in the system, or a top-ranking focus of categories.

It is recognized that at this highest level, the theorem on a posteriori probability by Patrick applies and there are both classes and categories (only classes and complex classes). It further is recognized that features (with feature values) are the lowest level in the hierarchy. There are different types of features (Type Ø, Type 1 complex and other complex features) corresponding to whether feature values are mutually exclusive, binary embedded, complex with $F \rightarrow F$ relationships, and so on.

Many researchers have realized that there can be a complex relationship from the lowest level to highest level in such a hierarchy. There are an infinite number of such relationships but fortunately the field of knowledge imposes constraints on the possible relationships. For example, in medical diagnosis and treatment, anatomy and physiology impose $F \rightarrow F$-type relationships. Pathology, internal medicine and pediatrics impose $F \rightarrow H$-type relationships. Clearly, these latter $F \rightarrow H$-type relationships are uncertain and learning by example from prospective studies can be expected to improve this knowledge. A model is needed to capture this knowledge at various levels.

In medicine, for instance, values for signs, symptoms, and lab tests are at the lowest level. But a symptom such as pain cannot be described by a single feature and, therefore, various models of complex features can be proposed. Even so, the ability to convert a particular complaint of pain to a complex feature, capturing the inference ability of an expert physician, is difficult *because the expert physician can hear and see the patient and therefore infer a more complex feature than can a computer without hearing and vision.*

There is not one model for the hierarchy, but it depends upon the problem. For example, in medicine both a total system model and a subsystem model have application.

6-2 LITERATURE REVIEW

An early model relating features to categories is the Perceptron of Rosenblatt presented in 1958, often criticized because of its lack of structure. The idea was to input many examples from a category, with the hope that resulting interconnections could produce discrimination to distinguish that category from others. It was an idea that had to be tried! Studies in statistical pattern recognition during the 1960s showed why the perceptron was not adequate and in 1972 Patrick proposed integrating statistical pattern recognition with artificial intelligence as a way to introduce both statistical knowledge and problem knowledge.

Hierarchical structure in the form of a network of subsystems was suggested by Patrick in 1969. This was elaborated on in 1975 by Patrick and Shen (1975) and Patrick, Stelmack, and Garrett (1975). In the latter publication classes, subclasses, features, and complex features were defined. In medicine, a complex class is where multiple diseases can be active at the same time. Structures consisting of networks, trees, and causal networks were discussed by Patrick in 1979. Patrick (1972) suggested the expert system integrating artificial intelligence with statistical pattern recognition in "A Priori Problem Knowledge and Training Samples," *Frontiers of Pattern Recognition.*

Psychological researchers Anderson and Bower (1973) defined a network structure intended to model long-term memory, which is a form of a complex feature. Minsky in 1975 defined *frames,* which is a form of complex feature; it was also studied by researchers including Jourbert *and others* in 1983. Brodie *and others* (1984) discuss relational data bases and network structures. A discussion of hierarchical knowledge representation for describing control tasks is found in Rasmussen (1985).

In 1983 Blois distingished between the science and art of medicine, indicating that science deals with "universal" properties while art deals with the uniqueness of individual patients. He feels medical science deals with the properties which all patients share while the art of medicine deals with the ways in which patients, even with the same disease, differ. He feels that we are increasingly diagnosing and treating diseases at the generalized level. This suggests that a hierarchical model should capture as much medical science as needed for quality diagnosis and treatment. An upshot is not to try to capture too much knowledge.

The new theorem on a posteriori probability in 1983 by Patrick shows the relationship between classes, complex classes, and only classes; and it sets the stage for a new hierarchical model of a posteriori probability explaining ad hoc methods such as **CASNET** and **EXPERT** (Kulikowski and Weiss, 1982).

Pople (1982) considered a hierarchical structure bearing considerable similarity to that of Patrick, Shen, and Stelmack (1974). Pople defined operations in the network consisting of subclassification specification, subclassification interaction, causal specialization, and causal intersection.

6-3 CASNET AND EXPERT

In this section we take a closer look at the **CASNET/EXPERT** project (Kulikowski and Weiss, 1982; Weiss and Kulikowski, 1984; Kastner and others, 1984; Kulikowski, 1983) to show its place in artificial intelligence and statistical pattern recognition. First, it is a subsystem approach which attempts to separate the disease knowledge base from decision-making strategies. We recognize that there are three levels in ascending order as features, complex features, and categories.

To construct an inference, the following rules are used:

1. *F–F Rules:* These involve (cause) that one feature depends on another feature (effect). *F–F* rules are analogous to frames and complex features and columns in **CONSULT-I®**. The *F–F* rule is represented

$$f_i \rightarrow f_j,$$

but values for f have been limited to binary values.

2. *F–H Rules:* Suppose a *conjunction of findings* is true for a patient, $B(\{f_i\})$; then

$$B(\{f_i\}) \xrightarrow{W_j} h_j$$

means that hypothesis h_j is true with weight W_j.

Alternatively, a *disjunctive form* is "if *n* of the following findings have been specified true values, infer the following hypothesis." A Type-1 complex feature in **CONSULT-I®** can have this disjunctive facility. The conjunction facility is not only present in a complex feature of **CONSULT-I®** but throughout any given column for a category.

3. *H–H Rules.* Context of a pattern is presumed recognized if two or more hypotheses about that pattern are true. The rule

$$B(\{f_i, h_j\}) \xrightarrow{W_k} h_k$$

indicates that with hypothesis h_j true and finding f_i we know hypothesis h_k is true with certainty W_i. CASSNET/EXPERT modules are not aware of only classes and complex classes as in **CONSULT-I®**. But the above *H–H* rule could be considered for generating only classes or complex classes.

Ultimate hypothesis generation is achieved by combining *F–H* rules and *H–H* rules. The methods of combining are guided by the strong theories of statistical pattern recognition although not specifically stated by the authors (Kulikowski and Weiss, 1982).

6-4 HIERARCHICAL STRUCTURE PROPOSED FOR *INTERNIST-I*

Patrick, Stelmack, and Shen (1974) used concepts of subsystems with categories and subcategories and methods of activation rules for subsystems along with formation of new subsystems. Recently, researchers including Pople (1982) have advocated this approach. Pople's vantage point was to obtain a focus of differential diagnosis, but he realized that differential diagnosis previously used in Internist had problems with respect to theory, efficiency, and performance.

Pople (1982, (p. 151) proposed "well-structured subproblems" after Patrick *and others* (1974). Pople also proposed categories with subcategories (see Figs. 1 and 2 in Pople 1982).

Pople further proposed operations or modules for branching

down to a subcategory from a category, combining two subcategories as a complex subcategory, and local inductive inference.

6-5 HIERARCHICAL KNOWLEDGE WITH A POSTERIORI PROBABILITY

6-5-1 Notation

Indexing notation for the knowledge base hierarchy used in this section consists of

r: level

indexing the rth level. At the rth level there are subsystems indexed by s,

r_s: sth subsystem at rth level

and subsubsystems indexed by t,

r_{s_t}: tth subsubsystem of sth subsystem at rth level.

A subsystem (or subsubsystem) contains classes and categories (only classes and complex classes). As always a class or category can have subclasses and subcategories, respectively. For each class or category entity there exists a c.c.p.d.f.

For the rth level,

$\omega_{r_{s_{t_i}}}$

is the ith class in the tth subsubsystem of the sth subsystem.

6-5-2 Theorem on A Posteriori Probability by Patrick Applies at Multiple Levels in the Hierarchy

At any level r, the theorem on a posteriori probability by Patrick applies. In particular

$$p(\omega_{r_i}, \mathbf{x}) = p(\omega^*_{r_i}, \mathbf{x}) + \sum_{\omega_{r_i} \in \Omega^*_\eta} p(\Omega^*_\eta, \mathbf{x}) \tag{1}$$

without regard to subsystem (or subsubsystem). Concept formation can take place at any rth level either by learning by example (with a teacher) or by discovery (without a teacher).

It is clear how the theorem on a posteriori probability by Patrick applies at any *r*th level, but what is it in terms of a hierarchy of classes and categories? Properties at the *r*th level are as follows:

1. Category concepts can be formed at any level limited by the a priori class structure.
2. Dependence of higher-level classes on lower-level classes is through the dependence of higher-level categories on lower-level categories. Fan-down dependence to *nonformed categories* at any time is *potential dependence* with zero probability until such time as the lower-level category concept has been formed (with nonzero probability).
3. At any level a class has subclasses and a category has subcategories as columns.
4. At a low level, features (complex features) can have subfeatures.
5. The features of a category or class at a higher level are categories at the next lower level.
6. Classes are not in the decision space as are categories and feature values (which can be categories).

These properties are illustrated in Figure 6.1. Until a concept (category) is formed at some level, a "link" cannot eixst to it from a higher level.

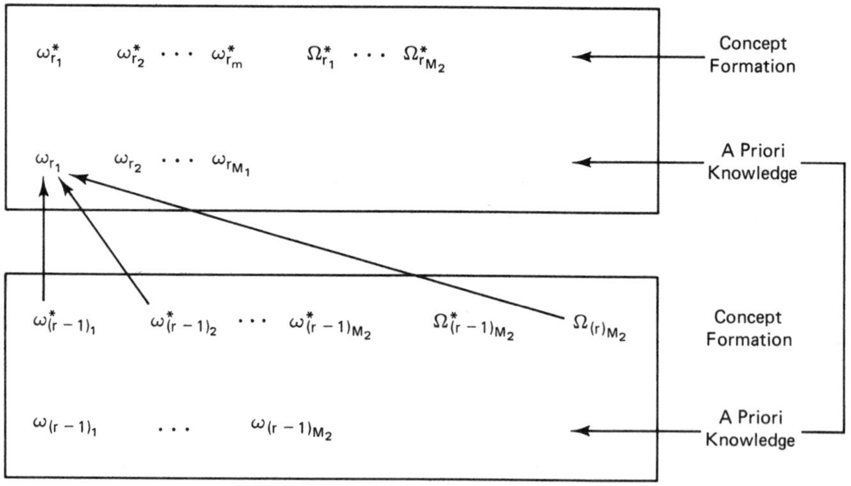

FIGURE 6.1. Illustration that categories at a lower level are features for classes at the higher level.

Classes can be formed as concepts either by example (with a teacher) or by discovery (without a teacher), but usually they are formed a priori by being told.

At any level a class or category can be considered a module with a c.c.p.d.f. involving its feature from the next lowest level.

The formation of a category concept at one level does not elevate that category to a higher level.

A higher level may have increased dimensionality as a result of feature influence outside of that available to a lower level.

Aspects of the theorem on a posteriori probability by Patrick are as follows:

1. At any level, categories are mutually exclusive and exhaustive.
2. The final decision space consists of categories at the highest level.
3. The new theorem on a posteriori probability by Patrick applied to a hierarchy includes the viewpoint of a causal network but more. For example, added by the new theorem is concept formation by learning without a teacher at multiple levels.
4. At any level a class or category incorporates multiple columns for completeness in knowedge and performance.

6-6 VIEWPOINT OF HIERARCHY OF CONSULT-I® SUBSYSTEM

The **CONSULT-I®** subsystem can be viewed as a basic unit for concept formation as shown in Figure 6.2. At the lowest level, respective sets of features $\mathbf{x}_1, \mathbf{x}_2, \ldots$ input to the respective subsystem. The output of the subsystem are categories which can be ordered by their a posteriori probabilities. These are then input as statistical feature values to the second level subsystem as shown in Figure 6.2. A concept at any level can be taken as the probable category or the concept formation can remain probabilistic. The output of the highest-level subsystem is a set of categories with associated a posteriori probabilities.

An iterative expression for category γ_i^* at the rth level can be derived. The categories $\{\gamma^*_{(r-1)_{s_k}}\}_{k=1}^{M_{(r-1)_s}}$ in the sth subsystem are mutually exclusive. The set of categories containing one category from each subsystem is denoted

$$\{\gamma^*_{(r-1)_{s_k}}\}_{s=1}^{S_{r-1}}$$

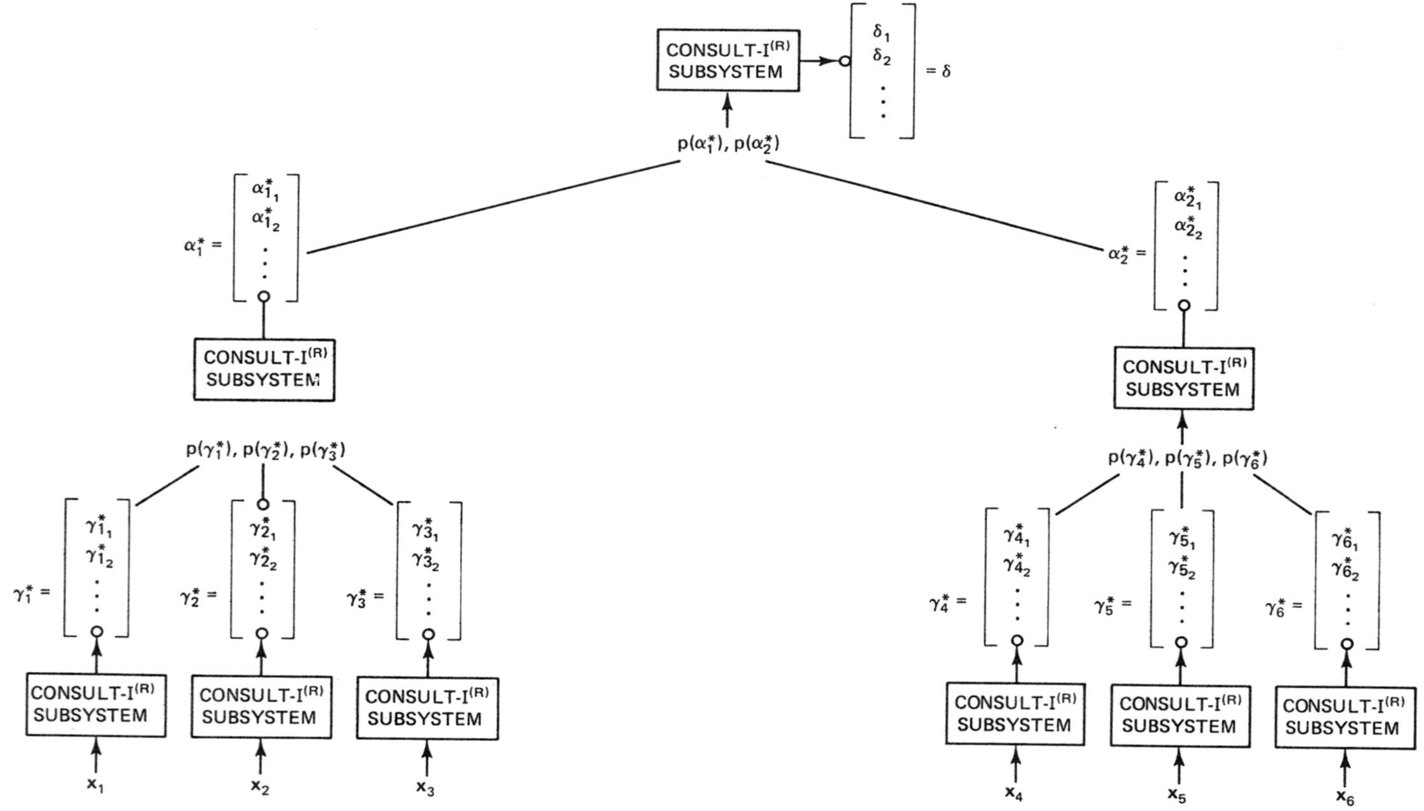

FIGURE 6.2. Hierarchy of **CONSULT-I®** subsystems for concept formation.

where there are S_{r-1} subsystems at level $(r - 1)$. Sets of the above form are mutually exclusive. Thus,

$$p(\gamma^*_{r_i}|\mathbf{x}) = \sum_{\delta} p(\gamma^*_{r_i}, \{\gamma^*_{(r-1)_{s_k}}\}_{s=1}^{S_{r-1}}|\mathbf{x})$$

where δ is the domain of sets where one category is taken from each subsystem at level $(r - 1)$. Further

$$p(\gamma^*_{r_i}|\mathbf{x}) = \sum_{\delta} p(\gamma^*_{r_i}|\{\gamma^*_{(r-1)_{s_k}}\}_{s=1}^{S_{r-1}}) \;\; p(\{\gamma^*_{(r-1)_{s_k}}\}_{s=1}^{S_{r-1}}|\mathbf{x})$$

By construction of the hierarchy, category outputs from respective subsystems are statistically independent. Thus

$$p(\gamma^*_{r_i}|\mathbf{x}) = \sum_{\delta} p(\gamma^*_{r_i}|\{\gamma^*_{(r-1)_{s_k}}\}_{s=1}^{S_{r-1}}) \prod_{s=1}^{S_{r-1}} p(\gamma^*_{(r-1)_{\delta_s}}|\mathbf{x})$$

The iteration next can be continued down to level $(r - 2)$ and so on.

Assume that the output from subsystem s at level $(r - 1)$ is taken as the maximum a posteriori probability category $(\gamma^*_{(r-1)_s})_{\max}$. Then

$$p(\gamma^*_{r_i}|\mathbf{x}) = p(\gamma^*_{r_i}|\{\gamma^*_{(r-1)_{s_{max}}}\}_{s=1}^{S_{r-1}})$$

6-7 MUTUALLY EXCLUSIVE CATEGORIES THAT ARE STATISTICALLY DEPENDENT

Further insight into the differences between the new theorem on a posteriori probability by Patrick and Bayes theorem are provided in this section. Acknowledgment of classes as well as categories in the new theorem on a posteriori probability by Patrick allows a complex class category Ω^*_{ij} to be related to only class categories ω^*_i and ω^*_j while Ω^*_{ij}, ω^*_i, and ω^*_j remain *mutually exclusive*. That is, Ω^*_{ij}, ω^*_i, and ω^*_j are mutually exclusive but are related. We now will show how this relationship is a dependence (*statistical dependence*) through the feature space.

It is not surprising that a reader could have difficulty with the new theorem because, indeed, there are two major concepts to apply simultaneously: *mutual exclusiveness of categories* and *statistical dependence of categories.*

A key is that we are learning about the category γ^*_η (ω^*_i, ω^*_j, or Ω^*_{ij}) and this learning takes place over time. There is a *time dimension.* Consider the inference function,

$$p(\gamma_\eta^*|\mathbf{x}_1, \mathbf{x}_2, \ldots, \mathbf{x}_n) = \frac{p(\gamma_\eta^*|\mathbf{x}_1, \mathbf{x}_2, \ldots, \mathbf{x}_{n-1})\, p(\mathbf{x}_n|\gamma_\eta^*, \mathbf{x}_1, \ldots, \mathbf{x}_{n-1})}{p(\mathbf{x}_n|\mathbf{x}_1, \ldots, \mathbf{x}_{n-1})}.$$

During the course of iteration over $\mathbf{x}_1, \ldots, \mathbf{x}_{n-1}, \mathbf{x}_n$, knowledge about statistical dependence of one category on another is learned, assuming that the categories are active in the learning session. Over time it is learned how the feature space of one category depends upon the feature space of another category. Let the feature space domain for the respective categories ω_i^*, ω_j^*, Ω_{ij}^* be defined X_i, X_j, and X_{ij}, respectively. Let $\dot{\mathbf{x}}_i$ and $\dot{\mathbf{x}}_j$ be two sets of learning examples, the first for ω_i^* and the second for ω_j^*. What can we say about

$$p(\Omega_{ij}^*, X_{ij}|\omega_i^*, \dot{\mathbf{x}}_1;\ \omega_j^*, \dot{\mathbf{x}}_2)?$$

We can define a candidate domain $D(\Omega_{ij}^*)$ for Ω_{ij}^* and let

$$D(\Omega_{ij}^*) = \bar{\omega}_i^* \cap \bar{\omega}_j^*,$$

which is a region of hyperfeature space where both ω_i^* and ω_j^* have not occurred with some threshold of relative frequency. We now can predict that a set of learning examples $\dot{\mathbf{x}}_3$ from Ω_{ij}^* "probably" will be in $D(\Omega_{ij}^*)$. If, further, we expect that Ω_{ij}^* will "look something like ω_i^* and something like ω_j^*," then this further helps our prediction.

This example is illustrated in Figure 6.3 for a three-dimensional example (three features). In the example ω_i^* is "heavily characterized" by features x_1 and x_2 while ω_j^* is "heavily characterized" by x_1 and x_3. A region $D^2(\Omega_{ij}^*)$ captures the concept of being in $D(\Omega_{ij}^*)$ but also being like ω_i^* and like ω_j^*. Based on the model, *we predict or expect that a feature sample from Ω_i^* will be in $D^2(\Omega_{ij}^*)$. This is statistical dependence of event Ω_{ij}^* on previous events* ω_i^* and ω_j^*.

Thus, although $(\Omega_{ij}^*, \dot{\mathbf{x}}_3)$ is mutually exclusive of $(\omega_i^*, \dot{\mathbf{x}}_1)$ and $(\omega_j^*, \dot{\mathbf{x}}_2)$ during learning it is statistically dependent on them. An aspect of the new theorem on a posteriori probability by Patrick might be represented

$$(\omega_i, \dot{\mathbf{x}}_1, \dot{\mathbf{x}}_2, \dot{\mathbf{x}}_3) = (\omega_i^*, \dot{\mathbf{x}}_1) + (\Omega_{ij}^*, \dot{\mathbf{x}}_3),$$

which shows that class ω_i consists of examples from *two different time segments during learning*. Class ω_i is not mutually exclusive of ω_i^* and Ω_{ij}^*.

A posteriori probability is a dynamic process involving learning in the new theorem on a posteriori probability by Patrick. A class ω_i generated during the learning process is not mutually exclusive of ω_i^* and ω_j^*. *Bayes theorem is derived from axiomatic probability theory and did not anticipate learning by example* and especially not by discovery (learning with-

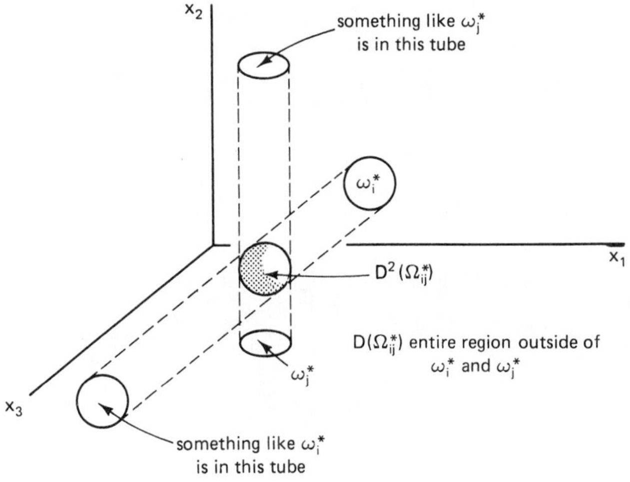

FIGURE 6.3

out a teacher). Bayes theorem applies as long as no attempt is made to introduce additional a priori concepts to relate Ω^*_{ij} to ω^*_i and ω^*_j.

The new theorem on a posteriori probability by Patrick also is derived from axiomatic probability theory. But its added structure of classes provides the interplay during learning for statistical dependence of one category on another. The new theorem provides for anticipating complex classes in the category space and a structure to introduce a priori knowledge for learning complex classes without a teacher.

7

Discussion of Classes, Only Classes, Categories, and Statistically Dependent Categories

7-1 DEFINITIONS

7-1-1 Events, Categories, Complex Categories

Define a category space $\mathcal{Y}$ consisting of mutually exclusive and exhaustive categories $\gamma_1^*, \gamma_2^*, \ldots, \gamma_M^*$. Being mutually exclusive, these categories are events which cannot occur together. Let

$$\{\omega_i^*\}_{i=1}^{M_1} = \omega_1^*, \omega_2^*, \ldots, \omega_{M_1}^* \tag{1}$$

be a subset of the categories in the category space and name ω_i^* "the only class ω_i." The notation *only class* ω_i^* is used to distinguish this category from categories consisting of class ω_i and one or more other classes. The M_1 *only classes* [Eq. (1)] are mutually exclusive and thus cannot occur together. Thus, the event ω_i^* means

$$\omega_i^*: \quad \text{Only class } \omega_i. \tag{2}$$

Thus, ω_i^* and ω_j^*, $i \neq j$, cannot occur together because the former is only the class ω_i while the latter is only the class ω_j by definition.

Let

$$\{\Omega_\xi^*\}_{\xi=1}^{M_2} = \Omega_1^*, \Omega_2^*, \ldots, \Omega_{M_2}^* \tag{3}$$

be a subset of categories, also events in the category space, and name Ω_ξ^* complex class ξ. The M_2 complex classes [Eq.(3)] are mutually exclusive and thus cannot occur together. The event Ω_ξ^* means:

$$\Omega_\xi^*: \quad \text{Complex class } \Omega_\xi.$$

It may be convenient to let $\xi \rightarrow (i, j)$ and define

$$\Omega^*_{ij} \triangleq \text{only } (\omega_i, \omega_j) \tag{4}$$

meaning the event class ω_i and class ω_j. The event ω_i means:

$$\omega_i\text{:} \quad \text{Class } \omega_i. \tag{5}$$

Contrast Eq. (5) with Eq. (2), and it may help to realize that we are dealing with *events* in the category space in Eqs. (2) and (3). As an extension define

$$\Omega^*_{abc\,\ldots\,x\,\ldots} \triangleq \text{only } \{\omega_a, \omega_b, \omega_c, \ldots, \omega_x \ldots\}. \tag{6}$$

By definition (by construction), all *only classes* and *complex classes* are mutually exclusive. The right-hand side of Eq. (6) is the event class ω_a and class ω_b . . . and class ω_x. In like manner, the left-hand side of Eq. (6) is

$$\Omega^*_{abc\,\ldots\,x}\text{:} \quad \text{Complex class } \Omega_{\text{abc}\,\ldots\,x}.$$

The practical significance of classes is that, in designing a classification system utilizing artificial intelligence, the best starting point in development is to describe the patterns corresponding to *only classes.* Even with a small number M_1 of classes, the number of complex classes can be very large. A priori knowledge can be introduced to constrain this number to "possible" complex classes or "probable" complex classes. A priori knowledge and the scientific method can be used to generate patterns for the complex classes from patterns of the classes in their complex.

Again, it is prudent to *issue a warning that complex classes cannot just be "found to occur"* or learned to exist without some prior knowledge. This learning is a form of learning without a teacher. Certain a priori knowledge must exist for learning without a teacher.

7-1-2 Primitives, Features, Measurements

Define a primitive space $\mathcal{A}$ consisting of primitives a_d:

$$\{a_d\}_{d=1}^{D} = a_1, a_2, \ldots, a_d, \ldots, a_D. \tag{7}$$

A primitive has meaning either True or False or is integral to other primitives (see Type Ø below). Features are defined

$$\{x_j\}_{j=1}^{L} = x_1, x_2, \ldots, x_L, \tag{8}$$

and we will discuss the difference betwen a primitive and a feature. *A*

Type Ø feature is defined as a string of V primitives where only one primitive is True; setting $V = 9$,

$$x_j = \{a_{j_1}, a_{j_2}, \ldots, a_{j_9}\}; \text{ with only } a_{j_v} \text{ TRUE.} \tag{9}$$

It is convenient to redefine the a_{j_v} as x_{j_v} and let x_{j_v} denote the vth value of feature x_j.

A Type 1 embedded feature is defined as a single primitive,

$$x_j = a_{j_v}, \; a_{j_v} \quad \text{True or False.} \tag{10}$$

It is convenient to redefine a_{j_v} as x_{j_v}, a value of x_j.

Thus, a feature x_j is either Type Ø with V mutually exclusive and exhaustive values or Type 1 with two (2) values, True or False. In practice, Type 1 features often are embedded by an interviewer into a display called a *Type 1 Measurement,* whereas Type Ø features are displayed as a single measurement (and simply called a Type Ø feature). Other types of features can be defined in terms of primitives and are presented elsewhere in this book (see Section 8-9).

7-2 EVENT–CONDITIONAL PROBABILITY DENSITY FUNCTION

For each event γ^*_η in the category space $\boldsymbol{\gamma}$, there exists a category conditional probability density function

$$p(\mathbf{x}|\gamma^*_\eta), \tag{11}$$

where

$$\mathbf{x} = [x_1, \ldots x_L] \tag{12}$$

is defined the feature vector (series of feature values).

Considering ω_i and ω_j, what is the relationship between

$$p(\mathbf{x}|\omega^*_i), \quad p(\mathbf{x}|\omega^*_j), \tag{13}$$

and

$$p(\mathbf{x}|\Omega^*_{ij}), \tag{14}$$

where

$$\Omega^*_{ij} = (\omega_i, \omega_j) \; ?$$

Can Eq. (14) be obtained from Eq. (13) ?

In artificial intelligence with statistical pattern recognition, patterns corresponding to $p(\mathbf{x}|\omega^*_i)$ and $p(\mathbf{x}|\omega^*_j)$ are part of the knowledge base just as is $p(\mathbf{x}|\Omega_{ij}^*)$. Some systems try to use relatively high values of $p(\mathbf{x}|\omega_i^*)$ and/or $p(\mathbf{x}|\omega_j^*)$ as "flags" or subgoals representing data base changes used to help calculate $p(\mathbf{x}|\Omega_{ij}^*)$. We will again investigate the generation of Eq. (14) from Eq. (13).

7-3 A PRIORI CATEGORY PROBABILITIES

Define an a priori category probability,

$$p(\gamma_\eta^*) = P_\eta, \tag{15}$$

where

$$\sum_{\eta=1}^{M} P_\eta = 1. \tag{16}$$

The a priori *only class* probabilities are

$$p(\omega_i^*) = P_i \tag{17}$$

and sum to one only if the probability of each *complex class* is zero.

7-4 MIXTURE PROBABILITY DENSITY

The probability density of $\mathbf{x}$ can be computed realizing that categories $\gamma_1^*, \gamma_2^*, \ldots \gamma_M^*$ are mutually exclusive:

$$p(\mathbf{x}) = \sum_{\eta=1}^{M} p(\mathbf{x},\gamma_\eta^*) \tag{18}$$

$$= \sum_{\eta=1}^{M} p(\mathbf{x}|\gamma_\eta^*)p(\gamma_\eta^*). \tag{19}$$

Complex classes consist of combination of classes taken m at a time; the number of complex classes consisting of exactly m classes is

$$\binom{M_1}{m} = \frac{M_1!}{m!\,(M_1 - m)!} \tag{20}$$

where M_1 is the number of classes.

Equation (19) can be rewritten

$$p(\mathbf{x}) = \sum_{i=1}^{M_1} p(\mathbf{x}|\omega_i^*)P_i +$$

$$\sum_{\xi(i,j)=1}^{\binom{M_1}{2}} p(\mathbf{x}|\Omega_{ij}^*)P_\xi +$$

$$\sum_{\xi(i,j,k)=1}^{\binom{M_1}{3}} p(\mathbf{x}|\Omega_{ijk}^*)P_\xi + \ldots + . \tag{21}$$

Fortunately, complexes over classes for "large m" are expected to be rare, although not impossible. A truth table can be used to index possible events, whether *only classes* or *complex classes* (but rarely classes). Thus, processing time would not be used to process for an impossible complex class. Concept formation using Patrick's theorem is used to prevent this combinatorial explosion.

7-5 CLASSES AND COMPLEX CLASSES

The event ω_i (which is class ω_i) occurs if the event ω_i^* and/or any event Ω_ξ^* occurs where Ω_ξ^* is a *complex class* containing ω_i.

Events

$$\{\omega_i^*\} \quad \text{and} \quad \{\Omega_\xi^*\} \tag{22}$$

are mutually exclusive and exhaustive and constitute the category space. Thus,

$$p(\omega_i) = p(\omega_i^*) + \sum_{\omega_i \in \Omega_\xi^*} p(\Omega_\xi^*), \tag{23}$$

where the second term on the right involves all complex classes containing class ω_i. Equation (23) is an expression that class ω_i occurred either alone as an "only class" or in one or more complex classes. *Note that ω_i is not one of the basic categories γ_ξ^** in the category space. The basic categories (events) ω_1^*, Ω_{12}^*, . . . are mutually exclusive.

The class ω_i is an event defined in terms of basic events (categories) in the category space, through Eq. (23).

Both ω_i^* and Ω_{ij}^* "contain" the class ω_i. Complex classes Ω_{ij}^* also "contain" other classes. Equation (23) is a theorem the proof of which involves:

1. Union of mutually exclusive events:

$$\omega_i = \omega_i^* \cup [\cup \Omega_\xi^*], \qquad \Omega_\xi^* \text{ contains } \omega_i. \tag{24a}$$

2. Joint Probability

$$p(\omega_i, \mathbf{x}) = p(\omega_i^*, \mathbf{x}) + \sum_{\omega_i \,\varepsilon\, \Omega_\xi^*} p(\Omega_\xi^*, \mathbf{x}). \tag{24b}$$

Given a feature vector **x**, it follows that

$$p(\omega_i|\mathbf{x}) = p(\omega_i^*|\mathbf{x}) + \sum_{\omega_i \,\varepsilon\, \Omega_\xi^*} p(\Omega_\xi^*|\mathbf{x}). \tag{25}$$

is a conditional probability of class ω_i. The a posteriori probabilities,

$$p(\omega_i^*|\mathbf{x}) = \frac{p(\mathbf{x}|\omega_i^*)p(\omega_i^*)}{p(\mathbf{x})} \tag{26}$$

$$p(\Omega_\xi^*|\mathbf{x}) = \frac{p(\mathbf{x}|\Omega_\xi^*)p(\Omega_\xi^*)}{p(\mathbf{x})} \tag{27}$$

are calculated given the category conditional probability density functions:

$$p(\mathbf{x}|\omega_i^*) \tag{28}$$

$$p(\mathbf{x}|\Omega_\xi^*) \tag{29}$$

It needs to be stressed that the goal is to calculate the a posteriori category probablities, Eqs. (26) and (27); *the a posteriori class probability, Eq. (25), is an intermediate step generated or created during concept formation.* There are many applications in practice where it is unnecessary to perform the intermediate calculations; the p.d.f.'s of the categories are directly estimated.

On the other hand, Eq. (25) suggests that knowledge of a posteriori event

$$p(\omega_i^*|\mathbf{x}), \tag{30}$$

and/or a posteriori event

$$p(\Omega_\xi^*|\mathbf{x}) \tag{31}$$

infer knowledge about

$$p(\omega_i|\mathbf{x}) \tag{32}$$

and, *by feedback,* about the former a posteriori events. This is axiomatic. In practice, training samples (*relative frequency*) *separated by time or space* is a concept workable into a model of feedback from the engineering standpoint. It is important to realize that training sessions take place over time where in each session only one category is active. This training session provides for learning more about the class containing that category and thus about other categories in that class.

7-6 MODELS FOR COMPLEX CLASSES

7-6-1 Introduction

In practice it is not unusual to have knowledge of only class conditional probability density functions,

$$p(\mathbf{x}|\omega_i^*);$$

but often knowledge of complex class conditional probability density functions,

$$p(\mathbf{x}|\Omega_\xi^*)$$

is not directly available. This poses a challenge to discover knowledge of complex classes. This discovery may never have been accomplished by researchers up to this point. For example, in medical diagnosis it may never have occurred to practicing physicians or research physicans whether an event is an only class or a complex class. They deal with the class which is the union of only class and complex classes containing that class. An example noted by Fattu and Patrick (1983a) is the complex class hyperthyroiditis, whereas at one time only classes hyperthyroidism and thyroiditis were known but the complex class was unknown. These classes were viewed as only classes if you thought about it at all. An "open mind" lets you wonder if they can occur together. They can.

The mixture, Eqs. (19) or (21), is a fundamental expression for the data base; but unless all event conditional probability density functions in Eq. (21) are known, there results an unsupervised learning problem (learning without a teacher). In the following sections, several models for $p(\Omega_\xi^*|\mathbf{x})$ are discussed.

7-6-2 Classes in Terms of Only Classes

Consider that there exist two classes, ω_i and ω_j. Then the *only class* ω_i^* and class ω_i are, respectively,

$$\omega_i^* = (\omega_i, \bar{\omega}_j)$$

$$\omega_i = (\omega_i, \bar{\omega}_j) + (\omega_i, \omega_j). \tag{33}$$

Likewise for *only class* ω_j^* and class ω_i, respectively,

$$\omega_j^* = (\omega_j, \bar{\omega}_i)$$

$$\omega_j = (\omega_j, \bar{\omega}_i) + (\omega_j, \omega_i). \tag{34}$$

In general,

$$p(\Omega_{ij}^*|\mathbf{x}) = p(\omega_i, \omega_j|\mathbf{x}) = p(\omega_j|\omega_i, \mathbf{x})p(\omega_i|\mathbf{x}) \tag{35}$$

$$\begin{aligned} p(\omega_i^*|\mathbf{x}) &= p(\omega_i, \bar{\omega}_j|\mathbf{x}) = p(\bar{\omega}_j|\omega_i, \mathbf{x})p(\omega_i|\mathbf{x}) \\ &= [1 - p(\omega_j|\omega_i, \mathbf{x})]p(\omega_i|\mathbf{x}). \end{aligned} \tag{36}$$

7-6-3 Classes Occurring Independently with Complex Class Dependent on Both

By definition, *only classes* ω_i^* *and* ω_j^* *are mutually exclusive, which means that they cannot occur together to give rise to feature vector* $\mathbf{x}$ *of a pattern. On the other hand, classes* ω_i *and* ω_j *can occur together to give rise to feature vector* $\mathbf{x}$.

Assume that there exists $\mathbf{x}_1$ and $\mathbf{x}_2$, both subsets of $\mathbf{x}$, such that

$$\mathbf{x} = \mathbf{x}_1 + \mathbf{x}_2, \qquad \mathbf{x}_1 \cap \mathbf{x}_2 = \emptyset \tag{37}$$

and

$$p(\omega_i|\mathbf{x}) = p(\omega_i|\mathbf{x}_1)$$

$$p(\omega_j|\mathbf{x}) = p(\omega_j|\mathbf{x}_2). \tag{38}$$

The expressions in Eq. (38) presume that ω_i is *completely* characterized by $\mathbf{x}_1$ and ω_j by $\mathbf{x}_2$.

Imposing Eqs. (37) and (38) on Eq. (35), Eq. (35) becomes

$$p(\Omega_{ij}^*|\mathbf{x}) = p(\omega_j|\omega_i, \mathbf{x}_1, \mathbf{x}_2)p(\omega_i|\mathbf{x}_1, \mathbf{x}_2) = p(\omega_j|\mathbf{x}_2)p(\omega_i|\mathbf{x}_1) \tag{39}$$

and imposing Eq. (38) on Eq. (36) in like manner, Eq. (36) becomes

$$p(\omega_i^*|\mathbf{x}) = [1 - p(\omega_j|\mathbf{x}_2)]p(\omega_i|\mathbf{x}_1). \tag{40}$$

Equations (37) and (38) impose a dependence between the two classes ω_i and ω_j through the feature vector, and Eqs. (39) and (40) result from the use of this dependence by forming the product of the two class conditional probability density functions. This product combination can be contrasted with the more familiar linear combination of functions, which is a summation.

Equations (39) and (40) have an interesting practical interpretation. In Eq. (39), feature subset $\mathbf{x}_2$ is explained by class ω_j while feature subset $\mathbf{x}_1$ is explained by class ω_i, which together explain the *complex class* Ω^*_{ij}.

Yet probability of ω_j does not depend on ω_i either through the occurrence of event ω_i or the features characterizing it, $\mathbf{x}_1$. *The two classes ω_i and ω_j occur independently but the complex class is dependent on both* (in this model).

In Eq. (40), feature subset $\mathbf{x}_1$ explains class ω_i but "does not explain class ω_j;" thus, explained is the *only class* ω_i, ω^*_i. As an example, consider an individual with hepatitis (ω^*_2) characterized by a positive hepatitis antigen (x_2) and also with a Strep. throat (ω^*_1) characterized by a positive throat culture. The two diseases are assumed to arise independently and x_2 never explains ω^*_1 while x_1 never explains ω^*_2.

Example: Statistically Independent Features

Assuming the model of independently occurring classes with complex class depending on both, suppose that we know

$$p(\mathbf{x}_1|\omega_i) \quad \text{and} \quad p(\mathbf{x}_2|\omega_j).$$

In addition, also assume that the features of each probability density function are statistically independent:

$$p(\mathbf{x}_1|\omega_i) = \prod_{x_j \,\varepsilon\, \mathbf{x}_1} p(x_j|\omega_i)$$

$$p(\mathbf{x}_2|\omega_j) = \prod_{x_j \,\varepsilon\, \mathbf{x}_2} p(x_j|\omega_i). \tag{41}$$

In practice the developer can, for example, determine the subset $\mathbf{x}_1$ using a threshold:

$$x_j \,\varepsilon\, \mathbf{x}_1 \quad \text{if } p(x_j|\omega_i) > T$$

and

$$x_j \,\varepsilon\, \mathbf{x}_2 \quad \text{otherwise.}$$

Then substituting Eq. (41) in Eq. (39) results in

$$p(\Omega_{ij}^*|\mathbf{x}) = \frac{\left[\prod_{x_k \, \varepsilon \, \mathbf{x}_2} p(x_k|\omega_j)p(\omega_j)\right]}{p(\mathbf{x}_2)} \frac{\left[\prod_{x_w \, \varepsilon \, \mathbf{x}_1} p(x_w|\omega_i)p(\omega_i)\right]}{p(\mathbf{x}_1)} . \tag{42}$$

Similarly, the a posteriori probability can be calculated for ω_i^*.

Assumptions in Eqs. (37) and (38) are bold assumptions that should be satisfied for some problems in practice (but not all).

7-6-4 Complex Class Dependent on Statistically Independent Classes

Assuming that classes ω_i and ω_j are conditionally statistically independent, we get

$$p(\Omega_{ij}^*|\mathbf{x}) = p(\omega_i, \omega_j|\mathbf{x}) = p(\omega_i|\mathbf{x})p(\omega_j|\mathbf{x}), \tag{43}$$

which bears *some* resemblance to Eq. (39). The difference is that in Eq. (43), there is no assumption that one subset of features is "significant" for ω_i and another subset for class ω_j. A companion equation to Eq. (43) is

$$\begin{aligned} p(\omega_i^*|\mathbf{x}) = p(\omega_i, \bar{\omega}_j|\mathbf{x}) &= p(\bar{\omega}_j|\mathbf{x})p(\omega_i|\mathbf{x}) \\ &= [1 - p(\omega_j|\mathbf{x})]p(\omega_i|\mathbf{x}). \end{aligned} \tag{44}$$

In Eq. (43) the assumption is that

$$p(\omega_i|\omega_j, \mathbf{x}) = p(\omega_i|\mathbf{x}).$$

It is more instructive to realize that the assumption is equivalent to

$$p(\mathbf{x}|\omega_i,\omega_j) = \frac{p(\mathbf{x}|\omega_i)p(\mathbf{x}|\omega_j)}{p(\mathbf{x})},$$

which places a significant constraint on the features. There is little reason to expect such a constraint to be satisfied in practice.

7-6-5 Fuzzy Set Approximation—Statistically Independent Classes

The left-hand side of Eq. (43) is "small" if either $p(\omega_i|\mathbf{x})$ or $p(\omega_j|\mathbf{x})$ is "small"; it is "large" otherwise. This suggests that the fuzzy set AND operation applied to Eq. (43) results in

$$p(\Omega_{ij}^*|\mathbf{x}) = \min\{p(\omega_i|\mathbf{x}), p(\omega_j|\mathbf{x})\} \tag{45}$$

and Eq. (44) becomes

$$p(\omega_i^*|\mathbf{x}) = \min\{[1 - p(\omega_j|\mathbf{x})], p(\omega_i|\mathbf{x})\}. \tag{46}$$

Equation (45) has intuitive appeal because it suggests that *both class* ω_i *and class* ω_j *are present only if each independently has a minimum probability.* A disadvantage of this model is that no provision is made for some features to explain class ω_i while others explain class ω_j. *Also, no provision is made for* $\mathbf{x}$ to be affected by the occurrence of both ω_i and ω_j.

To this point we have considered the following properties for constructing a complex class model:

1. One subset of $\mathbf{x}$ may be explained by class ω_1 while another subset is explained by class ω_2.
2. Classes ω_1 and ω_2 can occur independently to give complex class Ω_{12}^*.
3. Features in a subset $\mathbf{x}_1$ may be statistically independent for class ω_1 while features in a subset $\mathbf{x}_2$ may be statistically independent for class ω_2.

In addition, there are the following considerations:

4. Contrary to point 1 above, a subset of features $\mathbf{x}_3$ of $\mathbf{x}$ may be explained only by Ω_{12}^*.
5. Given Ω_{12}^*, there may be statistical dependence among $\mathbf{x}_1$, $\mathbf{x}_2$, $\mathbf{x}_3$ as subsets of $\mathbf{x}$.
6. $p(\mathbf{x}|\Omega_{12}^*)$ may have to be characterized separately from that for ω_1 and ω_2 because a reasonable relationship cannot be determined or the accounting is more complex than the separate characterization.

7-6-6 Optimum Calculation of Complex Class A Posteriori Probabilities

A complex class conditional probability density function exists for each complex class; and for some problems, its direct construction is the desired approach. In general

$$p(\Omega_{ij}^*|\mathbf{x}) = \frac{p(\mathbf{x}|\omega_i, \omega_j)p(\omega_i, \omega_j)}{p(\mathbf{x})}, \tag{47}$$

where $p(\mathbf{x}|\omega_i, \omega_j)$ is the complex class conditional probability density function. Certainly various structures other than those imposed in the previous section can be proposed for relating Ω_{ij}^* to ω_i and ω_j. These structures can involve trees, networks, sets, graphs, etc. Basically, the same considerations apply as those for only classes ω_i^* and ω_j^*. Relationship structures are useful, however, if they can *simplify inductive generation* of a complex class from only classes and *simplify unsupervised learning of the existence of a complex class when trained for only classes,* or when training for a complex class can through *deduction* provide knowledge about an only class through the new theorem by Patrick.

Unsupervised learning provides a means for reasoning whereby a new category is created in the category space. To qualify as a category, it must be determined that this event is mutually exclusive of other events in the category space (only classes and complex classes). Then this is a new event which cannot be generated as an only class through deduction from a complex model and cannot be generated by induction as a complex class. Instead, the a priori knowledge (meta-knowledge) built into the system provides for learning without a teacher to form a new category.

Three processes are identified:

1. Generation of Planned Complex Classes through Induction.
2. Generation of Planned Only Classes through Deduction.
3. Generation of a New Unplanned Category through Learning Without a Teacher.

Process 3 is Reasoning.

7-6-7 Either Or, Only Classes

Let ω_i^* and ω_j^* be two only classes in the category space. Then, because ω_i^* and ω_j^* are mutually exclusive, the a posteriori probability of *either* ω_i^* *or* ω_j^* is

$$
\begin{aligned}
p(\omega_i^* \text{ or } \omega_j^* | \mathbf{x}) &= \frac{p(\mathbf{x}, \omega_i^* \text{ or } \mathbf{x}, \omega_j^*)}{p(\mathbf{x})} \\
&= \frac{p(\mathbf{x}, \omega_i^*) + p(\mathbf{x}, \omega_j^*)}{p(\mathbf{x})} \\
&= \frac{p(\mathbf{x}|\omega_i^*)p(\omega_i^*)}{p(\mathbf{x})} + \frac{p(\mathbf{x}|\omega_j^*)p(\omega_j^*)}{p(\mathbf{x})} .
\end{aligned} \tag{48}
$$

This has application in medical diagnosis where the treatment is the same for ω_i^* and ω_j^*. *Then Eq. (48) is the a posteriori probability of an event* *identified by the treatment.* Another application is for only classes ω_i^* and ω_j^* for which urgent attention is desired.

Equation (48) extends to multiple only classes

$$p(\omega_{\xi_1}^* \text{ or } \omega_{\xi_2}^* \text{ or} \ldots \omega_{\xi_n}^*) = \sum_{i=1}^{n} \frac{p(\mathbf{x}|\omega_{\xi_i}^*)p(\omega_{\xi_i}^*)}{p(\mathbf{x})}, \tag{49}$$

where the subscript i or ξ is used to index a subset of only classes.

7-6-8 Neither *Only Classes*

The a posteriori probability of neither $\omega_{\xi_1}^*$ nor $\omega_{\xi_2}^*$ nor . . . $\omega_{\xi_n}^*$ is

$$\begin{aligned} &p(\text{not } \omega_{\xi_1}^*, \text{ not } \omega_{\xi_2}^*, \ldots \text{ not } \omega_{\xi_n}^*|\mathbf{x}) = \\ &1 - p(\omega_{\xi_1}^* \text{ or } \omega_{\xi_2}^* \ldots \text{ or } \omega_{\xi_n}^*|\mathbf{x}) = \\ &1 - \sum_{i=1}^{n} \frac{p(\mathbf{x}|\omega_{\xi_i}^*)p(\omega_{\xi_i}^*)}{p(\mathbf{x})}. \end{aligned} \tag{50}$$

7-6-9 A Class But Not the *Only Class*

The event class ω_i but not ω_i^* is denoted

$$(\omega_i, \text{ not } \omega_i^*) \tag{51}$$

and is the union of all *complex classes* containing class ω_i. Thus,

$$p(\omega_i, \text{ not } \omega_i^*) = \sum_{\omega_i \in \Omega_\xi^*} p(\Omega_\xi^*). \tag{52}$$

7-6-10 Example—Incorrectly Training for a Complex Class when the Objective Is to Train a Single Class

Consider an example where $\omega_1, \omega_2, \ldots, \omega_{M_1}$ are classes in the class space; and attention is given to the *complex class,*

$$(\omega_i, \bar{\omega}_j), \tag{53}$$

which is the event class ω_i but not class ω_j. It is important to be aware of such complex classes to avoid incorrectly training for $(\omega_i, \bar{\omega}_j)$ when the objective is to train for ω_i.

An example of incorrect training is now provided from a *Hearing Loss Subsystem:*

R: Hearing loss in right ear
L: Hearing loss in left ear.

There exists a complex class:

$\Omega_{RL} = (R, L)$: Hearing loss in the right ear and hearing loss in the left ear

$$p(\text{hearing loss at least left ear}) = p(L, R) + p(L, \bar{R})$$
$$p(\text{hearing loss at least right ear}) = p(R, L) + p(R, \bar{L}).$$

Note that

$$p(L) = P(L, R) + p(L, \bar{R}).$$

Recall that

$$P(L \text{ only}) = p(L, \bar{R}) = p(L^*).$$

Events L and R above correspond to classes. The developer must be careful not to confuse an event L with (L, R) or event R with event (R, L).

What are the categories? They are only classes L^* and R^* and complex class (L, R). The event (L, R) is a *complex class* different from the class L and different from class R. Incorrectly, the developer could train a category (in fact, an only class)

$$p(L \text{ only}) = p(L, \bar{R}),$$

imposing Can'ts to prevent class (L, R) when one thinks one is training the class L, i.e., event $(L, R) + (L, \bar{R})$. One would be surprised that hearing loss in the L ear is not recognized when there is bilateral hearing loss. One actually had trained a category which is an only class, L^*.

7-6-11 "At Least" Complex Class and "Not" Complex Class

For the same class space as is in the previous section, the event "at least class ω_i" is expressed by:

$$(\text{At least class } \omega_i) = \bigcup_{\forall_j} (\omega_i, \omega_j), \tag{54}$$

where

$$(\omega_i, \bar{\omega}_j) \triangleq \omega_i^*: \text{ Only class } \omega_i.$$

The event, "Not Class ω_i," is expressed by

$$(\text{Any class but Not class } \omega_i) = \cup\omega_j \quad \forall_j, j \neq i. \tag{55}$$

7-7 HOW ONLY CLASSES AND COMPLEX CLASSES CAN HELP EACH OTHER DURING TRAINING

7-7-1 Introduction: Training—Where Is It From?

The theorem on a posteriori probability by Patrick demonstrates feedback at several levels. Consider the theorem in the form

$$p(\mathbf{x}|\omega_i) = p(\mathbf{x}|\omega_i^*)\frac{p(\omega_i^*)}{p(\omega_i)} + \sum_{\omega_i \,\varepsilon\, \Omega_\xi^*} p(\mathbf{x}|\Omega_\xi^*)\frac{p(\Omega_\xi^*)}{p(\omega_i)}. \tag{56}$$

There is a practical problem when given training samples for "class ω_i." Are these samples from ω_i, ω_i^* or one or more *complex classes* containing ω_i? First of all, it is reasonable to require supervised training to avoid all the problems of unsupervised estimation (Patrick, 1972, 1968, 1965). Second, it is reasonable to expect that training is more nearly often available for ω_i^* than for ω_i or Ω_ξ^* (as in medical diagnosis). There may be exceptions where training thought to be from ω_i^* actually is from a larger set in ω_i; but presumably this can be handled by the hypercubes characterizing ω_i^*. Exceptions can be considered individually. Third, if training is available for ω_i^* and any existing *complex* classes Ω_ξ^*, then it is available for ω_i through Eq. (56).

7-7-2 Calculating Likelihood Functions

Given a recognition vector, there exists a fixed number $p(\mathbf{x}|\omega_i)$. Concerning the components in Eq. (56) for fixed a priori probabilities, we know the following.

Given $p(\mathbf{x}|\omega_i)$ fixed:

1. $p(\mathbf{x}|\omega_i^*)$ decreases as any $p(\mathbf{x}|\Omega_\xi^*)$ increases.
2. The union of complex class probabilities decreases as $p(\mathbf{x}|\omega_i^*)$ increases.

This is *Negative Feedback.*

There exists a relationship between $p(\mathbf{x}|\Omega_\xi^*)$ and $p(\mathbf{x}|\omega_i)$ in certain cases. According to Eq. (56): Given a relationship, $p(\mathbf{x}|\Omega_\xi^*)$ increases as $p(\mathbf{x}|\omega_i)$ increases for ω_i in Ω_ξ^*.

This is *Positive Feedback.*

7-7-3 Iterative System for Sequential Acquisition of Feature Values

A possible iterative system is to process $x_1, x_2, \ldots, x_n$ sequentially:
Stage 1

$$p_1(x_1|\omega_i) = p_1(x_1|\omega_i^*)$$

and our best estimate of the c.c.p.d.f. for Ω_{ij}^* is

$$p_\emptyset(x_1|\Omega_{ij}^*) = p_1(x_1|\omega_i^*), \quad \text{any } \Omega_\xi^* \text{ containing } \omega_i. \qquad x_1 \text{ Like } \omega_i \tag{57a}$$

Stage 2

We now have, from Eq. (57a), terms for the right-hand side of Eq. (56) to obtain

$$p_2(x_1,x_2|\omega_i) = p_2(x_1,x_2|\omega_i^*) \frac{p(\omega_i^*)}{p(\omega_i)} + \sum_{\omega_i \, \varepsilon \, \Omega_\xi^*} p_\emptyset(x_1|\Omega_{ij}^*) \frac{p(\Omega_\xi^*)}{p(\omega_i)}.$$

But because of Stage 1,

$$p_1(x_1, x_2|\Omega_{ij}^*) = p_2(x_1|\omega_i)\, p_2(x_2|\omega_j) \qquad x_1 \text{ Like } \omega_i \; x_2 \text{ Like } \omega_j \tag{57b}$$

Stage n

By induction, at some stage n

$$p_n(x_1, x_2, \ldots, x_n|\omega_i) = p_n(x_1, x_2, \ldots, x_n|\omega_i^*) \frac{p(\omega_i^*)}{p(\omega_i)} + \sum_{\omega_i \, \varepsilon \, \Omega_{ij}^*} p_{n-1}(x_1, x_2, \ldots, x_{n-1}|\Omega_{ij}^*) \frac{p(\Omega_\xi^*)}{p(\omega_i)}.$$

Analogous to Eq. (57b):

$$p_{n-1}(x_1, x_2, \ldots, x_{n-1}|\Omega_{ij}^*) = \prod_{n_i \text{ Like } \omega_i} p_n(x_k|\omega_i).$$

Analogous to the second part of Eq. (57b),

$$\prod_{m_{ji} \text{ Like } \omega_j \text{ but Unlike } \omega_i.} p_n(x_k|\omega_i) \tag{57c}$$

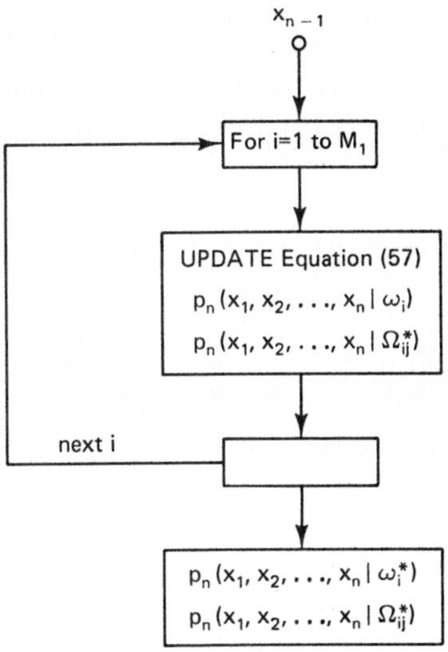

FIGURE 7.1. Training components of the Theorem on A Posteriori Probability (Patrick).

n_i is the number of features $\{x_k\}$ like ω_i while m_{ji} is the number of features $\{x_k\}$ like ω_j but unlike ω_i.

In this system, we assume that training is available for *only classes* ω^*_i. *At Stage Ø,* an estimate of the likelihood of only class ω^*_i is available [first part of Eq. (57a)]. This gives an estimate of the likelihood of class ω_i; but *all complex classes containing* ω_i *are equally probable at this point.*

At Stage 1, a better estimate of the likelihood of ω^*_i is available as is a "primitive" estimate of all complex class likelihoods for ω_i. In turn, an improved estimate of the likelihood of ω_i is available, giving the next improved estimate of complex classes.

Computation of *complex class* probabilities can be accomplished at the same time that *only class* probabilities are computed, as illustrated in Figure 7.1.

The iteration began with a training record from only class ω^*_i and one from only class ω^*_j. This taught about Ω^*_{ij} and ω_i and ω_j. At Stage 2 a better estimate of ω_i and ω_j is obtained because of the estimate of Ω^*_{ij} at Stage 1; then the estimate of Ω^*_{ij} is improved. This process continues to any Stage n.

8

Primitives, Features, Complex Features, and Insignificant Features

8-1 INTRODUCTION

A diagram of the knowledge base structure for integrating **AI** and **SPR** is presented in Section 1-4 of Chapter 1. In Section 1-2 of Chapter 1 primitives, features, and complex features are discussed. In this chapter many aspects of these constructions are considered. Then in Chapter 9 the engineering of the category conditional probability density function will be developed. Chapters 8 and 9 are integral in that the knowledge base structure defined in Chapter 8 allows the engineering in Chapter 9.

A classification system requires a knowledge base structure; and the feature structure (along with classes and categories) must be postulated a priori. This structure can be changed or adapted. Studies in dimensionality reduction (Patrick, 1972) have shown that the developer should engineer the feature structure as carefully as possible to reflect a priori knowledge to understand how incorrect engineering can lead to misclassifications. To obtain a minimal size set of features a helpful construction is that of *linear independence.* It is essential to understand how to handle *features with mutually exclusive values but which may be concepts* rather than numerical numbers.

Sets of *binary features* (features with two values—True and False) must be studied to learn how they can form a single variable called a *complex feature* value that can be composed of concepts rather than ordered numerical numbers or ranges. A complex feature can be a significant way up the hierarchical ladder toward categories and for this reason needs to be considered as integral to the category conditional probability density function.

There are features with *Rule-in* values and values which impose a *Can't,* implementing a form of "common sense."

Statistical dependence and independence of features must be understood as a different construction from linear independence. The former requires samples for learning **(SPR).**

We introduce constructions called *critical* and *noncritical features* where the latter also can be an *insignificant feature.*

A *missing feature value* is a property of the pattern to be recognized or classified (findings) whereas an *insignificant feature* is a property of the previously trained system!

Another consideration is that an observation or finding (feature value) has some probability of being in error. A way of making a classification system less sensitive to observation error is desirable. One can anticipate that there is a trade-off between increasing observation error and decreasing diagnostic performance. Ideally, we would like to design a system presuming no observation error, a situation resulting in highest diagnostic performance. *This places more responsibility with the user (feature extractor) but the system is more sensitive.*

Finally, statistical methods for dimensionality reduction are considered but the reader is referred to such books as *Fundamentals of Pattern Recognition* (Patrick, 1972). Statistical dimensionality reduction concerns the problem of learning from example the "best" subset of features or some "best" set of combinations of features. Presumed is that the initial set of features are redundant, correlated, dependent, and that some constitute a nuisance. These methods usually are based on models.

In this book a *measurement* will be taken as some collection of features placed together for interaction between a user and the *interviewer.* It is a construction of convenience and may not affect diagnostic performance unless it is a complex feature.

8-2 LINEAR INDEPENDENCE

Feature vectors $\mathbf{x}_1, \mathbf{x}_2, \ldots, \mathbf{x}_L$ are basis vectors such that a particular category's presentation $\mathbf{x}$ can be represented as:

$$\mathbf{x} = \sum_{j=1}^{L} x_j \mathbf{x}_j \tag{1}$$

where

$$x_j = (\mathbf{x}, \mathbf{x}_j) \tag{2}$$

is an expression of the projection of **x** onto x_j. The coefficient x_j is an expression of how much of the basis vector $\mathbf{x}_j$ "is in **x**."

The basis vectors $\mathbf{x}_j$ should be *linearly independent,* satisfying

$$(\mathbf{x}_j, \mathbf{x}_\xi) = \emptyset \qquad \forall\, \xi \neq j. \tag{3}$$

The vector space spanned by $\mathbf{x}_1, \mathbf{x}_2, \ldots, \mathbf{x}_L$ is *complete* if any vector **x** in the space can be represented by Eq. (1) with coefficients given by Eq. (2).

The coefficients $x_j = (\mathbf{x}, \mathbf{x}_j)$ are numbers on the real line and thus are ordered. Ordered numbers are mutually exclusive, giving rise to the requirement of mutually exclusive feature values. The construction of linear independence suggests that if a feature is appended to each of these dimensions then the features are not redundant—all are needed. That is, a pattern is represented by projections onto these dimensions.

8-3 FEATURES AND FEATURE VALUES

A *j*th feature is a name or title given to the basis vector $\mathbf{x}_j$; a feature value of $\mathbf{x}_j$ is the coefficient $x_j = (\mathbf{x}, \mathbf{x}_j)$. In **CONSULT-I®**, **CONSULT LEARNING SYSTEM®**, and **The OUTCOME ADVISOR®** the feature vectors (basis vectors) may be considered the *L*-tuples.

$$\begin{aligned}\mathbf{x}_1 &= \{1, \emptyset, \emptyset, \ldots, \emptyset\}\\ \mathbf{x}_2 &= \{\emptyset, 1, \emptyset, \ldots, \emptyset\}\\ &\ \ \vdots\\ \mathbf{x}_L &= \{\emptyset, \emptyset, \emptyset, \ldots 1\}.\end{aligned}$$

It is easy to verify that

$$\begin{aligned}(\mathbf{x}_i, \mathbf{x}_j) &= 1,\ i = j\\ &= \emptyset,\ i \neq j.\end{aligned}$$

Each one of these feature vectors has a name. For example, in medicine, $\mathbf{x}_1$ might be a thyroid function test with the name T_4, $\mathbf{x}_2$ a test with the name T_3, $\mathbf{x}_3$ the symptom name weakness, and so on.

The feature values,

$$x_{j_v} = (\mathbf{x}, \mathbf{x}_j),\ v = 1,2, \ldots V,$$

the possible projections of $\mathbf{x}$ onto $\mathbf{x}_j$ *must be mutually exclusive.* This is a rule which incorrectly might be violated by a developer, constructing a V-tuple of feature values

$$\{x_{j_v}\}_{v=1}^{V},$$

who does not understand or abide by the rule. The rule is easy to apply to continuous feature values which can be discretized or intervalized, such as, temperature, heart rate, age, respiration, laboratory test values, and so on. It is more difficult to apply to subjective concepts such as weakness, history information, nausea and skin wetness. The problem usually arises when one attempts to create user friendliness by embedding feature values in a measurement, using more than one feature. Then, the values of that measurement may not be mutually exclusive.

Features should be carefully selected realizing that they correspond to basis vectors and should be linearly independent. *A feature should contribute to completeness and should not be redundant.*

8-4 MEASUREMENTS

A measurement can be a feature value (if Type Ø) or an embedded feature value (if Type 1)†. A measurement is an interviewer convenience which does not contribute to the mathematics of decision making. However, the ability of a user to interact with **CONSULT-I®** requires user friendliness with respect to having the user supply feature values. When there are large numbers of features, it may be necessary to utilize special techniques to simplify the interviewer.

The values of a measurement are indexed $v = 1,2, \ldots, V$. In **CONSULT-I®** a variable MEAS(v) is defined to indicate the user's response regarding the value indexed by v. The interpretation of MEAS(v) depends on the type of measurement. Measurement types are indicated by Ø, 1, 2, 3,. . . . Most attention in this book is given to Type Ø and Type 1 features.

†It is convenient to dispense with the word "measurement" except that to be precise it is necessary to describe the collection of features summarized by Type 1. We conveniently drop measurement and use the term Type 1 feature, although it is not rigorous.

8-5 INTERVIEWER

8-5-1 Interaction between User and Recognition Vector (Findings)

The interviewer provides the interaction between the user and the *recognition vector* $\mathbf{x}_r$. Once the recognition vector $\mathbf{x}_r$ is specified, **CONSULT-I®** follows an optimum system model when making decisions with respect to the training provided. Considerations in designing the interviewer are now discussed.

8-5-2 User–Activated Features—No Feature Prompt

Without a prompt, the user supplies a feature name with its value. The interviewer searches the feature list, furnishes the feature and inserts the user-supplied feature value in the recognition vector $\mathbf{x}_r$. The user can supply feature values in sequence.

Theoretically, a *differential diagnosis* M_D can be formed and suggests the "next best feature" for which to supply a value. Various such methods of feature selection are considered in Chapter 10, starting with optimum feature selection strategies.

8-5-3 User–Activated Features—Feature Prompt

8-5-3-1 Sequential Feature Prompt

Sequential feature prompt is where the interviewer supplies, in sequence, one feature after the other to which the user supplies feature values. *This implies that a subsystem is involved rather than a total system since otherwise a very, very long list of features would have to be reviewed by the user.*

8-5-3-2 Selected Feature Prompt

Selected feature prompt is where the user has an external list of features available. By number, the user selects a feature for which to select a value. This method is, relatively, extremely fast.

8-6 MISSING FEATURE VALUES (OF THE FINDINGS)

A feature of the findings for which no value is available is said to have a missing value as previously discussed. *The interviewer reserves the response*

"M" for the user to specify the value as missing. Mathematically, the response "M" is not a feature value. The set of feature values $\{x_{j_v}\}$ does not include the value "M". A missing feature results in computation of category conditional probability density functions in a marginal space not including the feature(s) with missing value(s).

For nonsequential interviewing, all features are initialized as having missing values at the beginning of the interview.

8-7 TYPE Ø MEASUREMENT

A Type Ø measurement *is a feature* with two or more values, and the values are mutually exclusive. Examples of Type Ø measurements (features) include sex, age, weight, heart rate, respiration, many laboratory tests, net worth, income, waiting time, and so on.

Only one value† of Type Ø measurement (feature) is selected in **CONSULT-I®**. Thus

MEAS = 1, value number v selected.
= Ø otherwise.

Type Ø measurements are especially user friendly. A flow diagram for a Type Ø measurement is shown in Figure 8.1.

Dependence among Type Ø features results from column training with appended minicolumn training for any column. Columns and minicolumns are introduced in Chapter 9.

8-8 TYPE 1 MEASUREMENT

A Type 1 measurement contains an ordered list indexed by $v = 1,2, \ldots, V$. Each index corresponds to a single feature having two values: True, False (called a Binary Feature). Thus

MEAS(v) = 1, if feature indexed by v is True.

MEAS(v) = 2, if feature indexed by v is False.

MEAS(v) = "M" if feature indexed by v is missing.

The string R$($J$) = "M" is reserved for the user to indicate that all features in the list have missing feature values. Note that MEAS(v) = "M" signifies that the feature (of the findings) indexed by v has a miss-

†An exception is the logical OR of feature values to take into account uncertainty.

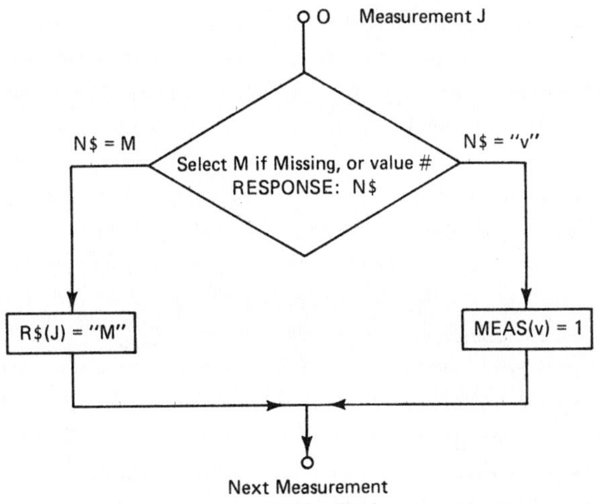

FIGURE 8.1 Flow Diagram for Type Ø measurement.

ing feature value but says nothing about the other features. It is possible *to specify that at least some number of features have True values without specifying which features have the True values. This is an example of a complex feature.*

Features in the Type 1 measurement list are said to be *embedded.* Each feature has a value True, False, or Missing. *Because each feature is processed individually, AND capability is preserved among embedded features.* AND as used here is a property of the training and thus construction of the category conditional probability density function discussed in Chapter 9. It is important that the process of embedding features does not cause ANDing capability to be lost. A special consideration is dependence among the features of a Type 1 measurement. Each feature in a Type 1 measurement expresses a property (*primitive*) of the category. Given the category, the probability of one feature value clearly can depend on the values of other features. Methods to express this dependence will be discussed. The flow diagram for a Type 1 measurement is shown in Figure 8.2.

8-9 OTHER TYPES OF MEASUREMENTS

8-9-1 Type 2 Measurement

A Type 2 measurement consists of a set of embedded features for which each feature can have more than two values. It is not discussed further at this time but it is a form of complex feature.

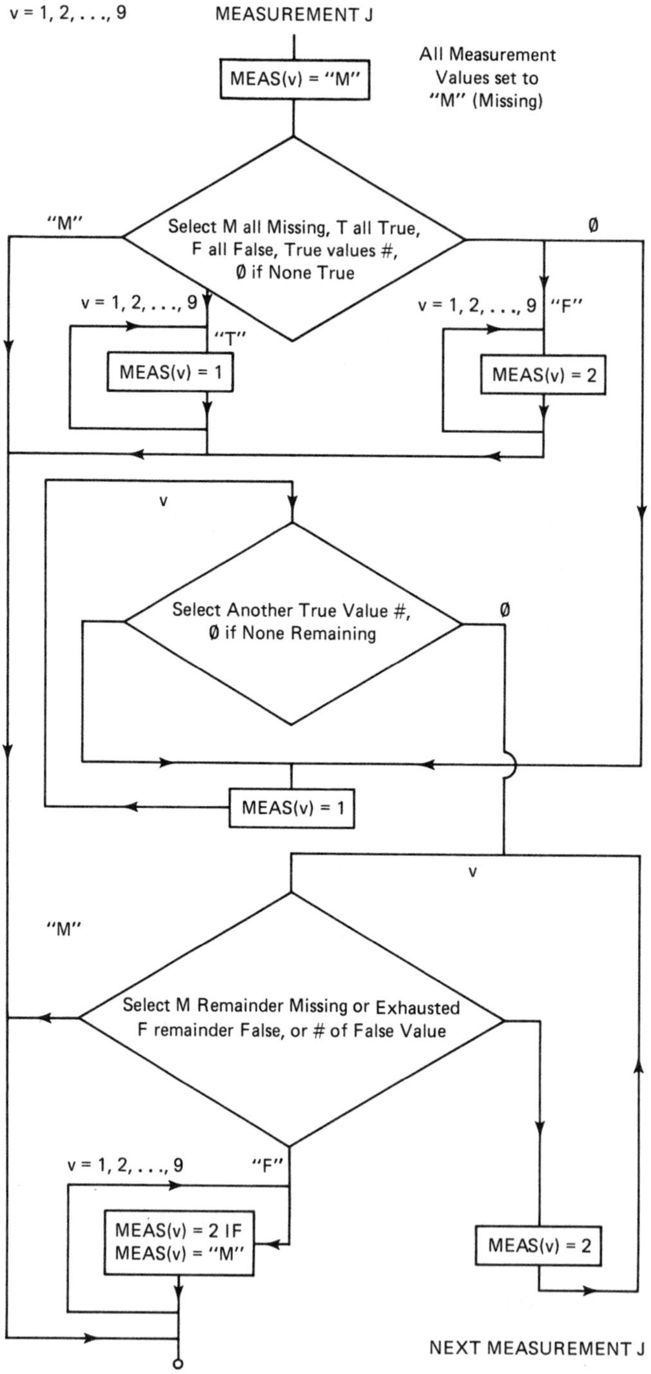

FIGURE 8.2 Flow Diagram for Type 1 measurement.

8-9-2 Type 3 Measurement

A Type 3 measurement implements a linear or nonlinear function of supplied measurement values. The functional creates a feature with mutually exclusive values and thus satisfies the requirement for a Type Ø feature. The functional utilizes addition, multiplication, division or exponentiation (or logarithm). It can involve the solution of simultaneous equations with specified dependent variables, independent variables being the output of the complex feature.

A Type 3 measurement has capability for enormous complexity reduction and dimensionality reduction. It is an example of mapping from a measurement space to a feature space; and it is an example of a complex feature. Special uses include time dependence and complex physiological expressions. It can be used to incorporate a priori physical constraints. It eliminates combinatorial explosion.

8-9-3 Type 4 Measurement

A Type 4 measurement is a Type 1 measurement where each embedded feature has a value with a continuous range of values. Possible probability density functions for embedded feature x_j, $p(x_j|\gamma_i^*)$ include the following:

		Supplies	Parameters	
$p(x\|\gamma_i^*) = \frac{1}{\sqrt{2\Pi\sigma_i}}$	$\exp\{-(x - m_i)^2/2\sigma_i^2\}$	σ_i	m_i	(4)
$p(x\|\gamma_i^*) = \frac{1}{V}$	$x_0 \leq x \leq x_o + V$	x_0,	V	
$p(x\|\gamma_i^*) = a_x$	$x_0 \leq x \leq x_o + V$ $a_x = 2V$			

8-9-4 Type 5 Measurement

A Type 5 measurement is a special case of a Type 1 measurement where individual features $x_1, x_2, \ldots, x_9$ have dependent continuous feature values. These variables have a multidimensional Gaussian probability density function.

$$p(x_1, x_2, \ldots, x_9|\gamma_i^*) = \frac{1}{(2\Pi_i)^{9/2}|A|} \exp\{-(\mathbf{x} - \mathbf{M}_i)^t\mathbf{A}(\mathbf{x} - \mathbf{M}_i\} \tag{5}$$

where

$$A = \begin{bmatrix} a_{11} & a_{12} & \cdots & a_{19} \\ a_{21} & a_{22} & \cdots & \\ \vdots & & \ddots & \\ a_{91} & \cdots & & a_{99} \end{bmatrix}$$

$$(\mathbf{x} - \mathbf{M}_i)^t A(\mathbf{x} - \mathbf{M}_i) = \sum_{\eta=1}^{9} \sum_{\xi=1}^{9} (\mathbf{x}_\xi - M_{i_\xi})(\mathbf{x}_\eta - M_{i_\eta})a_{\xi_\eta} \qquad (6)$$

the vector $\mathbf{M}_i$ is the mean vector and $\mathbf{A}$ is the inverse of the covariance of matrix $\boldsymbol{\Phi}_i$ for these variables for category γ_i^*.

8-10 STATISTICALLY INDEPENDENT AND DEPENDENT FEATURES

The feature vector previously defined can consist of a subset of independent features denoted $\mathbf{x}_I$ and a subset of dependent features noted $\mathbf{x}_D$:

$$\mathbf{x} = [\mathbf{x}_I, \mathbf{x}_D]. \qquad (7)$$

In general, we provide that $\mathbf{x}_D$ consists of subsets (or subsubsets) of dependent features. The subsubsets of dependent features have local dependencies, sometimes referred to as *packets* of information.

8-11 CRITICAL FEATURE, CAN'T

A *critical feature* x_j for a category γ_i^* is one for which

$$p(x_j = x_{j_v}|\gamma_i^*) = 1 \qquad (8)$$

for some feature value x_{j_v}. That is, all the probability density is at a single feature value.

A *noncritical feature* is one for which the probability density is nonzero at more than one feature value.

A **"CAN'T"** is imposed on category γ_i^* when

$$p(x_j = x_{j_v}|\gamma_i^*) = \emptyset \qquad (9)$$

for some feature value x_{j_v}. The category "Can't" occurs when $x_j = x_{j_v}$, i.e., the category is "Ruled-out."

8-12 RULE-IN FEATURE VALUE

A "Rule-In" feature value x_{j_v} for category γ_i^* exists if

$$\begin{aligned} p(x_j = x_{j_v}|\gamma_i^*) &= 1, \text{ for category } \gamma_i^* \\ p(x_j = x_{j_v}|\gamma_\xi^*) &= \emptyset, \text{ for all categories } \gamma_\xi^* \text{ not } \gamma_i^*. \end{aligned} \tag{10}$$

The Rule-in *feature implies interaction between all the categories.* If nature were training the category patterns with a *Can't,* she would never allow category γ_i^* to have a pattern with feature value x_{j_v}. An expert is hard pressed to declare a *Rule-in* feature because the expert has to declare all categories not γ_i^* as never having feature value x_{j_v}.

8-13 COMPARING TYPE Ø FEATURES WITH TYPE 1 FEATURES

8-13-1 Type Ø Feature

Because the values of a Type Ø feature are mutually exclusive, a response for one value precludes a response for another (when training)†. Thus operations AND and NOT are possible. The operation MISSING for the whole feature is allowed.

The advantage of a Type Ø feature is that, in effect, different "weights" can be given for respective "true" values. As indicated previously, one "true" value precludes other values for this feature.

A Type Ø feature is a primitive but also is the most fundamental decision to be made in the knowledge base hierarchy. It cannot be decomposed further. A Type Ø feature also is a measurement in that it is a basic way of observation.

8-13-2 Type 1 Feature

A Type 1 feature usually is embedded in a Type 1 measurement. These Type 1 features of a measurement, taken together, can form a Complex feature value. Because respective Type 1 features in a Type 1 measurement can have a True or False value, possible operations among the embedded Type 1 features are AND, BUT, NOT, NEITHER, ALL, and MISSING. The weight for a particular logical operation can be variable through columns or minicolumns.

---

† Multiple values of a Type Ø feature can be specified in the recognition vector. This corresponds to ORing multiple inputs.

8-14 INTERACTION BETWEEN FEATURES

The Type 1 measurement forms a concept about a pattern (sample). A concept formed by one Type 1 measurement may make it *unnecessary* to form another Type 1 measurement value. This is analogous to the AI Frame construction proposed by Minsky, 1975. Translated into practical terms in **CONSULT-I®**, this means that the interviewer would be prevented from asking (or inclined not to ask) certain additional questions.

The constraint not to ask additional questions also is an example of behavioral performance as compared with diagnostic performance. *Obviously this should be an essential aspect of feature selection in the interviewer.*

Feature selection (see Chapter 10) from the **SPR** standpoint considers the next feature to select that would result in highest diagnostic performance. Interaction between features can rule out selecting certain features, an AI construction (i.e., Frame). But, in reality, dependence among features must be learned by example (an **SPR** construction).

8-15 SUBOPTIMUM DEPENDENCE AMONG TYPE 1 FEATURES

8-15-1 Introduction

In the absence of accurate estimates of event (categories) probabilities, various approaches can be devised to let true properties of a category enhance without false properties overly dehancing the category. For the most part, knowledge about a pattern is incorporated in a Type 1 measurement for that pattern.

8-15-2 Average Property of a Pattern Incorporated in a Type 1 Measurement

The *average truth* of a Type 1 measurement can be defined,

$$\bar{T}_j = \frac{1}{9} \sum_{v=1}^{9} p(x_{j_v} = T|\gamma_i^*)T_v \tag{11}$$

$$T_v \neq \emptyset \text{ if value } v \text{ true}$$

$$T_v = \emptyset \text{ if value } v \text{ false,}$$

and the *average false* of a Type 1 measurement

$$\bar{F}_j = \frac{1}{9} \sum_{v=1}^{9} \quad p(x_{j_v} = F|\gamma_i^*)F_v \tag{12}$$

$$F_v \neq \emptyset \text{ if value } v \text{ false}$$

$$F_v = \emptyset \text{ if value } v \text{ true}$$

If $\emptyset \leq T_v \leq 1$ and $\emptyset \leq F_V \leq 1$, then

$$\bar{T}_j \text{ and } \bar{F}_j \text{ range from } \emptyset \text{ to } 1.$$

These averaging functions can be viewed as filters protecting against fluctuations, but a disadvantage is that sensitivity of the measurement is decreased. This material could well be discussed in Chapter 14 which deals with considerations when training expert systems. The developer of an expert system may want to protect against faulty feature extraction and thus decrease the sensitivity of a Type 1 measurement to responses given as values for its embedded Type 1 features.

8-15-3 Average Joint Truth of Features

Likewise, average truth for pairs of feature values being present can be defined (Average Joint False also can be defined).

8-15-4 Maximum Type 1 Feature

Define a functional

$$p(x_1, x_2, \ldots, x_9|\gamma_i^*) = \underset{\substack{j \\ \text{TRUE} \\ j=1,2,\ldots 9}}{\text{MAX}} \{p(x_{j_v} = \text{True}|\gamma_i^*)\} \underset{\substack{j \\ \text{FALSE} \\ j=1,2,\ldots 9}}{\text{MAX}} \{p(x_{j_v} = \text{False}|\gamma_i^*)\} \tag{13}$$

which "gives one chance" for the presence of a property to affect the category conditional probability density function and one chance for the absence of a property to affect the category conditional probability density function. The reader can derive modifications.

8-15-5 Significant Type 1 Measurement

A functional for a complex feature derived and discussed in Chapter 9 is

$$\prod_{j=1}^{9} (1 - p_{\delta_j}) + p_{\delta_j} p(x_{j_v}|\gamma_i^*, \delta_j) \tag{14}$$

where

p_{δ_j} = Probability that an embedded Type 1 feature is significant.

Setting

$$(1 - p_{\delta_j}) = \epsilon, \text{ say, } \epsilon = 1/10$$

allows for making a feature "somewhat" insignificant. On the other hand, setting

$$(1 - p_{\delta_j}) = 1/2$$

makes the feature just as likely significant as insignificant; this has a smoothing effect but sensitivity is decreased.

8-15-6 Product of True Probabilities

The functional

$$\begin{gathered}\Pi\ p(x_{j_v}|\gamma_i^*) \\ x_{j_v} = \text{True},\ v = 1,2,\ldots 9\end{gathered}$$

regards absence of a property as complete insignificance.

8-15-7 Log Parametric Measurement

Define a parameter S and variable probability p_v, where

$$\begin{gathered}\emptyset \leq p_v \leq 1 \\ S = 1, 2, 3, 4, \ldots\end{gathered}$$

consider the functional

$$g(\mathbf{p};\ \mathbf{S}) = \frac{\prod_{v=1}^{9} \ln\{S + p_v\}}{\prod_{v=1}^{9} \ln\{S + 1\}} \tag{15}$$

This functional is sketched versus $p_v = p$ for various values of the parameter S in Figure 8.3.

The intent is to define

$$p_v = p(x_{j_v}|\gamma_i^*).$$

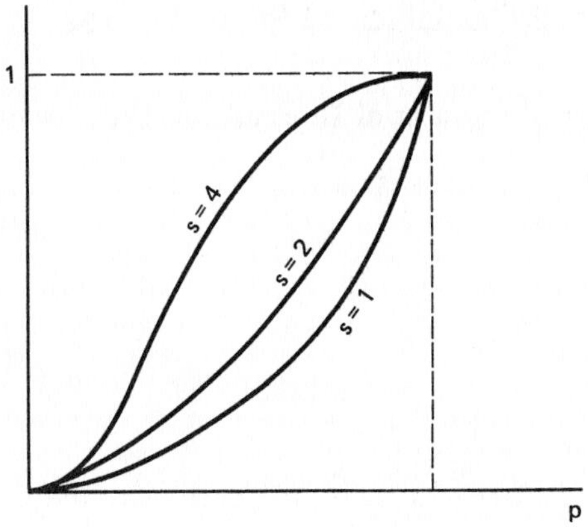

FIGURE 8.3. Log parametric function.

Advantages of the functional are:

1. $\emptyset \leq g \leq 1$
2. $g(p)$ is an increasing function of p_v.
3. Increasing S causes an increasing amount of the range of the function to be located in high values.

A modification of the function in Eq. (15) is

$$g(\mathbf{p}; \mathbf{S}) = \frac{\prod_{v=1}^{9} \ln \{S_v + p_v\}}{\prod_{v=1}^{9} \ln \{S_v + 1\}} \tag{16}$$

which allows weighing the rise of the functional with each p_v individually.

Other variations are the:

Log Parametric Maximum Probability

$$g(\mathbf{p}; \mathbf{S}) = \frac{\{\ln\{S + \mathrm{MAX}\,\{p_v\}\}^9}{\{\ln\,\{S + 1\}\}^9} \tag{17}$$

and

Log Parametric Maximum Minimal Probability

$$g(\mathbf{p}; \mathbf{S}) = \frac{\{\ln\,\{S + \mathrm{MAX}\{p_v\}\}\}^5\,\{\ln\{S + \mathrm{MIN}\{p_v\}\}\}^4}{\{\ln\,\{S + 1\}\}^9}\,. \tag{18}$$

8-15-8 Mechanical Conditional Probabilities

8-15-8-1 Sequential Increase of True Features

Denote as usual the features in a Type 1 measurement $x_j, j = 1,2, \ldots,$ 9 as usual ($v = 9$). Denote by

$$\{T_{j_v}\}$$

and

$$\{F_{j_v}\}$$

those embedded features having respectively, True and False values. One objective can be sequentially to increase the probability of True features and decrease the probability of False features based on the sequential number of True features.

Let

$NT(J)$ = Number of True Features for jth measurement. Modify p_{j_v} for True Features

$$p_{j_v} \text{ (modified)} = \frac{n_{j_v} + NT(J)}{9 + NT(J)}, \text{ True Features} \qquad (19a)$$

$$p_{j_v} \text{ (modified)} = \frac{n_{j_v}}{9 + NT(J)}, \text{ False Features} \qquad (19b)$$

These modified probabilities reflect that as the number of True properties increases then the category is more likely; and thus, *a conditional probability of a True feature is mechanically adjusted upward.* On the other hand, the conditional probability of a False feature is mechanically adjusted downward (the reverse of this latter model will be discussed).

If there are NO true features, then nothing is changed. As soon as there are one or more True features, the functional becomes "suspicious" that there should be more. With the presence of True features, the functional is less willing to let False features "have their marginal probabilities."

Extending this concept leads to the minicolumn approach (see Chapter 9, Section 9-11). Ideally, the true probabilities are learned using the **CONSULT LEARNING SYSTEM®** or **The OUTCOME ADVISOR®**.

The last model is ad hoc and whether it improves performance needs to be tested on the particular application. There is another construction that must be examined, however. This is *the construction that*

Insignificance of unobserved increases as the number of observed True properties increases. Using this concept, just the opposite of Eq. (15) is achieved. Complex features formed using these models can be tested for their ability to represent a category presentation, whether typical or atypical.

8-15-8-2 Sequential Increase in Insignificance

An interesting concept is that the significance of a Type 1 feature being false can decrease as the number of True features increases. Consider Eq. (14) when significance approaches zero. That is

$$\{(1 - p_{\delta_j}) + p_{\delta_j}\, p(x_{j_v}|\gamma_i^*, \delta_j) \rightarrow 1$$
$$p_{\delta_j} \rightarrow \emptyset$$

whether x_{j_v} = True or x_{j_v} = False.

This suggests a mechanical conditional probability where, given

$$NT(J) = \text{Number of True features for } j\text{th measurement,}$$

$$p_{j_v}\ (\text{modified}) = \frac{n_{j_v} + NT(J)}{9 + NT(J)}, \quad \text{False Features} \qquad (20)$$

Thus, the category conditional probability of a false feature increases as the number of True features increases. This is just the opposite of Eq. (19b).

Equation (20) reflects the construction that insignificance increases as the category likelihood increases. There is less inclination to let a false reading cause an error as insignificance increases. *This is consistent with the goal of achieving high likelihood,* and may be necessary when the probabilities are not available from the scientific method.

In medical diagnosis nature doesn't play games, as far as we know, by changing the rules for significance and insignificance. Such is not the case in military game theory or when there is time variation.

How much intelligence can be built into a Type 1 feature with 9 embedded binary features? Up to this point particular embedded features have not had more effect and have not depended in a deterministic way on other embedded features. Now consider this: each Type 1 measurement is itself a classification system, mapping the 9 responses to an outcome. That is the nature of a complex feature—a natural part of the knowledge base hierarchy. You can see that a Type 1 feature itself provides cause (condition) and effect (outcome). Causal network approaches to classification in effect involve the mathematics of the complex feature such as a Type 1 measurement. A Type 1 feature describes a particular property of a pattern such as history, orientation, size, shape, severity, risk, drug status, organ condition, state, and so on.

9

Engineering Construction of the Category Conditional Probability Density Function

9-1 INTRODUCTION

The category conditional probability density function (c.c.p.d.f.) is the inference function in **CONSULT-I®** that measures the "closeness" of a pattern† called the recognition sample, $\mathbf{x}_r$, to each category in $\{\gamma_{ij}^*\}$ in the knowledge base. Outwardly it implements inductive inference but inwardly deductive inference operates for marginal projections when feature values are missing and when imposing Can't operations for "common sense." Presentations not previously seen during training are "generated" by these operations which are in addition to those generated by probabilistic inference rules called columns with minicolumn modification. Columns can be viewed as inductive conjunctions (ANDs of subsets of features) of production rules guided in their construction by the field of knowedge about the category. Minicolumns can be viewed as local packets of knowledge (subsets of features) that can modify a column.

Statistical dependence among features for a category exists within the column; and *local* statistical dependence is imposed by minicolumns.

Categories not previously seen during training, in particular complex classes, are generated by deduction if required. The basic entry point for training usually is as only classes $\{\omega_{ij}^*\}$.

The theorem on a posteriori probability by Patrick describes this inductive inference function with concept formation of new categories

†We use closeness rather than distance to avoid the need for mathematical jargon. As used in this book, a closeness measure can satisfy the requirements of a distance measure.

while all categories in the knowledge base remain mutually exclusive. There are a very large number of complex class categories that are *potential* and never generated in the knowledge base. On the other hand, a complex class can be provided a priori just as can an only class.

This engineered c.c.p.d.f. is an integration of **SPR** and **AI** made possible through the theorem on a posteriori probability by Patrick *whereby categories remain mutually exclusive although they can be statistically dependent during concept formation* (**SPR**). Statistical dependence among features can be localized and their construction reflects F→F rules, F→H rules, and H→H rules of **AI** and "Bayes networks."

Flexibility results by being able to introduce simplifying (though accurate) conditions of independent features for certain features while providing for dependence among features where appropriate. For a very large system with M_1 (number of classes) in the thousands and L (number of features) in the thousands plus complex classes, most features are insignificant for any given category. Provision is available to optimally use knowledge that features are insignificant for a category. Definitions of insignificance are capable of reflecting knowledge of feature value uncertainty.

It is possible to construct $\{p(\mathbf{x}|\gamma_i^*)\}$ for each of several subsystems whose interconnection constitutes a *total system.* This occurs when the data base is accumulated by experts working in specialties, thus suggesting they are working on subsystems. The method of subsystem interconnection should be optimum for the problem.

In general, we will consider a problem consisting of M categories: $\gamma_1^*, \gamma_2^*, \ldots \gamma_M^*$. A category is an *only class* ω_i^* or a *complex class* Ω_ξ^*.

9-2 COLUMNS OR SUBCATEGORIES

Let K be the initial maximum number of *probabilistic presentations* (each called a column or hypercube or subcategory) for a category. Then

$$p(\mathbf{x}|\gamma_i^*) = \sum_{k=1}^{K} p(\mathbf{x}, \gamma_{i_k}^*|\gamma_i^*)$$

$$= \sum_{k=1}^{K} p(\mathbf{x}|\gamma_{i_k}^*, \gamma_i^*)p(\gamma_{i_k}^*|\gamma_i^*) \tag{1}$$

$$= \sum_{k=1}^{K} p(\mathbf{x}|\gamma_{i_k}^*)\, p(\gamma_{i_k}^*|\gamma_i^*)$$

The term $p(\mathbf{x}|\gamma^*_{i_k})$ is considered the column-conditional probability density function for the kth column of category γ^*_i. It follows that

$$\sum_{k=1}^{K} p(\gamma^*_{i_k}|\gamma^*_i) = 1 \tag{2}$$

and each term $p(\gamma^*_{i_k}|\gamma^*_i)$ reflects the relative frequency that presentation $\gamma^*_{i_k}$ occurs for category γ^*_i. The term $p(\gamma^*_i)$ is the a priori category probability.

9-3 A PRIORI SUBCATEGORY PROBABILITIES

The a priori subcategory probabilities are constrained by

$$p(\gamma^*_i) = \sum_{k=1}^{K} p(\gamma^*_{i_k}). \tag{3}$$

If $p(\gamma^*_i) = 1/M$, then

$$\sum_{k=1}^{K} p(\gamma^*_{i_k}) = \frac{1}{M} \forall\, i \tag{4}$$

If the a priori subcategory probabilities are equal, then

$$p(\gamma^*_{i_k}|\gamma^*_i) = \frac{1}{K} \forall\, k \tag{5}$$

9-4 STATISTICALLY INDEPENDENT AND DEPENDENT FEATURES

Features x_r and x_j are statistically independent given category γ^*_i if

$$p(x_r, x_j|\gamma^*_i) = p(x_r|\gamma^*_i)p(x_j|\gamma^*_i). \tag{6}$$

It is convenient without loss of generality to define the features $\mathbf{x}$ to consist of subsets of *independent features* denoted $\mathbf{x}_I$ and *dependent features* denoted $\mathbf{x}_D$. That is,

$$\mathbf{x} = [\mathbf{x}_D, \mathbf{x}_I] \tag{7}$$

where I and D denote the independent and dependent subsets. Then

$$\begin{aligned} p(\mathbf{x}|\gamma^*_i) &= p(\mathbf{x}_D, \mathbf{x}_I|\gamma^*_i) \\ &= p(\mathbf{x}_I|\gamma^*_i, \mathbf{x}_D)p(\mathbf{x}_D|\gamma^*_i) \\ &= p(\mathbf{x}_I|\gamma^*_i)p(\mathbf{x}_D|\gamma^*_i). \end{aligned} \tag{8}$$

A set of statistically independent features $\{x_\xi\}_{\xi \epsilon I}$ given category γ_i^* satisfies

$$p(x_1, x_2, \ldots, x_{L_I}|\gamma_i^*) = \prod_{\xi=1}^{L_I} p(x_\xi|\gamma_i^*) \tag{9}$$

where L_I is the number of features in the set I. This of course will provide considerable complexity reduction. The set of dependent features D have values that vary in a dependent way among themselves but do not depend on the subset of statistically independent features. There are L_D features in the dependent subset. Let

$$x_{\xi_v}$$

denote the vth value of feature x_ξ; then

$$Cp(x_{1_v}, x_{2_v}, \ldots, x_{L_{D_v}}|\gamma_i^*) \tag{10}$$

is the probability density for category γ_i^* at the particular point represented by

$$x_{1_v}, x_{2_v}, \ldots x_{L_{D_v}} \tag{11}$$

where L_{D_v} is the number of dependent features, and C is the numerical value of Eq. (9) for the independent subset of features.

9-5 MAXIMUM LIKELIHOOD

Equation (1) is a likelihood function biased by $p(\gamma_{i_k}^*|\gamma_i^*)$; and this imposes some practical considerations on the developer of a subsystem as discussed below.

Under the requirement that subcategories $\{\gamma_{i_k}^*\}$ are mutually exclusive, it follows that (fuzzy set operation)

$$p(\mathbf{x}|\gamma_i^*) = \max_k \{p(\mathbf{x}|\gamma_{i_k}^*)\} \tag{12}$$

since only one of the subcategories in $\{p(\mathbf{x}|\gamma_{i_k}^*)\}$ can be true.

In practice, Eq. (12) can be used in place of Eq. (1) when it is understood that Eqs. (4) and (5) are valid and the subcategories $\{\gamma_{i_k}^*\}$ truly are mutually exclusive. Eq. (12) can be viewed as a *fuzzy set* disjunction operation. Considerable effort in this chapter is directed at how to engineer the construction of $p(\mathbf{x}|\gamma_{i_k}^*)$.

9-6 INDEPENDENT SETS OF DEPENDENT FEATURES

The set of dependent features D can be decomposed into mutually exclusive subsets

$$D = D_1 + D_2 + \ldots D_U. \tag{13}$$

Let

$$\{x_\xi^u\} = D_u \tag{14}$$

be the dependent features in dependent subset D_u. Then

$$p(\mathbf{x}_D|\gamma_{i_k}^*) = \prod_{u=1}^{U} p(x_1^u, x_2^u, \ldots, x_{L_u}^u|\gamma_{j_k}^*) \tag{15}$$

is the joint probability density function for subcategory $\gamma_{i_k}^*$ where

U: Number of dependent subsets
u: uth dependent subset
L_u: Number of dependent features in uth subset.

It is reasonable to presume that dependencies are limited to features in a subset while $\gamma_{i_k}^*$ as a column provides for dependencies among subsets in Eq. (15).

The functionals (probabilities) in Eq. (15) can be viewed as packets of knowledge or production rules; but their "interconnection" is engineered by the direction provided in Eq.(15) for subcategory $\gamma_{i_k}^*$ of category γ_i^*. The construction includes "Bayes networks" from AI.

Equation (15) suggests considerable complexity reduction because it is the product of relatively less complex probability densities. It reflects facility to impose *local dependencies* in the feature space while allowing interconnecting subsets of dependent and independent features. This situation occurs in practice where dependencies are among features in a subset rather than among all the features.

9-7 INDEPENDENCE AND DEPENDENCE—COLUMN SPECIFIC

The vector $\mathbf{x}$ can have both independent and dependent subsets, the structure of which depends on the kth column; i.e.,

$$\mathbf{x} = \{\mathbf{x}_{D(k)}, \mathbf{x}_{I(k)}\} \tag{16}$$

for the kth column.

Then, imposing Eq. (16), equations analogous to (8), (9), and (15) respectively exist for the *k*th column:

$$p(\mathbf{x}|\gamma^*_{i_k}) = p(\mathbf{x}_{I(k)}|\gamma^*_i)\, p(\mathbf{x}_{D(k)}|\gamma^*_i) \tag{17}$$

$$p(x_1, x_2, \ldots, x_{L_{I(k)}}|\gamma^*_{i_k}) = \prod_{\xi=1}^{L_{I(k)}} p(x_\xi|\gamma^*_{i_k}) \tag{18}$$

$$p(\mathbf{x}_{D(k)}|\gamma^*_{i_k}) = \prod_{u=1}^{U(k)} p(x^u_1, x^u_2, \ldots, x^u_{L_{u(k)}}|\gamma^*_{i_k}), \tag{19}$$

and Eq. (1) becomes

$$p(\mathbf{x}|\gamma^*_i) = \sum_{k=1}^{K}\left[\prod_{\xi=1}^{L_{I(k)}} p(x_\xi|\gamma^*_{i_k}) \prod_{u=1}^{U(k)} p(x^u_1,x^u_2, \ldots, x^u_{L_{u(k)}}|\gamma^*_{i_k})\, p(\gamma^*_{i_k}|\gamma^*_i)\right] \tag{20}$$

where

$U(k)$ = Number of dependent subsets for *k*th column.
$u(k)$ = *u*th dependent subset for column *k* (generically *u*).
$L_{I(k)}$ = Number of independent features for column *k*.
$\gamma^*_{i_k}$ = *k*th subcategory or column of category γ^*_i.

Equation (20) appears quite mathematical but has been implemented in **CONSULT-I®**. That is, there are *K* columns† of inductive inference for each category. Each column consists of a large number (disjunctions) of injunctions of weights that are true probabilities.

The knowledge base structure directly represented in Eq. (20) includes categories with subcategories. However, the *dependent subsets of features can be viewed as subsubcategories.* Going deeper, since a feature can be a Type 1 measurement, i.e., a *complex feature* itself a function of features, this suggests a subsubsubcategory. Usually we will accept a dependent subset as a complex feature, the first level of concept formation. More generally, subsubcategories are introduced in Eq. (20) by introducing a Σ for a mixture of subsubcategories. A fuzzy set max can replace the Σ.

†A column in a probabilistic "cloud" or quantum region in hyperspace where patterns of a category are gathered together as a presentation of that category. The column contains particular dependencies among features specialized to the presentation.

This facility of engineering a category with increasing depth of local statistical dependencies provides the potential for separating categories in hyperspace. The objective is to engineer complex mathematical surfaces for each category so that the category can consist of complex presentations. Subsubcategories also can be generated as solutions to physical equations which are functions of feature values. This in some cases is equivalent to Type 3 features previously discussed.

9-8 STRUCTURE OF INDEPENDENT PROBABILITY DENSITY FUNCTIONS

9-8-1 Type Ø Independent Feature

A Type Ø Independent Feature is one where

$$p(x_\xi|\gamma_i^*) = p_{\xi_v},\ x_\xi = x_{\xi_v} \tag{21}$$

$$\text{with} \sum_{v=1}^{V} p_{\xi_v} = 1$$

where V is the number of feature values for feature indexed by ξ, x_{ξ_v} denotes the vth value of feature x_ξ, and p_{ξ_v} is the probability density at feature value x_{ξ_v}.

9-8-2 Type 1 Binary Feature (Independent)

A Type 1 Independent Feature is a special case of Eq. (21) where

$$V = 2, \qquad p_{\xi_2} = (1 - p_{\xi_1}),$$

and x_{ξ_1} is associated with TRUE and x_{ξ_2} is associated with NOT TRUE (FALSE).

9-8-3 Uniform Probability Density

Type Ø (and Type 1) independent features have a uniform probability density if

$$p_{\xi_v} = \frac{1}{V} \tag{22}$$

or

$$p_{\xi_v} = \frac{1}{V - NZZ}$$

where NZZ is the number of feature values not used in a Type Ø feature.

9-8-4 Special Feature Values

For a Type Ø feature, it *can be* convenient but not necessary to reserve the feature value

$$x_\xi = 5 : \text{Normal, None}$$

to denote None or Normal.

9-9 INSIGNIFICANT FEATURE FOR PRESENTATION (COLUMN) OF A CATEGORY

The features $x_1, x_2, \ldots, x_L$ are designed so that a subset is useful for representing a category in the subsystem. For any given category, some of the features can be Insignificant. Significant features used to represent members of the category do not depend on any Insignifcant feature and Insignificant features do not depend on each other; thus, *an Insignificant feature is statistically independent of other features* for the category concerned.

By an Insignificant Type Ø feature for a category we mean that *no value of that feature, if present in a recognition or test vector (findings), can convey information about that category relative to other classes.* For a Type 1 feature (embedded in a Type 1 measurement), there are two feature values, TRUE and FALSE. *If the Type 1 feature is insignificant a value FALSE is most probable, with probability approaching one.* All categories for which this feature is insignificant have no knowledge (F→H knowledge) in the data base about this feature to distinguish these categories (H→H knowledge). On the other hand, a category for which the feature is significant does have information conveyed when a recognition vector has a nonmissing value for that feature and its (the category's) likelihood is increased over that for the Insignificant categories.

On the other hand, when a category with an Insignificant feature has a value, FALSE, the likelihood for that category can become relatively higher than for a category having the same feature significant.

Formally, an Insignificant Type 1 feature, x_j, is defined as

$$p(x_j = \text{TRUE}) = \epsilon; \; p(x_j = \text{FALSE}) = 1-\epsilon$$

for some "small" ϵ. A judgment must be made as to how close ϵ is to zero, since $\epsilon = \emptyset$ makes the feature a Rule-out feature (imposes a Can't). In practice we have chosen $\epsilon = 0.1$, which is justified because of uncertainty in training. In summary:

Insignificant Features†

Type $\emptyset$: x_ξ.

A statistically independent feature with uniform probability density function over its range of values:

$p(x_\xi|\gamma^*_{i_k})$: Uniform.

Type 1: x_ξ

$$p(x_\xi = \text{TRUE}|\gamma^*_{i_k}) = \epsilon, \; \epsilon << 1$$
$$p(x_\xi = \text{FALSE}|\gamma^*_{i_k}) = 1 - \epsilon.$$

9-10 SPECIAL CASE: CONTINUOUS PROBABILITY DENSITY FOR INDEPENDENT FEATURE

A Type $\emptyset$ feature can become a continuous feature by letting‡ $V \rightarrow \infty$. An example of such a continuous probability density function is the Gaussian probability density function,

$$p(x_\xi|\omega_i) = \frac{1}{\sqrt{2\pi}\,\sigma} \; e \left[\frac{-(x_\xi - m)^2}{2\sigma^2} \right]$$

where

$$m = E[X_\xi]$$
$$\sigma^2 = E\,[X_\xi - m)^2]$$

are the mean and variance, respectively (X_ξ denotes a random variable, with x_ξ a value of that random variable).

†Alternatively, the probability density of the values for the category can be "normal" as for many other categories. For example, there is a normal range for the white blood cell count but the probability density is not uniform. An insignificant feature is a relative concept. The distribution of its values is "normal." For example, the normal category or reference category has the reference probability density over the values of the feature. **The OUTCOME ADVISOR®** or **CONSULT LEARNING SYSTEM®** can be used to learn the probabilities for feature values corresponding to insignificance.

‡To be mathematically precise, this limit must be taken under specified constraints.

9-11 CREATING MINICOLUMNS IN THE KNOWLEDGE BASE STRUCTURE

The general equation for $p(\mathbf{x}|\gamma_i^*)$, given category γ_i^*, (from Section 9-7) can be expressed:

$p(\mathbf{x}|\gamma_i^*) =$

$$\sum_{k=1}^{K} \prod_{\xi=1}^{L_{I(k)}} p(x_\xi|\gamma_{i_k}^*) \left[\prod_{u=1}^{U(k)} \prod_{s=1}^{S_k(u)} p_{i_{k_s}}^u \right] p(\gamma_{i_k}^*|\gamma_i^*) \tag{23}$$

and requires specification of the following:

1. $I(k)$, $D(k)$: Subsets of independent and dependent features for column k.
2. $u = 1,2, \ldots, U(k)$: uth disjoint subset of dependent features for column k.
3. $L_{I(k)}$: Number of statistically independent features for the kth column.
4. $p(x_\xi|\gamma_{i_k}^*)$: Probability density function given subcategory $\gamma_{i_k}^*$ of an independent feature x_ξ, given the kth column.
5. $p(\gamma_{i_k}^*|\gamma_i^*)$: Relative frequency of the kth column given category γ_i^*. Included: reset $p(\gamma_{i_k}^*|\gamma_i^*) = 1$ if $p(\gamma_{i_k}^*|\gamma_i^*)$ is maximum over all k, Ø otherwise.
6. $p_{i_{k_s}}^u$ Probability density for sth feature in the uth minicolumn modification of dependent features for kth column.
7. $S_k(u)$: Number of features in uth subset of features for column k.

Equation (23) results from Eq. (20) by representing

$$p(x_1^u, x_2^u, \ldots, x_{L_{u(k)}}^u) = \prod_{s=1}^{S_k(u)} Lu(k)\ p_{i_{k_s}}^u$$

9-12 DEDUCTIVE OPERATION OF ALLOWING MISSING FEATURE VALUES

9-12-1 Partitioning the Recognition Vector: Missing Features

Let $\mathbf{x}_r$ be the *recognition (or test vector)* (the findings) consisting of a subset $\mathbf{x}_M$ of features with missing values and a subset $\mathbf{x}_p$ with values present:

$$\mathbf{x}_r = \begin{bmatrix} \mathbf{x}_p \\ \mathbf{x}_M \end{bmatrix} \tag{24}$$

Then the category conditional probability density function for those features that are present is obtained by the well known projection operation in probability theory, mathematically the following integral:

$$p(\mathbf{x}_p|\gamma_i^*) = \int p(\mathbf{x}_M, \mathbf{x}_p|\gamma_i^*)\, d\mathbf{x}_M \tag{25}$$

where the integration is over the domain of all features with missing values. That is, a feature(s) that is missing can have any feature value—all values are possible. A feature with a missing feature value will be referred to as a *missing feature.*

9-12-2 Partitioning a Subset of Missing Features into Independent and Dependent Subsets

Let

$$\mathbf{x}_M = \begin{bmatrix} \mathbf{x}_{M_I} \\ \mathbf{x}_{M_D} \end{bmatrix} \tag{26}$$

be the vector or set of *missing* independent and dependent features respectively. Then applying Eq. (25) to Eq. (23) results in

$$p(\mathbf{x}_\mathrm{p}|\gamma_i^*) = \int\int p(\mathbf{x}_{M_I}, \mathbf{x}_{M_D}, \mathbf{x}_p|\gamma_{i_k}^*)\, d\mathbf{x}_{M_I}\, d\mathbf{x}_{M_D}$$

$$= \sum_{k=1}^{K} \int \prod_{\xi=1}^{L_{I(k)}} p(x_\xi|\gamma_{i_k}^*) d\mathbf{x}_{M_I} \left[\int \prod_{u=1}^{U(k)} \prod_{s=1}^{S_k(u)} p_{i_{k_s}}^u d\mathbf{x}_{M_D} \right] p(\gamma_{i_k}^*|\gamma_i^*). \tag{27}$$

9-12-2-1 Missing Independent Features

The integral for the independent features on the right-hand side of Eq. (27) evaluates in terms of Nonmissing and Missing features as follows:

$$\int \prod_{\xi=1}^{L_{I(k)}} p(x_\xi|\gamma_{i_k}^*) d\mathbf{x}_{M_I}$$

$$= \prod_{\text{Nonmissing}} p(x_\xi|\gamma^*_{i_k}) \quad \prod_{\text{Missing}} \int p(x_\xi|\gamma^*_{i_k})d\mathbf{x}_\xi \tag{28}$$

$$= \prod_{\text{Independent nonmissing features.}} p(x_\xi|\gamma^*_{i_k})$$

This results because the features are independent and the missing independent features integrate to one.

9-12-2-2 Missing Dependent Features

For the term

$$\int \prod_{u=1}^{U(k)} \prod_{s=1}^{S_k(u)} p^u_{i_{k_s}} \, d\mathbf{x}_{M_D} \tag{29}$$

in Eq. (27), recall that $s = 1,2, \ldots, S_k(u)$ indexes minicolumns. Missing dependent features means one or more of the features characterizing a minicolumn is missing. Also, note that respective subsets of independent features are mutually exclusive.

Let

$$\mathbf{x}_{M_{D_S}}$$

be the missing features for minicolumn u where the M denotes Missing. Then the term inside the integral in expression (29) becomes

$$\prod_{u=1}^{U(k)} \prod_{s=1}^{S_k(u)} \delta^u_{i_{k_s}} (p^u_{i_{k_s}}) \tag{30a}$$

where

$$\begin{aligned} \delta^u_{i_{k_s}} (y) &= (y) \text{ if } u\text{th feature present.} \\ &= 1 \text{ if } u\text{th feature missing.} \end{aligned} \tag{30b}$$

For any subset s, the effect of one or more missing features is to project the probability density to a lower dimensional space containing a projection of the minicolumn. Any minicolumn in Eq. (23) having intersecting feature spaces defined by the present features $p_{i_{k_s}}$ contributes $p^u_{i_{k_s}}$ which, corresponding to respective features, is added. This projection theorem for minicolumns when features are missing is presented without proof.

9-12-3 Expression for c.c.p.d.f. when Features Are Missing

Putting these results together, Eq. (27) becomes

$$p(\mathbf{x}_p|\gamma_i^*) = \sum_{k=1}^{K} \underset{\substack{\text{Independent,}\\ \text{nonmissing}\\ \text{features}}}{\Pi\, p(x_\xi|\gamma_{i_k}^*)} \left[\prod_{u=1}^{U(k)} \prod_{s=1}^{S_k(u)} \delta_{i_{k_s}}^u (p_{i_{k_s}}^u)\, p(\gamma_{i_k}^*|\gamma_i^*) \right] \tag{31}$$

where $\delta_{i_{k_s}}^u(\ )$ is given by Eq. (30b).

9-12-4 Special Case—One Minicolumn

For the case of one minicolumn for the kth column, $(U(k) = 1)$, Eq. 31 reduces to

$$p(\mathbf{x}_p|\gamma_i^*) = \sum_{k=1}^{K} \underset{\substack{\text{Independent,}\\ \text{nonmissing}\\ \text{features}}}{\Pi\, p(x_\xi|\gamma_{i_k}^*)} \prod_{s=1}^{S_k(u)} \delta_{i_{k_s}}^u (p_{i_{k_s}}^u)\, p(\gamma_{i_k}^*|\gamma_i^*) \tag{32}$$

Thus, for $S\ (k) = 1$ Eq. (23) becomes

$$p(\mathbf{x}|\gamma_i^*) = \sum_{k=1}^{K} \underset{\substack{\text{Independent,}\\ \text{nonmissing}\\ \text{features}}}{\Pi\, p(x_\xi|\gamma_{i_k}^*)} \prod_{s=1}^{S_k(u)} \delta_{i_{k_s}}^u (p_{i_{k_s}}^u) * p(\gamma_{i_k}^*|\gamma_i^*) \tag{33}$$

Equation (33) reflects that *without minicolumns, dependence information is reflected entirely by the column direction.* For some problems, Eq. (33) represents the practical description of the category conditional probability density function. A *hypercube* of points is generated by Eq. (33) as $\mathbf{x}$ varies over its range.

An objective in the **CONSULT-I®** system of artificial intelligence with statistical pattern recognition is a user-friendly developer's system allowing a developer to train a subsystem by first creating directed columns. First level dependence naturally is accounted for by the column direction. Other columns also are directed for recognized different presentations from the expert field of knowledge. Modification of a column is accomplished by minicolumns also directed by Expert knowledge. Insignificant features are established during initialization so that training is automatic. Dependence through columns and minicolumns is a natural growth process for a category accomplished by the developer.

If the a priori probability of the minicolumn is not known, a fuzzy set approach can be used whereby the minicolumn resulting in maximum likelihood is chosen.

9-13 LEARNING THE COMPLEX CLASS CONDITIONAL PROBABILITY DENSITY FUNCTION BY DEDUCTION

9-13-1 Engineering in *CONSULT-I®*

As presented several times before, the approach is first to use training sessions to learn about the *only classes* $p(\mathbf{x}|\omega_i^*)$, $i = 1,2, \ldots, M_1$. These training sessions can involve direct training of column probabilities using expert knowledge. Alternatively, the **CONSULT LEARNING SYSTEM®** can be used to process hard data to estimate (learn by example) the probabilities needed for a column in **CONSULT-I®**.

Recall from Section 9-7 that the c.c.p.d.f. whether for an only class or complex class is

$$p(\mathbf{x}|\gamma_c^*) = \sum_{k=1}^{K} \prod_{\xi=1}^{L_{i(k)}} p(x_\xi|\gamma_{c_k}^*) \prod_{u=1}^{U(k)} p(x_1^u, x_2^u, \ldots, x_{Lu(k)}^u|\gamma_{c_k}^*) * p(\gamma_{c_k}^*|\gamma_c^*) \tag{34}$$

where category γ_c^* has K columns (hypercubes) with $U(k)$ minicolumns for the kth column. Reviewing Chapter 8 where Type Ø and Type 1 features were discussed, we see that each feature x_ξ has values $\{x_{\xi v}\}$ with corresponding probabilities $p_{c_{\xi_v}}$ for the cth category. Our objective is to determine these probabilities for complex class $\gamma_c^* = \Omega_{ij}^*$ given those for only classes ω_i^* and ω_j^*. A reasonable model will be required for relating Ω_{ij}^* to ω_i^* and ω_j^*. The model used here will involve likeness and unlikeness.

9-13-2 Model Involving Likeness and Unlikeness

The c.c.p.d.f. $p(\mathbf{x}|\omega_i^*)$ for only class ω_i^* is assumed characterized by regions of significance and insignificance S_i^* and I_i^*, respectively, domains in the feature space.

Regions of likeness and/or unlikeness can be defined as follows:

$$S_i^* \cap S_j^*: \text{ region like } \omega_i^* \text{ and } \omega_j^*. \tag{35a}$$

$$S_i^* \cap I_j^*: \text{ region like } \omega_i^* \text{ but unlike } \omega_j^*. \tag{35b}$$

$$I_i^* \cap S_j^*: \text{ region like } \omega_j^* \text{ but unlike } \omega_i^*. \tag{35c}$$

$$I_i^* \cap I_j^*: \text{ region unlike } \omega_i^* \text{ and unlike } \omega_j^*. \tag{35d}$$

for any two only classes ω_i^* and ω_j^*.

A model for Ω_{ij}^* includes necessarily that it has regions

$$S_i^* \cap I_j^*$$

and

$$I_i^* \cap S_j^*$$

"Weight" is given heaviest to these regions. Next, there can be regions

$$S_i^* \cap S_j^*$$

but they are given less weight. Regions

$$I_i^* \cap I_j^*$$

are considered insignificant.

Regions are characterized by significant features and their feature values.

9-13-3 The Complex Class c.c.p.d.f.

Complex class Ω_{ij}^* given samples $\dot{\mathbf{x}}_n = \mathbf{x}_1, \mathbf{x}_2, \ldots, \mathbf{x}_n$, can be expressed

$$p(\mathbf{x}|\Omega_{ij}^*, \dot{\mathbf{x}}_n) = p(\mathbf{x}|S_i^* \cap I_j^*, I_i^* \cap S_j^*)\, p(S_i^*|\dot{\mathbf{x}}_n) * p(S_j^*|\dot{\mathbf{x}}_n)\, p(I_i^*|\dot{\mathbf{x}}_n)\, p(I_j^*|\dot{\mathbf{x}}_n) \tag{36}$$

Let

$$p_{c_{\xi_v}}$$

be the probability for this complex class when the feature is x_ξ with value x_{ξ_v}. Denote by $p_{j_{\xi_v}}$ and $p_{i_{\xi_v}}$ the respective probabilities for only classes ω_j^* and ω_i^*. Partition $\mathbf{x}$ into components as follows:

$\mathbf{x}_{ij}^- \varepsilon\ S_i^* \cap I_j^* \neq \emptyset$:	Use probabilities from ω_i^* for S_i^*	(37a)
$\mathbf{x}_{ji}^- \varepsilon\ S_j^* \cap I_i^* \neq \emptyset$:	Use probabilities from ω_j^* for S_j^*	(37b)
$\mathbf{x}_{ij}\ \varepsilon\ S_i^* \cap S_j^* = \emptyset$:	Set probability in intersection to insignificance	(37c)
$\mathbf{x}_{ij}\ \varepsilon\ S_i^* \cap S_j^* \neq \emptyset$:	Set probability in intersection to min $[p_{i_{\xi_v}}, p_{j_{\xi_v}}]$	(37d)

Probabilities from the c.c.p.d.f.s of ω_i^* and ω_j^* are extracted as above, feature by feature, and placed in Eq. (35) for Ω_{ij}^*.

9-13-4 Discussion

This method of complex class generation is practical. Conditions can be set for completion of computation of a complex class probability. For example, a condition can be set that

$$S_i^* \cap I_j^* \neq \emptyset$$

and

$$S_j^* \cap I_i^* \neq \emptyset$$

but this requires almost as much computation as completion would take.

To perform a complete computation, the probabilities $\{p_{i_{\xi_v}}\}$ and $\{p_{j_{\xi_v}}\}$ are stored during computation for only classes. Then, to compute for Ω_{ij}^*, initially set its c.c.p.d.f. to that of either ω_i^* or ω_j^*; regions (37a) and (37b) are identified and Eq. (35) for Ω_{ij}^* modified accordingly. Region (37b) need not be identified because the initially selected c.c.p.d.f. will have insignificant probabilties in this region. Region (37d) can be the last to implement.

A focusing technique can be used to determine whether to process for Ω_{ij}^*. For example, if no a posteriori probability for only classes exceeds a threshold, one can look for a complex class starting with the only class with highest a posteriori probability; with this only class, complex classes are formed.

The reader will note that the subsystem (or several subsystems) itself is a focusing technique indicating candidate only classes and thus complex classes.

Using a threshold to focus for complex classes must be modified if all probabilities for only classes are below the threshold because it still could be true that a complex class would have higher probability than any only class.

9-14 LIKELIHOOD FUNCTION FOR CATEGORY USED IN SUBSYSTEM OR TOTAL SYSTEM

9-14-1 Deriving the Likelihood Function

In Section 9-11 the likelihood function $p(\mathbf{x}|\gamma_i^*)$ is constructed in terms of columns and mini-columns for γ_i^*, a category in a subsystem. Suppose now we wish to use this functional in a total system. The key is to realize that *features for the total system not included in the construction of* $p(\mathbf{x}|\gamma_i^*)$ *are insignificant.*

Suppose the expression $p(\mathbf{x}|\gamma_i^*)$ has been computed for a *total system* and has the following structure as previously described:

$$p(\mathbf{x}|\gamma_i^*) = \sum_{k=1}^{K} \prod_{\eta=1}^{L_I(k)} p(x_\eta|\gamma_{i_k}^*) \left\{ \prod_{u=1}^{U(k)} \prod_{s=1}^{S_k(u)} \delta_{i_{k_s}}^{u} (p_{i_{k_s}}^{u}) \, p(\gamma_{i_k}^*|\gamma_i^*) \right. \tag{38}$$

where

K : Number of columns.
$U(k)$: Number of minicolumns for column k.
$L_I(k)$: Number of statistically independent features for kth column
$p(x_\eta|\gamma_{i_k}^*)$: Probability density function of statistically independent feature x_η for kth column. (39)
$p(\gamma_{i_k}^*|\gamma_i^*)$: Mixing probability for kth column.
$\prod_{s=1}^{S_k(u)} (p_{i_{k_s}}^{u})$: Probability density for uth minicolumn.

The statistically independent features I in Eq. (38) can be decomposed into Insignificant (ISIG) and Significant (SIG) features:

$$I = I_{\text{SIG}} + I_{\text{ISIG}}. \tag{40}$$

That is

$$\prod_{\eta=1}^{L_I(k)} p(x_\eta|\gamma^*_{i_k}) = \prod_{I_{\text{SIG}}} p(x_\eta|\gamma^*_{i_k}) \prod_{I_{\text{ISIG}}} p(x_\eta|\gamma^*_{i_k}). \tag{41}$$

Now, because Eq. (38) is for category γ_i^* in a total system where the total number of features is very large, there will be a very large number of insignificant features in that total system insofar as category γ_i^* is concerned. We now place γ_i^* in a zth subsystem consisting of categories $\mathcal{S}_z$. The categories in $\mathcal{S}_z$ may be considered a differential diagnosis or focus as follows.

Grouping Categories into a Differential Diagnosis (Subsystem)

Without loss of generality a differential diagnosis thus can be viewed as the categories in a subsystem. The categories in this subsystem have Independent, Insignificant features denoted I_{ISIG}, which are in common within the total system; denote the latter by I_{ISIG_C}. Thus,

$$I_{\text{ISIG}} = I_{\text{ISIG}_\text{NC}} + I_{\text{ISIG}_\text{C}}$$

where $I_{\text{ISIG}_\text{NC}}$ are those insignificant features that may not be considered in common within the total system. Recall that an independent, insignificant feature has a "uniform" probability density function if Type Ø; and for Type 1 features, it has probability ϵ if True and probability $(1 - \epsilon)$ if False.

Define

$$\prod_{I_{\text{ISIG}_\text{C}}} p(x_\eta|\gamma_i^*) = \tag{42}$$

$$C_z = \text{Constant}$$

$$\gamma_i^* \in \text{Differential Diagnosis of } \mathcal{S}_z$$

which applies to those features of categories in $\mathcal{S}_z$ which, in common within the total system, are insignificant.

Substituting Eq. (42) into Eq. (41) and that result into Eq. (38) results in

$p(\mathbf{x}|\gamma_i^*) =$

$$C_z^* \sum_{k=1}^{K} \prod_{I_{\text{SIG}}} p(x_\eta|\gamma^*_{i_k}) \prod_{I_{\text{SIG}_\text{NC}}} p(x_\eta|\gamma^*_{i_k}) \left\{ \prod_{s=1}^{U(k)} \prod_{u=1}^{S_k(U)} \delta^u_{i_{k_s}} (p^u_{i_{k_s}}) * p(\gamma^*_{i_k}|\gamma_i^*). \right. \tag{43}$$

The only independent insignificant features remaining in Eq. (43) are those insignificant features not in common among all the categories within the total system. The constant C_z applies for all categories in the differential diagnosis and is a property of the insignificant features in common within the total system.

9-14-2 Subsystems Likelihood Functions as Modules in a Total System

Equation (43) can be considered an expression for a category likelihood function designed for a subsystem which can be inserted in a total system. To operate in a total system it is necessary only that the constant C_s be computed for subsystem z with respect to the total system. More than one subsystem can contain category γ_i^* but the constant C_z will vary with the subsystem z.

In this regard *subsystems can be viewed as an a priori convenience in which to group knowledge by area of expertise.* Dynamically, however, a subsystem can be formed automatically as a new subsystem or as a focus for a differential diagnosis. Forming subsystems on line is relatively time consuming using state of the art 1986 computing. Therefore, *activation rules* and *networking* provide a practical approach to total system construction.

9-15 HOW KNOWLEDGE OF STATISTICAL DEPENDENCIES IMPOSED IN COLUMNS OR MINICOLUMNS IMPROVES PERFORMANCE

9-15-1 Introduction

Consider a two-class (two only classes ω_1^* and ω_2^*) and a two-dimensional (two features, i.e., $L = 2$) example. Suppose that feature variation is trained uniform for each dimension of each only class as illustrated in Figure 9.1a. An area of overlap between the two only classes is shown as the shaded area. How, because of statistical dependence between x_1 and x_2 given category ω_2^*, could it result that category ω_2^* does not overlap category ω_1^*?

An answer is illustrated in Figure 9.1b where two subcategories $\omega_{2_1}^*$ and $\omega_{2_2}^*$ of category ω_2^* are shown. Subcategory $\omega_{2_1}^*$ is a presentation where x_1 increases as x_2 increases. Subcategory $\omega_{2_2}^*$ is a presentation where x_1 decreases as x_2 increases.

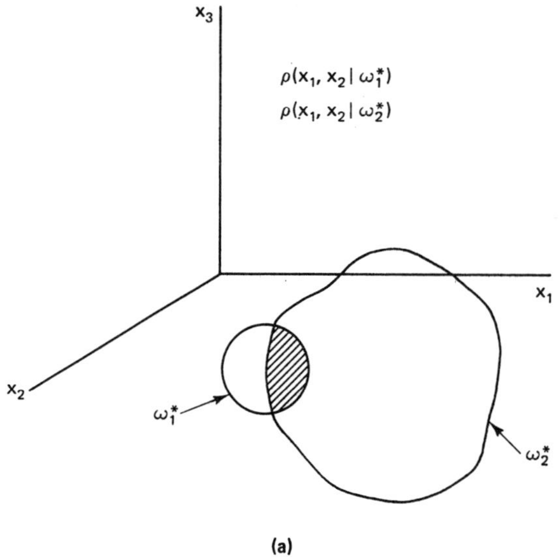

FIGURE 9.1a Two categories (only classes) ω_i^* and ω_2^* with uniform training for each dimension of each category.

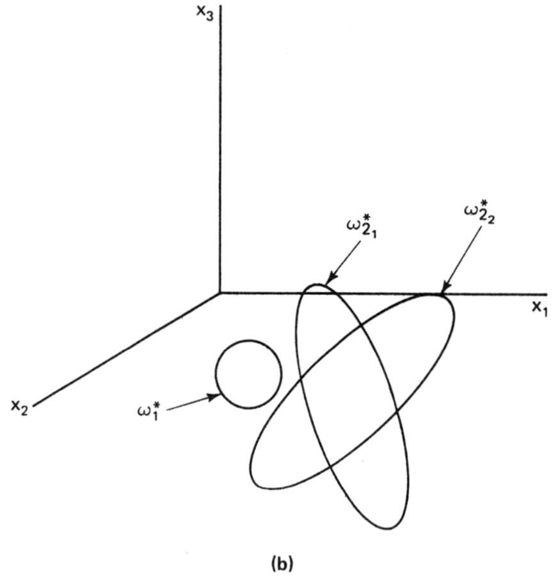

FIGURE 9.1b Illustration of category ω_2^* with two presentations (subcategories) where each has dependent features x_1 and x_2.

This example illustrates that if a feature is allowed to take on feature values over its range without regard to other features on which it is dependent, then *presentation points for the category can be generated by deduction which in fact do not occur in practice.* Performance can be degraded by this process and care must be taken to protect against it.

9-15-2 Example from Thyroid Disease Subsystem

Training vectors for two presentations of ω_1^*, Hashimoto's Thyroiditis, are shown in Figure 9.2a, and for two presentations of ω_2^*, Idiopathic Hypothyroidism, are shown in Figure 9.3a. For each only class, the respective presentations correspond to early and late presentations. Two columns (subcategories) are used for each category to account for the dependencies.

If a single column is used for each category, then the training for each category is more nearly spherical as illustrated in Figures 9.2b and 9.3b, respectively.

The single column training of category ω_1^* contains three error points as illustrated in Figure 9.2b, all corresponding to category ω_2^*. The single column training of category ω_2^* contains an error point corresponding to category ω_1^*, as illustrated in Figure 9.3b.

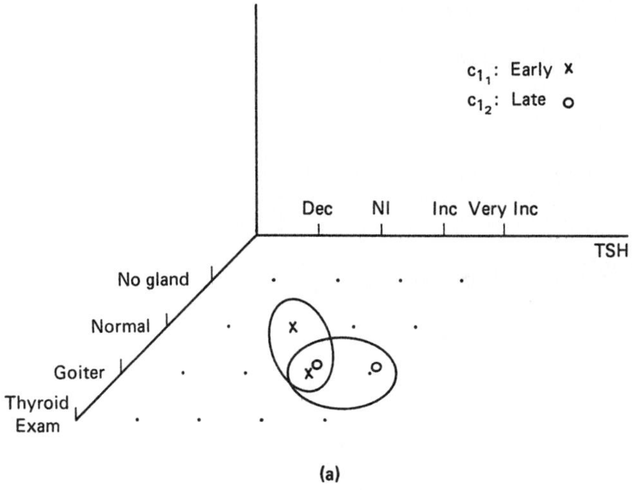

FIGURE 9.2a ω_1^*: Hashimoto's Thyroiditis.

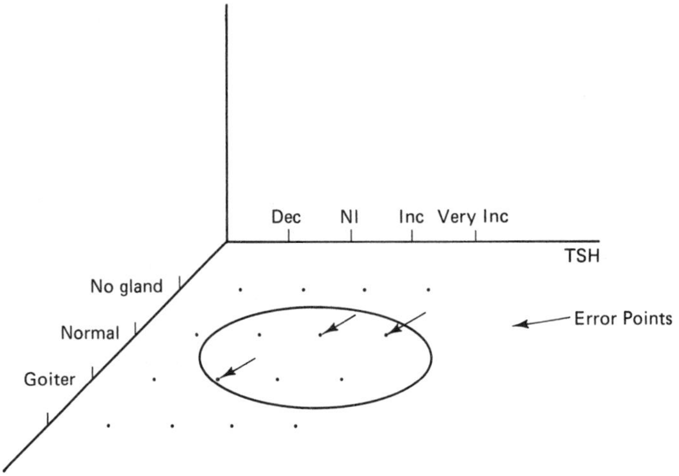

(b)

FIGURE 9.2b

9-15-3 Discussion

Training a category by subcategories utilizing columns or by sub-subcategories using minicolumns reflects either problem knowledge or statistical knowledge of dependencies. It is important to identify and provide for such dependencies in training. The reader should carefully examine various closeness measures of systems to see if this dependence can be accommodated.

9-16 MODIFICATIONS OF THE INFERENCE FUNCTIONS

9-16-1 Either/Or Maximum Likelihood with Columns

Let category γ_ξ^* be defined to occur if

$$\gamma_\xi^* = \bigcup_{z=1}^{K} \gamma_{\xi_z}^* \text{ occurs} \qquad (44)$$

That is, category γ_ξ^* occurs if either $\gamma_{\xi_1}^*$, or $\gamma_{\xi_2}^*$, or . . ., or $\gamma_{\xi_k}^*$ occurs. In practice, this corresponds to a problem where $\gamma_{\xi_1}^*, \gamma_{\xi_2}^*, \ldots, \gamma_{\xi_K}^*$ *are different presentations of the same category* γ_ξ^*.

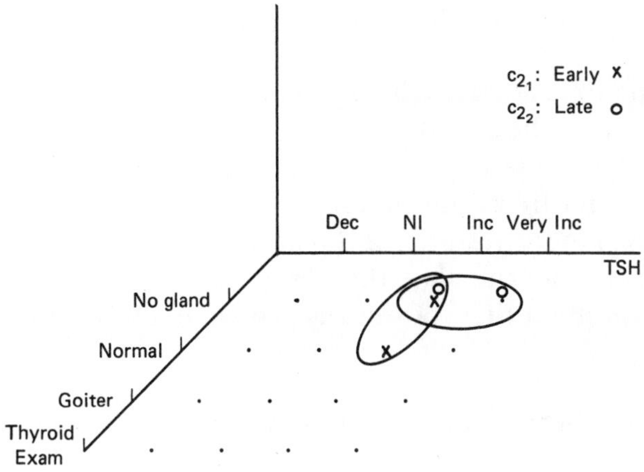

(a)

FIGURE 9.3a ω_2^*: Primary Idiopathic Hypothyroidism.

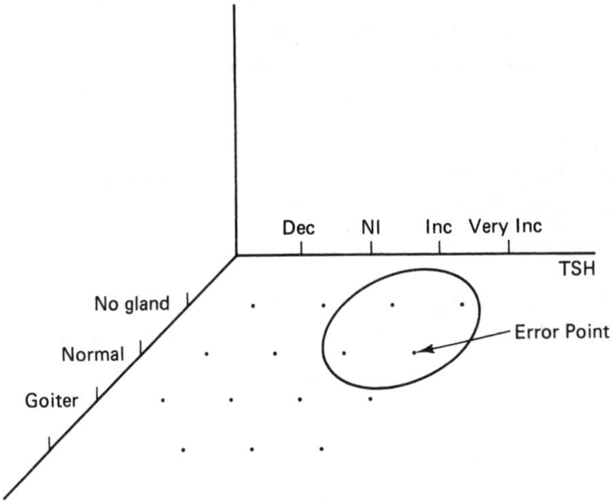

(b)

FIGURE 9.3b

If the presentations $\{\gamma_{\xi_z}^*\}$ are mutually exclusive, then

$$p(\gamma_\xi^*|\mathbf{x}) = p(\gamma_{\xi_1}^*|\mathbf{x}) + p(\gamma_{\xi_2}^*|\mathbf{x}) + \cdots + p(\gamma_{\xi_k}^*|\mathbf{x}). \tag{45}$$

In general, there may be overlap in the a posteriori probabilities of the presentations. In that case, the fuzzy set operation for OR is one approach to obtain a form similar to Eq. (45).

$$p(\gamma_\xi^*|\mathbf{x}) = \max_z \{p(\gamma_{\xi_z}^*|\mathbf{x})\} \tag{46}$$

Equation (46) calculates the a posteriori probability of category γ_ξ^* as the maximum of the a posteriori probabilities of subcategories $\gamma_{\xi_z}^*$. A subcategory representation of category γ_ξ^* has been referred to as a *column.* The column directs the composition of feature types, dependencies, *Can'ts, insignificant features,* and feature variations for the category.

Likewise, we can calculate the a posteriori probability of category γ_ξ^* as the maximum of the a posteriori probabilities of subsubcategories $\gamma_{\xi_{z_s}}^*$.

9-16-2 Either/Or Maximum Likelihood with Minicolumns

Let category γ_ξ^* be as in Eq. (44), but each $\gamma_{\xi_z}^*$ is composed of subcategories. These subcategories consist of a unique subset of features. The subset of features is one of the following:

1. *A Column Partition.* The wth subset of features indexed by $\xi_{z_w}^*$ and designates the marginal probability density function associated with these features for the zth column (presentation) of category ξ. Denote this partition of a column $\mathscr{C}_{\xi_{z_w}}$.
2. *A Minicolumn.* The subset of features associated with the sth minicolumn appended to column ξ has an associated probability density function. The sth minicolumn is indexed by ξ_{z_s} and denoted $\mathfrak{M}_{\xi_{z_s}}$.

A presentation then exists for the union of subsets from (1) with the union of subsets from (2). This presentation is denoted by:

$$\bigcup_w \mathscr{C}_{\xi_{z_w}} \cup \mathfrak{M}_{\xi_{z_s}} : \mathrm{SUB}_{\xi_{z_\delta}} \tag{47}$$

w = ranges over subsets of partitions of ξth column.
s = ranges over minicolumn for ξth column.

$\mathrm{SUB}_{\xi_{z_\delta}}$ is the δth subsubcategory for category ξ, column z.

Multiple marginal projections are utilized to eliminate intersection in the union in Eq. (47). Denoting acceptable subcategories of the form in Eq. (47) by:

$$\gamma_{\xi_{z_\delta}} \triangleq \mathrm{SUB}_{\xi_{z_\delta}}. \tag{48}$$

Equation (46) is extended to

$$p(\gamma_\xi^*|\mathbf{x}) = \max_{z,\delta} \{p(\gamma_{\xi_{z_\delta}}^*|\mathbf{x})\}. \tag{49}$$

δ ranges over all presentations in Eq. (47). In practice possible presentations in Eq. (47) are limited by problem knowledge. Equation (47) provides a means of incorporating many packets of local dependence in constructing a presentation indexed by δ for column ξ.

9-17 MIXTURE PROBABILITY DENSITY IN TERMS OF SUBCATEGORIES

9-17-1 The Mixture Probability Density Functions for Columns

Equations (16)–(20) of Section 9–7 express the probability density function $p(\mathbf{x})$ in terms of category conditional probability density functions $p(\mathbf{x}|\gamma_\xi^*)$, $\xi = 1, 2, \ldots, M$. These categories γ_ξ^* are *only classes* ω_i^* or *complex classes* Ω_ξ^*.

A category γ_ξ^* has subcategories defined

$$\{\gamma_{\xi_z}^*\}$$

as described in Section 9-2 (subsubcategories are also permitted). These subcategories are mutually exclusive for any category, and

$$p(\mathbf{x}) = \sum_{\xi=1}^{M} p(\mathbf{x}, \gamma_\xi^*) = \sum_{\xi=1}^{M} p(\mathbf{x}|\gamma_\xi^*)p(\gamma_\xi^*) \tag{50}$$

where

$$p(\mathbf{x}|\gamma_\xi^*) = \sum_{z=1}^{K} p(\mathbf{x}|\gamma_\xi^*, \gamma_{\xi_z}^*)\, p(\gamma_{\xi_z}^*|\gamma_\xi^*). \tag{51}$$

Thus

$$p(\mathbf{x}) = \sum_{\xi=1}^{M} \sum_{z=1}^{K} p(\mathbf{x}|\gamma_\xi^*, \gamma_{\xi_z}^*)\, p(\gamma_{\xi_z}^*|\gamma_\xi^*)\, p(\gamma_\xi^*). \tag{52}$$

Contrast Eq. (51) with Eq. (46). In Eq. (51), the event γ_ξ^* is either $\gamma_{\xi_1}^*$ or $\gamma_{\xi_2}^*$, or . . ., or $\gamma_{\xi_k}^*$; in Eq. (46) the event $\mathbf{x}$ is either $(\mathbf{x}\gamma_{\xi_1}^*)$, or $(\mathbf{x}\gamma_{\xi_2}^*)$, or . . ., or $(\mathbf{x}\gamma_{\xi_k}^*)$. In the former, the category space is partitioned while in the latter, the feature space is partitioned.

As before, the categories γ_ξ^* are sets of *only classes*

$\{\gamma_i^*\}$

and sets of *complex classes*

$$\{\Omega_\xi^*\}$$

where Ω_ξ^* contains classes $\omega_1, \omega_2, \ldots, \omega_M$ in some combination.

We now define *only subclasses*

$$\{\omega_{i_z}^*\}_{z=1}^{K} \tag{53}$$

of *only class* ω_i^* and *subcomplex classes*

$$\{\Omega_{\xi_z}^*\}_{z=1}^{K} \tag{54}$$

of complex class Ω_ξ^*, Thus, Eq. (52) can be rewritten

$$p(\mathbf{x}) = \sum_{i=1}^{M_1} \sum_{z=1}^{K} p(\mathbf{x}|\omega_i^*, \omega_{i_z}^*)\, p(\omega_{i_z}^*|\omega_i^*) p(\omega_i^*).$$

$$+ \sum_{\xi=1}^{M_2} \sum_{z=1}^{K} p(\mathbf{x}|\Omega_\xi^*, \Omega_{\xi_z}^*)\, p(\Omega_{\xi_z}^*|\Omega_\xi^*)\, p(\Omega_\xi^*) \tag{55}$$

9-17-2 Example

Consider a subsystem, Breast Disease Subsystem, consisting of M_1 *only classes*,

$$\{\omega_i^*\} = \text{Cancer, Fibrocystic, Fibroadenoma, } \ldots .$$

Only subclasses of cancer are the "clusters" or "typical and atypical presentations" of cancer; for example:

$$\begin{aligned} \omega_{1_1}^* &= \text{early cancer.} \\ \omega_{1_2}^* &= \text{late cancer.} \\ \omega_{1_3}^* &= \text{cancer with observer errors.} \\ \omega_{1_4}^* &= \text{cancer with fuzzy training.} \end{aligned} \tag{56}$$

On the other hand, examples of *complex classes* are:

$$\begin{aligned} \Omega_1^* &= (\omega_1, \omega_2) : \text{(Cancer, fibrocystic)} \\ \Omega_2^* &= (\omega_1, \omega_3) : \text{(Cancer, fibroadenoma).} \end{aligned} \tag{57}$$

Both examples of *subclasses* and *complex classes* are practical and are encountered during development of many subsystems.

The *complex classes* $\{\Omega_\xi^*\}$ can have "typical and atypical" presentations just as for *only classes*. This motivates the definition of *subcomplex classes*.

During development, one must be careful to distinguish subclasses from complex classes.

9-18 DISCUSSION

A minicolumn modification of a column of a category provides for describing a subsubcategory of a category. As such it can be thought of as down two levels in the knowledge base hierarchy from the category level. It can be a complex feature (i.e., a function of feature values). *The minicolumn provides a way for engineering a particular complex feature specialized to the category.* Furthermore, the complex features as a minicolumn can have a name. You could think of a feature value causing a complex feature (subsubcategory) causing a subcategory causing a category as a *causal system,* perhaps a causal method in some cases. Note, however, that mathematics are used to allow us to understand any assumptions if they are made. *A posteriori category probabilities given findings are indeed computed.* A priori knowledge precisely is introduced in the engineering of the inference function. If a priori probabilities of subsubcategories are not available, then ask, "what do you know? Are they best presumed equal?" If yes, then select the minicolumn with highest ultimate category likelihood.

Is a minicolumn a production rule? Production rule theory has never addressed knowledge base structure, categories, subcategories, likelihoods, a posteriori probabilities, concept formation, unsupervised learning, fuzzy sets, and so on—all integrated together as artificial intelligence with statistical pattern recognition.

Models for subsubcategories can take various forms. For example let

$$p(x_1^{\mathrm{u}}, x_2^{\mathrm{u}}, \ldots, x_{L_{u(k)}}^{\mathrm{u}} = \sum_{e=1}^{E} \left[\prod_{s=1}^{S_k(u)} p_{i_{k_s}}^{u}\,(\mathrm{e}) \right] p(\gamma_{i_{k_e}} | \gamma_{i_k}^{*}) \tag{58}$$

where previously in this chapter E = 1. Consider replacing the Σ in (58) by a fuzzy set operation, max.

At the extreme every possible **x** (record) can direct a column. **The OUTCOME ADVISOR®** and **THE CONSULT LEARNING SYSTEM®** accomplish this using a focus at the findings to prevent combinatorial explosion.

10

Selecting the Next Feature Automatically

10-1 INTRODUCTION TO OPTIMUM FEATURE SELECTION

Selecting the next feature optimally† can be a difficult computation in practice. Optimum mathematical theory is essential to guide one in understanding suboptimum approaches.

In this chapter, concept formation of categories can take place on-line by deduction. Learning of only class c.c.p.d.f.s is assumed done off-line. Thus, the results apply to classification systems (such as expert systems) where **CONSULT LEARNING SYSTEM®** is not used on-line.

The problem formulation begins by assuming ℓ features have been processed and the objective is to determine the next "best feature" or next "best features."

Feature selection can be viewed as a function of the interviewer; but it involves the knowledge base structure and the inference functions for categories. *The problem is formulated by assuming that ℓ features have been processed and the next feature(s) is to be selected from the remaining $(L - \ell)$ features.* First an optimum approach is presented and then practical suboptimum approaches are presented.

10-2 OPTIMUM SINGLE FEATURE SELECTION AT STAGE ℓ

Let ℓ of the L features ($\ell < L$) already have been processed at stage ℓ, with the present (processed) $\mathbf{x}_{p_\ell}$ and missing (unprocessed) $\mathbf{x}_{M_{\ell-1}}$ features in $\mathbf{x}$ indicated as

$$\mathbf{x}_\ell = \{\mathbf{x}_{p_\ell}, \mathbf{x}_{M_{L-\ell}}\}. \tag{1}$$

†Optimum is defined by some criterion such as minimizing probability of error or minimizing risk.

If L_{ji} is the loss in deciding category γ_j^* when category γ_i^* is True, the loss in deciding category γ_j^* is

$$\sum_{i=1}^{M} L_{ji}\, p(\gamma_i^* | \mathbf{x}_\ell) \tag{2}$$

A Minimum Risk Decision at stage ℓ is to announce the category γ_j^* minimizing the risk expressed by Eq. 2; i.e.,

$$\operatorname*{Min}_{j} \left\{ \sum_{i=1}^{M} L_{ji}\, p(\gamma_i^* | \mathbf{x}_\ell) \right\} \tag{3}$$

The objective in optimum feature selection is to select that feature indexed by $\ell + 1$ to produce

$$\mathbf{x}_{\ell+1} = \{\mathbf{x}_{p_{\ell+1}}, \mathbf{x}_{M_{L-\ell-1}}\} \tag{4}$$

which minimizes risk at stage $\ell + 1$. There are

$$(L - \ell) \tag{5}$$

ways to select the $(\ell + 1)$ st feature, denoted x_ξ, with V possible values

$$x_{\xi_v},\ v = 1,2, \ldots, V. \tag{6}$$

Utilizing Eq. (2), the $(\ell + 1)$ st feature is selected† with an updated minimum risk

$$\min_{\xi} \left\{ \operatorname*{Min}_{j} \left\{ \sum_{i=1}^{M} L_{ji} \frac{p(x_{\xi_v} | \mathbf{x}_\ell, \gamma_i^*)\, p(\mathbf{x}_\ell | \gamma_i^*)\, P_i}{p(x_{\xi_v}, \mathbf{x}_\ell)} \right\}\right\} \tag{7}$$

(where ξ is one of the $L - \ell$ remaining features) *for the specific feature value* x_{ξ_v} at stage $(\ell + 1)$. Since x_{ξ_v} is one of V values and all possible values must be considered, the optimum criterion of *minimum expected risk* is obtained, utilizing Eq. (7):

$$\min_{\xi} \left\{ \operatorname*{Min}_{j} \left\{ \sum_{i=1}^{M} L_{ji} \sum_{v=1}^{V} \frac{p(x_{\xi_v} | \mathbf{x}_\ell, \gamma_i^*)\, p(\mathbf{x}_\ell | \gamma_i^*) P_i}{p(x_{\xi_v}, \mathbf{x}_\ell)} \right\}\right\} \tag{8a}$$

where

$$p(\mathbf{x}_{\xi_v} | \gamma_i^*, \mathbf{x}_\ell) \triangleq p_{\xi_v}. \tag{8b}$$

†There are $L - \ell$ remaining features to select from.

Equation (8a) illustrates that the expected feature value depends on past feature values. For example, a particular subcategory can be active.

A special case of the minimum risk decision rule is the Minimum Probability of Error Decision Rule obtained when we set $L_{ji} = 1$ for $j \neq i$ but $L_{ji} = \emptyset$ for $j = i$. For this case, optimum feature selection to minimize probability of error is a simplification of Eq. (8a).

First, we note that for L_{ji} having such values, called zero-one loss values, Eq. (3) reduces to

$$\operatorname*{Max}_{i} \{p(\gamma_i^* | \mathbf{x}_\ell)\}$$

which is the minimum probability of error decision rule.

Equation (8a) for optimum feature selection under this assumption reduces to

$$\operatorname*{Max}_{\xi} \left\{ \operatorname*{Max}_{i} \left\{ \sum_{v=1}^{V} \frac{p(x_{\xi_v} | \mathbf{x}_\ell, \gamma_i^*)\, p(\mathbf{x}_\ell | \gamma_i^*)\, P_i}{p(x_{\xi_v}, \mathbf{x}_\ell)} \right\}\right\} \tag{9}$$

Assuming computation of likelihood of category γ_i^* is for a subcategory (within a column), then Eq. (9) reduces to

$$\operatorname*{Max}_{\xi} \left\{ \operatorname*{Max}_{i} \left\{ \sum_{v=1}^{V} \frac{p(x_{\xi_v} | \gamma_i^*)\, p(\mathbf{x}_\ell | \gamma_i^*)\, P_i p_{\xi_v}}{p(x_{\xi_v}, \mathbf{x}_\ell)} \right\}\right\}$$

10-3 OPTIMUM SELECTION OF REMAINING FEATURES AT STAGE ℓ

The calculations in Eqs. (8) and (9) assume that the system already is at stage ℓ when a single next feature is sought. A more general problem is to look ahead from an arbitrary stage and select the remaining $(L - \ell)$ features. Of course, $\ell = 1$ is at stage one.

At stage ℓ, there are

$$(L-\ell)! \tag{10}$$

sequences in which to select the remaining features. Denote this set of feature vectors by

$$\mathbf{x}_\eta,\ \eta = 1,2, \ldots, (L-\ell)! \tag{11}$$

The features in $\mathbf{x}_\eta$ are denoted

$$x_{\eta_\xi},\ \xi = 1,2, \ldots, (L-\ell) \tag{12}$$

A particular look-ahead sequence of feature values for sequence

$$x_{\eta_{\xi_v}}, \ \xi = 1,2, \ldots, (L - \ell) \tag{13}$$

where $x_{\eta_{\xi_v}}$ is the vth value of the ξth feature in sequence η, and has probability density function

$$\prod_{\xi=1}^{(M-\ell)} p_{\eta_{\xi_v}}(\gamma_i^*) \triangleq p_\eta(\gamma_i^*, s) \tag{14}$$

where s indexes the sth of the $(v)^{M - \ell}$ sets of feature values assuming statistical independence among the features. (Dependence is handled by allowing this probability to be that for a specific kth column and/or minicolumn.) Utilizing Eqs. (13) and (14), Eqs. (7) and (8) become

$$\operatorname*{Min}_{\eta} \left\{ \operatorname*{Min}_{j} \right\} \sum_{i=1}^{M} \frac{L_{ji}\, p_\eta(\gamma_i^*, s)\, p(\mathbf{x}_\ell | \gamma_i^*) P_i}{p(x_\xi, \mathbf{x}_\ell)} \Bigg\}\Bigg\} \tag{15}$$

and

$$\operatorname*{Min}_{\xi} \left\{ \operatorname*{Min}_{j} \left\{ \sum_{i=1}^{M} L_j \prod_{\eta=1}^{(M-\ell)} \sum_{s=1}^{(V)^{M-\ell}} \frac{p_\eta(\gamma_i^*, s)\, p(\mathbf{x}_\ell | \gamma_i^*) P_i p_\eta(\gamma_i^*, s)}{p(x_\xi, \mathbf{x}_\ell)} \right\}\right\} \tag{16}$$

$$\eta = 1,2, \ldots (M - \ell)!$$

Computing time to implement Eq. (15) is *extremely long*. In practice feature selection using Eq. (8) takes time but much, much less time than Eq. (16). The former has been implemented in **CONSULT-I®**; however, simplified suboptimum versions which we will consider in the following sections have also been used.

10-4 SUBOPTIMUM METHODS OF FEATURE SELECTION

10-4-1 Introduction

Various forms of suboptimum feature selection can be devised. They can involve feature rank, category risk, maximum versus average approaches and other constructions.

10-4-2 Maximizing Expected Likelihood of Top Class

The approach here is to seek the best next feature to rule in the currently top ranking category. The ith category conditional probability density for feature x_j with value x_{j_v} is

$$p(x_j = x_{j_v}|\gamma_i^*) \triangleq p_{i_{j_v}} \tag{17}$$

Let $\mathcal{L}_i(j-1)$ be the probability density function (likelihood function) for category i utilizing features up to the current stage $(v - 1)$. Then the likelihood function for category γ_i^* after selecting the next feature j with vth value is

$$[\mathcal{L}_i(j-1)] * p_{i_{j_v}} \triangleq \mathcal{L}_i \, p_{i_{j_v}}. \tag{18}$$

The expected likelihood of the ith category, with expectation with respect to values of feature x_j, is

$$E\,\{\mathcal{L}_i \, p_{i_{j_v}}\} = \mathcal{L}_i \sum_{v=1}^{V} p_{i_{j_v}} p_{i_{j_v}} \tag{19}$$

since the feature has V values. Now we can determine the category γ_i^* having highest likelihood at stage (j).

The feature j resulting in a maximum of the expression Eq. (19) for the category γ_i^* with maximum likelihood at stage (j) can be determined. A disadvantage of this approach is that emphasis is placed on the top category at previous stage $(j - 1)$, which may not be the correct decision at stage j. Formally, this method of feature selection is to select feature x_j to achieve the following:

$$\max_{j} \left\{ \mathcal{L}_i \sum_{v=1}^{V} p_{i_{j_v}} p_{i_{j_v}} \right\} \tag{20}$$

This method of feature selection determines the next best feature x_j for the top category γ_i^* at stage $(j - 1)$. Of course, any other category (second ranking, third ranking) could be used as focus.

There is no guarantee that the top ranking category at stage $(j - 1)$ remains top ranking at stage j. Nevertheless, a top ranking category eventually will emerge (well separated); retain this category rank until all features are processed. This same method can be used to select subsystems.

10-4-3 Maximizing Expected Rank Likelihood of Top Category

By introducing a rank R_{i_j} for the *j*th feature of the *i*th category the cost or risk of the *j*th feature is introduced. We define that the higher the rank R_{i_j}, the more important is the feature because of decreased feature cost and/or danger, or because of increased importance of the test for category γ_i^*. Eq. (20) is modified to obtain Eq. (21).

Select Feature x_j:

$$\max_j \left\{ R_{i_j} \mathcal{L}_i \sum_{v=1}^{V} p_{i_{j_v}} p_{i_{j_v}} \right\}. \tag{21}$$

10-4-3-1 Maximize by Selecting a Feature for D Categories

A straightforward extension of Eq. (21) is to maximize over the average of the top D categories in set **D**:

Select feature x_j:

$$\max_j \left\{ \sum_{i_i \in D} \mathcal{L}_i \mathrm{R}_{i_j} \sum_{v=1}^{V} p_{i_{j_v}} p_{i_{j_v}} \right\}. \tag{22}$$

The desire is that one of the categories in the differential **D** will emerge after feature selection x_j with highest *expected ranked likelihood,* and that the true category is in **D.**

10-4-3-2 Maximizing the Maximum Rank Likelihood of Top Class

A straightforward approach to simplify Eq. (21) is to apply a fuzzy set operation obtaining:

Select feature x_j:

$$\max_j \left\{ R_{i_j} \max_v \{\mathcal{L}_i \, p_{i_{j_v}}\} \right\} \tag{23}$$

where the largest probability density for some value v is selected for the top event.

10-4-3-3 Maximize in Set D by Using a Fuzzy Set Operation

A straightforward simplification (but approximation of Eq. (22) is to maximize over the top D events in set **D** using a fuzzy set operation:

Select feature x_j:

$$\max_j \left\{ \sum_{i \varepsilon D} \mathcal{L}_i \mathrm{R}_{i_j} \max \{p_{i_{j_v}}\} \right\}. \tag{24}$$

10-4-4 Maximizing Maximum Likelihood Difference

For category ξ, the likelihoods when selecting feature j are:

$$\{\mathcal{L}_\xi p_{\xi_{j_v}}\}_{v=1}^{V}.$$

The difference between $M\mathcal{L}_{i_j}$ and $M\mathcal{L}_{\xi_j}$ for some other category γ_i^* is for feature x_j:

$$\max_v \{\mathcal{L}_i \, p_{i_{j_v}}\} - \max_v \{\mathcal{L}_\xi \, p_{\xi_{j_v}}\} \triangleq M\mathcal{L}_{i_j} - M\mathcal{L}_{\xi_j} \tag{25}$$

where $M\mathcal{L}_{i_j}$ is the maximum likelihood over feature values for feature j of category i. Eq. (25) is defined as the maximum likelihood difference between a category i and any other category ξ, when selecting feature j.

The *Maximum Likelihood Difference* with respect to category i is defined:

$$M\mathcal{L}D_{i_j} \triangleq \sum_{\forall \xi \neq i} (M\mathcal{L}_{i_j} - M\mathcal{L}_{\xi_j}). \tag{26}$$

10-4-4-1 Maximizing $M\mathcal{L}D_i$ for Top Category

The method

$$\max_j \{M\mathcal{L}D_{i_j}\}_{i=1}^{F} \tag{27}$$

selects the feature j maximizing the maximum likelihood difference for a category, where F is the number of categories in **D** less one.

10-4-4-2 Maximizing $M\mathcal{L}D_i$ for γ_i^* in a Differential Diagnosis

An extension of Eq. (27) is

$$\max_j \{\{ \sum_{i \varepsilon D} M\mathcal{L}D_{i_j}\}_{j=1}^{F}\}$$

for categories i in a differential diagnosis **D**. Defining a set **D** smaller than the entire category space reduces computation time; however, completeness is lost. If **D** is the entire category space, then the feature x_j leading to maximum $M\mathcal{L}D_{i_j}$ can be found.

10-5 GOAL-DIRECTED FEATURE SELECTION AND THE STUDY OF THRESHOLDS

The problem of assigning thresholds as considered by Greenes (1979) can be applied to the feature selection problem. Given a differential diagnosis and associated management goals, how can a posteriori probability of feature values derived from execution of a feature be used in a rule? A "goal rule" *G* that *replaces a goal* is defined:

G → ‹cond-string›[|‹cond-string›|]

where

- Square brackets [] indicate that the items within them may be indefinitely repeated.
- Vertical bars | | separate alternative productions from one another: disjunction of condition strings.
- A condition string is defined either as a simple condition or a conjunction of simple conditions separated by commas.

An *antecedent* of *G* can become a *subgoal* whereby a rule is searched to obtain the subgoal. New subgoals can be successively pursued to increasing depth until a point is reached where the immediate goal can be established. At that point, any higher level goal is further evaluated in relation to additional *conjunctive* conditions.

A *threshold* is defined as the probability of an antecedent condition or subcondition above which the condition is considered satisfied. If the threshold is not reached, the condition is considered unsatisfied.

In medicine a *condition* is a treatment, a diagnosis, or a feature request. A treatment usually is a condition of the highest level system goal rule. A condition of a treatment usually is a diagnosis rule.

A *Goal Tree* can be defined as follows:

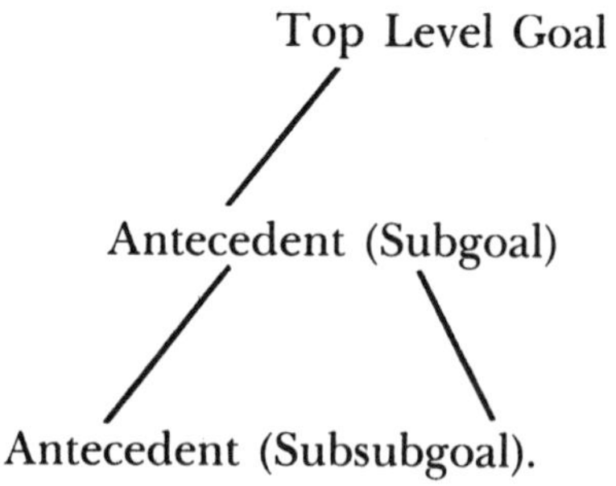

Subgoals (antecedents) are processed by obtaining necessary data and satisfying any probability threshold.

Greenes states that decision analysis (see Patrick, 1979) is the classical representation of the problem of solving a Goal Tree but that artificial intelligence models can be used to avoid direct investigation of the entire tree. He calls "certainty factors" (**MYCIN**) and "numerical strengths" or "weights" (**INTERNIST**) *surrogates of probability.* The threshold is a means for translating *experience* into *knowledge* utilizing data and statistics derived therefrom.

The Goal Tree itself does not implement inference but requires an inference rule. The rules for feature selection discussed in this chapter are all orientated toward the goal of causing a top ranking category to emerge and hold onto the top ranks. A threshold could be used to end feature selection. For example, this could be when a category has emerged with relatively high rank, or a top ranking category does not hold top rank after so many features are processed. The threshold allows one to implement the human behavior of success or to give up for this case.

11

Total System: Integrating CONSULT-I® Subsystems

Subsystems are a modular construction for acquiring a knowledge base and making decisions. There are problems where it is desired to process categories or features from another subsystem or even from complex classes that are complexed with classes in another subsystem. This problem is handled by constructing a knowledge base structure that crosses subsystems.

The key is that *a category has insignificant features for features not in the subsystem.* Ideally this is how a subsystem should be designed. An alternative is for one or more features of a category to have values which are called *intermediate categories* (Patrick *and others*, 1973, 1974; Patrick, 1979; Patrick *and others*, 1985). An intermediate category is a decision from another subsystem that affects the subsystem. This follows the construction of a network of adaptive estimation systems introduced by Patrick (1969, 1972). An intermediate category is a concept in the knowledge base structure of the total system. It can be viewed as a complex feature for the subsystem although it is constructed in another subsystem.

11-1 INTRODUCTION TO THE TOTAL *CONSULT-I®* SYSTEM

A total classification system has a knowledge base consisting of "all" categories and features. The total system is *modular* (subsystems) if categories and category feature relationships are arranged in modules for ease of review and updating. The classes and categories suggest a natural *hierarchy* because *only classes* and *complex classes* are formed from classes. This hierarchy is a property of the feature space and category space and applies to the modules as well as the total system. At the bottom of the hierarchy are *primitives,* which are the basic components used to identify *classes, only classes,* and *complex classes.*

A *primitive is a feature* (a Type 1, binary feature). Usually, a class, only class, or complex class is measured by a multivariate function of primitives (the inference function). However, a primitive can be the sole component of inference for an only class, class, or complex class. That is, a primitive can be a class or category.

This hierarchical structure is important for a total system where it may be desirable to identify a primitive as a category. For example, increased sodium, a primitive, can be the category hypernatremia.

In practice a variety of classification problems arise. There are classifications where the problem is known to be confined to one subsystem or several subsystems. There can be problems where the total system must be considered, but some form of subsystem activation usually is required. For example, the same approaches for feature selection in Chapter 10 can be used for subsystem selection. To accomplish this, subsystem conditional probability density functions are required.

11-2 PARAMETERS OF THE TOTAL SYSTEM

A total classification system (diagnostic system) consists of M categories γ_i^*, $i = 1, 2, \ldots, M$, M_c classes, and L features. There exists an optimum decision strategy for the total system. The total system consists of S subsystems where the sth subsystem is characterized as follows:

Subsystem† $\mathcal{S}_s$: (s = 1, 2, . . ., S)

M_s : Number of categories in subsystem s.

M_{c_s} : Number of classes in subsystem s.

L_s : Number of features in subsystem s.

K_s : Number of columns for categories or classes in subsystem s. (1)

A method is needed to index all categories, classes, features, other subsystems and categories of other subsystems *associated with (affecting) subsystems* $\mathcal{S}_s$; the latter is called the *reference subsystem*. This is accomplished with vectors for the sth subsystem:

$\mathbf{x}_s = \{x_{s_j}\}$, x_{s_j} = 1 if jth feature (primitive) is included in the reference subsystem s, Ø otherwise.

$\boldsymbol{\gamma}_s^* = \{\gamma_{s_i}^*\}$, $\gamma_{s_i}^*$ = 1 if ith category γ_i^* is included in the reference subsystem s, Ø otherwise.

†We will refer to subsystem $\mathcal{S}_s$ as subsystem s for convenience.

$\mathbf{c_s} = \{c_{s_i}\}, \quad c_{s_i} = 1$ if ith class is included, Ø otherwise.
$\mathbf{s}_s = \{s_e\}, \quad s_e =$ if subsystem $\mathcal{S}_e$ is associated with the reference subsystem $\mathcal{S}_s$, Ø otherwise. (2)

A category $\gamma^*_{s_i}$ in reference subsystem $\mathcal{S}_s$ can depend on categories in other subsystems. The existence of this dependence is denoted by

$\mathrm{d}^*_{s_i} = \{\gamma^*_{s_{i_{e_\xi}}}\}$, 1 if category $\gamma^*_{s_i}$ in the reference subsystem $\mathcal{S}_s$
$\gamma^*_{s_{i_{e_\xi}}} = 1$ depends on category $\gamma^*_{e_\xi}$ in subsystem e. The supervisor in running the interviewer for feature selection extracts category decisions from one subsystem for use as feature values in the reference subsystem, and so on. (3)

Categories $\gamma^*_{e_\xi}$ outside of subsystem $\mathcal{S}_s$ which can affect a category $\gamma^*_{s_i}$ in subsystem $\mathcal{S}_s$ are called *intermediate categories* (Patrick *and others,* 1973, 1974; Patrick, 1979) and denoted by

$\gamma^*(s)$: Set of intermediate categories for subsystem $\mathcal{S}_s$ (4)

These intermediate categories are used to interconnect subsystems. Optimally "interconnecting" two subsystems could require that all features of the second subsystem are involved in joint probability density functions for categories in the first reference subsystem. This often is unrealistic and unnecessary in practice and can contradict the reasons for defining subsystems in the first place. Intermediate categories are a practical model for obtaining joint probability density functions of a category affected by another subsystem(s).

11-3 PRIMITIVES IN A TOTAL SYSTEM

A *primitive* is the basic characteristic of a category presentation. A *feature value* is the next higher level characteristic.† A Type 1 embedded feature is a primitive that is either TRUE or FALSE. *Each* feature value of a Type Ø feature can be a primitive. A *complex feature* is at a higher level‡ in the feature space hierarchy and is a function of primitives.

The primitive is important because it is the basic storage unit for features and complex features and is the basic building block of the knowledge base structure. The interviewer can incorporate primitives

†A feature value can be a primitive.

††A Type 1 measurement with embedded Type 1 features provides a complex feature.

in a grammar for user interaction; but the diagnostic system operates on primitives, "not the grammar."

Linearly independent basis functions discussed elsewhere in this book (Chapter 7) have coefficients which are primitives. Considering each value of a TYPE Ø feature as a primitive leads to an unnecessary expansion of dimensionality. Furthermore, since feature values of a TYPE Ø feature are mutually exclusive, this expansion of dimensionality leads to mathematical violations. For these reasons, *the TYPE Ø feature is taken as a single primitive (or primitive group).*

A convenient way to order primitives is alphabetically; but associate with each primitive an integer p to indicate its order, the primitive name, and the primitive TYPE (Ø or 1).

Categories also are ordered by the index c when the category is referred to as in the total system and by index i within any subsystem. Associated with each category† indexed by c is a set of primitives denoted $\mathbf{p}_c$. Within a subsystem $\mathcal{S}_s$ a category $\gamma^*_{s_i}$ has associated primitives $\mathbf{p}_{s_i}$ and associated categories $\mathbf{d}_{s_i}$. Included in $\mathbf{p}_c$ (and $\mathbf{p}_{s_i}$) is the primitive type.

A category in $\mathbf{d}^*_{s_i}$ *can be a feature value for category* $\gamma^*_{s_i}$ *in subsystem s.* In this case, the category in $\mathbf{d}^*_s$ is an *intermediate category.* If the intermediate category has non-zero probability as output from any subsystem, then it can affect the category in the reference subsystem. An application with the network of an Acid Base Subsystem with an Electrolyte Subsystem is found in Patrick *and others,* 1985.

11-4 CATEGORY PRIMITIVE RELATIONSHIP

11-4-1 Optimum Total Subsystem

For the total system, the category indexed by c has a category conditional probability density function

$$p(\mathbf{x}|\gamma^*_c, \mathbf{p}_c) \tag{5}$$

where $\mathbf{x}$ is the feature vector of the findings. Knowledge of Eq. (5) $\forall c$ results in an optimum system.

†A category itself is a primitive. The concept "In The Beginning There Was Hyperspace" views categories of values of a feature called the category feature. These categories are feature values and are primitives.

11-4-2 Optimum Subsystem—Complete Subsystem

We now consider the subsystem $\mathcal{S}_s$ with categories $\gamma^*_{s_i}$ and features (primitives) **x.** A *complete subsystem* is defined as a subsystem where decision making does not depend on any other subsystem. A category γ^*_i in this subsystem depends only on $\mathbf{p}_i$ and thus has probability density function

$$p(\mathbf{x}|\gamma^*_i, \mathbf{p}_i) \; : \text{For a complete subsystem.} \tag{6}$$

Notation γ^*_i will be used instead of $\gamma^*_{s_i}$ for simplicity.

Let $\mathfrak{X}_s$ be the feature space for subsystem $\mathcal{S}_s$; then Eq. (6) can be rewritten

$$p(\mathbf{x}\varepsilon\mathfrak{X}_s|\gamma^*_i, \mathbf{p}_i). \tag{7}$$

More generally, the probability density function in Eq. (7) depends on $\boldsymbol{d}_s$ which contains those categories in other subsystems on which γ^*_i depends. Thus, we redefine Eq. (7)

$$\begin{aligned}
&\mathbf{p}(\mathbf{x}\varepsilon\mathfrak{X}_s|\gamma^*_i, \mathbf{p}_i, \mathbf{d}_s)\\
&\mathfrak{X}_s = \text{Feature space for subsystem } \mathcal{S}_s.\\
&\gamma^*_i = i\text{th category in subsystem } \mathcal{S}_s.\\
&\mathbf{p}_i = \text{Primitives for } i\text{th category.}\\
&\boldsymbol{d}_s = \text{Categories in other subsystems on which category } \gamma^*_i \text{ in subsystem } \mathcal{S}_s \text{ depends. } \mathbf{d}^*_s = \{d^*_{s_i}\}
\end{aligned} \tag{8}$$

11-4-3 Discussion of d_s

The vector $\mathbf{d}_s$ contains categories in other subsystems upon which category γ^*_i in reference subsystem $\mathcal{S}_s$ depends. We reserve the option for $\mathbf{d}_s$ to contain the category feature relationship for any category $\mathbf{d}_s$.

11-5 TOTAL SYSTEM LIKELIHOOD FUNCTIONS

For any category γ^*_c in the total system, the results in Chapter 9 apply, and from Section 9-7,

$$p(\mathbf{x}|\gamma^*_c) = \sum_{k=1}^{K} \prod_{\eta=1}^{L_1(k)} p(x_\eta|\gamma^*_{c_k}) \left[\sum_{u=1}^{U(k)} \prod_{t=1}^{S(u)} (p^u_{c_{k_t}}) \right] p(\gamma^*_{c_k}|\gamma^*_c) \tag{9}$$

where

K	: Number of columns	
$U(k)$	: Number of mini-columns in column k for kth column.	
$L_{I(k)}$	: Number of statistically independent features for kth column.	(10)
$p(x_\eta \mid \gamma^*_{c_k})$	: Probability density function of statistically independent feature x_η for kth column.	
$p(\gamma^*_{c_k} \mid \gamma^*_c)$	: Mixing probability for kth column; i.e., subcategory probability given category γ^*_c.	
$\prod_{t=1}^{S_k(u)} (p^u_{c_{k_t}})$	: Probability density for uth minicolumn of column k (subcategory k) involving $S(u)$ packet probabilities.	
$S(u)$ K	: # of features involved in the uth minicolumn (subsubcategory) of subcategory K.	

Before using Eq. (9) in a Total System or a subsystem, the equation can be *greatly* simplified. Let the statistically independent features I in Eq. (9) be decomposed into Insignificant (ISIG) and Significant (SIG) independent features:

$$\mathrm{I} = \mathrm{I}_{\mathrm{SIG}} + \mathrm{I}_{\mathrm{ISIG}}. \tag{11}$$

That is,

$$\prod_{\eta=1}^{L_I(k)} p(x_\eta \mid \gamma^*_{c_k}) = \prod_{\mathrm{I_{SIG}}} p(x_\eta \mid \gamma^*_{c_k}) \prod_{\mathrm{I_{ISIG}}} p(x_\eta \mid \gamma^*_{c_k}). \tag{12}$$

11-6 GROUPING CATEGORIES INTO A DIFFERENTIAL DIAGNOSIS (SUBSYSTEM)

A differential diagnosis, without loss of generality, can be viewed as the categories in a subsystem. Without loss of generality we have denoted this differential diagnosis by subsystem $\mathcal{S}_s$. Referring to Eq. (2), the categories in this subsystem generally have a subset of Independent, Insignificant features from I_{ISIG} which are common and the subset is denoted by $\mathrm{I}_{\mathrm{ISIG}_\mathrm{C}}$. Thus,

$$\mathrm{I}_{\mathrm{ISIG}} = \mathrm{I}_{\mathrm{ISIG}_{\mathrm{NC}}} + \mathrm{I}_{\mathrm{ISIG}_\mathrm{C}}$$

where $\mathrm{I}_{\mathrm{ISIG}_{\mathrm{NC}}}$ is the subset of those insignificant features in $\mathrm{I}_{\mathrm{ISIG}}$ which are not in common. Recall that independent, insignificant features have a "uniform" probability density function if Type Ø; and for Type 1 features, they have probability ϵ if True and probability $(1 - \epsilon)$ if False (see Chapter 8).

Define

$$\prod_{I_{ISIG_C}} p(x_\eta|\gamma_i^*) = C_s \tag{13}$$

$$C_s = \text{Constant}$$
$$\gamma_i^* \in \text{Differential Diagnosis of } \mathcal{S}_s.$$

This is the constant C_s in Eq. (14).

Substituting Eq. (12) into Eq. (9) results in

$$p(\mathbf{x}|\gamma_c^*) = C_s * \sum_{k=1}^{K} \prod_{I_{SIG}} p(x_\eta|\gamma_{c_k}^*) \prod_{I_{ISIG_{NC}}} p(x_\eta|\gamma_{c_k}^*) \left\{ \sum_{u=1}^{U(k)} \prod_{t=1}^{S_k(u)} (p_{c_{k_t}}^u) \right\} * p(\gamma_{i_k}^*|\gamma_i^*). \tag{14}$$

The only independent insignificant features remaining in Eq. (14) are those not in common among all the categories. The constant† C_s is common to all categories in the differential diagnosis, which are in the reference subsystem $\mathcal{S}_s$; and C_s accounts for features from the total system which are insignificant with respect to the reference subsystem $\mathcal{S}_s$. There may be a subset of features for category γ_i^* that are insignificant but not in common ($I_{ISIG_{NC}}$).

11-7 DIFFERENTIAL DIAGNOSIS WITH MISSING FEATURES

For a total system, the number of features in the recognition vector $\mathbf{x}_r$ can be very large (L dimensional). In practice a recognition vector $\mathbf{x}_r$ for findings (a pattern) has most (or at least many) features missing. Accordingly, partition the *recognition vector* into

$$\mathbf{x}_r = [\mathbf{x}_M, \mathbf{x}_p]$$
$$\mathbf{x}_p\text{: present features in recognition vector} \tag{15}$$
$$\mathbf{x}_M\text{: missing features in recognition vector}$$

A missing feature is a property of the recognition vector; whereas, an insignificant feature is a property of the category-feature relationship which is part of the knowledge base.

---

†This constant is a normalization factor which does not affect relative a posteriori probabilities of the categories.

Using the Projection Theorem previously developed in Section 9-12, it follows that after applying expression (15), Eq. (14) becomes

$$p(\mathbf{x}|\gamma_c^*) = C_s^* \sum_{k=1}^{K} \prod_{\substack{\text{Independent}\\ \text{significant}\\ \text{nonmissing}\\ \text{features}}} p(x_\eta|\gamma_{c_k}^*) \prod_{\substack{\text{Independent}\\ \text{insignificant}\\ \text{noncommon}\\ \text{nonmissing}\\ \text{features}}} p(x_\eta|\gamma_{c_k}^*) *$$

$$\prod_{u=1}^{U(k)} \left\{ \prod_{t=1}^{S_k(u)} (p^{u}_{c_{k_t}}) \right\} * p(\gamma_{i_k}^*|\gamma_i^*). \tag{16}$$

Equation (16) is the expression of inference for category γ_c^* in the total system relative to a reference subsystem $\mathcal{S}_s$. For the reference subsystem, many features from the total system are insignificant and this is accounted for by the constant† C_s. Put differently, *when an inference function for a category is placed in a total system, it is multiplied by a constant C_s for the reference subsystem.*

11-8 ACTIVATION RULES

11-8-1 Introduction

Activation Rules provide a method for arriving at a differential diagnosis given a recognition vector $\mathbf{x}_r$. Undoubtedly, the best procedure for activation often will be interactive with the user choosing a subsystem. *Automatic "focusing" techniques are of value for some problems but, in general, are wasteful in terms of processing time and storage requirements.* Furthermore, they can result in decreased decision-making performance. Various methods of activation including optimum methods will be considered.

The constant C_s reflects off-line learning to observe insignificant features to reduce the complexity of any on-line focusing.

---

†A total system could have thousands of features with most absorbed into the constant C_s.

11-8-2 Optimum Activation Rule

Given

$$\mathbf{x}_r = \begin{bmatrix} \mathbf{x}_p \\ \mathbf{x}_M \end{bmatrix}$$

an optimum activation rule (see Chapter 10 on feature selection) is:

$$\begin{aligned} &\text{Activate } \gamma_i^* : p(\mathbf{x}_p|\gamma_i^*) > \delta \\ &\text{Do not Activate } \gamma_i^* : p(\mathbf{x}_p|\gamma_i^*) \leq \delta \end{aligned} \qquad (17)$$

The constant δ is a threshold which itself is knowledge.

11-8-3 Activation of Category by Feature Value

A suboptimum method of activating categories is to activate any category having a significant feature value in $\mathbf{x}_p$ with nonzero probability density. This method requires checking L features for each of the M categories in the total subsystem. The number of checks is:

M * L = Number of checks required to determine categories to be activated.

As an example, suppose both M and L are of the order 2×10^3; then $M * L = 4 \times 10^6$ is the number of checks required.

11-8-4 Activation of Subsystems by Rules

Considerable simplification results by activating subsystems by rules.† This is accomplished through a *subsystem activation program,* itself a subsystem. Depending on the problem, either a *single subsystem or multiple subsystems* are activated.

11-9 OPTIMUM TOTAL SYSTEM PROCESSING

The optimum total system theoretically can be implemented by a series of operations. This implementation "crosses" subsystems, "pulling out" each category feature relationship. Subsystems thus can be viewed as

†The threshold technique of Section 11-8-2 is an elementary rule.

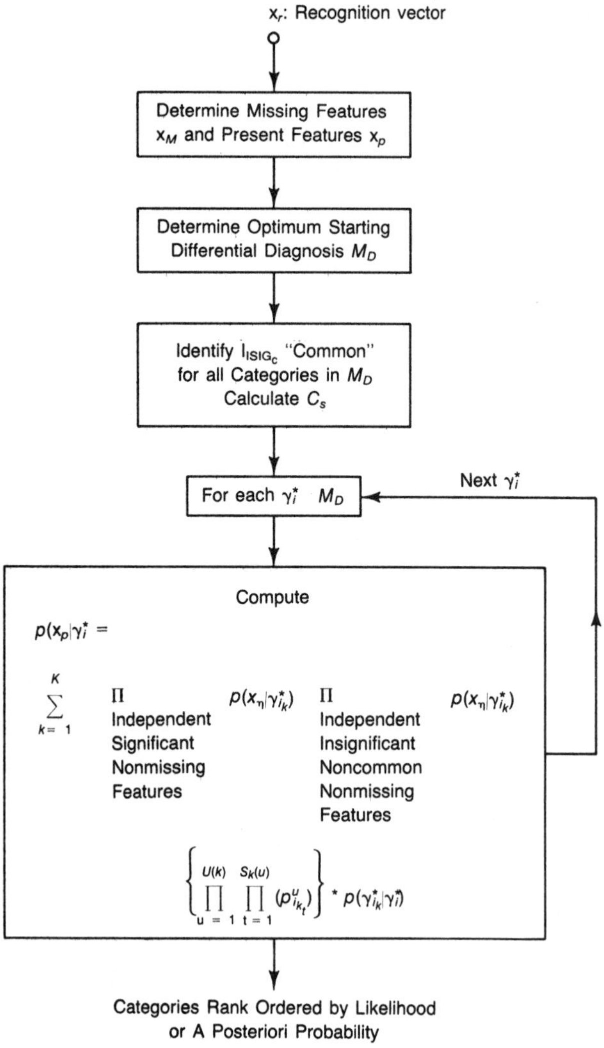

FIGURE 11.1 Optimum total system processing.

organizing knowledge: used as a reference to locate particular category feature relationships. The steps in the implementation are as follows, and illustrated in Figure 11.1.

1. Given a recognition vector $\mathbf{x}_r$, obtain

$$\mathbf{x}_r = \begin{bmatrix} \mathbf{x}_p \\ \mathbf{x}_M \end{bmatrix}$$

2. Determine an optimum starting differential diagnosis M_D either by using Eq. (17) or category activation by feature values.

3. Determine $\mathbf{x}_M$ and $\mathbf{x}_p$ for the union of all categories in M_D. Let this be a new subsystem—a reference subsystem $\mathcal{S}_s$.
4. Identify independent insignificant features that are common to all categories in M_D, denoted by the set I_{ISIG_C} and determine C_s.
5. Calculate Eq. (16) for each category γ_i^* in the differential diagnosis, taking into account missing features, features in the set $I_{\text{ISIG}_\text{NC}}$ and minicolumns for each column of a category.

This implementation assumes that the recognition vector $\mathbf{x}_r$ is made available by the interviewer either through serial feature acquisition, random feature selection or adapting a previous feature vector with one or more new feature values.

11-10 DEVELOPING A TOTAL SYSTEM

11-10-1 The Steps

The theory presented in this book has been used to develop a total diagnostic system both with or without subsystems.† Steps in this development are outlined below.

1. Create and Store Primitives. The creation of primitives is an ongoing process; but by storing them *alphabetically,* updating is simplified. The order of a primitive is indicated by an *integer p,* as discussed in Section 11-3. When a primitive is created and stored, a vector $\mathbf{x}_s$ is updated for each subsystem $\mathcal{S}_s$ for which that primitive is *significant.* Often new primitives are created when developing or modifying a subsystem $\mathcal{S}_s$. Automatic techniques can be used to add a new primitive to $\mathfrak{X}_s$ of any appropriate subsystem $\mathcal{S}_s$ or to transfer a subsystem primitive to the total system's primitive list.
2. Categories are indexed γ_c^* in the total system with γ_s^* indicating those categories in subsystem $\mathcal{S}_s$. Classes associated with categories are naturally part of the subsystem.
3. Subsystems are created in the total system through an initialization process whereby for each subsystem $\mathcal{S}_s$, parameters M_s, M_{l_s}, L_s, and K_s are specified;‡ appropriate data files are created and formatted. For subsystem $\mathcal{S}_s$, a set of *intermediate categories* $\mathbf{d}_s$ is determined. The intermediate categories are indexed in the total system; and through $\mathbf{d}_s$, we indirectly know each subsystem having a category

†A total system could be one large subsystem.

‡M_{l_s} is the number of classes or only classes in subsystem $\mathcal{S}_s$.

d(s) as an intermediate category for subsystem $\mathcal{S}_s$. Intermediate categories that can be feature values for the reference subsystem constitute the links among subsystems. Category conditional probability density functions for categories of one subsystem are themselves conditioned on the intermediate categories of other subsystems. This is consistent with the knowledge base structure engineered in Chapter 9.

4. Develop Category Feature Relationships. A category feature relationship is a module—a *likelihood packet.* This likelihood packet consists† of multiple columns ("hypercubes"). It is expressed by Eq. (16).

   The *likelihood packet* initially is designed for the total system and has *likelihood packets falling in respective subsystems.* Of particular interest is *Likelihood Packet Corollary,* where *the Likelihood Packet is the Product of Likelihood Subpackets in respective subsystems.*

   Except for where local minicolumn packets "cross subsystems," the above applies. The "crossing of subsystems" with local packets should be avoided by the developer.

   The Likelihood Packet Corollary is a powerful concept for the total system, consistent with the concept of intermediate categories. The knowledge base for the total system can, without loss of generality, consist of *Likelihood Packets* for categories in respective subsystems. The same likelihood packet can be used in a system or a total system.

5. Decision Rule. Decisions are made either by computing category likelihood functions or the a posteriori probability of categories.

6. Explanation. The differential diagnosis can be explained by Basic Consulting, using respective marginal likelihoods for each feature of a category, or presenting the relative importance of each feature of the recognition vector and the correlation level‡ with the column.

7. Reasoning Process. Reasoning is shown for decisions by columns, minicolumns, features with Can't, probabilities, likelihood or relative feature ranks, and correlation level.

---

†The word "hypercube" is used to emphasize that a subcategory is a "statistical cloud" of possible patterns for a category. Some patterns in the "cloud" have higher probabilities than other patterns.

‡Correlation Level is an expression of the degree of correlation of the findings with the closest subcategory or subsubcategory. High correlation level requires high degree of multiple features in the findings being like those of patterns of the category.

8. Induction. **CONSULT-I®** uses Induction in the final inference (decision making) program by first looking for Insignificance, then Missing, and then likelihood for the respective columns (hypercubes) of each category.

11-10-1-1 Approach in CONSULT-I®

With regard to the above, **CONSULT-I®** uses the following approach:

1. Stores primitives (or feature values) with an index for the type of measurement (if the feature is to be used by the interviewer as Type Ø or Type 1).
2. Stores $p(x|\gamma^*_{i_k})$, where $\gamma^*_{i_k}$ is a subcategory.
3. Uses Activating Rules where appropriate.
4. Stores intermediate category probabilities.
5. Optimum Decision Rule based on Theorem of A Posteriori Probability (Patrick).
6. Deductions for Complex Class Formation, Missing Features.
7. Induction—Inference, Likelihood Function.
8. Provision for Total System to integrate Subsystems.
9. Compatible with CONSULT LEARNING SYSTEM® which can learn column presentations by example.

11-10-1-2 Definitions

The following are definitions used in describing the CONSULT-I® total system:

THIST: Interviewer for total system.

PRIMITIVE: Basic feature with index number, kind, size.

KIND: (1) Laboratory test, (2) Sign, (3) Symptom, (4) History (if a medical system).

SIZE: Number of feature values.

MEASUREMENT: A primitive or collection of primitives where the primitive cannot occur at the same time for any one category.

11-10-1-3 Menu–Driven Interviewer

A Menu-Driver Interviewer is constructed by utilizing primitives in association with the following:

Numbers 1, 2, 3, ... for feature number.
Increased, Decreased are represented by numbers for features.
5 is reserved for Normal for Type Ø features when appropriate.

Feature values must be mutually exclusive for Type Ø features. Since more than one primitive can be used to compose a feature, feature values cannot be mutually exclusive in forming a Type 1 Measurement.

11-10-1-4 Final Decision–Making Program Properties

The final decision-making program, DEC4, has the following properties:

DEC4 uses Parameters.
M = Number of categories.
L = Number of features.
K = Number of columns per category.
F = Number of significant features.

11-10-1-5 Blanking

Blanking vector with uniform probability density function is provided for insignificant features of any category whether the category is in a subsystem or the whole system. The DEC4 program overlays the subsystems or new subsystems. Features with values from the interviewer are output as hard copy for each subsystem in which they are significant.

11-10-1-6 Categories

Set of categories for the sth subsystem are numbered 1, 2, 3, . . ., M. A Modifier, s, indicates the subsystem when required to avoid confusion.

11-10-1-7 Feature Vector Identifier

Modifiers are added to identify the subsystem and category for which the feature vector is being processed. This is necessary to Size DEC4 with respect to M, L, K, and Blanking for the subsystem.

11-10-1-8 Differential Diagnosis for Subsystem I

A subsystem I can be processed with a HISTNI feature vector resulting in category conditional probability estimate of $p(\mathbf{x}|\gamma_i^*)$ with values 1, 2, 3, 4. This is the differential diagnosis.

11-10-1-9 New Subsystem

A new subsystem is the union of categories activated by Activation Rules whereby these categories have ranked category conditional probabilities $p(\mathbf{x}|\gamma_i^*)$: 1, 2, 3, 4.

The preceding steps are illustrated in Figure 11.2. After categories are activated, a new subsystem is formed consisting of these categories. An interviewer consistent with these categories, named NEWHIST, is used to obtain feature values for categories in the new subsystem. This interviewer NEWHIST is constructed from the vertical total system interviewer, THIST.

Finally, the process illustrated in Figure 11.1 is implemented in a program DEC4.

A new subsystem obeys the rules of a subsystem insofar as a posteriori probability calculations are made.

11-10-1-10 Activation Rules

Subsystem. Subsystems may be activated by a laboratory test value(s), a sign(s), or symptom(s), or combinations of these. Modifiers are used as follows:

Modifiers: *I*: Laboratory test value Increased
D: Laboratory test value Decreased
O: Laboratory test value does not matter
Positive: Self-explanatory
Negative: Self-explanatory

Categories. The same rules apply for Activating Categories. Note that there are many more categories than subsystems.

11-10-2 Interconnecting Subsystems in CONSULT-I®

Statistically Independent Subsystems. An interesting simplification of the total system results by an assumption that subsystems are statistically independent. This construction will now be described.

As before, let $\mathbf{x}_s \in \mathcal{X}_s$ denote the feature vector for subsystem $\mathcal{S}_s$. Assuming that, given respective category conditional probability density functions of $\mathbf{x}_1, \mathbf{x}_2, \ldots, \mathbf{x}_s$, are statistically independent, it follows that:

$$p(\mathbf{x}|\gamma_i^*) = p(\mathbf{x}_1, \mathbf{x}_2, \ldots, \mathbf{x}_s|\gamma_i^*) = \prod_{s=1}^{S} p(\mathbf{x}_s|\gamma_i^*) \quad (18)$$

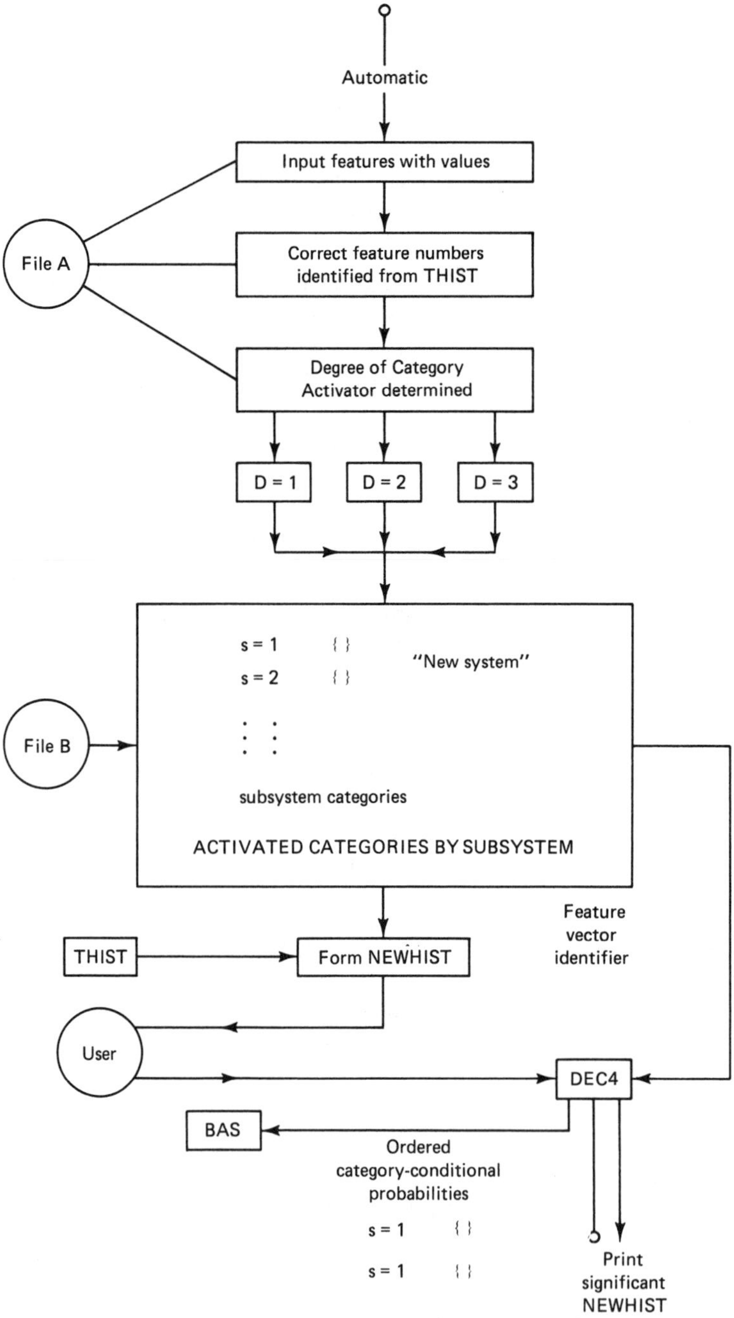

FIGURE 11.2 Subsystem activation.

Suppose that $\mathbf{x}_s \in \mathfrak{X}_s$ is insignificant for category γ_i^*; it follows that

$$p(\mathbf{x}_s|\gamma_i^*) = \prod_{\substack{x_{s_j}\text{ Type } \emptyset \\ \text{Feature}}} \frac{(9|n_{x_j})}{9} \prod_{\substack{x_{s_j}\text{ Type 1} \\ \text{Feature}}} \frac{[\delta(\text{True})\epsilon+\delta(\text{False})(1-\epsilon)]}{9} \tag{19}$$

$$\triangleq \mathscr{C}_s;$$

$$n_{x_j} = \text{Number of feature values for } x_{s_j}$$

Thus

$$p(\mathbf{x}_1,\mathbf{x}_2,\ldots,\mathbf{x}_s|\gamma_i^*) = \prod_{\substack{x_{s_j}\text{ in } \mathfrak{X}_s \\ \text{significant} \\ \text{for category} \\ \gamma_i^*}} p(\mathbf{x}_s|\gamma_i^*) \prod_{\substack{\text{No Feature in} \\ \mathbf{x}_s\text{ significant} \\ \text{for category} \\ \gamma_i^*}} \mathscr{C}_s \tag{20}$$

Equation (20) along with Eqs. (4) and (5) show how a category can cross subsystems. The inference function becomes greatly simplified when there are statistically independent features:

For both Eqs. (1) and (3),

$$p(\mathbf{x}_s|\gamma_i^*) = \prod_{k=1}^{K} p(\mathbf{x}_s|\gamma_{i_k}^*)\, p(\gamma_{i_k}^*|\gamma_k^*) \tag{21}$$

or, as previously discussed,

$$p(\mathbf{x}_s|\gamma_i^*) = \max_k \{p(\mathbf{x}_s|\gamma_{i_k}^*)\} \tag{22}$$

where k indexes the kth column. There also exist minicolumns in Eqs. (21) and (22).

11-10-3 CONSULT-I® Category Modules

11-10-3-1 Introduction

A very interesting aspect of **CONSULT-I®** is the facility to create knowledge modules for each category γ_i^* in a total system. Usually, these modules are created first in a particular subsystem. Then, category modules can be collected to form a new subsystem or placed in multiple subsystems. The **CONSULT-I®** theory of statistical pattern recognition with artificial intelligence provides an optimum theory under which individual category probability density functions can be trained and stored as knowledge modules. A collection of *these modules can be collected and a system encompassing the modules automatically generated. This includes automatic generation of primitives,* an interviewer and, of course, the category list.

11-10-3-2 CONSULT-I® Category Modules

Let $p(\mathbf{x}_s^*|\gamma_i^*)$ be a likelihood function complete for category γ_i^*, designed for some reference subsystem $\mathcal{S}_s^*$. By complete we mean that there are no features characterizing the category feature relationship of γ_i^* that are not in subsystem $\mathcal{S}_s$.

It is desired to use this module designed for subsystem $\mathcal{S}_s^*$ in another subsystem $\mathcal{S}_s$. To achieve this, let

L_s^* = Number of features in subsystem $\mathcal{S}_s^*$
L_s = Number of features in subsystem $\mathcal{S}_s$

and proceed as follows:

1. Append those primitives in $\mathbf{x}_s^*$ not in $\mathbf{x}_s$ to $\mathbf{x}_s$.
2. Determine features ε $(\mathbf{x}_s\text{-}\mathbf{x}_s^*)$ by type (Type Ø or Type 1).
3. Define C_s^* for $\mathbf{x}_s\text{-}\mathbf{x}_s^*$ according to previous formulation.

Then

$$f(\mathbf{x}_s|\gamma_i^*) = f(\mathbf{x}_s^*|\gamma_i^*)\ C_s^*.$$

This formulation is important because a category module can be designed without regard to other category modules. This presumes that appropriate rules are followed and that the primitive set is known.

12

Inference Functions as Closeness Measures and the Comparison of Classification Systems

12-1 INTRODUCTION

A category is described by its c.c.p.d.f. $p(\mathbf{x}|\gamma_i^*)$, an inference function or likelihood function that measures the closeness of a pattern $\mathbf{x}$ to the category γ_i^*. Closeness is an important viewpoint because the description of categories can be multimodal with a second category pattern slipped in "the holes" between modes of the first category. The ability to learn and characterize the multimode aspect of a category is essential. This is accomplished in **CONSULT-I®** through columns and minicolumns for each category. A column or column with minicolumn modification is a collection of patterns for a presentation of a category. The effective number of patterns in a column can be very large (billions, trillions, and so on). It can be thought of as a hyperspace quantum level or region.

In this chapter the **CONSULT-I®** closeness measure, derived with the guide of the theorem on a posteriori probability by Patrick, will be used as a reference for comparing other systems. The theorem on a posteriori probability by Patrick provides for constructing a knowledge base structure, collecting hard data to create the knowledge base, learn, and incorporate knowledge about dependence among features for a category.

Various systems compared with **CONSULT-I®** include measure of Belief used in **MYCIN** (Shortliffe, 1976), the Promise closeness measure (Gini and Gini, 1980), interpretation of a closeness measure used in **CASNET** and **EXPERT** (Kulikowski and Weiss, 1982; Weiss *and others,* 1978), and the closeness measure in **INTERNIST** (Miller *and others,* 1982; Myers *and others,* 1982; Pople, 1982).

The systems to be reviewed were not constructed with viewpoints of only classes, complex classes, complex categories, and so on. Therefore, we take editorial privilege to review the systems in terms of the new constructions.

12-2 CONSIDERATION IN A CLOSENESS MEASURE

The struggle to develop the ideal closeness measure for expressing the closeness of a recognition vector sample $\mathbf{x}$ (findings) to a category γ_ξ^* is well documented over decades. Considerations to take into account when designing a closeness measure are:

1. Independence versus dependence of features x_j in $\mathbf{x}$.
2. Type of feature x_j.
3. Typical and atypical presentations of category γ_j^*.
4. Local dependencies in the feature vector $\mathbf{x}$.
5. Sequence in which x_j's of findings are processed.
6. Desire to use feature values x_{j_v} for explanations of how a decision was reached.
7. Missing feature values x_{j_v} in a recognition vector (findings).
8. Insignificant features for a category.
9. Errors in observing feature values in the findings.
10. Errors or uncertainty in the feature values of a training record.

12-3 CATEGORY CONDITIONAL PROBABILITY DENSITY FUNCTIONS

An important closeness measure or inference function associated with Bayes theorem utilizes:

$$p(\mathbf{x}|\gamma_\xi^*) = \prod_{j=1}^{L} p(x_j|\mathbf{x}_{j-1},\gamma_\xi^*),\ \mathbf{x}_\theta \text{ the null vector,} \tag{1}$$

the category conditional probability density function. *If* $\mathbf{x}_{j-1}$ *is dropped, statistically independent features are assumed.* An objective in a learning system is to utilize dependencies among the features for accurate classification of findings. The method of direction is here defined Column-direction with minicolumn modification (in **CONSULT-I®**).

When subcategories and subsubcategories of γ_ξ^* are allowed with a closeness measure for each, *dependence among features is accounted for.*

This closeness measure is used in **CONSULT-I®.** Methods of accounting for dependence locally have included Sebestyen's adaptive sample set construction (Sebestyen, 1962; Patrick, 1972), Spect's expansion in terms of polynomials (Spect, 1966; Patrick, 1972), Patrick *and others'* Generalized K Nearest Neighbor rule (1970, 1972). From the theorem on a posteriori probability (Patrick).

$$p(\mathbf{x}|\omega_i^*) = p(\mathbf{x}|\omega_i) - \sum_{\omega_i \varepsilon \Omega_\xi} p(\mathbf{x}|\Omega_\xi^*) =$$

$$\prod_{j=1}^{L} p(x_j|\mathbf{x}_{j-1}, \omega_\xi) - \sum_{\omega_i \varepsilon \Omega_\xi} \prod_{j=1}^{L} p(x_j|\mathbf{x}_{j-1}, \Omega_\xi^*) \tag{2}$$

Sebestyen's adaptive sample set contruction has much to tell us about representing categories by subcategories. The idea is a good one, although our tools today are much stronger in terms of measuring closeness.

Options for constructing Eq. (2) include a direct approach on $p(\mathbf{x}|\omega_i^*)$ considering unions of subcategories reflecting respective dependencies. An indirect approach is to use a network structure with relationships between $\omega_i^*, \omega_i, \Omega_\xi^*$ and $\mathbf{x}$ along with search techniques to find a solution to Eq. (2). These procedures were discussed in Chapter 5.

12-4 GENERALIZED CONSULT-I® CLOSENESS MEASURE

The column-directed **CONSULT-I®** closeness measure has previously been discussed (see Patrick, 1972, 1979, 1983; Patrick *and others,* 1974; Patrick and Shen, 1975; Fattu and Patrick, 1983; Patrick and Fattu, 1984).

Column-Directed Basis Functions

Given a test vector (findings)

$$\mathbf{x} = [x_1, x_2, \ldots, x_L],$$

there exists an inverse closeness measure (inverse because the larger the measure the closer is the vector $\mathbf{x}$ to the category) $p(\mathbf{x}|\gamma_\xi^*)$ of the "closeness" of $\mathbf{x}$ to category γ_ξ^*.

Define

$$\{\gamma_{\xi_k}^*\}_{k=1}^{K} \tag{3}$$

as indexes of typical and atypical presentations of category γ_ξ^*.

Subcategories $\gamma_{\xi_k}^*$ define the kth column of packets for category γ_ξ^*. Let a subsubcategory (as in Section 9-2)

$$\gamma_{\xi_{z_\delta}}^* \tag{4}$$

be a particular set of packets (can be referred to as a subsubcategory) for the zth column consisting of:

$$\{C_{\xi_{z_w}}\} \text{ and } \{\mathfrak{M}_{\xi_{z_s}}\}. \tag{5}$$

Then (see Section 9-2)

$$p(\mathbf{x}|\gamma_{\eta_{z_\delta}}^*) \tag{6}$$

is the probability density function of the features in the δth set of packets of column z for category γ_η^*.

An inference function involving the zth column

$$\prod_w p(C_{\xi_{z_w}}|\gamma^* 2\xi_{z_\delta}) \prod_u p(\mathfrak{M}_{\xi_{z_u}}|\gamma_{\xi_{z_\delta}}^*),\ z = 1,2, \ldots, K \text{ (for each column)} \tag{7}$$

is an inverse closeness measure of the closeness of $\mathbf{x}$ to category γ_ξ^*. For some subsubcategory $\gamma_{\xi_{z_\delta}}^*$ (perhaps unique) the pattern $\mathbf{x}$ will be closest to the category γ_ξ^*. If K is sufficiently large and there are enough subsubcategories, we postulate that for some $\gamma_{\xi_{z_\delta}}^*$ of γ_ξ^*,

$$p(\mathbf{x}|\gamma_{\xi_{z_\delta}}^*) = 1 - \epsilon \tag{8}$$

for arbitrarily small ϵ. This is similar to saying that the functions $p(\mathbf{x}|\gamma_{\xi_{z_\delta}}^*)$, $k = 1, 2, \ldots, K$ are complete for describing $p(\mathbf{x}|\gamma_\xi^*)$. Note that $p(\mathbf{x}|\gamma_{\xi_{z_\delta}}^*))$ is a family of samples $\mathbf{x}$, not a single sample.

Equation (7) is the defining equation of the kth column *(hypercube for category* γ_ξ^* in **CONSULT-I®**.

Production rules used in production systems are a special case of Eq. (7). Of course, Eq. (7) could be used as an advanced production rule with column directed search; but then one is approximating the **CONSULT-I®** closeness measure.

Recall from Section 9-14 that the **CONSULT-I®** closeness measure (inference function) for category γ_ξ^* has the construction

$$p(\mathbf{x}|\gamma_\xi^*) = \sum_{k=1}^{K} \prod_{\eta=1}^{L_l(k)} p(x_\eta|\gamma_{\xi_k}^*) \left\{ \prod_{u=1}^{U(k)} \prod_{s=1}^{S_k(u)} \delta_{i_{k_s}}(p_{\xi_{k_s}}^u)\, p(\gamma_{\xi_k}^*|\gamma_\xi^*) \right\}$$

a more revealing form than Eq. (7).

12-5 ASPECTS OF THE CONSULT-I® CLOSENESS MEASURE

The closeness measure used in **CONSULT-I®** is individualized for each category in the category space. To help understand this closeness measure, consider a three-feature example where the objective is to construct

$$p(x_1,x_2,x_3)$$

from

$$p(x_2,x_3) \text{ and } p(x_1,x_2).$$

The problem is illustrated in Figure 12.1. To obtain $p(x_1,x_2,x_3)$, consider that

$$\begin{aligned} p(x_1,x_2,x_3) &= p(x_1,x_2|x_3)p(x_3) \\ &= p(x_2,x_3|x_1)p(x_1). \end{aligned} \quad (9)$$

The functions

$$p(x_1,x_2|x_3) \quad (10)$$

and

$$p(x_2,x_3|x_1)$$

are presumed not available to the knowledge engineer. This suggests that the *first function does not depend on* x_3, *and the second does not depend on* x_1 *until knowledge to the contrary is available.*

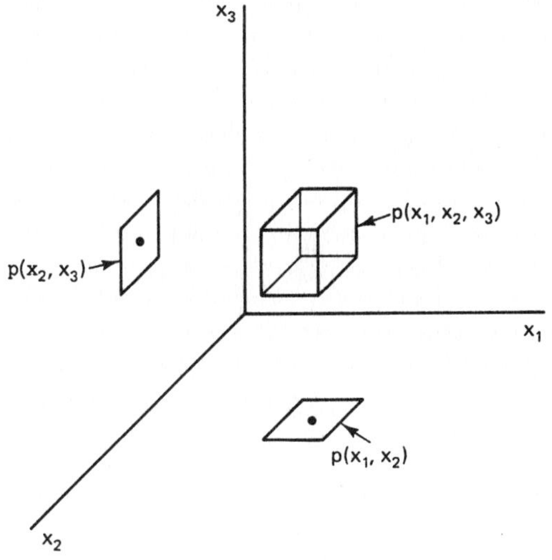

FIGURE 12.1 Packet-directed training.

Thus

$$p(x_1,x_2,x_3) = p(x_1,x_2)p(x_3) \qquad (11)$$
$$= p(x_2,x_3)p(x_1)$$

where

$$p(x_3) = \int p(x_2,x_3)dx_2 \qquad (12)$$

and

$$p(x_1) = \int p(x_1,x_2)dx_2. \qquad (13)$$

Without knowing how x_3 affects x_1 and x_2 or how x_1 affects x_2 and x_3, there *is no alternative method* to that of the above. If these dependencies are important, then they must be provided by a teacher or through estimation (learning using relative frequency—learning the correlation level by relative frequency in the feature space). The modules used in constructing the joint probability density functions are illustrated in Figure 12-1.

In the above example, there are two estimates of $p(x_1,x_2,x_3)$ that can be combined together. These two respective estimates are shown in Figure 12.2a and 12.2b.

Where there is no information, statistical dependence can be illustrated:

$$p(x_1,x_2,x_3) = p(x_1,x_2)p(x_3) \text{ when } x_3 \text{ is independent of } x_1,x_2.$$

But otherwise

$$p(x_1,x_2,x_3) = p(x_1,x_2|x_3)p(x_3).$$

There are three possibilities:

(1) $p(x_1,x_2|x_3) > p(x_1,x_2)$.
(2) $p(x_1,x_2|x_3) = p(x_1,x_2)$.
(3) $p(x_1,x_2|x_3) < p(x_1,x_2)$.

We are given that nothing is known about $p(x_1,x_2)$ as a function of x_3. Both (1) and (3) are true if there is some value of x_3 for which something is known about $p(x_1,x_2)$. This violates the given conditions. Thus, only (2) is possible. *Another model has been created.*† It will be verified by the scientific method using performance and estimation.

†This model is precise in view of the a priori knowledge available. Unfortunately, jargon such as "heuristic" has been used to describe something like this; but you can see the value of precisely devising a model to describe an inductive or deductive operation.

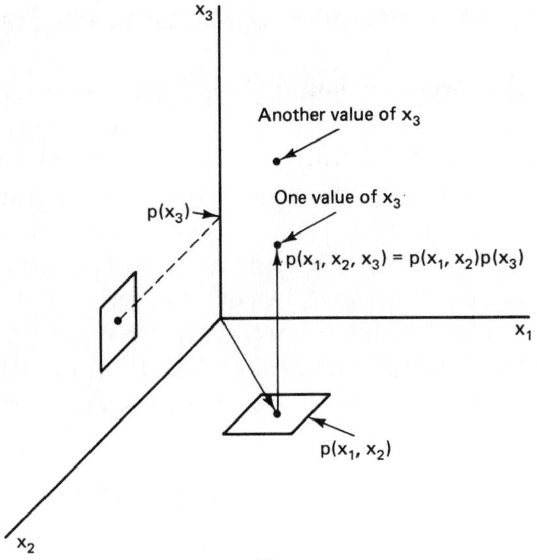

(a)

FIGURE 12.2a

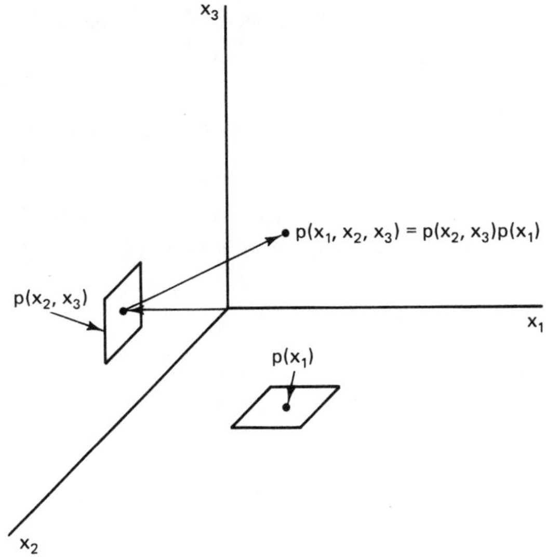

(b)

FIGURE 12.2b

12-5-1 Learning the Correlation Level: Concept Formation

A very powerful procedure would be one that can learn the degree of correlation at some point $\mathbf{x} = [x_1,x_2, \ldots, x_L]$ for category γ_i^*. This degree of correlation level is defined in this book as the *Correlation Level.* Training samples (records) from γ_i^* are used to determine the correlation or the correlation level.

The *correlation level* is a new approach measuring the closeness of $\mathbf{x}$ to the training records from γ_i^*. A correlation level of 4, for example, indicates that with high probability (relative frequency) up to four features at a time have values equal to or close to those values for the respective features in $\mathbf{x}$. If these four features are x_1,x_2,x_3,x_4 then we know that

$$p(x_1,x_2,x_3,x_4,x_5) = p(x_1,x_2,x_3,x_4)p(x_5)$$

and the right-hand side cannot be decomposed further at $\mathbf{x}$. *It is impossible for conventional Artificial Intelligence to deduce $p(x_1,x_2,x_3,x_4)$ from lower dimensional p.d.f.'s. Yet, Artificial Intelligence with Statistical Pattern Recognition can use relative frequency interaction in the feature space to learn this four-dimensional statistical dependence and thus accomplishes the desired deduction.*

12-6 STATISTICAL DEPENDENCE WHEN KNOWLEDGE IS INCOMPLETE

The discussion in the last section is presented as a theorem.

Theorem:

Given marginal probability density functions $p(x_i)$, and $p(x_j)$, if nothing is known about $p(x_j$ given $x_i)$, then the joint probability density function of x_i and x_j is given by†

$$p(x_i,x_j) = p(x_i)p(x_j).$$

Proof:

The conditional probability density function of x_j given x_i obeys one of three possible conditions:

(1) $p(x_j|x_i) > p(x_j)$.
(2) $p(x_j|x_i) = p(x_j)$.
(3) $p(x_j|x_i) < p(x_j)$.

---

†Yes, it is a statement of statistical independence. But look how it is derived.

A given is that nothing is known about $p(x_j \text{ given } x_i)$. But (1) and/or (3) is/are true if for some value of x_i there is something known about $p(x_j)$. Thus, (1) and/or (3)is/are impossible, proving the theorem.

This theorem on dependence can be applied recursively, factoring out "packets" of probability density functions for which nothing is known given any other "packet."

12-6-1 Packet–Directed Closeness Measure

The previous example illustrates a packet-directed closeness measure where the multidimensional probability density is estimated using packets that fit joint features or marginal projections of joint features. Features for which dependence information is not provided by packets are treated as statistically independent, avoiding a teacher to provide such dependence information.

This packet-directed closeness measure has the disadvantage of no over-all direction in construction of a presentation for a category. It assumes that subcategories of the category are disconnected and that training will be provided only for subcategories. Training may consist of many disconnected packets in such a case.

12-6-2 Category–Directed

An alternative approach is to train directly with a presentation in the high dimensional space as illustrated, for the three dimensional example, in Figure 12.3a. In Figure 12.3b two presentations are illustrated that depend on x_3. In the category-directed approach, packets are associated together as a presentation. *The association reflects dependencies among packets that can be provided no other way.*

Thus, a category-directed approach to training consists of presentations where a presentation is an association of packets, including marginal packets, where appropriate. This approach recognizes that associations among packets can be provided no other way.

12-6-3 Category-Directed, Packet-Modified

An extension of the category-directed approach is to allow for packet modification. This is illustrated in Figure 12.4 where $p_1(x_1,x_2,x_3)$ is

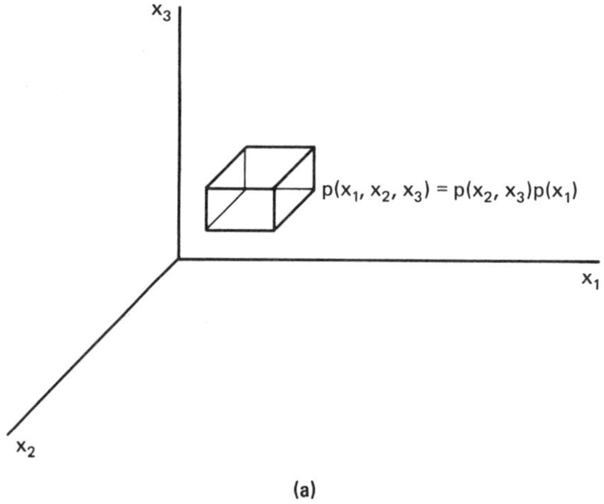

FIGURE 12.3a Presentation-directed training.

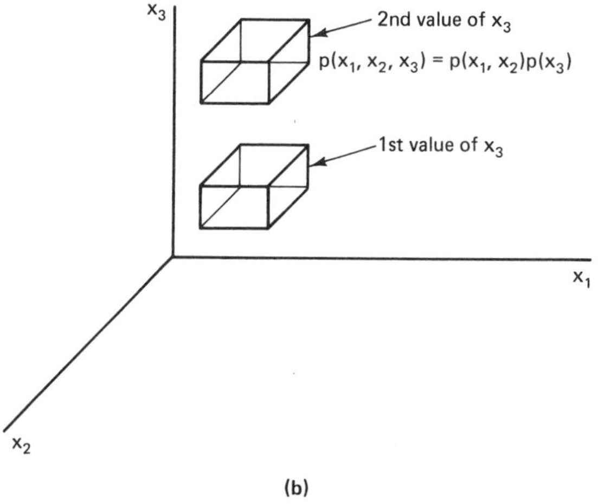

FIGURE 12.3b Presentation-directed training for two presentations (different values of x_3).

modified to $p_2(x_1,x_2,x_3)$ by a modification of x_1 and x_3 where x_3 increases when x_1 increases. Here,

$$p_1(x_1,x_2,x_3) = p_1(x_1,x_3)p_1(x_2) \tag{14}$$

$$p_2(x_1,x_2,x_3) = p_2(x_1,x_3)p_1(x_2) \tag{15}$$

recognize that changes in presentation do not depend on x_2; however, there are two respective presentations for different packets of depend-

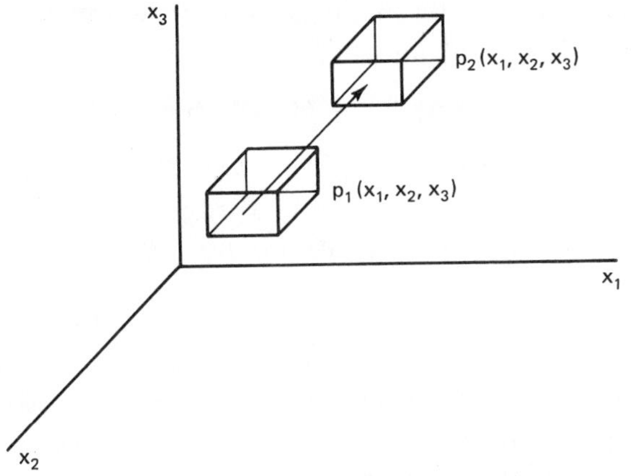

FIGURE 12.4 Category-directed, packet-modified.

ent variable x_1,x_3. Such packet modification is accomplished in **CONSULT-I®** *by minicolumns.*

We will return to the dicussion of the **CONSULT-I®** closeness measure but first some other approaches are considered.

12-7 OTHER CLOSENESS MEASURES FOR COMPARISON WITH THE *CONSULT-I®* INFERENCE FUNCTION

12-7-1 A Numerical Closeness Measure: A Complex Feature

Let the category space consist of $\omega_1^*,\omega_2^*, \ldots, \omega_M^*$ (i.e., no complex class).

Define

$$\begin{aligned} \alpha_{j_i} &= p(x_j^*|\omega_i^*) \\ \gamma_{j_i} &= p(x_j|\bar{\omega}_i^*) \text{ where } \bar{\omega}_i^* \text{ is the complement of } \omega_i^*. \end{aligned} \tag{16}$$

Let x_j be a measure of property y_j and define

$$p(y_i|x_{j_v},\omega_i^*) = \beta_{j_v i}. \tag{17}$$

Equation (17) is consistent with y_j being a *complex feature* defined by Patrick, 1979 (see Chapter 8). For example,

y_j : Fatigue

and

x_{j_1}: No fatigue
x_{j_2}: Little fatigue
x_{j_3}: Moderate fatigue
x_{j_4}: High fatigue

It is appealing to let $\beta_{i_{j_v}}$ be an increasing function of v.

Combining Eqs. (16) and (17), we obtain

$$A_{j_i} = \alpha_{j_i}\,\beta_{j_i} = p(x_j|\omega_i^*)p(y_j|x_j,\,\omega_i^*) \tag{18}$$

which is a result suggested by Cerutti and Timó Pieri, 1981. For the example of fatigue, Eq. (18) transfers a subjective value of "how much fatigue" to a subjective value of fatigue, both given category ω_i^*. In like manner,

$$\eta_{ji} = \gamma_{ji}\,\beta_{ji} \tag{19}$$

is a measure of fatigue when category ω_i^* is not active. More will be said about Eqs. (18) and (19) with regard to fuzzy set theory. However, note that a single probability density function can replace Eq. (18) while providing "weights" for $x_{j1}, \ldots, x_{j4}$ in the example. The fuzzy set concept amounts to partitioning y_j

$$(y_j, x_{j_v}),\ v = 1,2,\ldots,V;$$

and this is a matter of designing the property or attribute y_j to have appropriate intervalized values.

In this formulation, $p(x_j|\omega_i^*)$ is the relative frequency of fatigue given that observed value of fatigue. We can think of $p(y_j|x_j,\omega_i^*)$ as a measure that x_j is a significant indicator of fatigue. For example, we may wish to discount an observer's measure of "little fatigue" or even "no fatigue." We may not want such "absence" of a property to be taken seriously.

This approach should be compared with results elsewhere in this book where probability of observation significance is discussed (see Chapter 14).

12-7-2 Subjective Probabilities Approach

Cerutti and Timó Pieri (1981) placed a measure suggested by Shortliffe (1975) in perspective. It is called a measure of belief (Shortliffe and Buchanan, 1975). First, define

$MB[\omega_i^*, x_j] = x$: The Measure of increased Belief in category ω_i^* given x_j. (20)

$MD[\omega_i^*, x_j] = y$: The Measure of increased Disbelief in category ω_i^* given x_j. (21)

Define

$$MB[\omega_i^*, x_j] = \begin{cases} 1 \text{ if } p(\omega_i^*|\mathbf{x}_{j-1}) = 1 & (22) \\ \dfrac{\max\{(p(\omega_i^*|x_j, \mathbf{x}_{j-1}), p(\omega_i^*|\mathbf{x}_{j-1})\} - p(\omega_i^*|\mathbf{x}_{j-1})}{\max[1, \emptyset] - p(\omega_i^*|\mathbf{x}_{j-1})} & \text{otherwise} \end{cases}$$

$$MD[\omega_i^*, x_j] = \begin{cases} 1 \text{ if } p(\omega_i^*|\mathbf{x}_{j-1}) = \emptyset & (23) \\ \dfrac{\min\{(p(\omega_i^*|x_j, \mathbf{x}_{j-1}), p(\omega_i^*|\mathbf{x}_{j-1})\} - p(\omega_i^*|\mathbf{x}_{j-1})}{\min[1, \emptyset] - p(\omega_i^*|\mathbf{x}_{j-1})} & \text{otherwise.} \end{cases}$$

This measure is iterative, a summation (disjunctions), but no construction is available for the dependence among features.

Following Cerutti and Timó Pieri, 1981; Shortliffe and Buchanan, 1975, a certainty factor

$$CF[\omega_i^*, x_j] = MB[\omega_i^*, x_j] - MD[\omega_i^*, x_j]. \tag{24}$$

is defined. A suboptimum closeness function can be defined as in (Shortliffe and Buchanan, 1975) by *ignoring dependence* on $\mathbf{x}_{j-1}$. The closeness measure incorporates logical operations of fuzzy sets (Adlassnig, 1980; Wechsler, 1976; Zadah, 1979; Negoita, 1985).

Given x_j and x_{j+1}, iterative formulas for measures at $(j + 1)$ in terms of measures at (j) are:

$$MB[\omega_i^*, x_{j+1}, x_j] = \begin{cases} \emptyset \text{ if } MD[\omega_i^*, x_{j+1}, x_j] = 1 & (25) \\ MB[\omega_i^*, x_j] + MB[\omega_i^*, x_{j+1}]\,(1 - MB[\omega_i^*, x_j]) & \text{otherwise} \end{cases}$$

$$MD[\omega_i^*, x_{j+1}, x_j] = \begin{cases} \emptyset \text{ if } MB[\omega_i^*, x_{j+1}, x_j] = 1 & (26) \\ MD[\omega_i^*, x_j] + MD[\omega_i^*, x_{j+1}]\,(1 - MD[\omega_i^*, x_j]) & \text{otherwise.} \end{cases}$$

These functions form the basic decision element of a system called **MYCIN** (Shortliffe, 1976, 1975; Wallis and Shortliffe, 1982). Note that they are linear combinations as compared with the logarithm combination in the **CONSULT-I®** measure. *No provision is made for complex classes* (or otherwise for concept formation), only classes, subclasses, and so on. No provision is made for engineering the c.c.p.d.f. with a knowledge base structure involving primitives, complex features, Type Ø features, Type 1 features, and so on. There is a limited knowledge base structure. No provision is made for a priori probabilities and a posteriori probability cannot be computed. No provision is made for column direction instead of the less-structured packet directed. Also, no provision of using deduction to process missing features is provided.

12-7-3 Promise Closeness Measure

A closeness measure (inference function) designed, with feature selection in mind, by Gini and Gini (1980) is based on a unit called the MKB (Medical Knowledge Base). Each MKB is characterized by category ω_i^*, feature x_i and presentation k.

A state is defined as a set of L pairs,

$$\{(x_j,\ v_j)\}_{j=1}^{L} \tag{27}$$

where x_j has binary values, and

$$\begin{aligned} v_j &= \emptyset \ &&: x_j \text{ missing} \\ v_j &= 1 \ &&: x_j = T \text{ (True)} \\ v_j &= -1 \ &&: x_j = F \text{ (False).} \end{aligned}$$

That is, x_j denotes a feature, and v_j denotes the feature value. An *initial stage* is defined

$$\{(x_j,\ \emptyset)\}_{j=1}^{L}\text{: initial state.} \tag{28}$$

A *final state* for category ω_i^* is defined by the set

$$\{(x_j,\ v_j)_i\}_{j=1}^{L}\text{: final state for category } \omega_i^* \tag{29}$$

A state thus consists of the status of L binary features (i.e., features are either turned on or off) where

$$\begin{aligned} v_j = 1 &: x_j = T \\ v_j = -1 &: x_j = F \\ v_j = \emptyset,\ 1, \text{ or } -1 &: x_j = \text{insignificant.} \end{aligned}$$

The *set of final states* is the union set of final states with respect to different categories.

The kth description of category ω_i^* is defined

$$\{MKB(i,\ j,\ k)\}_{j=1}^{L}. \tag{30}$$

indicating that k is the kth presentation of category ω_i^*. A function of the following form is implied:

$$\begin{aligned} p(\text{MKB}(i,\ j,\ k) &= T) = 1 \\ p(MKB(i,\ j,\ k) &= \text{F}) = -1 \\ p(MKB(i,\ j,\ k) &= U) = \emptyset,\ 1, \text{ or } -1 \end{aligned} \tag{31}$$

where U indicates uncertain.

When a feature x_j obtains a value, the pair (x_j, v_j) in the state space is updated. The medical knowledge base Eq. (30) is indirectly updated. Presumably, a closeness measure can be defined,

$$p(MKB(i, k)) = \sum_{j=1}^{L} p(MKB(i, j, k)) \tag{32}$$

which is a "packet directed" measure for a kth column. This work is limited to binary features (single Type 1 features in **CONSULT-I®**).

An interesting function called the **PROMISE**—a concept in artificial intelligence search techniques—is defined as follows.

$$\textbf{PROMISE}\ (x_j, \omega_i) = \frac{1}{C_i} * \frac{1}{\mathrm{K}} \sum_{k=1}^{K} (\text{if } MKB(i, j, k) = Y \text{ then } 1) + \sum_{k=1}^{K} (\text{if } MKB(i, j, k) = N \text{ then } -1) \tag{33}$$

PROMISE is used for feature selection. The featue x_j which has the highest *promise* is selected next. A disadvantage of this function is that it is not directly related to selecting the next feature which minimizes probability of error, an optimum method of feature selection. The Promise of feature x_j is

$$\textbf{PROMISE}\ (x_j) = \sum_{i=1}^{M} \text{Promise } (x_j, \omega_i^*). \tag{34}$$

Discussion:

Equation (32) might be visualized as a kth presentation of category ω_i^*, i.e., the left-hand side of Eq. (32) is a measure of how close the findings given by Eq. (27) are to category ω_i^*. Taking a sum in Eq. (32) imposes statistical independence (see Chapter 7), and the structure of Eq. (32) shows that it is an approximation to the column closeness measure in **CONSULT-I®**.

A measure of the form Eq. (32) is motivated by the desire to achieve feature selection (see Chapter 10). The objective is not to be constrained by a particular next feature but to select the one with the most Promise. To achieve this, assumptions of statistical independence are made in the approach.

Equation (30) can be viewed as a kth training sample for category

ω_i^*. In this sense, the training samples are being stored as would be done in the generalized kth Nearest Neighbor technique developed by Patrick and Fisher (1970). An extension of Eq. (30) is to replace k by C_k, a set of paths, i.e.,

$$\{MKB\ (i, j, C_k)\}_{j=1}^{L}$$

C_k, analogous to a column in the **CONSULT-I®** closeness measure, shows how the *MKB* can be used to describe a column in **CONSULT-I®**.

12-7-4 CASNET

CASNET described in this section has been updated to a system called **EXPERT** (Kulikowski and Weiss, 1982; Kulikowski 1983; Weiss and Kulikowski, 1984).

12-7-4-1 Introduction

In **CASNET** (Weiss *and others,* 1978), a "state network" is described as follows:

(S, F, X, N)
S = set of starting "states"
F = set of final "states"
N = total set of "states"
X = set of mappings between "states" (35)

A "state" summarizes either events or relationships; and the ith state is denoted or indexed by

n_i, a node

The reader is warned to expect certain parts of the **CASNET** model to be incompletely described. By keeping the optimum **CONSULT-I®** model in mind, one can fill in undescribed aspects of **CASNET.** That is, consider primitives, features, complex features, and columns.

A "state" n_i is either confirmed or not confirmed as a result of processing features. In this sense, a "state" n_i is a *complex feature,* just as was the numerical closeness measure in Section 12-7-1.

12-7-4-2 Confirming "states" (Complex Features)

A noncausal, association relationship is said to exist between features $\{x_j\}$ and node n_i. Defining Q_{ji} as a confidence with a cost $C(j)$, a confidence measure $CF(n_i)$ is defined:

If $|CF(n_i)| < |Q_{ji}|$, then $CF(n_i) = Q_{ji}$ (Allows for error or uncertainty as in
If $CF(n_i) = -Q_{ji}$, then $CF(n_i) = \emptyset$ **CONSULT-I®**
If $|CF(n_i)| > \emptyset$, then n_i is confirmed. insignificant features.) (36)

Note that a sequence of features x_j can be processed before a node is confirmed. The exact form of the relationship between the features and a node is vague but it is a closeness measure. Another relationship is described next.

12-7-4-3 Forward Weights and Transitions between Nodes

A causal relationship is assumed to exist *between nodes,* defined by

$$n_j \xrightarrow{a_{ji}} n_i\text{: } n_j \text{ causes } n_i, \text{ independent of other events, with frequency } a_{ji}. \tag{37}$$

For a particular pathway starting at node n_ξ, the weight at node n_i is

$$W_F(i|\xi) = \prod_{\eta=\xi}^{i-1} a_{\eta,\ \eta+1}. \tag{38}$$

A total forward weight at node n_i is the sum of all $W_F(i|\xi)$ starting at the nearest confirmed or starting node n_i:

$$\begin{aligned} W_F(i) &= \sum_{\xi} W_F(i|\xi)\eta_\xi \\ &= a_i \text{ when } n_i \text{ is a starting node} \\ \eta_\xi &= a_\xi \textit{ when } n_\xi \text{ is an unconfirmed starting node} \\ &= 1 \text{ otherwise.} \end{aligned} \tag{39}$$

The forward weight could be minilikelihoods constructed from features appended to one node causing a category weight at another node.

A node thus can reflect (with a weight) that feature x_i has value x_i, and feature x_4 value x_4, and a complex of features have x_6 True, and x_7 False, and x_8 True. No provision is made for describing types of features, categories, subcategories, and so on. But **CASNET/EXPERT** has a few similarities to **CONSULT-I®**. **CASNET/EXPERT** is strongly "packet oriented" with pieces of knowledge being stored about a category. It is presumed that the association of these pieces of knowledge (at nodes) can be assembled as a further causal relationship (inference functions) for a category. The system does not store records as does **The OUTCOME ADVISOR®** or **CONSULT LEARNING SYSTEM®** and cannot generate Correlation Levels for a category at the findings.

Thus, dependence or correlation knowledge capability is reduced. The model presumes that a category should be described as an accumulation of small pieces of knowledge. *The number of required nodes could become astronomical since the approach does not have a focus at the findings* but rather must *store all pieces of knowledge (holes) as nodes.*

12-7-4-4 Discussion of Forward Weights

Equation (38) gives the weight of a node n_i as the product of weights of confirmed nodes for presentation ξ. This is a *packet-directed approach* rather than a column-directed approach. It could be made column directed and then have that desirable property of the **CONSULT-I®** closeness measure. Using a product rather than a sum is desirable(over the sum in **MYCIN**) as suggested by the optimum closeness measure in **CONSULT-I®**. The complex feature provides for introducing local dependencies (packets) but dependencies among packets is not directed. This is an approximation of the **CONSULT-I®** closeness measure.

Using the **CASNET** model, suppose that a node n_ξ can be a primitive, only class, or complex class. Thus, a_{ji} could be the a posteriori probability of a primitive, only class, or complex class at node i used to affect a class or complex class at node j. On the other hand, a_{ji} can be viewed as forming a complex feature at node j given a primitive at node i. Equation (39) demonstrates the complex feature effect where multiple primitives at starting nodes would be used to form a complex feature $W_F(i)$ at node i. A complex feature itself can be an only class or complex class.

Keep in mind that the goal is to decide an only class or complex class given primitive values. We know from the theorem by Patrick that knowledge of category conditional probability density functions (category is an only class or complex class) is the optimum solution to decision making. Feedback from categories to estimate conditional probability density functions of complex classes (induction) is not required if the conditional probability density functions for complex classes are known. These facts are buried in the **CASNET** framework, but are illustrated in these discussions.

CASNET lacks ability to store knowledge in an organized way about classes, only classes, and complex classes. The lack of models in **CASNET** precludes seeing that a model relationship must be constructed between a complex class and its classes (on only classes) if one is to learn about the other. Concept formation is vague in **CASNET.**

One could take the approach in **CASNET,** however, that first we will teach about only class ω_i^* at node n_i and then about only class ω_j^* at node n_j. These are pathways from primitive values to the nodes n_i and n_j. Such pathways look very much like parts of columns in **CONSULT-I®**. Some node n_{ij} then could causally be related to n_i and n_j; but if this is done with expert knowledge, a **CONSULT-I®**-like model will have to be used to form the complex class. Alternatively, a trained node n_{ij} through a **CONSULT-I®**-like model could be used to deduce knowledge about node n_i or node n_j.

Supervised training requires identification of the end node, an only class or complex class, prior to storing a pathway in the network. This, of course, is just category-related training.

12-7-4-5 Inverse Weights

In **CASNET,** provision is made for node n_i to have a weight that takes into account the confirmed nodes that are effects of node n_i. Define

$$W_I(i|\gamma^*) = \frac{W_F(\gamma^*|i)W_F(i)}{W_F(\gamma^*)} \tag{40}$$

where confirmed nodes are ignored in the pathway and forward weights are, therefore, computed from starting nodes. Define

$$W_I(i) = \max_{\gamma^*} \{W_I(i|\gamma^*)\}. \tag{41}$$

Equation (41) reflects feedback to node i from events γ^* (nodes) that are confirmed from features. The optimum formulation in Section 5-7 demonstrates the preceding as an example where i indexes a state in the true sense and γ^* indexes a complex class.

Together, Eq. (39), viewed as a weight for only class ω_i^* (state i), and Eq. (41), viewed as a feedback weight to node i due to state γ^*, are an example of a state equation. Using fuzzy set logic, Eqs. (39) and (41) can be combined:

$$W_i = \max \{W_F(i), W_I(i)\}. \tag{42}$$

In Eq. (42), *if W_i is viewed as the weight of state i, $W_F(i)$ can be viewed as the weight of state ω_i contributed by confirmation of only class ω_i^*. Then $W_I(i)$ can be viewed as a contribution to state ω_i from confirmation of an event containing state ω_i such as the complex class $\Omega^* = \gamma^*$ in Eq. (40).*

If $W_F(i)$ is interpreted as an only class ω_i^*, and is confirmed, then $W_I(i)$ has no effect on ω_i^*. *Realize that it is the* **CONSULT-I®** *model that has* *led to this facility to evaluate* **CASNET.** For example, suppose that $W_F(i)$ leads to confirmation of state i and thus only class ω_i^* through a causal link in the network to a node representing ω_i^*. Then **CONSULT-I®** would facilitate generation of complex class Ω^* through a causal link between ω_i^* and Ω^*, other only classes, and Ω^*, and the features $\{x_j\}$ and Ω^*. **CASNET** does not provide models for generation of Ω^* in this way, because the network is structure free except for its nodes and links. Models are used in **CONSULT-I®** for this generation.

12-7-5 INTERNIST Closeness Measure

12-7-5-1 Introducton

From Section 5-3, the theorem on a posteriori class probability (Patrick) provides the relationship

$$p(\omega_i|\mathbf{x}) = p(\omega_i^*|\mathbf{x}) + \sum_{\omega_i \in \Omega_\xi} p(\Omega_\xi^*|\mathbf{x}). \tag{43}$$

In Section 5-16-2 a result for a posteriori probability is derived assuming statistically independent features; and complex class conditional probability density function is constructed as the product of conditional probability density functions for classes in the complex. This equation does not provide for on-line concept formation but does provide for deductive problem solution. The result is

$$p(\mathbf{x}|\omega_i) = \frac{C(i, i)p(\mathbf{x}|\omega_i^*)}{1 - \sum_{\omega_i \in \Omega_{i\xi}^*} C(i_\xi, i)}. \tag{44}$$

The left-hand side is for a class, a concept used by deductive models to generate only classes ω_i^* and complex classes Ω_i^*. It follows that:

$$p(\omega_i|\mathbf{x}) = \frac{p(\mathbf{x}|\omega_i)p(\omega_i)}{p(\mathbf{x})} = \frac{C(i, i)p(\mathbf{x}|\omega_i^*)}{\left[1 - \sum_{\omega_i \in \Omega_{i\xi}^*} C(i_\xi, i)\right]} \frac{p(\omega_i)}{p(\mathbf{x})} \tag{45}$$

which results from the basic theorem on a posteriori class probability by Patrick involving both only classes and complex classes. Taking the log of both sides of Eq. (45) results in:†

†$C(i, i) = p(\omega_i^*)|p(\omega_i)$

$$\ln p(\omega_i|\mathbf{x}) = \ln p(\omega_i) + \ln p(\mathbf{x}|\omega_i^*) - \ln p(\mathbf{x}) + \ln C(i,i)$$
$$-\ln\left[1 - \sum_{\omega_i \in \Omega_\xi^*} C(i_\xi, i)\right] \qquad (46)$$

where

$$C(i_\xi, i) = \left[\prod_{\omega_{\xi_W} \in [\Omega_i^* - \omega_i]} \prod_{j=1}^{L} \delta_{j_{\xi_W}} p(x_j|\omega_{\xi_W})\right] \frac{p(\Omega_\xi^*)}{p(\omega_i)}. \qquad (47)$$

These results are directly derived from the **CONSULT-I®** closeness measure.

12-7-5-2 INTERNIST Closeness Measure (Score)

In the system named **INTERNIST**† (Miller *and others,* 1982; Myers *and others,* 1982; Pople, 1982; Miller 1984), *all features in effect are Type 1 (binary) with values*

$$x_{j_v} = T, F$$

or missing (*M*). This, of course, is a very restrictive construction. Also, there is no provision for embedding the Type 1 features as a Type 1 measurement or to form complex features. Given a recognition vector $\mathbf{x}_r$, define a *Master Differential Diagnosis* as

$$\{\omega_i^*\}_{\text{any } x_{j_v} = T, \text{ significant for } \omega_i^*}$$

which is a form of *feature consulting.* This is a simple *activation rule* resulting generally in a very large number of categories. That is, all categories are activated that have a significant feature with True values.

We translate what is called the **INTERNIST** score (Miller *and others,* 1982) as, using the **CONSULT-I®** notation,

$$\text{score}(\omega_i) = \sum_{x_{j_v} = T} a_i p(\omega_i^*|x_{j_v} = T)$$
$$+ \sum_{x_{j_v} = F} b_j\, p(x_{j_v} = F|\omega_i^*) + \sum c_j p(x_{j_v} = F) \qquad (48)$$
$$+ \sum_{\forall\, \Omega_{\xi_M} = F} 20\, p(x_{j_v} = T|\Omega_\xi^*)$$

where $\Omega_{\xi_M}^*$ is a complex class including class ω_i.

†Now known as Caduceus.

The last term in the score can be considered a simple way of providing feedback from a (any or all) complex class containing class ω_i. *A true feature for the class directly increases the score through the first term while a false feature value for the class concerned decreases the score but to a lesser amount (see weights below).* With regard to class, a false feature value decreases the score through the second to last term (for all classes). This is simply a normalization to decrease feature sensitivity for a false feature value (a model is used but not declared for review).

Because complex classes and only classes are not precisely defined in **INTERNIST**, there is some difficulty with the translation.

The functions a_i, b_j, and c_j are as follows:

$a_i(\emptyset) = +1$
$a_i(1) = +4$
$a_i(2) = +10$
$a_i(3) = +20$
$a_i(4) = +40$
$a_i(5) = +80$

$b_j(1) = -1$
$b_j(2) = -4$
$b_j(3) = -7$
$b_j(4) = -15$
$b_j(5) = -30$

$c_j(1) = -2$
$c_j(2) = -6$
$c_j(3) = -10$
$c_j(4) = -20$
$c_j(5) = -40$

12-7-5-3 Comparing INTERNIST Closeness Measure with CONSULT-I® Closeness Measure

Comparing the **INTERNIST** closeness measure (Miller *and others,* 1982) with that of **CONSULT-I®**, we see that the "spirit" of **INTERNIST** based on an ad hoc approach falls far short of the **CONSULT-I®** closeness measure. First, **INTERNIST** does not (cannot) distinguish classes ω_i from *only classes.* **INTERNIST** recognizes a complex class indirectly but fails to incorporate the rich feedback provided in **CONSULT-I®**'s closeness measure. ***INTERNIST** does not engineer category conditional probability density functional utilizing categories and subsubcategories, thus limiting performance ability.*

Correctly, in **INTERNIST** the constants $\{c_j\}$ are negative numbers. But lack of mathematical guidance caused the developing **INTERNIST** to change the terms in the score without explanation (see Pople *and others,* 1975; Pople, 1977 versus Miller *and others,* 1982).

Some properties worth mentioning include:

1. The weights a_i, b_j, c_j would appear necessary to try to enhance sensitivity loss by lack of a product effect as in a true likelihood function.
2. The weights impose a form of fuzzy sets.
3. Only Type 1 features are used.

12-7-5-4 Focus for a Differential Diagnosis

For ω_i in the master differential diagnosis, define

1. Class-Feature Status
   Relationships are recognized between features x_j and the *i*th category. We characterize them as the following union:
   $(x_{j_v} = T) \cap \omega_i^*$
   $(x_{j_v} = F) \cap \omega_i^*$
   $(x_{j_v} = T) \cap \bar{\omega}_i^*$: red herrings or second disease
   (x_j missing $\cap\ \omega_i^*$): missing significant features of ω_i^*.

These structures are interesting but incomplete.† Even limitation to the binary feature is a serious limitation. In any case, these category feature relationships provide a model with which to recognize a complex class and a missing feature.

2. A score rank
   r_j (score (ω_i))
   is determined for each *only class* ω_i^* *(only classes, classes,* and *complex classes* are not recognized by the developers of **INTERNIST**) in the differential diagnosis.
3. Two classes‡ are Competitive if:
   missing features "add the same for either class."
   This is an ad hoc combination of feature selection and focus; not enough basic theory has gone into its construction.

---

†Models for complex class generation described in this book for **CONSULT-I®** go far beyond this elementary model.

‡In **INTERNIST** there appear to be classes as opposed to *only classes,* but the developers seem not to have recognized it.

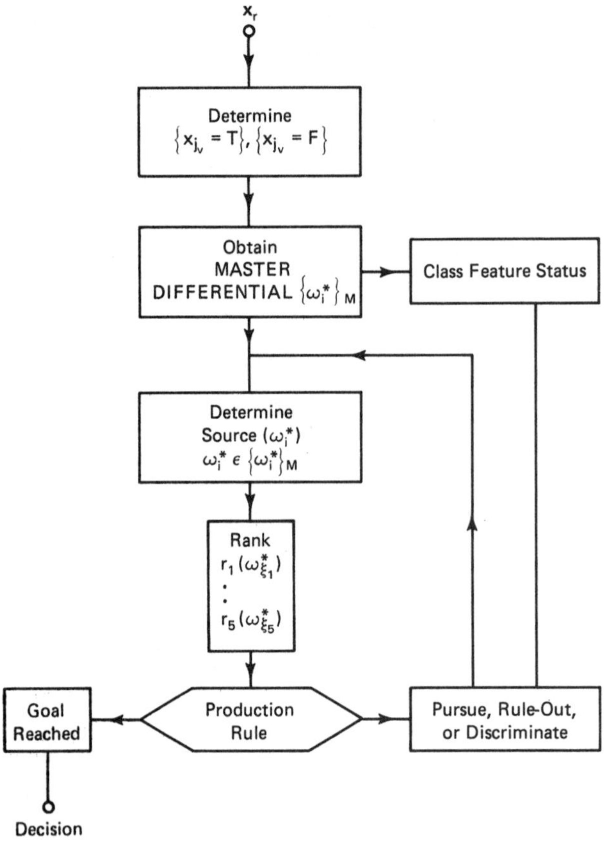

FIGURE 12.5

4. Two classes are Alternative if:
   above not true

Constructions (3) and (4) are not directed at a complex class model but rather at whether to keep a class in the differential diagnosis for item (5) below.

5. Goal and Production Rule
   The goal is to achieve a differential diagnosis such that
   $[r_1(\omega_i) - r_2(\omega_\xi)] > 90 \;\forall\; \xi \neq \omega_i,$
   at which time *only class* ω_i^* is decided.

   The production rule consists of:

   Pursuing. If $(r_1(\ ) - r_2(\ )) > 40.$

Rule-Out. If the goal is not reached and the pursuing condition is not reached, and $j > 5$ (more than 5 classes in differential diagnosis), then an only class with the lowest score is eliminated.

Discriminate. If the goal is not reached and $(r_1 - r_j) > 40$ for two or more values of j, $j > 1$.

In the case of Rule-Out, questions are asked utilizing the class-feature status in conjunction with the Production Rule. This may be diagrammed (Figure 12.5).

Disadvantages

1. No provision is made to focus on diseases in a well-defined subsystem such as Thyroid Diseases or Anemias, etc., as is done in **CONSULT-I®**.
2. Convergence and rate of convergence toward the goal are poorly described.
3. The counting rule score does not provide for handling multiple presentations of a category. There is confusion between classes and categories.
4. The production rules are suboptimum.
5. No provision is made for activating a well-defined subsystem, such as Breast Lumps in **CONSULT-I®**.
6. Without a model such as the **CONSULT-I®** model, it is not possible to optimally handle multiple presentations, subsubcategories, a priori probabilities, nonbinary features, and so on.

Advantage

Interconnected subsystems such as Breast Lumps and Pelvic Masses or Thyroid Diseases and White Blood Cell Diseases are activated *in the construction* because the production rule has no boundaries. In theory and practice, this is not true because the feature selection is *limited.*

13

Visualizing CONSULT-I®
Using Three–Dimensional Constructions

13-1 INTRODUCTION

In this chapter certain aspects of the **CONSULT-I®** inference function are described graphically from the standpoint of nodes in the feature space. These nodes are not synonomous with nodes corresponding to states in a state space network or in a causal network. The category conditional probability density function is interpreted using two- and three-dimensional drawings. Statistical pattern recognition constructions are related to operations or rules studied in artificial intelligence. For example, marginal probability density function calculations **(SPR)** are viewed as a *Marginal Projection Generator* **(AI).** A Type Ø feature has a probability density function, and there exists a construction **(SPR)** viewed as an Equivalence Generator **(AI)** or "fuzzy set." An *Insignificant Feature Generator* **(AI)** is used to describe inclusion as part of the category conditional probability density of an insignificant feature **(SPR).** *A Can't Generator* **(AI)** is used to view the process of establishing zero probability density **(SPR),** imposing a *common sense* **(AI)** constraint.

The a posteriori probability density calculation is viewed in this hyperspace context. *Training Columns and Classical Nodes are the "centers" of hypercubes described previously.*

13-2 NODES IN HYPERSPACE

Consider the feature vector when L = 3 (three features),

$$\mathbf{x} = \begin{bmatrix} x_1 \\ x_2 \\ x_3 \end{bmatrix} \tag{1}$$

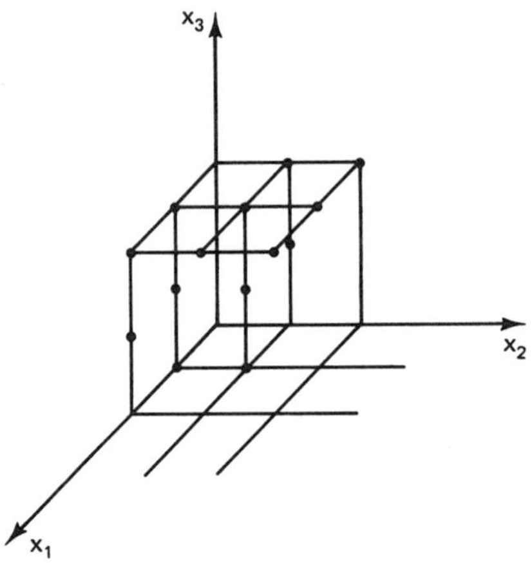

FIGURE 13.1 Nodes in hyperspace.

A feature has values x_{j_v} where in general there are $V(v = 1, 2, \ldots, V)$ values. Thus, there are V^L possible feature vectors. These V^L vectors are nodes (point to nodes) in the feature space. An illustration for $L = 3$ is shown in Figure 13.1. A particular feature vector (with feature values specified)

$$\mathbf{x} = [x_{11}, x_{22}, x_{33}] \tag{2}$$

is shown in Figure 13.2.

For the ith category, there exist *node probabilities*

$$\{p_{i_m}\}_{m=1}^{V^L}, \tag{3}$$

constrained by

$$\sum_{m=1}^{V^L} p_{i_m} = 1, \tag{4}$$

which characterize the ith category conditional probability density function. Of course, the objective is to estimate or learn each p_{i_m} for category γ_i^*.

An illustration of

$$p(\mathbf{x} \text{ at node } m|\gamma_i^*) = p_{i_m} \tag{5}$$

showing three node probabilities is found in Figure 13.3. The node probability is a basic building block for $p(\mathbf{x}|\gamma_i^*)$.

The **CONSULT LEARNING SYSTEM®** discussed in Chapter 15 can be used to estimate any p_{i_m}. In addition, interactive adaption using

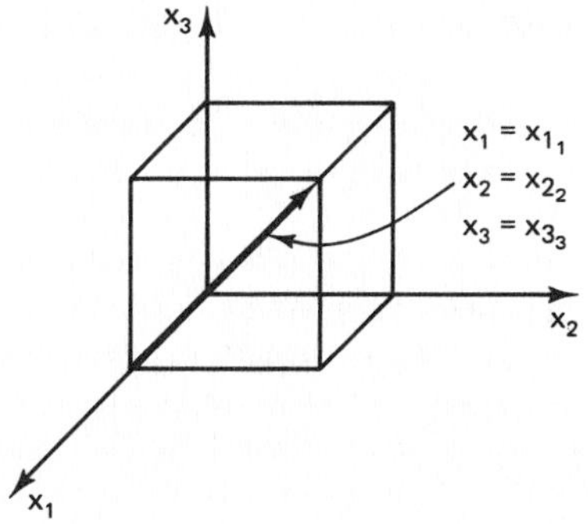

FIGURE 13.2 A feature vector.

a logical closeness measure allows combining nodes and then estimating the combined probability. Such combining of nodes in **CONSULT LEARNING SYSTEM®** or **The OUTCOME ADVISOR®** is illustrated in Figure 13.3.

13-3 MARGINAL PROBABILITY DENSITY OF A CATEGORY (MISSING FEATURE VALUES)

Suppose that values are specified for x_1 and x_2 but that x_3 has a missing feature. By convention in **CONSULT-I®**, "M" denotes a missing feature value (but is not itself a feature value). Thus the feature vector

$$\mathbf{x} = [x_{1_1}, x_{2_2}, M] \tag{6}$$

is at node i_1 or node i_2 *or* node i_3 for the example shown in Figure 13.3.

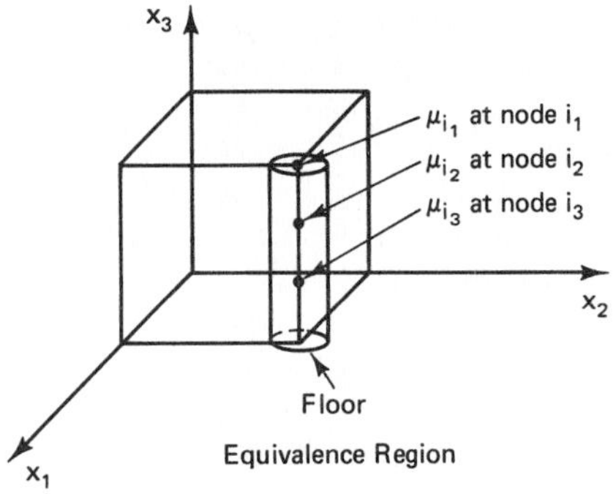

FIGURE 13.3 Example of nodes that happen to lie in an Equivalence Region.

The probability density of **x** given category γ_i^*, where

$$\mathbf{x} = [x_{1_1}, x_{1_2}, M] \text{ is}$$

$$p(\mathbf{x}|\gamma_i^*) = p_{i_1} + p_{i_2} + p_{i_3} \quad (7)$$

which is *the probability that* **x** *can be anywhere in the cylinder illustrated in Figure 13.3*. This basic theory is used in **CONSULT-I®**, **The OUTCOME ADVISOR®**, and **CONSULT LEARNING SYSTEM®** to handle missing feature values.

The effect of a missing feature value is to *project* node probabilities to the remaining subspace which does not include the feature with the missing value. Think of all the nodes in the cylinder shown in Figure 13.3 as "being projected to the floor."

The probability density at the feature vector $\mathbf{x} = [x_{1_1}, x_{1_2}, M]$ *is larger than* that for the feature vector $\mathbf{x} = [x_{1_1}, x_{2_2}, x_{3_3}]$; *the latter corresponds to more information.*† (See Section 3-11 on information theory.) This may appear surprising at first but becomes clearer when considering a posteriori probabilities. This illustration of the Marginal Projection Generator in **CONSULT-I®** corresponds to the theory of marginal probability discussed previously in Chapter 3.

13-4 EQUIVALENT FEATURE VALUES

Feature values of a Type Ø feature are equivalent for category γ_i^* if $p(\mathbf{x}|\gamma_i^*)$ is the same regardless of which of these values the feature has.‡ Considering the example in Figure 13.4, if feature values $x_{3_1}, x_{3_2}, x_{3_3}$ are equivalent, then $p_{i_1} = p_{i_2} = p_{i_3}$. This is an important concept because its use results in creation of *equivalence nodes* and reduces requirements to store probabilities at each of the equivalent nodes.§ Furthermore, if there is a need to estimate a node probability p_{i_1}, estimates of node probabilities p_{i_2} and p_{i_3} can be used in the estimation of p_{i_1}. *Equivalence reduces the number of training samples* required to estimate a node probability.

If the nodes i_1, i_2 and i_3 are equivalent in the example of Figure 13.4, then the cylinder shown is an *equivalence region.*

---

†This is consistent with a fact from *Information Theory* that more information is conveyed by the occurrence of a lower probability event.

‡Or there is a known relationship between probabilities of the feature values.

§Equivalence, studied in statistics and statistical pattern recognition, might be used in artificial intelligence as a heuristic.

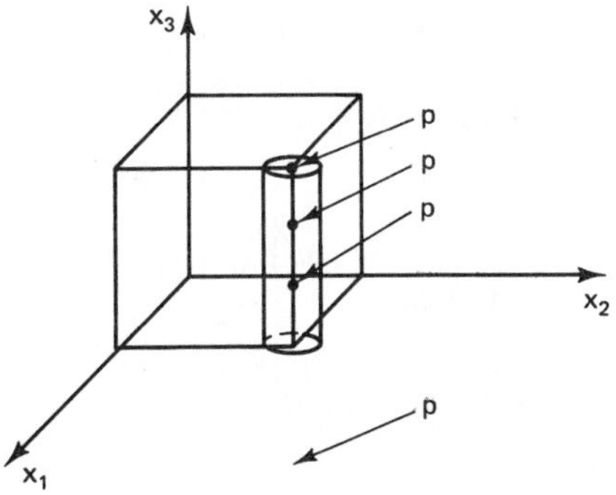

FIGURE 13.4 Example of Insignificant Feature (Feature x_3) for Category γ_i^*.

Equivalences are a special case of "dependence relationships," discussed elsewhere in this book. A *weighted* equivalence region is where the node probabilities are unequal but known relationship exists among them, as for a Complex feature.

13-5 INSIGNIFICANT FEATURE

An *insignificant feature* x_j for category γ_i^* is one for which $p(x_j|\gamma_i^*)$ is not affected by that feature's value. As far as category γ_i^* is concerned, a value for that feature contributes *no information* (perhaps relative to one category named normal).

Illustrated in Figure 13.4 is an insignificant Type Ø feature with $p_{i_1} = p_{i_2} = p_{i_3} = p_{i_4} = p$. No matter what value feature x_3 has, $p(\mathbf{x}|\gamma_i^*) = p$ when $\mathbf{x}$ is in the cylinder.

An insignificant feature cannot simply be ignored. The insignificant feature is a category property and not a subsystem or total system property. Given a category with an insignificant feature, the category conditional probability density is uniform for the insignificant feature.† This uniform probability density must be utilized in the overall calculation of joint category conditional probability density for all the features. An insignificant feature would be easiest to implement if it also were statistically independent of all other features. (It is!) It is reasonable to ex-

†Uniform is a relative concept as discussed in sections on insignificant features (for example, relative to a normal category).

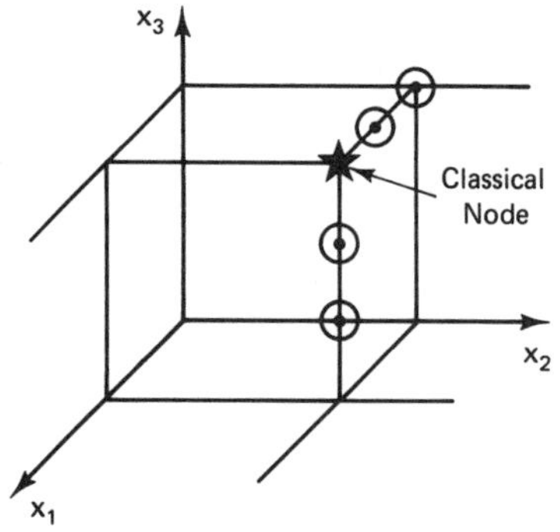

FIGURE 13.5 Example of a Classical Node (★) and a Hypercube.

pect that insignificance over multiple features means a uniform multi-dimensional probability which means independence because,

$$\begin{aligned} \int\int p(x, y)\, dx\, dy &= \int\int p(x|y)p(y)\, dx\, dy \\ &= \int p(y)\, dy \int p(x|y)\, dx \\ &= \int p(y)\, dy \int p(x)\, dx. \end{aligned} \tag{8}$$

13-6 CLASSICAL NODES

A classical node is that node at the center of a cluster of nodes having nonzero probabilities for the category. Simply, it is a "classical or typical presentation of the category;" it also can be an "atypical presentation of the category."

An example of a classical node is shown in Figure 13.5. Nodes, shown as "dots," are generated (AI) from the classical node shown as a "★" and taken together constitute a *hypercube*. These generated nodes are presentations never seen before for a category.

Appended to a classical node are all equivalences of feature values at the classical node or probabilities of feature values extending from the node. A classical node may or may not have zero probability. It may not directly be used for decision making since nodes in subspaces that contain a subset of the classical node's features may have the same probability or other nodes are generated from the classical node. The example shown in Figure 13.5 illustrates nodes that could have been generated by an "Equivalence Generator." An alternate operation, similar in some cases, is the *Insignificant Generator* which indicates the probability density does not change as noncritical feature values for x_3 and x_1 deviate from the classical node. These illustrations are analogous to uncertainty principles in nuclear physics or *information theory*.

The concept has been referred to as *heuristics* in AI. More generally, a Relative Frequency Generator **(SPR)** generates probabilities at values other than at the classical node. A classical node is important for *Basic Consulting* where all possible features with feature values are displayed for this presentation of the category. *Basic Consulting* (Patrick, 1979) is an operation in **CONSULT-I®** that can present as computer output the respective feature value probabilities for feature values characterizing a node. Basic Consulting allows implementation of one form of explanation for a decision.

13-7 THE CATEGORY CONDITIONAL PROBABILITY DENSITY FUNCTION

The collection of nodes with nonzero probabilities and their equivalences or generated probabilities along with all generated† nodes constitute the category conditional probability density function $p(\mathbf{x}|\gamma_i^*)$. A category conditional probability density function is constructed for each category in the subsystem.

Methods for locating nodes, assigning node probabilities, and assigning feature value equivalences are discussed elsewhere in this book. Methods of generating nodes from the typical and atypical nodes are also discussed elsewhere.

13-8 A POSTERIORI CATEGORY PROBABILITY

13-8-1 Introduction

Given the category conditional probability density functions $p(\mathbf{x}|\gamma_i^*)$, $i = 1,2,\ldots,M$ and a priori category probabilities P_i, $i = 1,2,\ldots,M$, we can calculate the probability of category γ_i^* given a test vector $\mathbf{x}$. The emphasis here is on, given the test vector (findings) $\mathbf{x}$. This test vector $\mathbf{x}$ is a new vector from a new record (findings). Contrast this with the training vectors used to construct the nodes and estimate their probabilities to form $p(\mathbf{x}|\gamma_i^*)$.

In considering $p(\mathbf{x}|\gamma_i^*)$, $\mathbf{x}$ is viewed as a "variable" (or variable vector) with values corresponding to each node used to construct $p(\mathbf{x}|\gamma_i^*)$. The probabilities attached to classical nodes were obtained through experience (expert knowledge) or estimation‡ (training). Pre-

†Generators include the following: Equivalence; Insignificant But (uses Can't); Noncritical; Dependence; Relative Frequency; Embedded Features; Complex Class; Subcategory; Rule-In (Inverse of Can't).

‡Using CONSULT LEARNING SYSTEM®.

sumably, there were records $\mathbf{x}_1, \mathbf{x}_2, \ldots, \mathbf{x}_n$ either in a professional's mind or in scientific data analysis (**CONSULT LEARNING SYSTEM®**) that led to the estimation of classical node probabilities. Generators referred to previously are used to generate possible nodes as extensions of the classical nodes. The "rules" used by these generators reflect problem knowledge about the category, its subcategories or "complex categories".

Suppose that we are presented with a new test vector **x.** We will use the previous experience stored as node probabilities for respective categories to recognize **x.**

The probability of category γ_i^*, given the test vector **x,** is expressed by the equation:

$$p(\gamma_i^*|\mathbf{x}) = \frac{p_i(\mathbf{x}|\gamma_i^*)\, P_i}{p(\mathbf{x})} = \frac{p(\mathbf{x}|\gamma_i^*)\, P_i}{\sum_{i=1}^{M} p(\mathbf{x}|\gamma_i^*)\, P_i}$$

Referring to Figure 13.6a, suppose that **x** is at node i_1. Then

$$p(\gamma_i^*|\mathbf{x} \text{ at node } 1) = \frac{p_{i_1}}{\sum_{\xi=1}^{M} p_{\xi_1}} \tag{9}$$

where $\sum_{\xi=1}^{M} p_{\xi_1}$ is a summation over the M categories of probabilities at node 1.

Several properties of $p(\gamma_i^*|\mathbf{x}$ at node 1) will help to clear up potential misunderstandings:

1. Dependence information among features is stored at node 1 (because it is multidimensional) for each category.
2. Between category information is expressed as follows:
   a. If node 1 has a feature value that "rules-in" category i, then for other categories that feature value invokes a Can't (or "rule-out") operation. Certain confirming tests are examples of "rule-in" feature values. By definition, only one category is active.

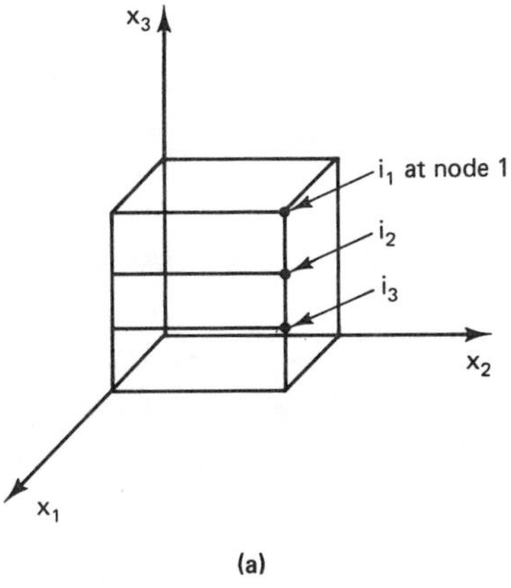

FIGURE 13.6a Node Probabilities in $p(\mathbf{x}|\gamma_i^*)$.

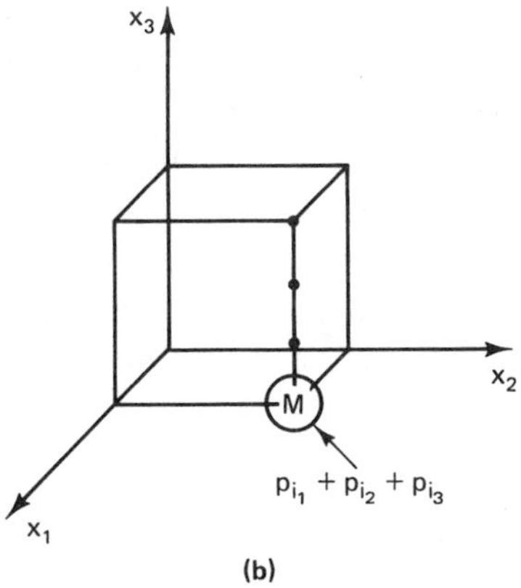

FIGURE 13.6b Marginal Projection of the Three-Node Probability in Figure 13.6a.

b. Because the a posteriori probability $p(\gamma_i^*|\mathbf{x}$ at node 1) expresses the relative probability of category γ_i^* at node 1 compared with the sum of probabilities for other categories, it is affected by the other categories.

The sketch in Figure 13.6b shows the projection of the three nodes i_1, i_2, i_3 onto the marginal node Ⓜ. Note that

$$p(\gamma_i^*|\mathbf{x}) \text{ at } Ⓜ) = \left\{ \frac{p_{i_1} + p_{i_2} + p_{i_3}}{\sum_{\xi=1}^{M} (p_{\xi_1} + p_{\xi_2} + p_{\xi_3})} \right\} P_{i}. \qquad (10)$$

We expect

$$p(\gamma_i^*|\mathbf{x} \text{ at node } 1) < p(\gamma_i^*|\mathbf{x} \text{ at } ⓜ)$$

because **x** at ⓜ means we do not know the value of feature x_3. *We expect to be less certain about a category if a significant feature value for that category is missing.* An unstated assumption is that this feature is not significant for the other categories and thus, according *to the above equation, the a posteriori probability* is reduced for those categories.

CONSULT-I® *automatically generates probabilities at marginal nodes through the Marginal Projection Generator* when a test vector has missing features. This important statistical pattern recognition operation can be viewed as *deductive reasoning to generate possible category presentations based on missing features.* Deduction proceeds utilizing knowledge stored at typical and atypical nodes and other nodes generated using the dependence generator, equivalence generator, and other generators. Through this deduction process, any one of millions–billions of nodes can be generated that never were previously stored in **CONSULT-I®**. This is *Reasoning*—the creation of knowledge.

In Figure 13.7, the a posteriori probabilities at node i_1 and the marginal node ⓜ are illustrated.

The *a posteriori probabilities at nodes* can be computed given the node probabilities in the category conditional probability density functions and the a priori category probabilities.

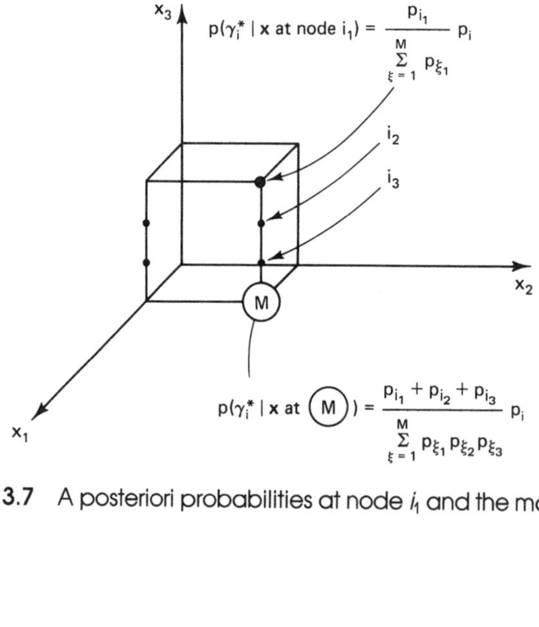

FIGURE 13.7 A posteriori probabilities at node i_1 and the marginal node ⓜ

13-9 TRAINING COLUMNS

13-9-1 Introduction

A priori training of the category conditional probability density function is accomplished by supplying typical and atypical nodes with relative frequency numbers for each category conditional probability density function for the subsystem concerned.

Each node is uniquely located by its coordinates in L dimensional space. An insignificant feature is given a uniform probability density function† with correction for error to identify it as insignificant. A relative frequency generator is used to assign probabilities to values (uniform if insignificant). Features significant for one category may not be significant for another category.

13-9-2 Storing Equivalences

A classical node (typical or atypical presentation) is used as a reference for generators. Relative frequency is generated over an independent feature by specifying probabilities for each value.

13-9-3 Storing Training Columns

A training column is the set of feature values defining coordinates of the node along with an assigned relative frequency number. If a feature is not significant, it is identified by a corrected uniform probability density function. A training column may have multiple features identified as insignificant.

The relative frequency assigned to a node (e.g., training column) is an estimate of the category conditional probability density at that node. This estimate is obtained from expert knowledge. Verified cases not previously published or known to experts can be used in the process. Knowledge of functional variation among features values is used by the Dependence Generator to create additional training nodes. These functional variations can be linear or nonlinear. Since dependence relationships can be imposed on subsets of feature values, **CONSULT-I®** has facility for imposing local measures of closeness more general than the mathematical concept of a metric.

---

†Or a normality probability density. We will continue to use uniform without loss of generality.

13-9-4 Type Ø Feature

For a Type Ø feature with $V = 9$ values (for example only),

$$p(x_{j_v}) = \frac{1}{9}, \; v = 1,2, \ldots, 9: \text{Insignificant Type Ø Feature.} \tag{11}$$

We are not "surprised" when a particular value x_{j_v} occurs. *All properties reflected by the Type Ø feature values are equally likely.*†

A category for which x_j is significant must have some feature value x_{j_v} for which

$$p(x_{j_v}) \neq 1/9 \tag{12}$$

The Insignificant feature contributes *no information.*

13-9-5 Type 1 Feature

For a Type 1 feature $V = 2$ and

$$p(x_{j_v}) = \frac{1}{2}, \; v = 1,2 \tag{13}$$

reflects the feature as contributing no information. Suppose, however, that

$$\begin{aligned} x_{j_1} &= \text{True} \\ x_{j_2} &= \text{False} \end{aligned} \tag{14}$$

is interpreted as reflecting the presence or absence of a property. Consider the property "probably is not present for most categories." For example, Q waves on an electrocardiogram are not present for most causes of chest pain. Thus, the probable situation is:

$$\begin{aligned} p(x_{j_v}) &= \epsilon, \; x_{j_v} \text{ True} \\ p(x_{j_v}) &= (1 - \epsilon), \; x_{j_v} \text{ False} \end{aligned} \tag{15}$$

for some "small" number ϵ. To be consistent, we define an *Insignificant Can't Type 1 feature* by Eq. (15) with $\epsilon = Ø$. We define an *Improbable Type 1 feature* by Eq. (15) with $\epsilon \neq Ø$. More generally, define

$$p(x_{j_v} | \mathbf{x}_{j-1}, \gamma_i^*) = \epsilon_j, \; x_{j_v} \text{ True: Improbable Feature} \tag{16}$$

$$p(x_{j_v} | \mathbf{x}_{j-1}, \gamma_i^*) = (1 - \epsilon_j), \; x_{j_v} \text{ False: For Category } \gamma_i^* \tag{17}$$

†Again, modification is possible to correspond to normality.

If $\epsilon = \emptyset$, then a "Can't" is imposed. To further investigate an improbable feature x_j for category γ_i^*, we "insert" the effect of an improbable feature x_j into the likelihood function as follows:

$$\begin{aligned} p(\mathbf{x}|\gamma_i^*) &= p(x_L, \ldots, x_{j+1}, x_j, \mathbf{x}_{j-1}|\gamma_i^*) \\ &= p(x_L, \ldots, x_{j+1}, x_j, |\mathbf{x}_{j-1}, \gamma_i^*) p(\mathbf{x}_{j-1}|\gamma_i^*) \qquad (18) \\ &= p(x_L, \ldots, x_{j+1}|x_j, \gamma_i^*) p(x_j|\mathbf{x}_{j-1}, \gamma_i^*) p(\mathbf{x}_{j-1}|\gamma_i^*) \\ &= p(x_L, \ldots, x_{j+1}|x_j, \gamma_i^*)(\epsilon_j)\, p(x_{j-1}|\gamma_i^*),\ x_{j_v} \text{ True} \end{aligned}$$

or

$$= p(x_L, \ldots, x_{j+1}|x_j, \gamma_i^*)(1 - \epsilon_j) p(\mathbf{x}_{j-1}|\gamma_i^*),\ x_{j_v} \text{ False}$$

One or more improbable features thus can drive the category-conditional probability density to near zero values when they are True, but not affect the conditional probability density much when False if $(1 - \epsilon)$ is a number $\cong 1$. On the other hand, if use of ϵ and $(1 - \epsilon)$ is standard for all categories in a subsystem, then all categories are equally affected by an insignificant feature. Any category having a feature significant, where the feature is insignificant for other categories, will have its probability density function (likelihood function) *increased above* ϵ by an amount reflecting the relative frequency of that feature value for the category concerned.

We again conclude that a feature that is insignificant for all categories in a subsystem has no effect on decisions made in that subsystem. This is important for optimally integrating subsystems to form a total system. In this case, there is a large set of features (primitives) and most may be insignificant for any one subsystem.

13-10 CATEGORY CONDITIONAL PROBABILITY DENSITY FUNCTIONS FOR UNCERTAIN OBSERVATION

13-10-1 Introduction

In this section we look at how to adjust training for a feature probability when the developer makes a judgment that the feature is not significant (with some probability).

Let δ_j be the event that feature j is significant and (δ_j, x_{j_v}) the event feature j is significant with value x_{j_v}; then consider the expression

$$p(\bar{\delta}_j + (\delta_j, x_{j_v})) \qquad (19a)$$

which is the probability that either feature j is insignificant† with any value or is significant with feature value x_{j_v}. Because events $\bar{\delta}_j$ and (δ_j, x_{j_v}) are mutually exclusive, it follows that:

$$p(\bar{\delta}_j + (\delta_j, x_{j_v})) = p(\bar{\delta}_j) + p(\delta_j, x_{j_v}) \tag{19b}$$

Given event γ_i^*, we condition Eq. (19b) to obtain

$$\begin{aligned} p(\bar{\delta}_j + (\delta_j, x_{j_v})|\gamma_i^*) &= p(\bar{\delta}_j|\gamma_i^*) + p(\delta_j, x_{j_v}|\gamma_i^*) \\ &= p(\bar{\delta}_j|\gamma_i^*) + p(x_{j_v}|\gamma_i^*, \delta_j)\, p(\delta_j|\gamma_i^*). \end{aligned} \tag{19c}$$

It is convenient to define $p(\bar{\delta}_j + (\delta_j, x_{j_v})|\gamma_i^*)$ as *the category conditional probability density function for uncertain observation.* Let

$$p(\delta_j|\gamma_i^*) \triangleq p_{\delta_j}.$$

Then

$$p(\bar{\delta}_j + (\delta_j, x_{j_v})|\gamma_i^*) = (1 - p_{\delta_j}) + p_{\delta_j}\, p(x_{j_v}\gamma_i^*, \delta_j). \tag{20}$$

Equation (20) applies for calculating probability *that either feature x_j is insignificant or, if significant, it has value $x_{j_v} = True$.* This expresses the knowledge about a possibly insignificant feature x_j.

Consider situations where knowledge can exist; first there are situations where we know nothing about whether feature x_j is significant for event γ_i^*; then

$$p_{\delta_j} = \tfrac{1}{2}\text{: We don't know if } x_j \text{ significant.} \tag{21a}$$

Second, if we "know" feature x_j is insignificant,

$$(1 - p_{\delta_j}) = \epsilon\text{: We know with little error that } x_j \text{ is significant.} \tag{21b}$$

Third, if we "know" feature x_j is significant,

$$p_{\delta_j} = 1. \tag{21c}$$

Equation (20) for these three situations becomes

$$p(\bar{\delta}_j + (\delta_j, x_{j_v})|\gamma_i^* = \tfrac{1}{2} + \tfrac{1}{2}\, p(x_{j_v}|\gamma_i^*, \delta_j)\text{: We don't know if } x_j \text{ is significant.} \tag{22a}$$

$$(1 - \epsilon) + (\epsilon)p(x_{j_v}|\gamma_i^*, \delta_j)\text{: We know feature } x_j \text{ is insignificant with small error.} \tag{22b}$$

---

†$\bar{\delta}_j$ denotes the event that feature j is insignificant.

$$\emptyset + p(x_{j_v}|\gamma_i^*, \delta_j)\text{: Feature } x_j \text{ significant.} \tag{22c}$$

One of these expressions can be inserted into Eq. (18); introducing p_{δ_j} into $p(\mathbf{x}|\gamma_i^*)$ (see Eq. (18)) results in

$$p(\mathbf{x}|\gamma_i^*) = p(x_L, \ldots, x_{j+1}|\mathbf{x}_j, \gamma_i^*)p(\mathbf{x}_{j-1}|\gamma_i^*)\ p(x_j|\mathbf{x}_{j-1}, \gamma_i^*)$$

$$p(\mathbf{x}|\gamma_i^*) = p(x_L, \ldots, x_{j+1}|\mathbf{x}_j, \gamma_i^*)p(\mathbf{x}_{j-1}|\gamma_i^*)\ \{p(\bar{\delta}_j + (\delta_j, x_{j_v})|\gamma_i^*)\} \tag{23}$$

It is tempting to use Eq. (22a) in Eq. (23) because Eq. (22a) is never Ø and has maximum value of 1. Suppose for example that

$$p(x_{j_v}|\gamma_i^*, \delta_j) = 0.1,\ x_{j_v} \text{ True.}$$

Then, for category γ_i^*

$$p(\bar{\delta}_j + (\delta_j, x_{j_v})|\gamma_i^*) = \tfrac{1}{2} + (\tfrac{1}{2})\ (0.1) = 0.55,\ x_{j_v} \text{ True}$$
$$\tfrac{1}{2} + (\tfrac{1}{2})\ (0.9) = 0.95,\ x_{j_v} \text{ False}$$

We don't know if x_j is significant.

Now for category γ_k^*, suppose that

$$p(x_{j_v}|\gamma_k^*, \delta_j) = 0.3.$$

Then

$$p(\bar{\delta}_j + (\delta_j, x_{j_v})|\gamma_k^*) = \tfrac{1}{2} + (\tfrac{1}{2})\ (0.03) = 0.65,\ x_{j_v} \text{ True}$$
$$\tfrac{1}{2} + (\tfrac{1}{2})\ (0.7) \ = 0.85,\ x_{j_v} \text{ False.}$$

What we are doing is observing an event $(\bar{\delta}_j + (\delta_j, x_{jv}))$ which is the event that either feature x_j is insignificant or significant with feature x_{j_v}. We have just calculated probability of this event for two different categories assuming probability of insignificance is (½).

Further, the category conditional probability density functions for γ_i^* and γ_k^*, respectively, were assumed 0.1 and 0.3 when x_{j_v} is True, or 0.9 and 0.7, respectively, when x_{j_v} is False. But, if there is an equally likely chance that x_j is not a significant feature, then the category conditional probability density functions when x_{j_v} is False are 0.95 and 0.85 for the respective categories.

Note that [(0.9) − (0.7)] = 0.2 while [(0.95) − (0.85)] = 0.1, the latter reflecting that smoothing has taken place.

Categories γ_i^* and γ_j^* *are not penalized as much for an absent property of a possibly insignificant feature.*

Equation (22a) may be considered a filter that smooths the ripples due to uncertainty. Sensitivity is reduced in that likelihood differences are not as great for two categories if the feature is always significant.

This explains an important experimental finding in developing expert systems: there are errors that for various reasons can prevent a category property from being observed. The developer wants to protect against these errors by increasing likelihood for an observation observed False over what normally would be supplied by the expert. *Some would have called this heuristic but, in fact, it is explained by the model just developed.*

13-10-2 Type 1 "Significated" Type 1 Measurement

If $x_1, x_2, \ldots, x_9$ are nine embedded Type 1 features in a Type 1 measurement (complex feature), then a model assuming independence within the column,

$$\prod_{j=1}^{9} \left\{ \frac{1}{2} + \frac{1}{2}\, p(x_{j_v} | \gamma_i^*, \delta_j) \right\} \tag{24}$$

is a segment (local module or complex feature value) of category conditional probability density function assuming uncertainty about the significance of the respective features. More generally, this condtional probability density function is

$$\prod_{j=1}^{9} (1 - p_{\delta j}) + p_{\delta j}\, p(x_{j_v} | \gamma_i^*, \delta_j) = \prod_{j=1}^{9} \{1 + p_{\delta j}\{p(x_{j_v} | \gamma_i^*, \delta_j) - 1\}\} \tag{25}$$

and reflects the probability $p(\delta_{\delta j}) = p_{\delta j}$ that the respective features x_j are significant.

Equation (25) *defines a complex of Type 1 features* for uncertain observations.

13-10-3 Probability of Significance Equals Probability of True

An interesting result is obtained by letting

$$p(x_{j_v} | \gamma_i^*, \delta_j) = p_{\delta j} \tag{26}$$

so that

$$1 + p_{\delta_j} \{p(x_{j_v} | \gamma_i^*, \delta_j) - 1\} = 1 + p_{\delta_j}^2 - p_{\delta_j}. \tag{27}$$

The derivative of the above function is

$$\frac{d}{d_{p_{\delta_j}}} \{1 + p_{\delta_j}^2 - p_{\delta_j}\} = 2p_{\delta_j} - 1; \tag{28}$$

and this slope of the function is sketched in Figure 13.8.

For the situation

$$p(x_{j_v}|\gamma_i^*, \delta_j) = (1 - p_{\delta_j})$$

$$1 + p_{\delta_j}\{p(x_{j_v}|\gamma_i^*, \delta_j) - 1\} = 1 - p^2_{\delta_j} \quad (29)$$

with derivative

$$\frac{d}{d_{p_{\delta_j}}}\{1 - p^2_{\delta_j}\} = -2_{p_{\delta_j}} \quad (30)$$

the function is sketched in Figure 13.9.

The interpretation of the results in Figures 13.8 and 13.9 is that with high probability of insignificance, neither True nor False feature values can affect the category conditional probability density, while with high probability of significance, either a True or False can have a significant effect.

Let

$$p(x_{j_v}|\gamma_i^*, \delta_j) = a\ p_{\delta_j},\ \emptyset \leq a \leq 1.$$

Then the respective functions are:

$$(1 + a^2_{p_{\delta j}}) - p_{\delta_j}$$

with slope

$$2ap_{\delta_j} - 1$$

and

$$1 - ap^2_{\delta_j}$$

with slope

$$-2ap_{\delta_j}$$

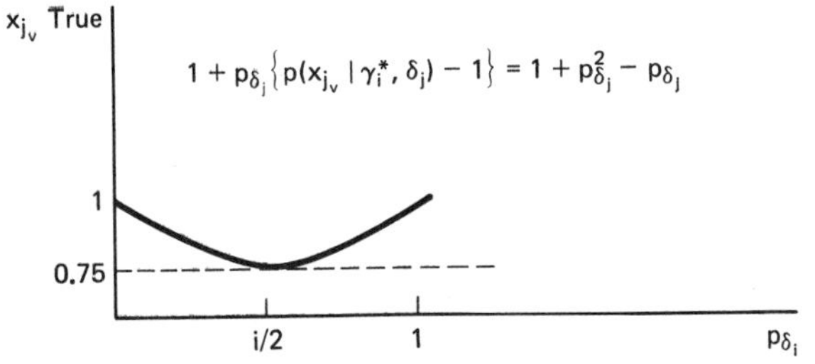

FIGURE 13.8 $p(x_{j_v}|\gamma_i^*, \delta_j) = p_{\delta_j}$

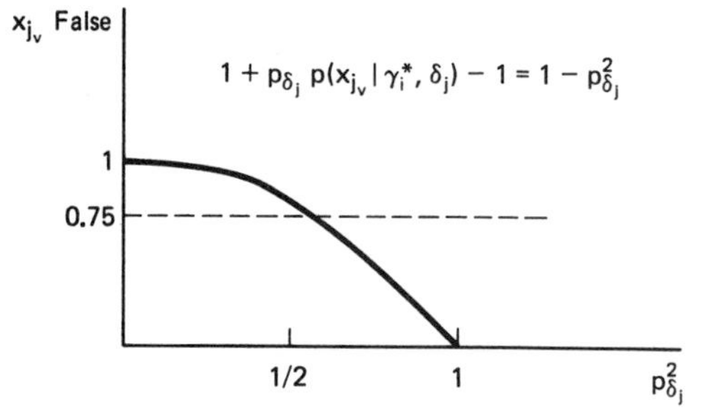

FIGURE 13.9 $p(x_{j_v}|\gamma_i^*, \delta_j) = (1 - p_{\delta_j})$

The effect of decreasing a is to "pull down" the derivative curve in Figure 13.8 while "pulling up" the curve in Figure 13.9.

13-10-4 Discussion

Eq. (25), for a complex of Type 1 features for uncertain observations,

$$\prod_{j=1}^{9} (1 - p_{\delta_j}) + p_{\delta_j} p(x_{j_v}|\gamma_i^*, \delta_j), \tag{31}$$

demonstrates many upshots. Letting $p(x_{j_v}|\gamma_i^*, \delta_j) = \epsilon$ allows setting category conditional probability density equal to $(1 - p_{\delta_j}) =$ constant $<< 1$ for the feature concerned. This results in enormous complexity reduction when considering a large system. Low probability False responses do not negate higher probability True responses, to the extent a simple product functional does, if $(1 - p_{\delta_j}) = ½$.

A disadvantage of the functional is that it causes some loss of sensitivity.

These calculations began with computation of p(Insignificant with either value or Significant with value x_{j_v}).

14

Considerations When Training Expert Systems

14-1 INTRODUCTION

Since 1977 we have been training **CONSULT-I®** as an expert system (Patrick *and others,* 1979; Fattu *and others,* 1982, 1983; Emerman *and others,* 1983; Franklin *and others,* 1983; Patrick *and others,* 1985; Detterman and Patrick, 1985). Much has been learned during this time about expert knowledge. First, it is not "hard knowledge" as is obtained when processing real data (records) in **The OUTCOME ADVISOR®** or **CONSULT LEARNING SYSTEM®** (Fattu *and others* 1985). It frequently is noted that expert knowledge may not be expert (for example, Lusted, 1968; deDombal *and others,* 1972, 1974; Christensen-Szalaneki *and others,* 1981; Lindberg, 1981; Wallsten, 1981; Wolf *and others,* 1985). Nevertheless, it may be all that is available before hard data are collected. Furthermore, expert knowledge can be the starting point for subsystem (problem) design.

Considerations include the effect of observation error on the category conditional probability density function for Type 1 features; numerical examples, difference between probability of True observed False and probability of False observed True, examples of training probabilities with unequal observation error, effect on probability where a feature is observed False given other features observed True for the category; (for Type Ø features).

Other considerations are constraints on the expert with respect to a priori category probabilities, equal number of training samples for each feature of a category and correction constants.

14-2 EXPERT TRAINING CONSTRAINTS

14-2-1 Introduction

Category γ_i^* with c.c.p.d.f. (consider one column or minicolumn) is trained with parameters $p_{i_{j_v}}$ for the vth value of the jth feature. A reasonable approach is to ask the developer to supply

$$p_{i_{j_1}}, p_{i_{j_2}}, \ldots, p_{i_{j_v}}$$

for feature j. As probabilities,

$$\emptyset \leq p_{i_{j_v}} \leq 1.$$

But there are other constraints. If training samples (records) are used to estimate the $p_{i_{j_v}}$ we know that

a. The number of samples is the same for each feature of category i.
b. Train each category with the same number of samples, i.e., a priori category probabilities are made equal here, to be modified later by a priori category probabilities extended to be c.c.p.d.f.'s.

Item (a) is achieved by Eq. (1) and Eq. (2) below where n_i does not depend on i.

Item (b) is achieved by requiring

$$n_{i_j} = n_i \;\forall\; j.$$

It is desirable to train all categories with equal a priori category probabilities while training category-feature relationships. The training of a priori category probabilities is a separate consideration. In general, training $p(x_1, x_2, \ldots, x_L|\gamma^*{}_i)$ utilizes n_i supervised training samples. Uncertainty in this estimator depends on n_i. With n the total number of training samples, the estimated a priori category probability for γ_i^* would be

$$\hat{P}_i = \frac{n_i}{n} : \text{Estimated a priori category probabilities.} \tag{1}$$

In a supervised mode, the prior estimates $\hat{P}_i$ $i = 1,2, \ldots, M$ are equal iff

$$n_i = n/M,\; i = 1,2, \ldots, M. \tag{2}$$

Keep this in mind as an internal constraint for each c.c.p.d.f.

14-2-2 Equal Number of Training Samples for Each Feature of a Category

When training $p(\mathbf{x}|\gamma_i^*)$, each marginal probability density function $p(x_j|\gamma_i^*)$ (for simplicity limit consideration to a column) should be trained with the same number of samples. This one-dimensional probability density function is characterized by probabilities $\{p_{i_{j_v}}\}_{v=1}^{V}$. An unbiased estimator of $p(x_j|\gamma_i^*)$ is

$$\hat{p}_{i_{j_v}} = \frac{n_{i_{j_v}}}{n_i}, \tag{3}$$

where

$$\sum_{v=1}^{V} n_{i_{j_v}} = n_i,\ j = 1,2,\ldots,L \tag{4}$$

since each jth feature is a component of the same training vector.

Violation of Eq.(4) can be one of the most practical difficulties encountered by experts. If actual hard data were utilized, obtained from nature, the problem does not occur.† But an expert, afforded the flexibility, often violates the rule. Note that

$$\sum_{v=1}^{V} \hat{p}_{i_{j_v}} \triangleq \frac{\sum_{v=1}^{V} n_{i_{j_v}}}{n_i} \triangleq \frac{n_{i_j}}{n_i} = 1 \text{ iff } n_{i_j} = n_i \tag{5}$$

Thus, by Eq. (2), Eq. (3) does not define a true probability density function unless $n_{i_j} = n_i$. This is necessary because *the number of samples for the respective dimensions are equal.*

Thus, the key is that

$$\sum_{v=1}^{V} n_{i_{j_v}} \underset{\text{MUST}}{=} n_i \tag{6}$$

and "must" not be violated. Any violation of this during training must be corrected.

---

†**The OUTCOME ADVISOR®** and **CONSULT LEARNING SYSTEM®** automatically satisfy Eq. (4) during training and the prior category probabilities depend on the population (Eq. 1).

Suppose that an *expert has supplied*

$$n^*_{i_{j_v}}$$

the problem is how to impose on the expert's training,

$$n^*_{i_{j_v}}$$

and the expert's implied training

$$n^*_{i_j} = \sum_{v=1}^{V} n^*_{i_{j_v}},$$

the constraints:

$$\begin{aligned} n^*_{i_j} &= n_i \ \forall\, j \\ n_i &= n \ \forall\, i \end{aligned} \tag{7}$$

For example, to see how errors occur if this is violated, consider:

$$n^*_{i_{1_v}} = \{2, 4, \emptyset, \emptyset, \emptyset, \emptyset, \emptyset, \emptyset\}, \text{ Feature 1,}$$

versus

$$n^*_{i_{2_v}} = \{2, 6, 2, 2, 6, 1, 3, \emptyset\}, \text{ Feature 2.}$$

For the second feature value ($v = 2$) of feature 1,

$$\hat{p}_{i_{1_2}} = 4/6$$

while for the second feature,

$$\hat{p}_{i_{2_2}} = 6/22,$$

a disaster if the second example was to have the "highest weight" on the second feature value.

14-2-3 Correction Constant

To insure constraints Eq. (7), define "correction" constants d_{i_j} such that

$$\sum_{v=1}^{V} n^*_{i_{j_v}} d_{i_j} = n_i. \tag{8}$$

Then, the *correction constant* is

$$d_{i_j} = n_i / \sum_{v=1}^{V} n^*_{i_{j_v}} = \frac{n_i}{n^*_{i_j}}. \tag{9}$$

This suggests modifying the number of samples per bin of feature *j* of category *i* to

$$\overset{u}{n}_{i_{j_v}} = n^*_{i_{j_v}} d_{i_j},$$

where *u* is used as a superscript with the property

$$\sum_{v=1}^{V} \overset{u}{n}_{i_{j_v}} = \sum_{v=1}^{V} n^*_{i_{j_v}} (n_i/n^*_{i_j}) = \frac{n^*_{i_j} n_i}{n^*_{i_j}} = n_i \qquad (10)$$

as desired.

An estimator for relative frequency,

$$\overset{u}{p}_{i_{j_v}} = p^*_{i_{j_v}} d_{i_j} = \frac{n^*_{i_{j_v}} d_{i_j}}{n_i} \qquad (11)$$

has the property

$$\sum_{v=1}^{V} \overset{u}{p}_{i_{j_v}} = \frac{\sum_{v=1}^{V} n^*_{i_{j_v}} d_{i_j}}{n_i} = \frac{n_i}{n_i} = 1, \forall j \qquad (12)$$

as desired. Thus, estimator $\overset{u}{p}_{i_{j_v}}$ Eq. (11),

$$\overset{u}{p}_{i_{j_v}} = \frac{n^*_{i_{j_v}}}{n_i} \frac{n_j}{n^*_{i_j}} = \frac{n^*_{i_{j_v}}}{n^*_{i_j}} = p^*_{i_{j_v}}$$

Comparing Estimators.

Both estimators

$$\overset{u_1}{p}_{i_{j_v}} = \frac{n^*_{i_{j_v}}}{n^*{}_{i_j}} C_{i_j} = \frac{n^*_{i_{j_v}}}{n^*_{i_j}} \frac{n^*/M}{n^*_{i_j}}$$

$$\overset{u_2}{p}_{i_{j_v}} = \frac{n^*_{i_{j_v}}}{n^*{}_{i_j}}$$

satisfy constraints:

Sum to one over $n = 1, 2, \ldots V$.

Number of samples per feature per class are equal.

14-2-4 Conclusion

During expert training, the following constraints apply:

1. Keep a priori category probabilities equal, Eq.(1), Eq. (2), when training the c.c.p.d.f.

2. Keep $n_{i_j} = n_i$; i.e., each feature x_j of category γ_i^* is trained with n_i samples (Eq. (6)). **If trained with $n_{i_j}^* \neq n_i$, correct using d_{i_j}. (Eq. (9)).

14-3 EFFECT OF OBSERVATION ERROR ON CATEGORY CONDITONAL PROBABILITY DENSITY FUNCTION—TYPE 1 FEATURES

14-3-1 Introduction

For a Type 1 feature, there are parameters $p_{i_{j_v}}$, $V = 2$, for the jth feature with two values, True or False.

A developer can supply two numbers

$$p_{i_{j_1}}, \; p_{i_{j_2}}$$

for the jth feature. For example

$$p_{i_{j_1}} = 0.8 : \text{True}$$
$$p_{i_{j_2}} = 0.2 : \text{False}$$

Suppose that the jth feature is observed False when it "should be or is true." The weight of 0.2 will hurt category i and we don't want it to if there is an observation error. Therefore, some method is needed for introducing the probability of observation error P_E.

As P_E increases, a False value for the jth feature will have decreasing effect on the inference of category γ_i^*. Unfortunately, the inference function then is less sensitive to distinguish categories, and more conservative.

For many reasons a feature value can be incorrectly observed. Limiting discussion here to a Type 1 feature with values T (True) or F (False), let E_{TF} denote the event that a false observation (in the language of game theory, "nature" knows it is False) is observed True. Likewise, E_{FF}, E_{FT}, E_{TT} exist where E_{FF} is the event that a False observation is observed False, F_{FT} the event that a True observation is observed False, and E_{TT} the event a True observation is observed True.

We have shown that it is natural for knowledge to be stored as a category conditional probability density function $p(x_j|\gamma_i^*)$ for feature x_j and category γ_i^*. This knowledge is acquired either as hard data (training samples) or expert knowledge. Training using expert knowledge is subject to considerable variability which is reducible by experience. For example, for category γ_i^*, the relative frequency that $x_j = T$ may be set at Ø because γ_i^* was never known to have $x_j = T$. Thus, $x_j = T$ is a Can't for category γ_i^*. The developer of an expert system learns, however, that in fact γ_i^* can occur with x_j observed True. For example, there can be observer error or a complex class may occur rather than a "pure" only class, in this case γ_i^*. Experience shows that correct decisions can be missed because of a Can't.

As another example, suppose that for a category γ_i^* an expert declares that $x_j = F$ is not possible. He/she then sets $p(x_j = F|\gamma_i^*) = 0.0$. For another category γ_k^* the expert declares that $x_j = F$ is very unlikely because x_j being True is a property of category γ_k^*. The expert then sets $p(x_j = F|\gamma_k^*) = 0.1$. Now suppose that γ_k^* is active and features x_1, $x_2, \ldots, x_{j-1}$ all have values characteristic of γ_k^*. Then along comes $x_j = F$ because of observer error, and the large difference of 1.0 versus 0.1 for $p(x_j = F|\gamma_i^*)$ versus $p(x_j = F|\gamma_k^*)$ causes a tenfold decrease in the likelihood of category γ_k^*. In practice this actually happens, usually because a presentation (subcategory) of γ_k^* was not known or a complex class occurred instead of γ_k^* and the complex class is not known to the developer. Considerations here are feature sensitivity and dependence of this sensitivity on other features.

We have found it useful to declare that an insignificant feature x_j for category γ_i^* has conditional probability density function $p(x_j = T|\gamma_i^*) = 0.1$, $p(x_j = F|\gamma_i^*) = 0.9$. For the category γ_k^* where x_j is significant, we increase $p(x_j = T|\gamma_i^*) > 0.1$ but often are reluctant to decrease $p(x_j = F|\gamma_k^*) < 0.9$, seemingly violating that $p(x_j = T|\gamma_i^*) + p(x_j = F|\gamma_i^*) = 1$. This has led us to understand that we are not observing what we think we are observing in x_j. This suggests redefining the observation event so as to model this violation.

The concept of an insignificant feature has proven to be very important. Naturally, for any category in a large system, most features can be insignificant. The concept of an insignificant feature allows an optimum approach whereby designed modules (subsystems) are integrated into a total system.

Returning to the specific problem of the observed feature x_j for category γ_i^*, x_j can either be observed T (True) or F (False). Thus

$$x_j = (x_j, T) + (x_j, F). \tag{13}$$

But

$$(x_j, T) = (x_j, T, E_{TT}) + (x_j, T, E_{TF}) \tag{14}$$

$$(x_j, F) = (x_j, F, E_{FF}) + (x_j, F, F_{FT}). \tag{15}$$

Since x_j *was* observed,

$$p(x_j) = p(x_j, T) + p(x_j, F). \tag{16}$$

To proceed, we need to distinguish between T (True) by nature and T (True) by the observer and likewise for F (False). Using O (Observer) and N (Nature) as subscripts, Eqs. (13), (14), and (15) become

$$\begin{aligned}(x_j, T_O) &= (x_j, T_O, E_{T_O T_N}) + (x_j, T_O, E_{T_O F_N})\\ (x_j, F_O) &= (x_j, F_O, E_{F_O F_N}) + (x_j, F_O, E_{F_O T_N}).\end{aligned} \tag{17}$$

Suppose an expert declares that

$$\begin{aligned}p(x_j, T_N) &= 0.2\\ p(x_j, F_N) &= 0.8\end{aligned}$$

for some category. According to Eq. (17), as depicted by the arrows, some of nature's probability crosses over. This problem was well recognized two decades ago for a channel problem in communications theory. In practice we observe that for certain problems

$$p(x_j, T_O) < p(x_j, T_N) \tag{18}$$

and

$$p(x_j, F_O) > p(x_j, F_N)$$

because of this "cross talk."

Feature Dependence or the Adaptive Model

Consider Eq. (17) in view of the fact that $j - 1$ features $\mathbf{x}_{j-1}$ have been processed prior to arriving at stage j. The probabilities for the events in Eq. (17) may be considered adaptive, depending on $\mathbf{x}_{j-1}$. Considering category γ_i^*, if $\mathbf{x}_{j-1}$ has been looking like γ_i^*, then it is more likely that a primitive characteristic of category γ_i^* is True and more likely that a primitive not characteristic of category γ_i^* is False. For this model

$$\begin{aligned}p(x_j, T_O, \mathbf{x}_{j-1}) &> p(x_j, T_N)\\ p(x_\mu, F_O, \mathbf{x}_{j-1}) &> p(x_\mu, F_N)\end{aligned}$$

where x_j is considered characteristic of category γ_i^* and x_μ not characteristic of γ_i^*, x_μ different from γ_i^*. This is a smoothing effect because the dependencies are not provided for exactly. The developer of an expert system tends to protect against a false observation carrying too much weight.

This suggests a set of adaptive models for the conditional probability density function of x_j depending on the previous number of features with true values for γ_i^*. One can envision a state space network or causal network as a vehicle for storing these adaptive probability densities. But that is not adequate since column direction for the categories' presentation(s) is needed. In this sense a **CONSULT-I®** column (with or without minicolumns) is pathed through a state space network. The concept of adaptive columns where the probability at x_j depends on $\mathbf{x}_{j-1}$ generates many columns through a state space network. Many problems do not require this amount of complexity so that adaptive columns are not needed.

14-3-2 Examples

In this section, we consider a Type 1 feature x_j with values

$$x_{j_v} = \begin{matrix} T_O & \text{(True)} \\ F_O & \text{(False).} \end{matrix} \tag{19}$$

As before, an error E occurs if T_N is observed False or F_N is observed True, opposite the truth known to nature, illustrated below:

There exists a probability of observer error

$$p(x \text{ observed in error}|\gamma_i^*) = p_E \tag{20}$$

where x is a random variable generically representing x_{j_v}. This is a special case of the model of Eq. (17). The observer probability of error p_E is assumed the same for both kinds of error in Figure 14.1.

Our objective is to obtain knowledge of the category conditional probability density function, $p(\mathbf{x}|\gamma_i^*)$, in particular its marginal for feature x_j. Because of observer error, this probability density function is different from that calculated without observer error.

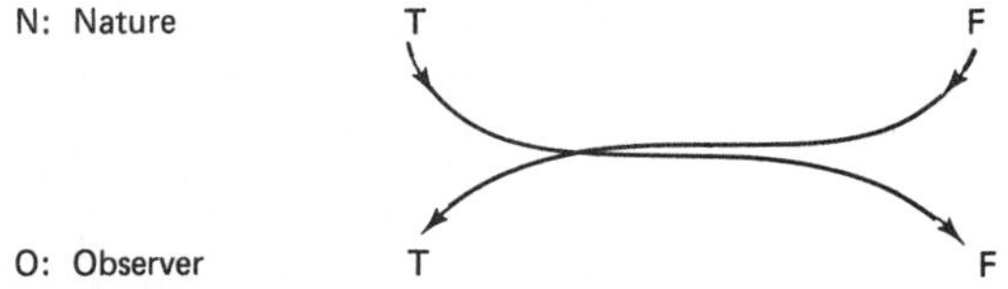

FIGURE 14.1 Illustration of Observer Error E.

14-3-3 Probability that a Feature Value Is Observed True

Let x generically denote a jth feature x_j. Then x_j can be observed True either with error (E) or without error ($\bar{E}$). Thus,

$$\begin{aligned} p(x = T_O|\gamma_i^*) &= p(x = T_O, E|\gamma_i^*) + p(x = T_O, \bar{E}|\gamma_i^*) \\ &= p(x = T_O|E, \gamma_i^*)p(E|\gamma_i^*) + p(x = T_O|\bar{E},\gamma_i^*)p(\bar{E}|\gamma_i^*) \\ &= p(x = T_O|E, \gamma_i^*)p_E + p(x = T_O|\bar{E},\gamma_i^*)(1 - p_E). \end{aligned} \tag{21}$$

where

$$p_E = p(E|\gamma_i^*),\ p(\bar{E}|\gamma_i^*) = (1 - p_E)$$

because of equality of events.

Further assume that it is just as likely that the observer will observe $x = T_O$ with error as $x = F_O$ without error.

$$p(x = T_O, E) = p(x = F_O, \bar{E}), \tag{22}$$

then

$$p(x = T_O|E, \gamma_i^*) = p(x = F_O|\bar{E}, \gamma_i^*). \tag{23}$$

Substituting Eq. (23) into Eq. (21) results in

$$p(x = T_O|\gamma_i^*) = p(x = F_O|\bar{E}, \gamma_i^*)p_E + p(x = T_O|\bar{E}, \gamma_i^*)(1 - p_E) \tag{24}$$

$$\begin{aligned} &= (1 - p_i)p_E + p_i(1 - p_E) \\ &= p_i(1 - 2p_E) + p_E. \end{aligned} \tag{25}$$

where generically

$$\begin{aligned} p_i &\triangleq p(x = T_O|\bar{E}, \gamma_i^*) \\ 1 - p_i &\triangleq p(x = F_O|\bar{E}, \gamma_i^*). \end{aligned} \tag{26}$$

14-3-4 Probability that a Feature Value Is Observed False

Feature x_j is observed False either with error (E) or without error ($\bar{E}$). Analogous to Section 14-3-3, there results

$$p(x = F_O|\gamma_i^*) = p(x = F_O|E, p_i)p_E + p(x = F_O|\bar{E}, \gamma_i^*)\,(1 - p_E) \tag{27}$$

$$\begin{aligned} &= p(x = T_O|\bar{E}, \gamma_i^*)p_E + p(x = F_O|\bar{E}, \gamma_i^*)\,(1 - p_E) \\ &= p_ip_E + (1 - p_i)(1 - p_E) \\ &= (1 - p_i) - (1 - 2p_i)p_E. \end{aligned} \tag{28}$$

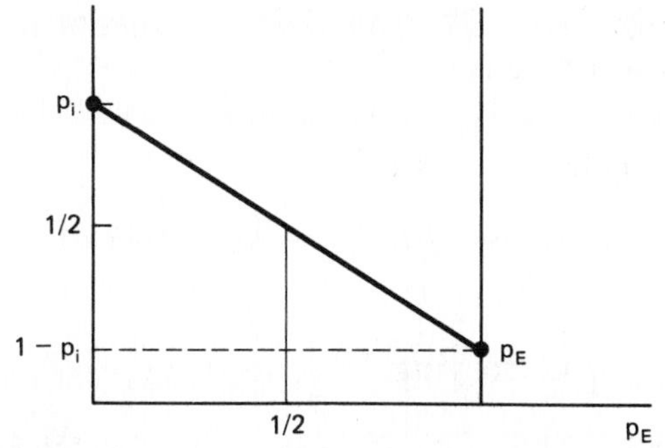

FIGURE 14.2 Sketch of $p(x = T_O|\gamma_i^*) = p_i(1 - 2p_E) + p_E$ versus p_E.

Equation (25) is sketched versus p_E in Figure 14.2 for $p_i > (1 - p_i)$. Note that the effect of $p_E = 1$ is to "reverse" the probability densities $p(x = T_O|\gamma_i^*)$ and $p(x = F_O|\gamma_i^*)$.

When

$$p_E = 1/2$$

then

$$p(x = T_O|\gamma_i^*) = p(x = F_O|\gamma_i^*) = 1/2. \quad (29)$$

14-3-5 Numerical Examples

Example 1

Suppose

$p_i = 0.2 \qquad (1 - p_i) = 0.8$
$p_E = 0.4.$

Then

$p(x = T_O|\gamma_i^*) = 0.44$
$p(x = F_O|\gamma_i^*) = 0.56$

which differ respectively from p_i and $(1 - p_i)$. Note that the effect of observer error is to increase probability $x = T$ but decrease probability of $x = F_O$.

Example 2

Suppose p_i is the same as in Example 1 but

$p_E = 0.2.$

Then

$p(x = T_O|\gamma_i^*) = 0.32$
$p(x = F_O|\gamma_i^*) = 0.68$

14-3-6 Probability True Observed False Different from False Observed True

In practice it is realistic to assume

$$p(E_{F_O T_N}\text{: Observing True as False}|\gamma_i^*) \triangleq p_{E_{F_O T_N}} \tag{30}$$

differs from

$$p(E_{T_O F_N}\text{: Observing False as True}|\gamma_i^*) \triangleq p_{E_{T_O F_N}} \tag{31}$$

Before considering examples, we derive an expression for $p(x = T_O|\gamma_i^*)$. As a generalization of the previous calculation,

$$\begin{aligned} p(x = T_O|\gamma_i^*) &= p(x = T_O, E_{TF}|\gamma_i^*) + p(x = T_O, E_{TT}|\gamma_i^*) \\ &= p(x = T_O, E_{TF}|\gamma_i^*)p_{E_{TF}} + p(x = T_O|\gamma_i^*, E_{TT})p(E_{TT}) \\ &= p(x = F_O|\bar{E}_{TF}, \gamma_i^*)p_{E_{TF}} + p(x = T_O|\gamma_i^*, E_{TT})p(E_{TT}) \\ &= (1 - p_i)p_{E_{TF}} + (p_i)p_{E_{TT}}. \end{aligned} \tag{32}$$

where we assume for illustration that

$$p(x = F_O, \bar{E}_{TF}|\gamma_i^*) = p(x = T_O, E_{TF}|\gamma_i^*)$$

In like manner, it can be shown that

$$p(x = F_O|\gamma_i^*) = p_i p_{E_{FT}} + (1 - p_i)p_{E_{FF}} \tag{33}$$

14-3-7 Examples of Probabilities with Unequal Observation Error

Typical situations in practice correspond to the following probabilities:

$p_{E_{TF}}$ ~Ø (very small)
$p_{E_{FF}}$ ~1 (very near 1)
$p_{E_{FT}}$ — (moderate)
$p_{E_{TT}}$ — (high).

Error probabilities $p_{E_{FT}}$ and $p_{E_{TF}}$ often cause greatest concern. An observation which nature knows is True may be observed False for a variety of reasons:

Inexperienced Feature Extraction ($p_{E_{FT}} > Ø$).
A breast lump may not be found, a goiter may not be noticed.
Early presentation ($p_{E_{FT}} > Ø$).

The time may be early and a breast lump may not yet be fixed for a case of breast cancer. This suggests a *separate presentation*—early breast cancer, a *complex feature incorporating time,* or *modifying the event-conditional probability density function* through Eq. (27) via $p_{E_{FT}}$.

Another very important consideration is that $p_{E_{FT}}$ *may be significant because of known dependence.* There is an event taken into account that other features of γ_i^* are True which affects the calculations of probability x is observed False. This is introduced in the following section.

14-3-8 Effect on Probability Where an Observation Is Observed False for γ_i^*, Given Other Features Observed True

Let

$$\alpha_{j_1, j_2, \ldots, j_t} \tag{34}$$

denote a set of Type 1 features which have been observed T (True). For feature x not in this set, consider:

$$p(x = F|\gamma_i^*, \alpha_{j_1, j_2, \ldots, j_t}) \tag{35}$$

Equation (35) can be expressed

$$\begin{aligned} p(x = F|\gamma_i^*, \alpha_{j_1, j_2, \ldots, j_t}) &= p(x = F, E_{FT}|\gamma_i^*, \alpha_{j_1, j_2, \ldots, j_t}) + \\ &\quad p(x = F, E_{FF}|\gamma_i^*, \alpha_{j_1, j_2, \ldots, j_t}) = \\ p(x = F|E_{FT}, \gamma_i^*, \alpha_{j_1, j_2, \ldots, j_t})\, &p(E_{FT}|\gamma_i^*, \alpha_{j_1, j_2, \ldots, j_t}) + \\ p(x = F|E_{FF}, \gamma_i^*, \alpha_{j_1, j_2, \ldots, j_t})\, &p(E_{FF}|\gamma_i^*, \alpha_{j_1, j_2, \ldots, j_t}). \end{aligned} \tag{36}$$

Suppose that we set

$$p(E_{FT}|\gamma_i^*, \alpha_{j_1, j_2, \ldots, j_t}) = \emptyset$$

given strong experience $\alpha_{j_1, j_2, \ldots, j_t}$ that γ_i^* is True, and thus set

$$p(E_{TT}|\gamma_i^*, \alpha_{j_1, j_2, \ldots, j_t}) = 1.$$

Assume

$$\begin{aligned} p(E_{FT}|\gamma_i^*, \alpha_{j_1, j_2, \ldots, j_t}) &= p(E_{FT}) \\ p(E_{FF}|\gamma_i^*, \alpha_{j_1, j_2, \ldots, j_t}) &= p(E_{FF}). \end{aligned} \tag{37}$$

Then Eq. (36) becomes

$$p(x = F|\gamma_i^*, \alpha_{j_1, j_2, \ldots, j_t}) = \tag{38}$$

$$p(x = F|E_{FT}, \gamma_i^*, \alpha_{j_1, j_2, \ldots, j_t})p(E_{FT}) + p(x = F|E_{FF}, \gamma_i^*, \alpha_{j_1, j_2, \ldots, j_t})\, p(E_{FF}).$$

Suppose

$$p(E_{FF}) = 1$$

such that Eq. (38) becomes

$$p(x = F|\gamma_i^*, \alpha_{j_1, j_2, \ldots, j_t}) =$$

$$p(x = F|E_{FT}, \gamma_i^*, \alpha_{j_1, j_2, \ldots, j_t})p(E_{FT}) + p(x = F|E_{FF}, \gamma_i^*, \alpha_{j_1, j_2, \ldots, j_t})$$

which *demonstrates an increase through the term* $p(x = F|E_{FT}, \gamma_i^*, \alpha_{j_1}, j_2, \ldots j_t)$ *because True values of* x_j *are observed as False.* The term $p(x = T|E_{TT}, \gamma_i^*, \alpha_{j_1, j_2, \ldots, j_t})$ increases given the set $\alpha_{j_1, j_2, \ldots, j_t}$. There are two effects to increase $p(x = F|\gamma_i^*, \alpha_{j_1, j_2, \ldots, j_t})$:

1. $p(E_{FT}) > \emptyset$ causes increase in probability x observed False
2. Set $\{\alpha_{j_1, j_2, \ldots, j_t}\}$ causes increase in probability x observed False.

The concept of not decreasing the likelihood for a feature with false feature values is suggested in the *measure of belief* distance measure used in **MYCIN** (Shortliffe, 1976).

14-4 EFFECT OF OBSERVATION ERROR ON CATEGORY CONDITIONAL PROBABILITY DENSITY FUNCTION—TYPE Ø FEATURES

14-4-1 Introduction

A Type Ø feature x_j has values

$$x_{j_v}, v = 1, 2, \ldots, V$$

and

$$\sum_{v=1}^{V} p(x_{j_v}|\gamma_i^*) = 1.$$

We are interested in

$$p(x_j = x_{j_v}|\gamma_i^*), \forall x_{j_v}$$

and how observation errors affect probability. Denoting x_j generically by x, $x = x_v$ can be observed with error.

$$E_{vv_\xi}: x \text{ observed as } x_v \text{ when nature's value is } x_{v_\xi}. \qquad (39)$$

Note that E_{vv_v} is no error.

14-4-2 Probability That Feature Value Is Observed x_{j_v}

Because the events E_{vv_ξ} are mutually exclusive for different v_ξ, it follows that

$$p(x = x_v|\gamma_i^*) = \sum_{\xi=1}^{V} p(x = x_v, E_{vv_\xi}|\gamma_i^*)$$

$$= \sum_{\xi=1}^{V} p(x = x_v|E_{vv_\xi}, \gamma_i^*)p(E_{vv_\xi}|\gamma_i^*). \quad (40)$$

Assuming

$$p(E_{vv_\xi}|\gamma_i^*) = p(E_{vv_\xi}),$$

it follows that

$$p(x = x_v|\gamma_i^*) = \sum_{\xi=1}^{V} p(x = x_v|E_{vv_\xi}, \gamma_i^*)p(E_{vv_\xi}).$$

Models for observation errors for Type Ø features can be developed further.

15

Discovering Knowledge Using The OUTCOME ADVISOR® and CONSULT LEARNING SYSTEM®

15-1 INTRODUCTION

The **CONSULT LEARNING SYSTEM®** is designed to be compatible with **CONSULT-I®.** The same feature format of Type Ø and Type 1 features, used in **CONSULT-I®**, is used in **CONSULT LEARNING SYSTEM®.** Marginal and joint events corresponding to packets or minicolumns in **CONSULT-I®** can be defined for the purpose of estimating probabilities used in **CONSULT-I®** columns. Using **AI** terms, this is learning by example and in **SPR** terms, it is estimation.

The **OUTCOME ADVISOR®** allows for construction of Type Ø features and estimation of conditional probabilities of events. The events are constructed using logical operations.

Using **SPR** language, learning takes place using supervised training samples.

Using learning systems such as **The OUTCOME ADVISOR®** or **CONSULT LEARNING SYSTEM®** for collection and analysis of multidimensional data bases was suggested by Patrick (1975, 1979). It has been applied to the study of food choking (Patrick, 1980c), thyroid disorders (Fattu, 1983; Blomberg *and others,* 1984), Nuclear Magnetic Resonance Imaging (Stein *and others,* 1984), chest pain (Patrick *and others,* 1977), Anemia (Blomberg *and others,* 1985) and reading disorders (Fattu *and others,* 1983). Multidimensional sensitivity and specificity can be learned using these systems (Patrick, 1979; Blomberg *and others,* 1984). A discussion of the relationship of Learning Systems to Expert Systems is in Fattu and Patrick (1986). Now we first discuss estimation of required probabilities in general terms without regard to feature type or specific column presentations.

Other systems have been developed for search of records for rule refinement using experts to focus the systems on experiments to form generalized or specialized rules. Such systems include **RX** (Blum, 1982), **SEEK** (Politatis and Weiss, 1984), and **MORE** (Kahn *and others*, 1985).

15-2 DEFINING EVENTS IN THE FEATURE SPACE

Let $x_1, x_2, \ldots, x_L$ be L features each with V values, x_{j_v}, $v = 1, L, \ldots, V$. The category conditional probability density function is

$$p(x_1, x_2, \ldots, x_L|\gamma_i^*). \tag{1}$$

In general, there are V^L sets with each set defined by L elements x_{1_w}, $x_{2_w}, \ldots, x_{L_w}$; for Type 1 embedded features, $V = 2$. The wth set can be denoted ν_w. For the v_wth set there exists a probability

$$p_{i_{w_1, w_2, \ldots, w_L}} = p(x_{1_w}, x_{2_w}, \ldots, x_{L_w}|\gamma_i^*).$$

Given n_i training samples from γ_i^* and letting the number of samples satisfying the set indexed by ν_w be (i.e., observed in the set)

$$n_{i_{w_1, w_2, \ldots, w_L}}, \tag{2}$$

then

$$\hat{p}_{i_{w_1, w_2, \ldots, w_L}} = \frac{n_{i_{w_1, w_2, \ldots, w_L}}}{n_i} \tag{3}$$

is a consistent, unbiased estimator for the set probabilities; i.e.,

$$E[\hat{p}_{i_{w_1, w_2, \ldots, w_L}}] = p_{i_{w_1, w_2, \ldots, w_L}} \tag{4}$$

and

$$n \overset{lim}{\rightarrow} \infty\ \hat{p}_{i_{w_1, w_2, \ldots, w_L}}] = p_{i_{w_1, \ldots, w_L}} \tag{5}$$

in probability or almost certainty (Eq. 5). The variance of this estimator is

$$\text{Variance } \{\hat{p}_{i_{w_1, w_2, \ldots, w_L}}\} = \frac{\sigma^2_{w_1, w_2, \ldots w_L}}{n_{i_{w_1 w_2 \ldots w_L}}} \tag{6}$$

where $\sigma^2_{w_1, w_2 \ldots w_L}$ depends on the true underlying probabilities:

$$\sigma^2_{w_1 w_2 \ldots w_L} = (p_{i_{w_1 w_2 \ldots w_L}})(1 - p_{i_{w_1 w_2 \ldots w_L}}). \tag{7}$$

One problem is to obtain a sufficiently large number of training samples n_i so that the variance (Eq. 6) of the estimate (Eq. 3) is small. In practice with L "large", it may be unreasonable to acquire a large enough number of samples $^{n}i_{w_1 w_2 \ldots w_L}$ for Variance $\hat{p}_{i_{w_1 w_2 \ldots w_L}}$ to be "acceptably small." For some sets $^{n}i_{w_1 w_2 \ldots w_L} = \emptyset$ and this is determined. In **CONSULT LEARNING SYSTEM®** and **The OUTCOME ADVISOR®** a method of adaptive set construction is constructed so as to "place the sets where there are samples." A closeness measure constructed through set operations effectively is "opened up" to accommodate more samples and thus decrease estimator variance.

15-3 ADAPTIVE SET CONSTRUCTION

An adaptive set is based on

$$x_1 \,\varepsilon\, [A_1] + x_2 \,\varepsilon\, [A_2] + \ldots + x_L \,\varepsilon\, [A_L]$$

where A_j is a set specified by OR operations (disjunctions) over the V feature values of x_j. That is

$$A_j = \delta_1 \, x_{j_1} + \delta_2 \, x_{j_2} + \ldots + \delta_v \, x_{j_v}$$

where $\delta_{j_v} = 1$ if feature value x_{j_v} is included in A_j and $\delta_{j_v} = \emptyset$ otherwise. The combination of AND operation with the above OR operation provides adaptive, interactive facility for defining sets (events).

15-4 CONSULT-I® COLUMNS WITH TYPE Ø AND TYPE 1 FEATURES

The kth column (hypercube) in **CONSULT-I®** has category conditional probablity density function

$$p(x_1, x_2, \ldots, x_L | \gamma^*_{i_k}) = \prod_{j=1}^{L} p(x_j | \mathbf{x}_{j-1}, \gamma^*_{i_k}) \qquad (8)$$

where minicolumns can modify this expression but are not specifically noted here (see Section 9-11). For a Type Ø feature in Eq. (8), the jth feature has values

$$x_{j_v}, \; v = 1,2, \ldots V.$$

A column structure reflects the STATISTICAL DEPENDENCE of the features in a "local region" of hyperspace (hyper feature space). A column can be discovered through unsupervised learning (see Patrick *and others,* 1965, 1967, 1968, 1970, 1971) and is local (see Sebastyen's adaptive sample set construction [1962]), Patrick and Bechtel [1969], Patrick and Fischer's Generalized K nearest neighbor rule [1970]).

The probability estimate

$$\hat{p}_{i_{j_v}} = \frac{n_{i_v}}{n_i} \tag{9}$$

is a simple estimator which rapidly converges to the true probability density with n_i increasing. It is an easy task to obtain these estimates for use in **CONSULT-I®** using the **CONSULT LEARNING SYSTEM.®**

As discussed in Section 7-10, a Type 1 feature in Eq. (8) has a complex probability density which can be expressed

$$p(x_1, x_2, \ldots, x_v | \gamma_i^*) = p_{i_{w_1 w_2 \ldots w_L}}. \tag{10}$$

For example, if $V = 9$ there are

$$2^9 = 512$$

sets of events in the set ν_v defined by $x_{1_w}, x_{2_w}, \ldots, x_{9_w}$ with probabilities to be estimated (Type 1 features). However, if column direction allows the assumption of statistical independence in Eq. (9), there are only 9 * 2 = 18 probabilities to be estimated. In practice it has been shown that provision for estimates of 512 probabilities is not efficient and not useful. A method such as column direction is desirable.

Independence is not assumed in Eq. (10). Thus, if a "sufficient number" of samples n_i are available, this approach converges to optimality. The developer needs to consider whether it is better to have low variance estimates with an independence assumption or questionable estimates with a dependence assumption. Of course, with the **CONSULT LEARNING SYSTEM®,** the marginals for the independence assumption can always be obtained from the joint set probabilities. For example, the marginal probability density function for the first Type 1 feature in the Type 1 measurement (assuming $V = 9$) is

$$p_{i_{v_1}} = \sum_{v_9=1}^{2} \cdots \sum_{v_3=1}^{2} \sum_{v_2=1}^{2} p_{i_{v_1 v_2 \ldots v_9}}. \tag{11}$$

This allows testing with estimates obtained using the **CONSULT LEARNING SYSTEM®** under either the independence assumption or the dependence assumption.

Both of these approaches can be compared with the approach of starting with independence and adding mechanical conditional probabilities to handle the dependence. Eventually, we are interested in verifying the quality of mechanical conditonal probabilities so that the approach of using the **CONSULT LEARNING SYSTEM®** without assuming independence always has a place.

15-5 AVERAGE CONDITIONAL PROBABILITY DENSITY OF DEGREE *n*

15-5-1 Introduction

Consider again the L features

$$x_1, x_2, \ldots, x_L$$

and category conditional probability density function

$$p(x_1, x_2, \ldots, x_L|\gamma_i^*).$$

Consider sets

$$\{x_{\xi_1}\}$$
$$\{x_{\xi_1}, x_{\xi_2}\}$$
$$\{x_{\xi_1}, x_{\xi_2}, x_{\xi_3}\}$$
$$\vdots$$
$$\{x_{\xi_1}, x_{\xi_2}, \ldots, x_{\xi_L}\}$$

Each combinaton of n elements consists of

$$\binom{L}{n} = \frac{L!}{n!\,(L-n)!} \tag{12}$$

elements where n is the number of features taken to compose an element of a set. The assumption of independence utilizes elements

$$\{x_{\xi_1}\}$$

and pairwise dependence would utilize

$$\{x_{\xi_1}\ x_{\xi_2}\}.$$

The situation of no independence utilizes

$$\{x_{\xi_1}, x_{\xi_2}, \ldots, x_{\xi_L}\}\ .$$

The probablity density

$$p(x_j|\mathbf{x}_{j-1}, \gamma_i^*)$$

can be considered in terms of the conditional probabilities

$$p(x_j|x_\xi,\gamma_i^*),\ \xi = 1,2,\ldots,j-1$$

when only pairwise dependence is utilized. Extension to higher order dependence can be considered but what follows is limited to at most third order.

15-5-2 Average Conditional Probability Density Degree Two

Given first-order dependence, denoted by D_1, define

$$\begin{aligned} p(x_j|\gamma_i^*, D_1) &= \frac{1}{(j-1)} \sum_{\xi=1}^{j=1} p(x_j|x_\xi, \gamma_i^*) \\ &= \frac{1}{(j-1)} \sum_{\xi=1}^{j=1} \frac{(p(x_j,x_\xi|\gamma_i^*)}{p(x_\xi|\gamma_i^*)}. \end{aligned} \tag{13}$$

The terms in the sum on the right hand side of Eq. (13) easily can be obtained by **The OUTCOME ADVISOR®**, or **CONSULT LEARNING SYSTEM®**.

Equation (13) represents a smoothing function which has a disadvantage of decreased sensitivity to any particular second order dependency. Again, we have seen the interesting property that smoothing can result from dependence among features.

15-5-3 Maximum Conditional Probability Density Degree Two

An alternative is to apply a fuzzy set operation to obtain

$$\begin{aligned} p(x_j|\gamma_i^*, D_1) &= \operatorname*{Max}_{\xi} \{ p(x_j|x_\xi, \gamma_i^*)\} \\ &= \operatorname*{Max}_{\xi} \left\{ \frac{p(x_j|x_\xi, \gamma_i^*)}{p(x_\xi|\gamma_i^*)} \right\}. \end{aligned} \tag{14}$$

This is not entirely satisfactory because a feature x_ξ with a value causing a "small" $p(x_j|x_\xi, \gamma_i^*)$ has no influence on the left-hand side of Eq. (14).

15-5-4 Rule-Based Conditional Probability Density Degree Two

Rules can be used as follows:

1. $p(x_j|x_\xi, \gamma_i^*) = \emptyset$ for some pair of feature values (x_{j_v}, x_{ξ_v}); thus, a Can't of Degree 2 is imposed.
2. $p(x_j|x_\xi, \gamma_i^*) = p(x_j|\gamma_i^*)$ for some pair of feature values; thus, statistical independence for certain values x_ξ.
3. $p(x_j|\gamma_i^*, D_1) = p(x_j|\gamma_i^*, x_\xi)$: Dominance of some feature x_ξ.

15-5-5 Average Conditional Probability Density Degree Three

$$p(x_j|\gamma_i^*, D_2) = \frac{1}{\binom{L}{n}} \sum_{\Omega} p(x_j|x_{\xi_1}, x_{\xi_2}, \gamma_i^*) \tag{15}$$

where Ω is the set of all pairs

$$(x_{\xi_1}, x_{\xi_2}),$$

for which there are

$$(L - 1)(L - 2).$$

For example,

$$\text{if } L = 10,\ (L - 1)(L - 2) = 9 * 8 = 72.$$
$$\text{if } L = 20,\ (L - 1)(L - 2) = 19 * 18 = 342.$$

Just as for Degree Two, Eq. (15) for Degree Three is a smoothing function.

15-5-6 Type Ø Measurements (Features): Example

For L Type Ø features the number of probabilities for degree n is

$$(V)^n \binom{L}{n}$$

For example, with $L = 9$, $V = 2$

Degree n	$2^n\binom{9}{n}$
1	$2\,\dfrac{9!}{1!\,(8)\,!} = 18$
2	$4\,\dfrac{9!}{2!\,(7)\,!} = 144$
3	$8\,\dfrac{9!}{3!\,(6)\,!} = 672.$

It is practical to use the **CONSULT LEARNING SYSTEM®** to obtain these probabilities for **CONSULT-I®**.

15-5-7 Type 1 Features

Dependence among Type 1 measurements usually is taken into account using hypercubes by **CONSULT-I®**. However, Eq. (14) or Eq. (15) can be applied to embedded Type 1 features in a Type 1 feature. For a Type 1 feature $V = 2$. For nine embedded Type 1 features there are, for degree n,

$$(2)^9\binom{9}{n}$$

probabilities. That is, for a single Type 1 feature with nine embedded Type 1 features, there are $(2)^9\binom{9}{n}$ probabilities for degree n.

15-6 UPDATING HYPERCUBES

15-6-1 Introduction

Once K hypercubes are established, the problem is how to update, given new training samples (records) for category γ_i^*. *This is an unsupervised estimation problem (Type 1) in that the training samples must be directed to one of the hypercubes or a new hypercube created.*† It is useful to define a closeness measure between a training vector $\mathbf{x}_r$ and the kth hypercube H_k,

$$d(\mathbf{x}_r,\ H_k).$$

---

†Blind training techniques in artificial intelligence can be expected to have serious problems here.

15-6-2 Closeness Measure Assuming Independence

Assuming independence, a closeness measure is just the inverse likelihood:

$$d(\mathbf{x}_r, H_k) = \frac{1}{\prod_{j=1}^{L} p(x_{r_{j_v}} | \gamma_i^*)}. \tag{16}$$

Training samples are directed to the nearest hypercube utilizing Eq. (16) and probabilities are updated as follows:

Type Ø Feature
Increase relative frequency by 1 in estimate of p_{j_v}.
Type 1 Feature
Increase relative frequency by 1 in estimate of p_{j_v}.

A criterion can be established to create a new hypercube if the distance is greater than a threshold. This involves the problems associated with unsupervised estimation including clustering problems (see Patrick, 1972).

15-7 CONDITIONAL DIFFERENTIAL DIAGNOSIS

Denote a conditional differential diagnosis at stage $j-1$ by

$$D(x_1, x_2, \ldots, x_{j-1}).$$

One question is whether the conditional differential diagnosis at stage $(j-1)$ can assist in decision making at stage j.

The optimum solution to decision making computes

$$p(\gamma_i^* | \mathbf{x}) = \frac{p(\mathbf{x} | \gamma_i^*) P_i}{\sum_{k=1}^{M} P_j p(\mathbf{x} | \gamma_k^*)}$$

assuming that all categories (concepts) γ_i^* have been formed. Consider

$$p(\gamma_i^* | \mathbf{x}_j, D_{j-1}) = \frac{p(\mathbf{x}_j, D_{j-1} | \gamma_i^*) P_i}{p(\mathbf{x}_j, D_{j-1})} = \frac{p(\mathbf{x}_j, D_{j-1} | \gamma_i^*) P_i}{\sum_{k=1}^{M} p(\mathbf{x}_j, D_{j-1} | \gamma_i^*) P_k}$$

or

$$p(\gamma_i^*|\mathbf{x}_j, D_{j-1}) = \frac{p(\mathbf{x}_j|\gamma_i^*, D_{j-1})\, p(D_{j-1}|\gamma_i^*)P_i}{\sum_{k=1}^{M} p(\mathbf{x}_k|\gamma_k^*, D_{j-1})\, p(D_{j-1}|\gamma_k^*)P_k}.$$

By D_{j-1} is meant that the a posteriori probabilities are known at stage D_{j-1}. Thus

$$p(D_{j-1}|\gamma_k^*) = 1$$

and we obtain

$$p(\gamma_i^*|\mathbf{x}_j, D_{j-1}) = \frac{p(\mathbf{x}_j|\gamma_i^*)P_i}{\sum_{k=1}^{M} p(\mathbf{x}_k|\gamma_k^*)P_k}$$

If $p(\mathbf{x}_j|\gamma_i^*)$ is known, then

$$p(\mathbf{x}_j|\gamma_i^*, D_{j-1}) = p(\mathbf{x}_j|\gamma_i^*).$$

indicating that the differential diagnosis at $(j-1)$ cannot help diagnosis at stage (j) in an optimum approach.

15-8 DISCOVERING KNOWLEDGE FOR TYPE Ø FEATURES USING *CONSULT LEARNING SYSTEM®*

15-8-1 Multiple Type Ø Features

In general, when there are L Type Ø features, the category conditional probability density for these L features expressed by

$$p(\mathbf{x}_1, \mathbf{x}_2, \ldots, \mathbf{x}_L|\gamma_i^*) \tag{17}$$

can be expressed as

$$p(x_1, x_2, \ldots, x_L|\gamma_i^*) = \prod_{j=1}^{L} p(x_j|\mathbf{x}_{j-1}, \gamma_i^*) \tag{18}$$

where

$$\mathbf{x}_{j-1} = \{x_1, x_2, \ldots, x_{j-1}\}.$$
$$\mathbf{x}_\phi = \text{empty set} \tag{19}$$

A feature x_j can have up to one of nine values (assuming 9 feature values). Thus, there are

$$9^{(j-1)}$$

possible probabilities at stage j.

In general, at stage L, there are

$$(V)^L$$

events each with a probability that must be estimated in order to optimally process L features (taking into account all correlations among the L features). For example, with $L = 8$, $V = 9$,

$$(V)^L = (9)^8 = 43{,}046{,}721 = 4.3 \times 10^7$$

which is a lot of probabilities. In practice, these event probabilities can all be estimated by the **CONSULT LEARNING SYSTEM®**. Storage of the data leading to the calculations is no problem. Of course, storing all the probabilities after calculation requires $(V)^L$ words of storage. As discussed previously, the **CONSULT LEARNING SYSTEM®** has a special construction for allowing formation of "adaptive" sets determined in part by OR operations on Type Ø feature values. This leads to a prodigious reduction in the number of possible computations $(V)^L$ assuming that hard data exists for events to provide estimation of statistical significance.

This suggests the desirability of discovering statistical independence among features (or subsets of Type Ø feature values) by utilizing problem knowledge. An alternative is to utilize the **CONSULT LEARNING SYSTEM®** to verify independence among two features (sets of Type Ø feature values) by estimating the joint probability and marginal probabilities,

$$p(x_{j_v}, x_{k_w}),\ p(x_{j_v}),\ p(x_{k_w})$$

for each value v of feature j and each value w of feature k. Statistical independence among the two features is "verified" if

$$\hat{p}(x_{j_v}, x_{k_w}) \cong \hat{p}(x_{j_v})\hat{p}(x_{k_w}),$$

to within a degree of confidence.† **CONSULT LEARNING SYSTEM®**, after defining the two events x_{j_v} and x_{k_w}, immediately leads to estimates of the probabilities with confidences in the estimates.

†A Type 1 measurement has embedded Type 1 features.

15-9 DISCOVERING DEPENDENCE KNOWLEDGE AMONG TYPE 1 FEATURES

15-9-1 Introduction

In general, a Type 1 feature† has a category conditional probability density function,

$$p(x_1, x_2, \ldots, x_V | \gamma_i^*), \tag{20}$$

which can be expressed as

$$p(x_1, x_2, , , , x_V | \gamma_i^*) = \prod_{j=1}^{V} p(x_j | \mathbf{x}_{j-1}, \gamma_i^*) \tag{21}$$

where

$$\mathbf{x}_{j-1} = \{x_1, x_2, \ldots, x_{j-1}\}$$
$$\mathbf{x}_\emptyset = \text{empty set.} \tag{22}$$

A feature x_j, being T (True) or F (False), expresses presence or absence of a property (primitive) of the event γ_i^*. Suppose, for example, that in $\mathbf{x}_{j-1}$ there are several True values; then it may be more likely that a property x_j is present than if properties in $\mathbf{x}_{j-1}$ are all False. This and other aspects of the Type 1 feature will be considered shortly.

15-9-2 *CONSULT LEARNING SYSTEM®* for Type 1 Measurements

The number of probabilities for feature j, for the probability denoted

$$p(x_j | \mathbf{x}_{j-1}, \gamma_i^*), \tag{23}$$

is

$$(2)^V$$

In a Type 1 measurement, there are V embedded features with (2) probabilities for each feature. Thus there are

$$(2)^V$$

---

†Since the terms in the expression are estimates, they are random variables. Thus at all times, the equality holds with some probability.

probabilities to be estimated for a Type 1 measurement consisting of V embedded Type 1 features.

In all, if $V = 9$,

$$2^9 = 512$$

probabilities need be estimated from training data. This is not unreasonable and can be accomplished by the **CONSULT LEARNING SYSTEM®**, a companion product to **CONSULT-I®**. Data stored in **CONSULT LEARNING SYSTEM®** can be processed to obtain estimates of probabilities of any events defined in terms of feature values. This applies to the 512 events needed for optimum performance of a Type 1 measurement.

Estimation of these 512 event probabilities, of course, takes time using the **CONSULT LEARNING SYSTEM®**; thus, it is desirable to process off line to obtain the 512 probabilities for decision making. *Note: The **CONSULT LEARNING SYSTEM®** utilizes an adaptive format to combine the 512 probabilities and it is these combined probabilities that are estimated. Thus, the number of parameters to be estimated* is greatly *reduced.* Furthermore, complex feature operations can be imposed on the V embedded Type 1 feature to greatly reduce complexity.

15-9-3 Example: Presence of Property Unduly Overridden by Nonpresence of Another Property

Consider as an example the class Pulmonary Emboli. For a series of 160 patients (Sasahara *and others,* 1973) with angiographically proven pulmonary emboli, we transfer the available statistics into Type 1 feature value probabilities:

	Feature	Value	p_j
x_1	Chest pain	True	0.88
x_2	Dyspnea	True	0.81
x_3	Respirations >16	True	0.88
x_4	Pulse >100/min.	True	0.44
x_5	Rales	True	0.53

Consider

$$p(x_2, x_4|\gamma_i^*) = p(x_4|\gamma_i^*, x_2)p(x_2|\gamma_i^*).$$

We know

$$p(x_2 = \text{True}|\gamma_i^*) = 0.81$$
$$p(x_4 = \text{False}|\gamma_i^*) = 0.56$$

If the recognition vector has sequence

$$(x_2 = \text{True}, x_4 = \text{False})$$

and assuming statistical independence,

$$\begin{aligned} p(x_2 = \text{True}, x_4 = \text{False}|\gamma_i^*) &= p(x_2 = \text{True}|\gamma_i^*)p(x_4 = \text{False}|\gamma_i^*) \\ &= (0.81) * (0.56). \end{aligned}$$

It may be that

$$p(x_4 = \text{False}|\gamma_i^*, x_2 = \text{True}) < (0.56).$$

If so, this class could be severely penalized by property x_4 being False when the class already is highly likely because x_2 is True. This situation frequently arises in practice.

Once x_2 is True, it is (may be) less likely that x_4 is False; but this cannot be reflected if independence is assumed.

In summary,

> A *false property may have less probability given another true property, which cannot be reflected using statistical independence.*

16

Conclusions

16-1 WHERE WE HAVE BEEN

This book is oriented to *Inference Systems and Classification Systems.* Patterns of categories are characterized by *Features* and *Feature values.* Basic to Inference or Classification is *engineering the category conditional probability density function.* In achieving this a *knowledge base structure* is created. It begins with the Primitives, Feature values, and proceeds upwards to *Complex Features, Subclasses, Classes, Categories of Only classes, and Complex Classes with their Subcategories, and Actions.* The Features are of various types including Fuzzy sets (Type Ø) and Complex (including Type 1).

The forerunner of all Inference functions is the conditional probability $p(B|A)$, where B is an Outcome and A is a Condition. For Multiple Outcomes $B1, B2, \ldots BM$ it becomes a *Classification function. Bayes theorem* teaches us about A Posteriori Probabilities and A Priori Probabilities. Furthermore, it utilizes "Relativity"—i.e., a posteriori probability is Relative. This results because Total Probability is involved in the theorem derivation. But Bayes theorem does not consider the engineering of its own Inference Function. That is accomplished through SPR and AI.

Two Fundamental Problems arose over the last two decades and both involve *concept formation.* The first is *how to "generate" new patterns* of a category; and the second is *how to generate new categories* in a Classification System. The first was necessary in order to recognize a category as a pattern never previously seen. The second was necessary for a system designed for single categories active at the same time when prospectively that isn't the case.

The first problem of generating patterns was indirectly handled by *closeness functions.* A common fixed closeness function used the multivariate Gaussian function or sums of multivariate Gaussian functions. These functions performed deduction and generated patterns; but they were found to be restrictive or not to model the problem properly. An alternative approach was to store all the records and wait for the findings to create a FOCUS. Then the CLOSENESS of stored patterns from each category was measured to the FOCUS. The *nearest neighbor rule* is a prototype using a simple closeness measure. Then came the *Generalized K-Nearest Neighbor rule* using a Closeness measure determined for each category from its patterns.

In generating records, **AI** would take the approach of using rules to deduce that "this" category looks like the findings more than any other category. A rigid viewpoint would prevent us from seeing that both **AI** and **SPR** use rules to generate records. *But **SPR** adds a dimension of repetition or relative frequency that conventional **AI** lacks.*

The second problem of generating categories required a new theorem. This *new theorem by Patrick* is similar to Bayes in that in both theorems categories are mutually exclusive. But *in the theorem by Patrick categories are statistically dependent during concept formation of new categories.* The new categories are generated from knowledge about existing categories. This is a new form of Learning without a Teacher.

The new theorem by Patrick does not give us answers to all the practical questions to generating categories but provides for divising models applicable to the problem. The practical problem remains of when to look for new categories. This is not a problem when there is low complexity. However, as complexity increases with more basic categories, an **AI** or interactive approach can be used. Nevertheless, the underlying theory is that of **SPR.** In this regard, the **AI** component reminds us more of search procedures; and indeed that is what the **AI** graphs accomplish. The new theorem by Patrick shows the importance of *learning significance and insignificance* in the feature space for the underlying categories. This takes repetition or relative frequency—an **SPR** concept. Conventional **AI** lacks this facility.

16-2 The OUTCOME ADVISOR®, CONSULT LEARNING SYSTEM®, and CONSULT-I®

The OUTCOME ADVISOR® and **CONSULT LEARNING SYSTEM®** store the patterns for each category. The findings to be classified provide a Focus. Then any basic inference can be made using these stored patterns. But it is recognized that a fundamental problem is to *learn the* *correlation* for each category at the Focus. The Focus itself has correlation (i.e., this feature value and that feature value . . .). But how much correlation does the category have with the Focus? How close is the category to the Focus? If a category *has* records (patterns) at the Focus then we can determine its correlation with some confidence. Otherwise records have to be "generated" from existing stored records.

In this book we presented the new approach that records not at the Focus can have some probability of being at the Focus (or some Expected Equivalence with the Focus). This insight follows from previous studies with Equivalence and the Generalized K–Nearest Neighbor Rule.

In effect, patterns are generated at a focus for a category as follows: Stored patterns of a category are used to learn *Significance and Insignificance* in a *lower dimensional space*. This becomes *Past knowledge*.

At the Focus, correlation for a Category is learned utilizing the stored past knowledge of significance and insignificance.

A *closeness measure results that brings each stored pattern to the Focus*. For stored pattern $\mathbf{x}_s$, it has probability $p(\text{Focus}|\text{vector } \mathbf{x}_i)$ of being at the Focus. The Focus is multidimensional.

Relative Frequency at the Focus is Expected Equivalence:

$$\frac{1}{n}\sum_{s=1}^{u} p(\text{Focus}|\text{vector } \mathbf{x}_s)$$

For Conventional relative frequency,

$$\begin{aligned} p(\text{FOCUS}|\text{vector } \mathbf{x}_s &= 1\text{: } \mathbf{x}_s \text{ Focus} \\ &= \emptyset\text{: } \mathbf{x}_s \neq \text{Focus} \end{aligned}$$

NOT TRUE with **The OUTCOME ADVISOR®** and **CONSULT LEARNING SYSTEM®**.

Note that for each pattern a multidimensional vector with correlation is brought to the Focus. We are learning multidimensional correlation of the Focus. Lower dimensional knowledge as "packets just 'prime the pump'."

If complete correlation were known at highest dimensionality L for all findings (Focuses), then the classification problem is deterministic—there is nothing to learn.

Processing takes place twice. First to obtain low-dimensional probabilities of significance and insignificance in the Feature space to be used to construct a closeness measure. The dimensionality at this point can be "only so high." But it then is used to project the pattern with high dimensionality to the Focus. Thereby the high-dimensional correlation for the category is learned at the Focus.

There are two learning processes. One learns a closeness measure to be used in the inference function model. Then one learns the inference function.

The first kind of learning is in the past and uses conventional relative frequency to learn probabilities. This tells us the behavior of features or feature pairs or three features taken together or as high dimensionality as practical. Ideally, even infrequent high-dimensional feature value relations should be recorded; but eventually as dimensionality increases these are the records (patterns) themselves. Call these Packets of Correlation (E) where E is the dimensionality (number of features of the Packet. There is a limit to the number of packets and the confidence we can have in the packets. For example, if there are $L = 20$ Features, the number of five-dimensional packets is 15,504 for each category. But then there are 4 *DIM,* 3 *DIM,* 2 *DIM,* and 1 *DIM* packets as well. It appears that we can "prime the pump" with packets of limited dimensionality. The true dimensionality at the Focus for the category will have to be determined by the equivalent relative frequency at the Focus of the patterns themselves.

The OUTCOME ADVISOR® and **CONSULT LEARNING SYSTEM®** have used 1 *DIM,* 2 *DIM,* and 3 *DIM* packets to shape the closeness measure for determining the equivalent relative frequency of patterns at the Focus.

This discussion shows the importance of limiting the Feature List to essential features and feature values. It can be dangerous to use expert knowledge to "hard wire packets" because then actual records could be precluded from contributing to correlation at the Focus. The learning system could be prevented from learning by "Expert Knowledge."

To illustrate the expected equivalence at a Focus for a record not itself at the Focus, consider Figure 16-1.

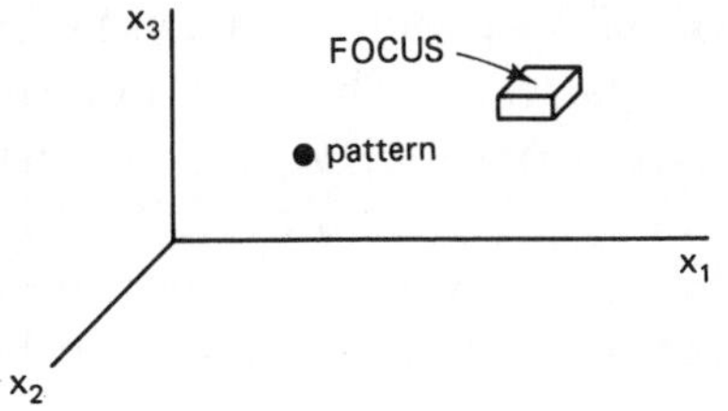

FIGURE 16.1

The pattern is not at the Focus but it can contribute an equivalent relative frequency to the focus. Consider that during past learning using all the patterns for the category, two dimensional packets were determined as in Figure 16.2. These packets are for two-dimensional regions which are projections from the three-dimensional Focus.

The probability that the pattern could have been at the Focus is

$$\prod_{j=1}^{3} p_j$$

for this example. If we knew 3 *DIM* packets and none were at the pattern, then the possibility the pattern can be at the Focus is zero (with some confidence). In this case the pattern simply would not be at the Focus. This is the same as saying that the patterns constitute total knowledge and no patterns can be generated by concept formation. The system then is hard wired or deterministic. There is nothing to learn!

Fortunately we learn packets of increasing dimensionality with decreasing confidence. Otherwise we never could learn at all. Thus, a rigid AI system with expert knowledge cannot learn.

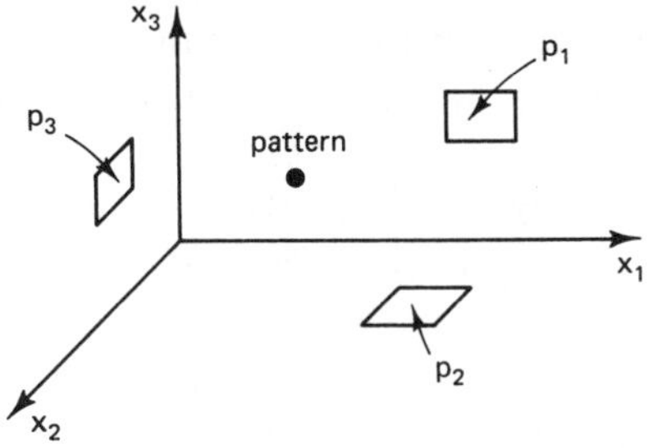

FIGURE 16.2 Two DIM packets which are projections from the Focus.

The OUTCOME ADVISOR® and **CONSULT LEARNING SYSTEM®** learn from the patterns. They are not rigid.

The Focus is at the Condition *A* and patterns for each category *B*1, *B*2, . . . , *BM* are brought to the Focus. This is accomplished every time there are new Findings and thus a new Focus. You can see how this is distribution free—not imposing an underlying probability density function as in conventional statistics. But it can use actual patterns not just expert knowledge as in conventional AI. The inference or classification involves multidimensions, not like the limited and restrictive regression analysis, discriminant analysis, and hypothesis testing, using these latter procedures.

For **The OUTCOME ADVISOR®** and **CONSULT LEARNING SYSTEM®** features need not have ordered feature values. The closeness measures use conditional probability of feature values, not less than or greater than as in conventional statistics.

The number of Focuses is unlimited in **The OUTCOME ADVISOR®** and **CONSULT LEARNING SYSTEM®**. That is one of their powers. Prior "expert" contraints do not limit the Focus to limit performance. For some problems we do learn that there are a limited number of "Global Focuses." For example, there are typical and atypical presentations of a disease or typical and atypical presentations of a problem in trouble shooting. At these global focuses there is some variation within but the global focus itself has a multidimensional correlation for a Category. We emphasize that the global focus is for the category.

Note that one of the jobs of **The OUTCOME ADVISOR®** and **CONSULT LEARNING SYSTEM®** was to learn the multidimensional correlate for a category at the Findings (Focus). This is one of the most fundamental problems in **AI** and **SPR**.

Now we are saying that *if we have learned a* Focus for a Category, then we also have learned Multidimensional Correlation for the Category. That learning can be used and in fact is used by **CONSULT-I®** is discussed next.

A Focus of multidimensional correlation is one of the expert's contribution to expert systems. **The OUTCOME ADVISOR®** and **CONSULT LEARNING SYSTEM®** learn these Focuses for use in **CONSULT-I®** or for the expert. There are many problems where this Focus of multidimensional correlation does not exist and **The OUTCOME ADVISOR®** or **CONSULT LEARNING SYSTEM®** are essential.

These Focuses of Multidimensional Correlation then are transition points from **The OUTCOME ADVISOR®** or **CONSULT LEARNING SYSTEM®** to **CONSULT-I®**.

CONSULT-I®

The Focuses of Correlation for each Category in **CONSULT-I®** are called columns (or hypercubes). The Column is oriented in hyperspace as determined by the feature value probabilities in the various dimensions. These feature value probabilities can be supplied by experts or from **The OUTCOME ADVISOR®** or **CONSULT LEARNING SYSTEM®**. In **CONSULT-I®**:

- For each Category there are Primary Focuses called Columns. Minicolumns modify the Columns.
- Findings are Projected to each Focus.
- Within a Focus the Closeness of Findings is adjusted by local correlation within the Focus.
- Because the Focus or Column contains multidimensional Correlation, for category γ_i^*,

$$p(\mathbf{x}|\gamma_i^*) = \prod_{j=1}^{L} p(x_j|\mathbf{x}_{j-1}, \gamma_i^*)$$

$$= \prod_{j=1}^{L} p(x_j|\text{Column}, \gamma_i^*)$$

Once you have learned about categories it is reasonable to want to condense the knowledge into Columns and minicolumns, a priori category probabilities, and feature selections based on this knowledge. Feature selections can be used for selecting the next test or another appropriate action.

16-3 OTHER APPROACHES

"In the Beginning There Was Hyperspace."™

Hyperspace is the common meeting ground for Inference and Classification systems. It is basic for comparing systems.

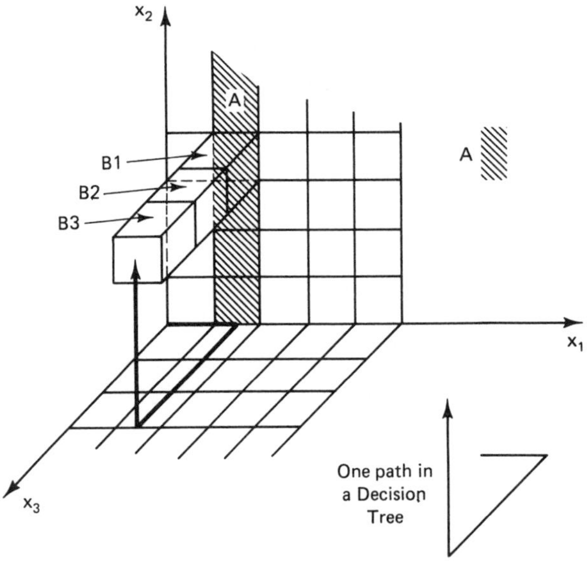

FIGURE 16.3 In the Beginning There Was Hyperspace.(TM)
Conditions **A** and Outcome **B** are defined in terms of the feature value. Outcomes **B1**, **B2**, and **B3** can be feature values as shown in Figure 16.3. The Inferences **A→B1**, **A→B2**, **A→B3**, and so on can be represented by the feature values in Hyperspace.

Hyperspace

Consider a Condition A and an Outcome B. In a three-dimensional space, let two of the dimensions x_1 and x_2 represent features as in Figure 16.3. The Condition A is a particular region in the space formed by x_1 and x_2. Another feature x_3 in this three-dimensional space can be used to index Outcomes B_1, B_2, B_3. *This shows the interrelationship between Features (Feature Values) and Categories. An Inference or Classification* is a transformation(s) in the hyperspace. All approaches to Inference or classification can be represented or described by this Hyperspace concept. Included are: Decision Trees, Bayes Theorem, Patrick's Theorem, Conditional Probability, Discriminant Analysis, Regression Analysis, Production Rules, Induction, and Deduction of Artificial Intelligence, or Statistical Pattern Recognition.

Decision Tree

A decision tree is a single path between Condition and Outcome as illustrated in Figure 16.3. Often decision trees fail because too many paths are required and can't be solved. The impracticability of storing transition probabilities limits the computation of an accurate Conditional Probability.

Production Rules

Production rules can be put together to perform Induction just as a path in a decision tree. Paths (individual production rules) are put together by a "supervisor" to represent FINDINGS (a particular path). But, Production Rules have the same deficiencies as Decision Trees.

Proper Solution

Accurate computation of

$$p\ (B_i|A),\ i = 1,2, \ldots M$$

is the desired inference. $A \rightarrow B_i$ is a particular path through the hyperspace. If each Feature has V values and there are L Features then there are V^L paths in the hyperspace. If $L=10$ and $V=9$, $(9)^{10}$ is a very large number.

The OUTCOME ADVISOR® and **CONSULT LEARNING SYSTEM®** can determine the probability of any path or combination of paths through Hyperspace using Examples. The Focus is on the Condition A and then the Examples are brought to the Focus. A decision tree is but a "bone fragment."

A Decision Tree loses correlation information. To see this, observe that there are $(V)^L$ paths and this is too many to remember. Further, there are too many Transition Probabilities to learn.

In ***The OUTCOME ADVISOR®*** *or* ***CONSULT LEARNING SYSTEM®*** *Inference of Closeness depends on the Past (Feature Histograms) and the Present (Focus). Then, Inference of Outcome Probability depends on the Present (Focus at Findings), Inference of Closeness, Focus, and Records allows Learning the Correlation by Deductions. Then A Posteriori Probability is Inferred by Induction using repetition of Correlations.*

For **CONSULT-I®**, Inference of Closeness is in the Past (Examples or Experts). Inference of Correlation also is in the past—Orientation of the Column. Inference of a posteriori probability then is by Induction. The Closeness and Correlation depend on the Findings if there are multiple columns.

Glossary

Action: The consequence of deciding a category or subcategory of a particular rank for the category or subcategory. The action can be the next Feature to select.

Activation Rules: Rules to activate one or more subsystems based on the findings.

AND/OR Graph Concepts: Search technique which consists of OR nodes and AND nodes. A node represents a goal or problem description. See Section 4-8.

A Posteriori Probability: The probability of a category given (conditioned on) findings. It is normalized with respect to the probability of the findings. The probability of the findings depends on all the categories.

A Posteriori Probability Using Correlation Levels: The a posteriroi probability of a category at the findings is computed iteratively using the training patterns from the category. The strength of the patterns for the category at the findings in the iteration is the correlation level for the pattern. *Since the findings are the same for all categories, the category with highest a posteriori probability is the one with highest iterative correlation level.* Another viewpoint is this: Given training patterns from a category, what is the probability that some future pattern from the category could agree with the findings? It is presumed that such findings never were previously observed for the category.

A Priori Probability: The probability of a category. An estimate of the a priori probability of a category is the relative frequency of occurrence of that category in a population of training records.

Associative Law of Addition: (see Section 3-2).

Associative Law of Product: (see Section 3-2).

Axiomatic Formulation: (see Section 3-5).

Basis Set: See Spanning Set.

Bayes Framework: See Bayes Theorem. A viewpoint introduced by Patrick in 1965 to emphasize the need to engineer the Likelihood (category conditional probability density function) using an integration of SPR and AI.

Bayes Theorem: Inference of one of a multiple number of categories given findings for categories which are mutually exclusive. The inference involves Likelihood and a priori probability for all the categories and the probability of the findings. Little is said about engineering the likelihood function.

Breadth-First Search: See Section 4-9.

Can't Feature: A feature with a value such that a category conditional probability density function is zero for that category at that feature value.

Can't Generator: The process of establishing zero probability density (SPR), imposing a *common sense* (AI) constraint.

Category: An *only class or complex class* mutually exclusive of other categories which are in the Category Space. A category is denoted γ_ξ^*.

Category Feature: A set of elements (feature values) where an element is a category in the decision space. Just as for regular features, each pattern of a category has a category feature value—the category. See "In The Beginning There Was Hyperspace.(TM)"

Category Space: Set of M categories which are mutually exclusive and having rules specialized to the space.

Category-Feature Relationship Space: A cross product space $\mathfrak{X}\ \boldsymbol{\gamma} = \mathcal{F}$; where $\mathfrak{X}$ is feature space and $\boldsymbol{\gamma}$ category space.

Category-Feature Relationship: Described by $p(\mathbf{x}|\omega_i^*)$ or $p(\mathbf{x}|\Omega_i^*)$. The set of all possible feature vectors for the category with some indication of their relative frequency of occurrence. Points can be placed in the set using examples, expert knowledge, or generated from existing points using deduction/induction operations.

Causal Network: A structure consisting of nodes and links. A condition at any node can affect another node through a link. Conventionally its relationship to hyperspace and other inference functions is not described.

Class Space: Set of M_1 classes not necessarily mutually exclusive with special rules separating categories (only classes or complex classes) from the classes. A class is denoted ω_i. (See only class and complex class.)

Classical Node: A category presentation considered typical or a starting point for engineering the *c.c.p.d.f.*

Classification System: An Inference System where there are multiple outcomes denoted $B_1, B_2, \ldots B_M$ and called categories. Often the categories are elements of a set called the Category Feature and are simple, non-complex events. As such the category feature is integral in forming "In The Beginning There Was Hyperspace.(TM)" An objective is to achieve high classification accuracy. A classification system also can improve actions and perform feature selection.

Closeness Measure: A measure of closeness, in particular how close findings are to a category.

Column: Denotes a subcategory conditional probability density function for a category whereby:

* A posteriori subcategory probability measures the closeness of findings to the column.
* Closeness is a complex correlation level with value the product of marginal probabilities for the column.

* All values of a feature have minimum probabilities corresponding to levels of insignificance (unless a Can't is imposed in which case probability is zero).
* Correlation is reflected by the column training. Correlation level is reflected by the number of features trained with significant feature values. Complex correlation level is reflected by the specific features trained with significant probabilities.

Columns/Minicolumns as a Focus at Findings: A column (minicolumn) was found by experience to summarize an important constellation of findings for a category.

Commutative Law of Addition: (See Section 3-2.)

Commutative Law of Product: (See Section 3-2.)

Complement of a Set: (See Section 3-2.)

Complex Class: An event consisting of two or more classes in the class space. A complex class is denoted Ω^*_ξ (being also a category, it is denoted γ^*_i).

Complex Event: An event defined by logical set operations of features and feature values used for a Condition A or an Outcome B.

Complex Feature: A feature whose values are functions of other feature values. Part of the knowledge base structure.

Concept Formation of Complex Class: Creating what we believe patterns from a complex class would look like given patterns from only classes. This is Type 2 Learning Without a Teacher. A model generates by deduction the complex class patterns. Conventional A.I. deals poorly with this concept formation in part because heuristics used for concept formation are poorly described as compared with models.

Concept Formation of Records: Creating records from existing records of a category that look like findings with some measure of probability or correlation.

CONSULT-I®: Expert system implementing Artificial Intelligence with Statistical Pattern Recognition discussed in this book.

CONSULT LEARNING SYSTEM®: System for "learning by example." Provides off-line or on-line learning of knowledge for CONSULT-I® using hard data (records). Can also be used as true classification system using hard data. Accepts TYPE Ø, TYPE 1, other Types, and Index features.

Constraints Affecting A Posterior Probabilities Using Correlation Levels: See A Posteriori Probabilities Using Correlation Levels. Certain constraints on the feature values of a category(ies) need be considered. They include CANT's, Rule-In's, ratios, products, frames, causality among features. *These constraints are applied to each training record (pattern)* used to iterate the category at the findings. Some of these constraints are from SPR and some from AI. For many problems there are records but no reliable constraints. A conventional AI approach could not be used. The approach using Correlation Levels always can be used since it has its base in SPR with AI integration. It would seem that for many problems even complex correlation levels are not required because the iterative effect of relative frequency from patterns for a category of the findings will be strong for one category relative to another.

Control Strategy: Component of a problem solving system used for deciding what to do next. Problem solving systems also consist of a data base and operators—the control strategy decides what operator to apply and in what sequence. CONSULT-I® has both local (event-conditional *p.d.f.*'s for a presentation) and global (ranking likelihoods) control strategy.

Correlation: A measure of the similarity of one element in a set to another element in the set. A conventional statistical definition of correlation is $E[(X - \bar{x})(X^t - \bar{x}^t)]$. In this book another concept of correlation is the relative frequency that patterns from a category are similar to findings using a similarity measure related to the correlation level. (See Learning Without a Teacher TYPE 3.)

Correlation Level: A measure of similarity between a pattern(s) in a category and findings. The correlation level concerns the features of the pattern(s) which have different values from those of the findings.

Correlation Level—Complex: (See Correlation Level.) The definition of a complex correlation level includes the specific features as well as the number of features for a category which agree with the findings. For two categories with equal iterative correlation levels, one category has highest a posteriori probability if it has highest complex correlation level.

Correlation Levels as Subcategories: (See Correlation, Correlation Level, Learning Without a Teacher TYPE 3.) A correlation level can be viewed as a subcategory of a category at a particular point in the feature space—the Findings. For example, it is possible that some patterns of a category are at Correlation Level 1, some at Correlation Level 2, some at Correlation Level 3, and so on up to Correlation Level L where L is the number of features.

Cross Learning: Refers to a construction where knowledge of an only class provides knowledge about a complex class or another only class.

Cylinder in Hyperspace: A collection of nodes along a particular dimension(s) in hyperspace. (See Chapter 13.)

Data Base: In reference to a search procedure, consists of data structures including arrays, lists, sets of predicate calculus sentences and/or semantic networks. In CONSULT-I® the data base includes the category-feature relationships.

Decision Space: Collection of categories where a category is the end result of explaining findings. Classes can be intermediate objects not in the decision space. A subset of the Category Space consisting of each and every category that could be the category of a pattern to be recognized.

Deductive Learning: Deducing a complex class from only classes. Deducing an only class from a complex class and class. Deducing a marginal probability density function from a higher order probability density function.

Depth-First Search: (See section 4-10.)

Discovery: Process of acquiring knowledge of something previously unknown (see section 2-1).

Distance Measure: A formal concept from mathematics dealing with the closeness of one point to another point in hyperspace. It has limited usefulness in classification theory where distance usually has no meaning in the conventional sense since features do not have ordered values.

Engineering the c.c.p.d.f.: (See Chapter 9.)

Equivalent Feature values: Feature values for which the category conditional probability density at the feature values are identical or have a known relationship.

Event: A basic component or element of a set. Conditions and Outcomes (Categories) are events.

Exhaustive Sets: Sets whose Union of elements in a set equals the whole space.

Experimental Probability of Error: Testing a classification system with records not used for training and computing the relative frequency of misclassifications.

Expert System: Implementation of a Classification or Inference rule where parameters are estimated by experts rather than by using hard data (actual records).

Feature: A feature is a topic used to describe each and every pattern of a category. A set of L features is considered required to describe patterns of each category and distinguish categories.

Feature Extraction: The process of observing, extracting and recording a feature value for a pattern.

Feature List: The feature list is the features with their feature values.

Feature Selection: Having already asked some questions resulting in feature values, Feature Selection is the process of determining the next feature (questions, topic) for which to solicit an answer (feature value). This is accomplished with some goal such as to minimize classification error or pursue a currently highest ranking category. Feature selection has serious limitations in the face of incomplete training.

Feature Sensitivity: A feature property reflecting to what extent a value for that feature can influence the a posteriori category probability. Decreasing feature sensitivity is a smoothing operation. Feature sensitivity is with respect to a particular category and is affected by the likelihood of other features for that category.

Feature Value: Each feature is itself a subset of subtopics called feature values. A pattern has precisely one feature value for each feature and these L feature values constitute a Record.

Findings: Set of feature values constituting a pattern for a class or category. The class or category of the findings is unknown but is to be inferred.

Findings as a Focus: The hyperspace concept of using the findings as a focal point around which patterns of a category are gathered to determine the correlation of those patterns (category) with the findings. This vastly different concept from conventional statistical decision making does not view correlation as a static property of a category but as a dynamic property changing with the finding and is computed at decision-making time.

First Order Logic: Extends predicate calculus through definitions of function which return objects and predicate equals (see section 4-4).

Focus: See findings as a focus.

Frame: A structure which provides instruction upon which other knowledge is interpreted (see section 4-16-4).

Fuzzy Set Theory: Theory of approximate reasoning (see section 3-13).

Generalized K-Nearest Neighbor Rule: A classification rule by Patrick and Fisher where patterns (records) of a category are brought to the Findings using a closeness measure. It is an early prototype for **The OUTCOME ADVISOR®** and **CONSULT LEARNING SYSTEM®**.

Heuristic: Rule for generating new knowledge or new representations of knowledge. A *domain* of structure and a control structure are implied. A heuristic is a model (see section 2-1).

Heuristic State-Space Search: (See section 4-11).

Hierarchical: System of things ranked one above the other. Used to build a knowledge structure from Feature values to Complex features to classes to categories to actions.

Hypercube: Concept-feature relationship involving subconcepts, miniconcepts. Training reflects typical and atypical presentations of a category. (See column.) A Category presentation or cluster.

"In The Beginning There Was Hyperspace"™: A concept which begins with all the features (and their values) and leads to the creation of mutually exclusive bins or boxes or holes, the collection of which fill the space. Bins can be identified which are patterns belonging to a category which itself is a bin. Relationships or operations among bins include probability, possibility, equivalence, relative frequency, category-feature relationship, class-feature relationship, complex feature, complex class, only class, probability density, event, complex event, inference, deduction, induction, marginal projection, correlation, closeness (or distance).

Index Feature: A feature usually having a large number of values. It is hierarchical. For example, it indexes multiple records for the same patient or DRG's (Diagnostic Related Groups).

Inductive Learning: (See Supervised Training Session).

Inference: A relationship of cause and effect between a Condition and an Outcome or Findings and a Category(s).

Inference System: A system whereby a Condition event A is said to cause an Outcome event B with some probability. Events *A* and *B* can be complex utilizing basic set theory and set operations.

Information: mathematically defined as

$$- \sum_{v=1}^{V} p(x_{j_v}|\gamma_i^*) \log_2 [p(x_{j_v}|\gamma_i^*)]$$

and is minus the expected value of a probability density function of feature x_j. If there were only one feature value then no information is conveyed by that feature (see section 3-11).

Insignificant Feature for a Category: A feature for which all feature values are equally likely for that category or have the same probabilities as for all other categories for which the feature is insignificant.

Interpreter: In a production system, the program that decides which production to process next. Resolves conflicts when multiple rules are active at a stage.

Interviewer: The man-machine interface between the Feature List and the user. It includes methods of interaction such as Sequential vs. Individual presentation of Features, Embedding multiple Features, Methods of Feature selection including Trees, Frames and optimum rules.

Intelligence: capacity for reasoning, understanding, gathering or distributing information (see Chapter 2).

Knowledge Base: Features and Feature values used to describe Events (Conditions and Outcomes) including categories and patterns (records) for the events. It includes the concept formation of records and categories not initially present or known.

Learning by Example: Process of obtaining or estimating parameters in an inference function or classification system using Examples (Records) of patterns of the Inference or Classifications.

Learning by Discovery: Using Deduction to learn what other Records of a Category *probably* could look like given a Record (Example) from the category or using Deduction to learn what other Categories could look like given Categories. The new Records and Categories were not seen previously.

Learning with a Teacher (supervised learning, supervised estimation): Using training records to learn the category conditional probability density function and/or a priori category probabilities where it *is known* to which category a training record (pattern) belongs.

Learning without a Teacher (unsupervised learning, unsupervised estimation): TYPE 1: Using training records to learn the category conditional probability density function and/or a priori category probabilities where it *is not known* to which category a training record (pattern) belongs.

Learning without a Teacher: TYPE 2: (See Concept Formation of Complex Classes. See Concept Formation of Records.)

Learning without a Teacher: TYPE 3: The process of learning how many and which features of a category are correlated at a particular point in the feature space—the Findings. This is accomplished even if the findings are at a hole in hyperspace where there is no previous training for the category (the findings never were previously seen for the category). (See Correlation, Correlation Level.)

Likelihood: The probability of findings given a category. It does not depend on the other categories or any a priori probability.

Loss: A constant or function used to modify the a posteriori probability of a Category to reflect the consequence of not recognizing or deciding that Category. Can be used to convert a minimum probabilitiy of error decision rule to a minimum Risk decision rule.

Marginal Projection Generator: Generates records never previously seen by projecting *c.c.p.d.f.* to a lower dimensional space created by Missing Features.

Maximum Likelihood Category: The category for which the Likelihood is maximum. Maximum is a fuzzy set operation that involves all the categories.

Meta-Knowledge: Self-knowledge. A system's meta-knowledge is its knowledge about its own knowledge. For example, how it will form Deduction or Induction.

Minicolumn: A minicolumn is a "perturbation" of a column which allows for the generation of many columns from a single column. A minicolumn

* Can modify the correlation level of a column.
* Can modify the complex correlation level of a column.
* Can be viewed as creating a subsubcategory of patterns.

Misclassified Findings for a Category: Findings that are misclassified for a category must be considered a focus for the generation of a new column for the category. New records incorrectly classified by association with the new column update the correlation level (and complex correlation level of the new columns).

Missing Feature: A missing feature is a property of the findings, not the training records. Given findings, a feature with an unknown feature value is a missing feature.

Mixture Probability Density: A sample $\mathbf{x}$ with *p.d.f.*, $p(\mathbf{x})$, can be decomposed as $p(\mathbf{x}) = P_1\, p(\mathbf{x}|\gamma_1^*) + P_2 p(\mathbf{x}|\gamma_2^*) + \ldots + P_M p(\mathbf{x}|\gamma_M^*)$. The P_i are called mixing parameters.

Model Space: A set of models denoted $\mathfrak{M}$ which contain the "glue" relating classes, only classes, and complex classes.

Modus Ponens: If sentence X is true and sentence $X \rightarrow Y$ is true, then we infer that sentence Y is true. Expressed as $(X \wedge (X \rightarrow Y)) \rightarrow Y$.

Mutually Exclusive Sets: Sets that have no elements in common.

Nodes in Hyperspace: Not to be confused with the nodes in a tree or network. Nodes in Hyperspace are regions or boxes containing a probability density (see Chapter 13).

Normalized Likelihood of a Category: The Likelihood for a category divided by the sum of the Likelihoods over all the categories. The normalized likelihood equals the a posteriori probability when the a priori probabilities are equal for all categories.

Null Category: For classes in the class space an event can be defined as not class 1, not class 2, not class . . . , not class M_1 and be a link to a second set of spaces. As such, the Null Category means "Other."

Observation Space: The feature space at decision making or recognition time where an observed set of feature values constitutes the findings.

Only Class: An event consisting of one and only one class in the class space. It is denoted ω_i^* (being also a category, it is denoted γ_ξ^*).

Operator: Rules of inference which modify the data base and cause a new state.

OUTCOME ADVISOR®, The: System for "learning by example." Provides learning of knowledge from records (hard data). Used as an inference system or as a classification system. Accepts only TYPE Ø features.

Ownership Feature: Feature that "crosses" subsystems in **CONSULT LEARNING SYSTEM®** or **The OUTCOME ADVISOR®**. Identifies a record in more than one subsystem as being "owned" by the same identifier.

Patrick's Theorem on A Posteriori Probability: Set of M (number of categories) expressions for inferring the categories from the findings. The categories including complex classes (multiple classes active at the same time) are mutually exclusive. The expressions internally involve classes which are not mutually exclusive.

Patrick's Theorem on A Posteriori Probability with Concept Formation Through Statistically Dependent Categories: (See Patrick's Theorem.) This is an iterative expression for the parameters characterizing all categories including only classes and complex classes. The iteration is performed by processing one training sample after another. The presentation of the theorem shows that although categories are mutually exclusive during iteration, they are statistically dependent. This statistical dependence provides for generating complex categories (concept formation).

Pattern: An element of a set of presentations of a category or class. A Record. A sample. A sample vector.

Potential Category: A complex class or only class that theoretically can be constructed from classes.

Predicate Calculus: Statement applied to one or more arguments and having values of either True or False (see section 4-3).

Primitive Class: Another name for a class in the class space used in constructing a complex class.

Primitive (Feature): The lowest level subtopic in the knowledge base used in describing patterns. Often the Feature value is a primitive.

Probability a Feature Is Significant: We can consider that a feature being significant is an event. We can attach a probability to this event. There are errors that for various reasons can prevent a category property from being observed. The developer wants to protect against these errors by increasing likelihood for an observation observed False over what normally would be supplied by the experts (see section 13-10).

Probability of the Findings: A mixture (sum) of the product of a posteriori probability and a priori probability of a category over all the categories.

Probability Space: The weights obeying laws of probability theory and SPR attached to the bins (boxes or holes) in the feature space for a category (or class).

Production Rule: In Production system, a Condition-Action pair—If (Condition) Then (Action). A part of the system's data base. Usually limited to a few of the features or feature values.

Probability of the Findings: A mixture (sum) of the product of a posteriori probability and a priori probability of a category over all the categories.

Propositional Calculus: (See Section 4-2.)

Reasoning in a System: A system is said to reason if it can do something it has not been explicity told how to do. For example, concept formation of Records or Categories never previously seen.

Recognition: The process of testing a classification system with a record not used for training and recording the category decided (or of highest a posteriori probability). Or the process of testing the outcome of an Inference System with a Condition.

Record: A collection or set of observed feature values for a problem. For a classification system, a record is a pattern of a category.

Regions of Insignificance in the Feature Space: Relative to a complex class, this is a region of the feature space where individual classes have never been observed to occur.

Relative Frequency: The relative number of times out of a fixed number that an event occurs during training. It is one of the classical approaches to Probability theory.

Relative Frequency as a Dimension(s): Relative frequency provides knowledge not representable by the category space, class space, feature space, or probability space. It provides a "glue" whereby a model provides concept formation of complex classes from only classes and concept formation of the correlation of findings with patterns from a category relative to other categories. Relative frequency as a dimension(s) arises from Statistical Pattern Recognition and is not possible with conventional Artificial Intelligence.

Relativity: For a classification system, relativity is the concept that things are exhaustive or bound. A category is classified or ranked *relative* to other categories. Concept formation of a complex class from only classes is relative to knowledge for the only classes. Correlation of findings with patterns of one category is relative to the correlation of the findings with other categories; correlation is not absolute. A posteriori probability of a category is relative to that for other categories and is not absolute. Likelihood of findings given a category is not relative to other categories and is absolute.

Rule-In Feature: A Feature with a value possible for one Category and impossible for all other Categories. When that Feature value is observed it "Rules-In" the Category.

Rule-Out Feature: A Feature with a value impossible for a Category(s).

Semantic Network: Network consisting of nodes (representing objects, concepts, situations) and arcs (representing relations between nodes). (See section 4-6).

Sentences as an Inference Rule: (See section 4-17).

Sentences of Propositional Logic: (See section 4-2-1).

Set: Collection of objects denoted $\xi_1, \xi_2, \ldots \xi_n$ and the set is denoted A, $B, \ldots$. ξ_i is an *element* of the set.

Set Operations: Equality, sum (or union), difference, subset, product (intersection, AND, complement, certain event, disjoint).

Significant Feature for a Category: A feature for which all feature values are not equally likely for that category or has a feature value(s) with probability different from that of at least one other category.

Space: A set of elements with definitions or imposed rules which are in addition to those for sets, i.e., relationships to other sets, a distance measure, a projection measure, a measure of similarity.

Spanning Set: A set of vectors $x_1, x_2, \ldots, x_L$ from E^L is said to span or generate E^L if every vector x in E^L can be written as a linear combination of x_1, $x_2, \ldots, x_L$.

State: A condition with respect to structure.

Statistical Independence: Two sets A and B are statistically independent if $p(AB)=p(A)p(B)$ (see section 3-8).

Subcategory Likelihood: A category occurs because one of its subcategories occurs. The likelihood of findings given a category is the likelihood of the findings given the subcategory, if that subcategory is known. If the subcategory is unknown, then the category likelihood involves all the subcategory likelihoods:

$$p(\mathbf{x}|\gamma_i^*) = \sum_k p(\mathbf{x}|\gamma_{i_k}^*) \frac{p(\gamma_{i_k}^*)}{p(\gamma_i^*)}$$

A fuzzy set approximation is

$$p(\mathbf{x}|\gamma_i^*) = \max_k \{p(\mathbf{x}|\gamma_{i_k}^*)$$

Subcategory of a Category: A subcategory is a subset of the pattern for a category. A category is said to occur if any of its subcategories occur. A subcategory has an a priori probability and the sum of a priori probabilities adds to the category a priori probability. In recognizing a category we are not trying to decide which subcategory occurred. Therefore, it is the a priori category probability and not the a priori subcategory probability that is used to compute a posteriori category probability.

Subsystem: A problem consisting of categories and a Feature List. Concept Formation of new Categories is possible.

Supervised Training Session: Records of known category (class if training for a class) are provided for Learning by Example.

Time: A dimension(s) allowing for repetition of events such as feature values of patterns in a category, pairs of feature values of patterns in a category, three features taken together and so on. Allows for adding features reflecting observations at different time.

Training: The process of observing and collecting records to learn by example existing or new parameters in the knowledge base.

Total System: (See Chapter 11.) System model of many subsystems consisting of L features, M categories, and M_c classes. Knowledge is grouped into S subsystems.

Unavailable Feature: An unavailable feature is a property of a training record. For that training record no value is available for the feature.

Unsupervised Training Session: Records from unknown categories are provided for Learning by Discovery.

Verification: The process of checking that observed feature values are recorded accurately in a record.

References

Adlassnig, K. P., G. Kolarz, W. Scheithauer, H. Effenberger, G. Grabner, "CADIAG: Approaches to Computer-Assisted Medical Diagnosis," *Comput. Biol. Med.* **15**:315–335, 1985.

Adlassnig, K. P., "A Fuzzy Logical Model of Computer-Assisted Medical Diagnosis," *Meth. Inform. Med.* **19**:141–148, 1980.

Aikins, J. S., J. C. Kunz, E. H. Shortliffe, and R. Fallat, "PUFF: An Expert System for Interpretation of Pulmonary Function Data," *Comp. and Biomed. Res.* **16**:199–208, 1983.

Alperovitch, A., and P. Fragu, "A Suggestion for an Effective Use of a Computer-Aided Diagnosis System in Screening for Hyperthyroidism," *Meth. Inform. Med.* **16**:93–95, 1977.

American Board of Internal Medicine, "Clinical Competence in Internal Medicine," *Ann. Int. Med.* **90**:402–411, 1979.

Anderson, J., and G. Bower, "Human Associative Memory," L. Erlbaum, Assoc., Hillsdale, N.J., 1973.

Balla, J., "The Use of Critical Cues and Prior Probability in Decision-Making," *Meth. Inform. Med.* **21**:9–14, 1982.

Balla, J., A. Elstein, and P. Gates, "Effects of Prevalence and Test Diagnosticity Upon Clinical Judgments of Probability, *Meth. Inform. Med.* **22**:25–28, 1983.

Barnett, A., C. Rutherford, J. Desforges, N. Gutensohn, and S. Davies, "Evaluating the Validity of a Bayesian Program for Predicting Stage in Hodgkin's Disease," *Meth. Inform. Med.* **20**:174–178, 1981.

Barr, A., and E. Feigenbaum, Eds., *The Handbook of Artificial Intelligence,* Volume II, W. Kaufmann, Inc., Los Altos, Ca., 1982.

Barr, A., and E. Feigenbaum, Eds., *The Handbook of Artificial Intelligence,* Volume I, W. Kaufmann, Inc., Los Altos, Ca., 1981.

Bayes, Rev. Thomas, "An Essay Toward Solving a Problem in the Doctrine of Chance," *Philos. Trans. R. Soc.* **53**:370, 1763.

Belforte, G., B. Bona, and R. Tempo, "Stability of Classification in Sequential Allocation Analysis," *Proc. 4th Symposium on Computer Applications in Medical Care,* 697–702, 1980.

Ben-Bassat, M., D. Teeni, "Human-Oriented Information Acquisition in Sequential Pattern Classification: Part I—Single Membership Classification," *IEEE Trans. on Systems, Man, and Cybernetics,* Vol. SMC-14, No. 1, 131–138, 1985.

Ben-Bassat, M., R. W. Carlson, V. K. Puri, M. D. Davenport, J. Schriver, M. Latil, R. Smith, L. Portigal, E. Lipnick, and M. Weil, "Pattern-Based Interactive Diagnosis of Multiple Disorders: The MEDAS System," *IEEE Trans. on Pattern Analysis and Machine Intelligence,* PAMI-2, (2), pp. 148–160, March 1980.

Bennett, J., and C. Hollander, "DART: An Expert System for Computer Fault Diagnosis," *Proc. Seventh International Joint Conference on Artificial Intelligence,* Vancouver, pp. 843–845, 1981.

Bjerregaard, B., S. Brynitz, J. Holst-Christensen, P. Jess, E. Kalaja, J. Lund Kristensen, and C. Thomsen, "The Reliability of Medical History and Physical Examination in Patients with Acute Abdominal Pain," *Meth. Inform. Med.* **22**:15–18, 1983.

Bleich, H. L., "Computer-Based Consultation: Electrolyte and Acid-Base Disorders," *Am. J. Med.* **53**:285, 1972.

Blois, M. S., "Information and Computers in Medicine: Can We Have a Theory of Medicine?" *MEDINFO '83,* J. Van Bemmel, M. Ball, O. Wigertz, eds, pp. 447–449, North Holland, Amsterdam, August 1983.

Blomberg, D. J., J. Guth, J. M. Fattu, E. A. Patrick, "Evaluation of a New Classification System for Anemias Using CONSULT LEARNING SYSTEM," *Proc. 9th Symposium on Computer Applications in Medical Care,* pp. 34–40, Baltimore, MD., 1985.

Blomberg, D. J., J. M. Fattu, and E. A. Patrick, "Learning Sensitivity and Specificity of Laboratory Diagnosis of Thyroid Disorders Using Consult Learning System™—An Example of Euthyroid Sick Syndrome," *Proc. 8th Symposium on Computer Applications in Medical Care,* Washington, D.C., 1984.

Blum, R. L., "Discovery, Confirmation, and Incorporation of Causal Relationships from a Large Time-Oriented Clinical Data Base: The RX Project," *Computers and Biomedical Res.* **15**:164–187, 1982.

Boom, R. A., L. Fonesca, C. Yanez, D. Gil, and T. Karson, "Differential Diagnosis Between Amoebic Liver Abscess and Acute Choleystitis," *J. Med. Systems* **7**:205–212, 1983.

Brodie, M. L., J. Mylopoulos, and J. W. Schmidt, Eds., *On Conceptual Modeling. Perspectives from Artificial Intelligence, Databases, and Programming Languages,* Springer-Verlag, New York, 1984.

Buchanan, B. G., and E. A. Feigenbaum, "DENDRAL and Meta-DENDRAL: Their applications dimension," *Artificial Intelligence* **11**:5–24, 1978.

Cerutti, S., and C. Timó Pieri, "A Method for the Quantification of the

Decision-Making Process in a Computer-Oriented Medical World," *Int. J. Bio-Medical Computing* **12**:29–57, 1981.

Christensen–Szalanski, J., and J. Bushyhead, "Physicians' Use of Probabilistic Information in a Real Clinical Setting," *J. of Experimental Psychology* **7**:928–935, 1981.

Clive, J., M. Woodbury, and I. Siegler, "Fuzzy and Crisp Set-Theoretic-Based Classification of Health and Disease," *J. Med. Systems* **7**:317–332, 1983.

Cobelli, C., and A. Salvan, A Medical Record and a Computer Program for Diagnosis of Thyroid Disease," *Meth. Inform. Med.* **14**:126–132, 1975.

Coomans, D., I. Broeckaert, M. Jonckheer, and D. Massart, "Comparison of Multivariate Discrimination Techniques for Clinical Data—Application to the Thyroid Functional State," *Meth. Inform. Med.* **22**:93–101, 1983.

Cooper, D. B., and P. W. Cooper, "Non-Supervised Adaptive Signal Detection and Pattern Recognition, *Information and Control,* Vol. 7, No. 3, pp. 416–444, 1964.

DeChardin, P. T., *Phenomenon of Man,* Harper & Row, New York, 1965.

deDombal, F. T., "How "Objective" is Medical Data?" In *Decision Making and Medical Care,* deDombal/Gremy, Eds., North Holland Publishing Co., Amsterdam, 33–37, 1976.

deDombal, F. T., J. Horrocks, G. Walmsley, and P. Wilson, "Computer–Aided Diagnosis and Decision Making in the Acute Abdomen," *J. R. Coll. Physicians (London)* **9**:212–218, 1974a.

deDombal, F. T., D. Leaper, J. Horrocks, J. Staniland, and A. McCann, "Human and Computer-Aided Diagnosis of Abdominal Pain: Further Report with Emphasis on Performance of Clinicians," *Brit. Med. Journal* **1**:376–380, 1974b.

deDombal, F. T., J. Horrocks, J. Staniland, and P. Guillou, "Pattern-Recognition: A Comparison of the Performance of Clinicians and Non-Clinicians—With a Note on the Performance of a Computer-Based System," *Meth. Inform. Med.* **11**:32–37, 1972.

deDombal, F. T., D. Leaper, J. Staniland, A. McCann, and J. Horrocks, "Computer–Aided Diagnosis of Acute Abdominal Pain," *Brit. Med. Journal* **2**:9–13, 1972.

Detterman, P. *Diagnostic Related Groups — A Synopsis,* Internal Publication, Patrick Consult Inc., Cincinnati, Oh, 1984.

Detterman, P. J., and E. A. Patrick, "A Nurse–Physician Team Approach to Abdominal Pain," Publication, Patrick Consult Inc., 1986.

Diamond, G., and J. Forrester, "Analysis of Probability as an Aid in the Clinical Diagnosis of Coronary Artery Disease," *N. Engl. J. Med.* **300**:1350–1358, 1979.

Duda, R. O., J. G. Gaschnig, and P. E. Hart, "Model design in the PROSPECTOR consultant system for mineral exploration." In D. Mitchie, Ed., *Ex-*

pert Systems in the Micro–electronic Age. Edinburgh University Press, Edinburgh, 1979.

Duda, R. O., P. E. Hart, and N. J. Nilsson, "Subjective Bayesian Methods for Rule-Based Inference Systems," *Readings in Artificial Intelligence,* N. Nilsson, Ed., Tioga Publ. Co., Palo Alto, Ca., pp. 192–198, 1980.

Eddy, D. M., and C. H. Clanton, "The art of diagnosis: Solving the clinicopathological exercise," *N. Engl. J. Med.* **306**:1263–1268, 1982.

Emerman, C. L., and E. A. Patrick, "Computer Aided Diagnosis of Drug Poisoning: A CONSULT-I® Subsystem," *Proc. Seventh Symposium on Computer Applications in Medical Care,* IEEE, Silver Springs, Md., pp. 126–128, 1983.

Engle, R. L., B. Flehinger, S. Allen, R. Friedman, M. Lipkin, B. Davis, and L. Leveridge, "HEME: A Computer Aid to Diagnosis of Hemotologic Disease," *Bull. N.Y. Acad. Med.* p. 52, 1976.

Esogbue, A. O., "Dynamic Programming, Fuzzy Sets, and the Modeling of R & D Management Control Systems," *IEEE Trans. System, Man, and Cybernetics,* SMC-**13**:18–29, 1983.

Evans, R., R. Gardner, A. Bush, J. Burke, J. Jacobson, R. Larson, F. Meier, H. Warner, "Development of a Computerized Infectious Disease Monitor (CIDM)," *Comp. and Biomedical Res.,* **18**:103–113, 1985.

Fagan, L. M., J. C. Kunz, J. Feigenbaum, and J. Osborn, "Representation of Dynamic Clinical Knowledge: Measurement Interpretation in the Intensive Care Unit," *Proc. Sixth International Joint Conference on Artificial Intelligence,* pp. 260–262, 1979.

Fattu, J. M. and E. A. Patrick, "Computer-Aided Diagnosis and Decision Making," In *Understanding Computers in Medicine,* J. Javitt, Ed., W. B. Saunders Co., Philadelphia, PA., 1986.

Fattu, J. M., D. J. Blomberg, E.A. Patrick, J. Guth, "An Expert System Developed from a Hard Data Knowledge Base: Example of a Laboratory Based Anemia Consultant," *Proc. 9th Symposium on Computer Applications in Medical Care,* pp. 257–262, Baltimore, MD., 1985.

Fattu, J. M., and E. A. Patrick, "Application of a New Theorem of A Posteriori Probabilities of Events to Medical Diagnosis," *Proc. Seventh Symposium on Computer Applications in Medical Care,* IEEE, Silver Springs, Md., pp. 844–847, 1983.

Fattu, J. M., and E. A. Patrick, "Training CONSULT-I® as an Expert System," *AAMSI Congress '83, Proceedings of the Congress on Medical Informatics,* D. Lindberg, E. van Brant, M. Jenkin, Eds., American Association for Medical Systems and Information, Bethesda, pp. 102–106, 1983.

Fattu, J. M., E. A. Patrick, N. A. Fattu, and L. Fay, "Application of CONSULT-I® to Develop Expert Systems," *MEDINFO '83,* J. van Bemmel/M. Ball/O. Wigertz, Eds., IFIP-IMPA, North Holland Press, Amsterdam, p. 457, 1983.

Fattu, J. M., E. A. Patrick, and W. Sutton, "Thyroid Disorders: Automatic Diagnosis in CONSULT-I®", *Comput. Biol. Med.* **12**:285, 1982.

Feigenbaum, E. A., and P. McCorduck, *The Fifth Generation. Artificial Intelligence and Japan's Computer Challenge to the World,* Addison-Wesley Publishing Co., Reading, Massachusetts, 1983.

Feinstein, A. R., "Clinical Biostatistics, XXXIX, the Haze of Bayes, the Aerial Palaces of Decision Analysis, and the Computerized Ouija Board," *Clin. Pharmacol, Ther.* **21**:482–496, 1977.

Feller, W., *An Introduction to Probability Theory and Its Applications,* John Wiley & Sons, New York, 1957.

Fieschi, M., M. Joubert, and D. Fieschi, "A System for Computer-Aided Diagnosis," *Meth. Inform. Med.* **21**:143–148, 1982.

Fralick, S. C., "Learning to Recognize Patterns Without a Teacher," *IEEE Trans. Information Theory,* Vol. IT–13, No. 1, pp. 57–64, 1967.

Franklin, P., and N. Angerman, "CONSULT-I®: Breast Disease," *Proc. AAMSI Congress '83,* D. Lindberg, E. vanBrant, M. Jenkin, Eds., American Association for Medical Systems and Information, Bethesda, Md., pp. 245–57, 1983.

Fu, K. S., *Sequential Methods in Pattern Recognition and Machine Learning,* Academic Press, Inc., New York, 1968.

Gini, G., and M. Gini, "A Serial Model for Computer Assisted Medical Diagnosis," *Int. J. Bio-Medical Computing,* **11**:99–113, 1980.

Goldman, L., and M. Weinberg, "A Computer–Derived Protocol to Aid in the Diagnosis of Emergency Room Patients with Acute Chest Pain," *N. Engl. J. Med.* **307**:588–596, 1982.

Gomez, F., and B. Chandrasekaran, "Knowledge Organizations and Distribution for Medical Diagnosis," *IEEE Trans. on Systems, Man, and Cybernetics,* SMC-**11**:36–42, 1981.

Gordon, B. L., "Terminology and Content of the Medical Record," *Comput. Biomed. Res.,* **3**:436, 1970.

Gorry, G. A., H. Silverman, and S. G. Pauker, "Capturing Clinical Expertise: A Computer Program that Considers Clinical Responses to Digitalis," *Amer. J. Med.* **64**:452–460, 1978.

Gorry, G. A., "Knowledge-Based Systems for Clinical Problem Solving," In *Decision Making and Medical Care,* F. T. deDombal, F. Gremy, Eds., North Holland Publishing Company, Amsterdam, pp. 23–31, 1976.

Gorry, G., J. Kassirer, A. Essig, and W. Schwarz, "Decision Analysis as the Basis for Computer-Aided Management of Acute Renal Failure," *Amer. J. Med.* **55**:473–484, 1973.

Gorry, G., and G. Barnett, "Experience with a Model of Sequential Diagnosis," *Comput. Biomed. Res.* **1**:490–507, 1968.

Greenes, R. A., "A Goal Directed Model for Investigation of Thresholds for Medical Action," *Proc. Third Symposium on Computer Applications in Medical Care, IEEE,* pp. 47–51, 1979.

Habbema, J.D.F., "Models for Diagnosis and Detection of Combinations of Diseases," *Decision Making and Medical Care,* F. T. deDombal F. Gremy, Eds., North Holland Publ. Co., Amsterdam, pp. 399–410, 1976.

Hayes-Roth, F., D. A. Waterman, and D. B. Lenat, Eds., *Building Expert Systems,* Addison-Wesley Publishing Company, Inc., Reading, Massachusetts, 1983.

Hudson, D. L., and T. Estrin, "EMERGE—A Data-Driven Medical Decision Making Aid," *IEEE Trans. on Pattern Analysis and Machine Intelligence,* Vol. PAMI-6, No. 1, 87–91, 1984.

Jacquez, John A., and M. J. Norusis, "The Importance of Symptom Non-Independence in Diagnosis," In *Decision Making and Mledical Care,* F. T. deDombal, F. Gremy, Eds., North Holland Publ. Co., Amsterdam, pp. 379–391, 1976.

Jagannathan, V., J. Bourne, B. Jansen, and J. Ward, "Artificial Intelligence Methods in Quantitative Electroencephalogram Analysis," *Computer Programs in Biomedicine* **15**:249–258, 1982.

Jourbert, M., M. Fieschi, D. Fieschi, G. Botti, and M. Roux, "Framed Knowledge for Medical Man–Machine Communication with Computer Programs," pp. 443–446, *MEDINFO '83,* J. van Bemmel, M. Ball and O. Wigertz, Eds., North Holland Press, Amsterdam, August 1983.

Kahn, G., S. Nowlan, and J. McDermott, "Strategies for Knowledge Acquisition," *IEEE Trans. Pattern Analysis and Machine Intelligence,* Vol. PAMI-7, No. 5, 511-522, 1985.

Kanal, L. N., "Patterns in Pattern Recognition: 1968–1974," *IEEE Trans. Information Theory,* IT-20, **6**:697–722, 1974.

Kassirer, J., and G. Gorry, "Clinical Problem Solving: A Behavioral Analysis," *Ann. Int. Med.* **89**:245–255, 1978.

Kastner, J. K., C. A. Dawson, S. Weiss, K. Kern, C. Kulikowski, "An Expert Consultation System for Frontline Health Workers in Primary Eye Care," *J. of Medical Systems* **8**:389-397, 1984.

Kastner, J., and S. Weiss, "A Precedence Scheme for Selection and Explanation of Therapies," *Proc. International Joint Conference on Artificial Intelligence,* pp. 908-909, 1981.

Kingsland, L. C., D. Lindberg, and G. Sharp, "AI/RHEUM. A Consultant System for Rheumatology,' *J. of Med. Systems* **7**:221–227, 1983.

Knill-Jones, R., "The Diagnosis of Jaundice by The Computation of Probabilities," *J. Roy. Coll. Physicians (London)* **9**:205, 1975.

Knill-Jones, R. Stern, D. Girmes, J. Maxwell, R. Thompson, and R. Williams, "Use of Sequential Bayesian Model in Diagnosis of Jaundice by Computer," *Brit. Med. J.,* **I**:530–533, 1973.

Krischer, J. P., "An Annotated Bibliography of Decision Analytic Applications to Health Care," Health Services Research and Development, Veterans Administration Hospital, Gainesville, Ga., 1979.

Kulikowski, C. A., "Expert Medical Consultation Systems," *J. of Medical Systems* **7**:229–234, 1983.

Kulikowski, C. A., and S. Weiss, "Representation of Expert Knowledge for Consultation: The CASNET and EXPERT Projects," In *Artificial Intelli-*

gence in Medicine, P. Szolovits, Ed., AAAS Selected Symposium 51, Westview Press, Boulder, Colorado, pp. 21–55, 1982.

Kulikowski, C., and J. Ostroff, "Constructing an Expert Knowledge Base for Thyroid Consultations Using Generalized AI Techniques," *Pro. 4th Symposium on Computer Applications in Medical Care,* IEEE, pp. 175–180, 1980.

Kullback, S., *Information Theory and Statistics,* John Wiley & Sons, New York, 1959.

Lasker, G. E., "Application of Sequential Pattern-Recognition Technique to Medical Diagnosis," *Bio-medical Computing* **1**:173-186, 1970.

Ledley, R. S., and L. B. Lusted, "Reasoning Foundations of Medical Diagnosis," *Science* **130**:9–21, July 1959.

Lesmo, L., M. Marzuoli, G. Molino, and P. Torasso, "An Expert System for the Evaluation of Liver Functional Assessment," *J. of Medical Systems* **8**:87–101, 1984.

Li, Ching-Chung, and King-Sun Fu, "Machine-Assisted Pattern Classification in Medicine and Biology," *Ann. Rev. Biophys. Bioeng.* **9**:393–436, 1980.

Lindberg, G., "Effects of Observer Variations on Performance in Probabalistic Diagnosis of Jaundice," *Meth. Inform. Med.* **20**:163–168, 1981.

Lindberg, D., L. Gaston, L. Kingsland, and H. Vanker, "AI/COAG, A Knowledge-Based System for Consultation About Human Hemostasis Disorders," Progress Report, *Proc. Fifth Symposium on Computer Applications in Medical Care,* IEEE, p. 253, 1981.

Ludwig, D., and D. Heilbronn, "The Design and Testing of a New Approach to Computer-Aided Differential Diagnosis," *Meth. Inform. Med.* **22**:156–166, 1983.

Lusted, L. B., *Introduction to Medical Decision Making,* Charles C. Thomas Publishers, Springfield, Il., 1968.

Mathlab Group, *MACSYMA Reference Manual,* Technical Report, Computer Science Laboratory, MIT, Cambridge, Mass., 1977.

McDermott, J., "R1: A Rule-Based Configurer of Computer Systems," *Artificial Intelligence* **19**:39–88, 1982.

Michalski, R. S., J. G. Carbonell, and T. M. Mitchell, Eds., *Machine Learning: An Artificial Intelligence Approach,* Tiogo Publishing Co., Palo Alto, CA, 1983.

Michalski, R., "A Theory and Methodology of Inductive Learning, Ch. 4 In *Machine Learning An Artificial Intelligence Approach,* R. Michalski, J. Carbonell, T. Mitchell, Eds., Tioga Publishing Co., Palo Alto, Ca., 1983.

Miller, R. A., "INTERNIST-1/CADUCEUS: Problems Facing Expert Consultant Programs," *Meth. Inform. Med.* **23**:9–14, 1984.

Miller, R. A., H. E. Pople, and J. D. Myers, "INTERNIST-1, An Experimental Computer-Based Diagnostic Consultant for General Medicine," *N. Engl. J. Med.* **307**:468, 1982.

Minsky, M., "A Framework for Representing Knowledge," in *The Psychology of*

Computer Vision, P. Winston, Ed., McGraw-Hill, New York, NY, pp. 211–277, 1975.

Minsky, M., "Steps Toward Artificial Intelligence," In Feigenbaum and Feldman, *Computers and Thought,* McGraw-Hill, New York, pp. 406–450, 1963.

Morgan, M., G. Barnett, E. Skinner, R. Lew, A. Mulley, and G. Thibault, "The Use of a Sequential Bayesian Model in Diagnostic and Prognostic Prediction in a Medical Intensive Care Unit," *Proc. Fourth Symposium on Computer Applications in Medical Care,* IEEE, pp. 213–221, 1980.

Myers, J., H. Pople, and R. Miller, "INTERNIST: Can Artificial Intelligence Help?" In D. Connelly, E. Benson, M. Burke, D. Fenderson, Eds., *Clinical Decisions and Laboratory Use,* University of Minnesota Press, Minneapolis, Mn., pp. 251–269, 1982.

Negoita, C. V., *Expert Systems and Fuzzy Systems,* the Benjamin/Cummings Publishing Company, Inc., Menlo Park, CA, 1985.

New Jersey State Department of Health, "A Prospective Reimbursement System Based on Patient Case Mix for New Jersey Hospitals, 1976–1983," Volume 1, *U.S. Health Care Financing Administration* Contract Number 600-77–0022, Trenton, NJ, 1980.

Newell, A., "The Knowledge Level," *Artificial Intelligence,* Vol. 18, p. 18, 1982.

Nilsson, Nils J., *Principles of Artificial Intelligence,* Tioga Publishing Co., Palo Alto, Ca., 1980.

Papoulis, A., *Probability, Random Variables, and Stochastic Processes,* McGraw-Hill, New York, 1965.

Patil, R., P. Szolovits, and W. Schwartz, "Modeling Knowledge of the Patient in Acid-Base and Electrolyte Disorders," In *Artificial Intelligence in Medicine,* P. Szolovitz, Ed., AAAS Selected Symposium 51, Westview Press, Boulder, Colorado, 1982.

Patil, R., P. Szolovitz, and W. Schwartz, "Causal Understanding of Patient Illness in Medical Diagnosis," *Proc. International Joint Conference on Artificial Intelligence,* p. 893, 1981.

Patrick, E. A., and J. M. Fattu, *CONSULT-I®: Artificial Intelligence with Statistical Pattern Recognition, An Expert System,* Patrick Consult Inc., Cincinnati, OH, 1985.

Patrick, E. A., and J. M. Fattu, *The Outcome Advisor®,* Patrick Consult Inc., Cincinnati, OH, 1985.

Patrick, E. A., J. M. Fattu, and D. Blomberg, "CONSULT-I® Network of Two Subsystems: CONSULT Electrolytes and CONSULT Acid Base," *Proc. 9th Symposium on Computer Applications in Medical Care,* Baltimore, Md., 1985.

Patrick, E. A., and J. M. Fattu, "Mutually Exclusive Categories Statistically Dependent During Concept Formulation" *Proc. Eighth Symposium on Computer Applications in Medical Care,* IEEE, 1984.

Patrick, E. A., "A Theorem of A Posteriori Probabilities of Events,"

MEDINFO '83, J. van Bemmel, M. Ball, O. Wigertz, Eds., IFIP-IMIA, North Holland Pub. Co., Amsterdam, pp. 454–456, 1983.

Patrick, E. A., "Survey of Medical Decision Analysis," In *Computer-Assisted Decision Making Using Clinical and Paraclinical (Laboratory) Data,"* B. Statland, S. Bauer, Eds., Mediad, Inc., Tarrytown, NY pp. 1–7, 1980a.

Patrick, E. A., Fundamentals of Pattern Recognition, translated into Russian, *MOCKBA COBETCHOE PA9UO,* 1980b.

Patrick, E. A., "Choking—A Questionnaire to Find the Most Effective Treatment," *Emergency,* Vol. 82, No. 7, p. 59, July 1980c.

Patrick, E. A., *Decision Analysis in Medicine: Methods and Applications,* CRC Press, Boca Raton, Fl., 1979.

Patrick, E. A., J. M. Fattu, and R. Uthurusanny, "CONSULT-I®: Consulting and Diagnosis for Doctors," *Proc. Fifth Illinois Conf. on Medical Information Systems,* Champaign, IL., May 3–4, 1979a.

Patrick, E. A., J. M. Fattu, and R. Uthurusanny, "CONSULT-I®: Automatic Diagnosis in Practice," *Proc. Third Symposium on Computer Applications in Medical Care,* IEEE, pp. 9–13, 1979b.

Patrick, E. A., E. Margolin, V. Sanghvi, and R. Uhurusanny, "Pattern Recognition Applied to Early Diagnosis of Heart Attacks," *Proc. Second World Conf. on Medical Information (MEDINFO '77),* Toronto, Canada, 203, 1977.

Patrick, E. A., "Pattern Recognition May Resolve Management of Breast Cancer: Limited Mastectomy versus Medical Mastectomy," *Science,* Vol. 187, p. 764, 1975.

Patrick, E. A., and L. Y. -L. Shen, "A Systems Approach to Applying Pattern Recognition to Medical Diagnosis," *TR-EE 75–12,* Purdue University Medical Computing Program, May 1975.

Patrick, E., F. Stelmack, and R. Garrett, "Theory for a Medical Decision Making and Consulting System," *Purdue University,* TR-EE 75–16, West Lafayette, In., May 1975.

Patrick, E. A., F. P. Stelmack, and L. Y. -L. Shen, "Review of Pattern Recognition in Medical Diagnosis and Consulting Relative to a New System Model," *IEEE Trans. Syst. Man Cybern.,* SMC-4, 1, pp. 1–16, 1974.

Patrick, E. A., L. Y.-L Shen, and F. P. Stelmack, "On the Theory of Medical Diagnosis and Consulting," *Proc. Intl. Joint Conf. Pattern Recognition,* IEEE, p. 231, 1973a.

Patrick, E. A., L. Y.-L. Shen, and F. P. Stelmack "Introduction to the Theory of Medical Consulting and Diagnosis," 1973 Nat. Comput. Conf., *AFIPS Conf. Proc., Vol 42, p. 455, 1973b.*

Patrick, E. A., *Fundamentals of Pattern Recognition,* Prentice-Hall, Englewood Cliffs, N.J., 1972.

Patrick, E. A., "A Priori Problem Knowledge and Training Samples," in *Frontiers of Pattern Recognition,* Academic Press, New York, 1972.

Patrick, E. A., K. Henry, J. Altman, "Computer Controlled Picture Scanning with Applications to Labeled Biological Cells," *Comp. Biol. Med.,* **2**:5–14, 1972a.

Patrick, E. A., L. Shen, G. Carayannopoulos, R. Agnew, F. Stelmack, D. Pamde, and J. Hardigg, "Computers and Pattern Recognition for Large Systems, *Purdue University TR-EE,* 72–27, 1972b.

Patrick, E. A., R. Wild, and J. Allman, "Computer Output of Cells and Cell Features," *Pattern Recognition,* Vol. 4, pp. 211–226, 1972c.

Patrick, E. A., F. Stelmack, L. Shen, R. Agnew, O. Panda, G. Carayannopoulos, R. Murray, J. Hardigg, S. Stopford, C. Kelley, C. Cunningham, J. Greist, R. Smith, R. Musselman, G. Larkin, G. Brunk, "Interactive Computing and Pattern Recognition with Applications to Health Care Delivery," *Purdue University TR-EE* 72–75, 1972c.

Patrick. E. A., and L. Y.-L. Shen, "Pattern Recognition Through Statistical Verification of a Priori Problem Knowledge," *Proc. Joint National Conference on Major Systems,* IEEE Anaheim, Ca., pp. 132–136, Oct. 1971.

Patrick, E. A., "Interactive Pattern Analysis and Classification Utilizing Prior Knowledge," *Pattern Recognition* **3**:No. 1, 53–71, 1971.

Patrick, E. A., and J. P. Costello, "On Unsupervised Estimation Algorithms," *IEEE Trans. Information Theory,* Vol. IT-16, No. 5, pp. 556–569, 1970.

Patrick, E. A., and G. Carayannopoulos, "Codes for Unsupervised Estimation of Source and Binary Channel Probabilities," *Information and Control,* Vol. 14, No. 4, pp. 358–375, 1970.

Patrick, E. A., and F. P. Fischer, "Generalization of *K*-Nearest Neighbor Decision Rules," *Proc. 1969 Int. Conf. Artificial Intelligence, Information and Control,* **16**:128–152, 1970.

Patrick, E. A., and L. Liporace, "Unsupervised Estimation of Parametric Mixtures," *Purdue University School of Electrical Engineering Tech. Rept.* EE 70–31, Aug. 1970.

Patrick. E. A., L. Shen, R. Agnew, "Computerized Detection and Classification Using Artificial Intelligence and Estimates," *Naval Ship Systems Command,* Contract N00024-70-C-448, August 10, 1970.

Patrick, E. A., "Concepts of an Estimation System, An Adaptive System, and a Network of Adaptive Estimation Systems," *IEEE Trans. on Systems, Science and Cybernetics,* Vol. SSC-5, No. 1, January 1969.

Patrick, E. A., and F. P. Bechtel, "A Nonparametric Recognition Procedure with Storage Constraint," *Purdue University TR-EE,* 69–24, Lafayette, In, August 1969.

Patrick E. A., and J. P. Costello, "On Some Approaches to Unsupervised Estimation," *Purdue University TR-EE* 68-7, August 1968.

Patrick, E. A., "On a Class of Unsupervised Estimation Problems," *IEEE Trans. Information Theory,* Vol. IT-14, pp. 407–415, 1968.

Patrick, E. A., F. C. Monds, G. L. Carayannopoulos, J. P. Costello, and T. A. Martin, "DEMO-I—A Supervised or Unsupervised Learning Computer Designed for Demonstration," *Purdue University TR-EE,* 67–18, 1967.

Patrick, E. A., "Learning Probability Spaces for Classification and Recognition of Patterns With or Without Supervision," Ph.D. Thesis, Purdue University, Lafayette, In., November 1965.

Pearson, K., "On the Systematic Fitting of Curves to Observations and Measurement," *Biometrika,* Vol. I, p. 1, 1902.

Pearson, K., "Contributions to the Mathematical Theory of Evolution," *Phil. Trans. Roy. Soc. London,* Vol. 185, p. 71, 1894.

Politakis, P. and S. M. Weiss, "Using Empirical Analysis to Refine Expert System Knowledge Bases," *Artificial Intelligence* 22:23-48, 1984.

Pople, H. E., "Heuristic Methods for Imposing Structure on Ill-Structured Problems: The Structuring of Medical Diagnosis," In *Artificial Intelligence in Medicine,* P. Szolovits, Ed., AAAS Symposium 51, Westview Press, Boulder, Colorado, 1982.

Pople, H. E., "The Formation of Composite Hypothesis in Diagnostic Problem Solving. An Exercise in Synthetic Reasoning," *International Joint Conference on Artificial Intelligence,* pp. 1030-1037, 1977.

Pople, H. E., J. D. Myers, and R. A. Miller, "DIALOG: A Model of Diagnostic Logic for Internal Medicine," *International Joint Conference on Artificial Intelligence,* pp. 848–855, 1975.

Prewitt, J., "Decision Theoretic Approaches to White Cell Differentiation." In *Decision Making and Medical Care,* F. T. deDombal, F. Gremy, Eds., North Holland Publ. Co., Amsterdam, p. 287, 1976.

Pryor, T. A., R. M. Gardner, P. D. Clayton, and H. R. Warner, "The HELP System," *J. of Medical Systems* **7**:87-102, 1983.

Raemer, H. R., *Statistical Communications Theory and Applications,* Prentice-Hall, Inc., Englewood Cliffs, N.J., 1969.

Raeside, D. E., "Bayesian Statistics: A Guided Tour," *Medical Physics* **3**(1):Jan./Feb. 1976.

Rasmussen, J., "The Role of Hierarchical Knowledge Representation in Decision-making and System Management," *IEEE Trans. on Systems, Man, and Cybernetics,* Vol. SMC-15, No. 2, 234–243, 1985.

Reggia, J., T. Pula, T. Price, and B. Perricone, "Towards an Intelligent Textbook of Neurology," *Proc. Fourth Symposium on Computer Applications in Medical Care,* IEEE, pp. 190–199, 1980.

Rich, E., *Artificial Intelligence,* McGraw-Hill Book Co., New York, 1983.

Roach, J., S. Lee, J. Wilcke, M. Ehrich, "An Expert System for Information on Pharmacology and Drug Interactions," *Comput. Biol. Med.* **15**:11–23, 1985.

Robbins, H., "Mixtures of Distributions," *Ann. Math. Statistics,* **19**(3):360-369, 1948.

Robinson, K., B. Ryack, G. Moeller, R. Post, and W. Schroeder, "A Computer-Based Diagnostic/Patient Management System for Isolated Environments," *Meth. Inform. Med.* **22**:131–134, 1983.

Rosenblatt, F., "The Perceptron: A Probabilistic Model for Information Storage and Organization in the Brain," *Psychological Review,* Vol. 65, pp. 386–417, 1958.

Rosenbloom, P., J. Laird, J. McDermott, A. Newell, E. Orciuch, "R1-Soar: An Experiment in Knowledge-Intensive Programming in a Problem-Solving Architecture," *IEEE Trans. on Pattern Analysis and Machine Intelligence,* Vol. PAMI-7, No. 5, 561–568, 1985.

Salamon, R., M. Bernadet, M. Samson, G. Derouesne, and F. Gremy, "Bayesian Method Applied to Decision Making in Neurology—Methodological Considerations," *Meth. Inform. Med.* **15**:174–179, 1976.

Sasahara, A. T. Hyers, C. Cole, F. Ederer, J. Murray, N. Wenger, S. Sherry, and J. Stengle, "The Urokinase Pulmonary Embolism Trial: A National Cooperative Study," *Circulation* 47 (Suppl. II):68, 1973.

Sebestyen, G. S., *Decision-Making Processes in Pattern Recognition,* Macmillan Co., New York, N.Y. 1962a.

Sebestyen, G. S., "Pattern Recognition by Adaptive Process of Sample Set Construction," *IEEE Trans. Information Theory,* Vol. 178, No. 5, September 1962b.

Shortliffe, E. H., "Hypothesis Generation in Medical Consultation Systems: Artificial Intelligence Approaches," *MEDINFO-'83,* J. vanBemmel, M. Ball, O. Wigertz, Eds., IFIP–IMIA, North Holland Publ. Co., Amsterdam, pp. 480–483, 1983.

Shortliffe, E., A. Scott, M. Bischoff, A. Campbell, W. vanMelle, and C. Jacobs, "ONCOCIN: An Expert System for Oncology Protocol Management," *IJCAI-'81,* pp. 876–881, 1981.

Shortliffe, E., B. Buchanan, and E. Feigenbaum, "Knowledge Engineering for Medical Decision Making: A Review of Computer-Based Clinical Decision Aids," *Proc. IEEE,* **67**:1207–1224, 1979.

Shortliffe, E. H., *Computer-Based Medical Consultation, MYCIN,* Elsevier Scientific Pub. Co., Amsterdam, 1976.

Shortliffe, E., and B. Buchanan, "Model of Inexact Reasoning in Medicine," *Math. Biosciences* **23**:351–379, 1975.

Simon, H. A., "Artificial Intelligence Systems That Understand," *Proc. International Joint Conference on Artificial Intelligence,* pp. 1059–1073, 1977.

Simon, Herbert A., "The Structure of Ill-Structured Problems," *Artificial Intelligence* **4**:181–201, 1973.

Slagle, J. R., H. Hamburger, "An Expert System for a Resource Allocation Problem," *Communications of the ACM,* **28(9)**:994–1004, 1985.

Slagle, J. R., M. W. Gaynor, and E. J. Halpern, "An Intelligent Control Strategy for Computer Consultation," *IEEE Trans. on Pattern Analysis and Machine Intelligence,* Vol. PAMI-6, No. 2, 129-136, 1984.

Smets, P., H. Vainsel, R. Bernard, and F. Kornreich, "Bayesian Probability of Fuzzy Diagnosis," *MEDINFO '77,* D. Shires, H. Wolf, Eds., IFIP, North Holland Publ. Co., Amsterdam, pp. 121–122, 1977.

Smith, J. W., C. Speicher, and B. Chandrasekaran, "Expert Systems as Aids for Interpretive Reporting," *J. of Medical Systems* **8**:373-388, 1984.

Spect, D. F., "Generation of Polynomial Discriminant Functions for Pattern Recognition," *IEEE Pattern Recognition Workshop,* Puerto Rico, October 1966.

Spragins, J. D., "Learning Without a Teacher," *IEEE Trans. Information Theory,* Vol. IT-12, No. 2, pp. 223–230, 1966.

Stein, A., A. V. Lakshiminarayanan, R. Gangarosa, E. A. Patrick, and J. M. Fattu, "Application of Artificial Intelligence to NMR Clinical Evaluation," *Proceedings of Third Annual Meeting, Society of Magnetic Resonance in Medicine,* August 13–17, New York, N.Y. 1984.

Swartout, W. R., "XPLAIN: A System for Creating and Explaining Expert Consulting Programs," *Art. Intell.* **21**:285–325, 1983.

Szolovits, P., and S. G. Pauker, "Categorical and Probabilistic Reasoning in Medical Diagnosis," *Artificial Intell.* **11**:115–144, 1978.

Taylor, T., "Computer-Guided Diagnosis," *J. Roy. Coll. Physicians* (London) **4**:188–194, 1970.

Teicher, H., "Identifiability of Finite Mixtures," *Ann. Math. Statistics,* **34**(4):1265–1269, 1963.

Teicher, H., "On the Mixture of Distributions," *Ann. Math. Statistics,* **31**(1):55–73, 1960.

Thomas, J. B., *An Introduction to Statistical Communication Theory,* John Wiley & Sons, New York, 1969.

Title Six, Social Security Act Amendment of 1983.

Tong, R. M., "A Retrospective View of Fuzzy Control Systems," *Fuzzy Sets and Systems,* **14**:199–210, 1984.

Tsotsos, J. K., "Knowledge of the Visual Process: Content, Form, and Use," *Proc. Sixth Int. Conf. on Pattern Recognition,* IEEE Computer Society, Oct. 19–22, 1982.

Wagner, G., P. Tautu, U. Wolber, "Problems of Medical Diagnosis—A Bibliography," *Meth. Inform. Med.* **17**:55–74, 1978.

Wallis, J. W., and E. H. Shortliffe, "Explanatory Power for Medical Expert Systems: Studies in the Representation of Causal Relationships for Clinical Consultation," *Meth. Inform. Med.* **21**:127–136, 1982.

Wallstein, T., "Physician and Medical Student Bias in Evaluating Diagnostic Information," *Med. Decision Making,* **1**:145–164, 1981.

Wardle, A., L. Wardle, "Computer Aided Diagnosis—A Review of Research," *Meth. Inform. Med.* **17**:15–28, 1978.

Warner, H., B. Rutherford, and B. Houtches, "A Sequential Bayesian Approach to History Taking and Diagnosis," *Comput. Biomed. Res.* **5**:256, 1972.

Wechsler, H., "A Fuzzy Approach to Medical Diagnosis," *Int. J. Bio-Medical Computing,* **7**:191–203, 1976.

Weiss, S. M. and C. A. Kulikowski, *A Practical Guide to Designing Expert Systems,* Rowman & Allanheld, Publ., Totowa, N.J., 1984.

Weiss, S., C. Kulikowski, and R. Galen, "Representing Expertise in a Computer Program: The Serum Protein Diagnostic Programs," *J. Clin. Lab. Automation* **3**:383–387, 1983.

Weiss, S., C. Kulikowski, and R. Galen, "Developing Microprocessor Based Expert Models for Instrument Interpretation," *Proc. International Joint Conference on Artificial Intelligence,* pp. 853–855, 1981.

Weiss, S., C. Kulikowski, S. Amarel, and A. Safir, "A Model-Based Method for Computer-Aided Medical Decision-Making," *Artificial Intelligence* **11**:145–172, 1978.

Weiss, S., C. Kulikowski, and A. Safir, "A Model-Based Consultation System for the Long-Term Management of Glaucoma," *Proc. International Joint Conference on Artificial Intelligence,* pp. 826–832, 1977.

Winkler, R. L., "Research Directions in Decision Making Under Uncertainty," Discussion paper for *NSF Workshop on Research Directions in the Operational Sciences,* May 1982.

Winston, P., *Artificial Intelligence,* Addison-Wesley Publishing Co., Reading, MA, 1977.

Winston, P. H., and K. A. Prendergast, Eds., *The AI Business. The Commercial Uses of Artificial Intelligence,* The MIT Press, Cambridge, Massachusetts, 1984.

Wirtschafter, D., J. Carpenter, and E. Mesel, "A Consultant-Extender System for Breast Cancer Adjuvant Chemotherapy," *Ann. Int. Med.* **90**:396–401, 1979.

Wolf, F. M., L. D. Gruppen, and J. E. Billi, "Differential Diagnosis and the Competing-Hypothesis Heuristic. A Practical Approach to Judgment Under Uncertainty and Bayesian Probability," *J.A.M.A.* **253**:2858-2862, 1985.

Yager, R. R., "Fuzzy Subsets with Uncertain Membership Grades," *IEEE Trans. on Systems, Man. and Cybernetics,* Vol. SMC-14, No. 2, pp 271-275, 1984.

Yakowitz, S., "A Consistent Estimator for the Identification of Finite Mixtures," *Ann. Math. Statistics,* Vol. 40, No. 5, pp. 1728–1735, 1969.

Yale University School of Organization and Management, *the New ICD-9-CM Diagnosis Related Groups Classification Scheme Users Manual,* prepared by the ICD-9-CM Project Staff, Health Systems Management Group, December 1981, Volume 1.

Zadah, L. A., "Linguistic Variables and Approximate Reasoning," *Proc. Sixth Symposium on Computer Applications in Medical Care,* IEEE, pp. 787–791, 1982.

Zadah, L. A., "A Theory of Approximate Reasoning," In *Machine Intelligence* 9, J. Hayes, D. Michie and L. I. Mikulick, Eds., Wiley, New York, pp. 149–194, 1979.

Zadah, L. A., "Fuzzy Sets," *Information and Control* **8**(3):338–353, 1965.

Index

F

G

H

I

N

O

P

U

V